Frontiers of Jewish Thought

The B'nai B'rith History of the Jewish People
is a project of the
B'nai B'rith Commission on Continuing Jewish Education.
The first five volumes appeared during the years 1959-1964
as the B'nai B'rith Great Books Series.
Their republication occurred in 1985.
In its entirety, it has been selected to be part of
the B'nai B'rith Judaica Library whose purpose is
to promote a greater popular understanding
of Judaism and the Jewish tradition.
The volumes in the series are:

The B'nai B'rith History of the Jewish People

FRONTIERS OF JEWISH THOUGHT

Edited by Steven T. Katz

B'nai B'rith Books
Washington, D.C.

Jerusalem • London • Paris • Buenos Aires • East Sydney

Library of Congress Cataloging-in-Publication Data

Frontiers of Jewish thought / edited by Steven T. Katz.
p.   cm.—(The B'nai B'rith history of the Jewish people)
Includes bibliographical references and index.
ISBN 0-910250-20-0   ISBN 0-910250-21-9 (pbk.)
1. Judaism—20th century. 2. Jews—Civilization. 3. Jews—Social
conditions. 4. Judaism—United States. 5. Jews—United States—
Civilization. 6. Jews—United States—Social conditions.
I. Katz, Steven T., 1944-   . II. Series.
BM565.F76   1992
296—dc20   91-46696

DEDICATION

This volume was made possible
through the generosity of Milton T. Smith,
who offers the following tribute:

A capable wife is a crown for her husband,
but an incompetent one is like rot in his bones.

אשת חיל עטרת בעלה
וכרקב בעצמותיו מבישה

– Mishle / Proverbs 12:4

To Helen, on our 54th year

– Milton

Contents

Foreword

It is a source of much gratification to see the steady demand for the five books which comprised the *B'nai B'rith Great Books Series*, retitled in 1985, *The B'nai B'rith History of the Jewish People*. These books presented the inner-content of Jewish tradition, the achievements of the great leaders and thinkers, the ideas, beliefs and religious movements of Judaism. In fact, they comprise a history of the Jewish People.

These books can been found on the shelves of countless family libraries, and in the studies of thousands of teachers and rabbis. Rarely do these volumes appear pristine. They were created to serve as texts for the classroom and for informal Jewish education, and that is how they have been used. There is nothing obscure in them. They have been written with an enviable clarity, and they inspire a curiosity about the ideas and accomplishments they describe. Because of the freshness and vigor of each essay, for more than thirty years these five volumes have been central texts in Jewish education in the United States.

In 1985 I organized a new edition which supplemented each essay with annotated bibliographies that reviewed the literature relevant to each essay's subject and published subsequently. The new edition proved to be very popular, and it rapidly went into a second printing. Its success highlighted the obvious limitation that the series stops at mid-century, and that there were important new developments in Jewish thought, new views on old subjects, and important new subjects which the series did not cover. As sound as the series was, it would become a period piece if it was not taken forward, and what better way to honor the achievements of the original fifty contributors and their editor Simon Noveck than to build upon their work and strive to equal the quality of their efforts.

It is just five years ago the I asked my good friend Steven Katz of Cornell University to consider the potential value of expanding the series with the purpose of carrying forward the intellectual history of the Jewish People from the 1950's to the end of the century. He believed the idea to be worthy, and he accepted my invitation to conceive and edit two new volumes, one devoted to critical issues and subjects in Jewish life, and the other focused on the principal interpreters of Jewish thought during the past forty years. A third volume, what will be the eighth in the series, will examine the lives of the principal public figures in Jewish life in the last half of this century.

Now with the publication of *Frontiers of Jewish Thought* I have the honor of thanking Steven publicly for his work. He enlisted the participation of a noteworthy group of essayists who when taken together with their editor may be justly described as among the principal figures in Jewish Studies in the 1990s. They are the intellectual heirs to the nearly fifty scholars, teachers and rabbis who contributed to the first five volumes. Because of the effective collaboration between the authors and the editor I believe the readers will find this volume to be free of unnecessary density and exceptionally well written. All of the essays were written especially for this volume.

The B'nai B'rith Commission on Continuing Jewish Education comprises a dedicated body of lay leaders who devote themselves to the creation of programs which achieve a greater understanding of Judaism and of the Jewish contribution to civilization. Three successive chairmen of the Commission have guided its return to book publishing—Abe Kaplan, Dr. A. J. Kravtin and Arthur Recht—each of them giving generously of their time and counsel to what is a complicated enterprise. Milton Smith of Austin, Texas, a senior member of the Commission and its current vice-chairman, has been a central figure in all of our efforts to publish important books and to have them used in the widest range of educational settings. His enthusiasm, encouragement and high standards have lightened my burdens and greatly increased the success of our book publishing program.

This Commission continues to enjoy the support, advice and commitment of Philip M. Klutznick who as the President of B'nai B'rith oversaw its establishment and placed its work at the center of the B'nai B'rith agenda. The B'nai B'rith Great Books Series was begun under his watchful eye. Today, B'nai B'rith's current President, Kent E. Schiner, encourages the Commission's activities in every way he can.

Among my professional colleagues I owe the greatest debt to Dr. Sidney M. Clearfield, the Executive Vice President of B'nai B'rith, who is providing the leadership and environment necessary for a Jewish educational program of quality to flourish. Within the Department of Continuing Jewish Education the administrative support and deep devotion which

Felice Caspar and Sandra Wiener provide have made this project proceed in a competent and orderly manner.

B'nai B'rith seeks to serve the Jewish People through a comprehensive set of programs which are devoted to the transmittal of one's Jewish identity from one generation to another, at the core of which are the ethics and values of Judaism. A tradition cannot endure or be passed on unless it is well understood, and the living faith which is Judaism in constantly in a state of creative tension and growth. *Frontiers of Jewish Thought* is offered to its readers as both a chronicle and a contribution to this process.

MICHAEL NEIDITCH
Director
B'nai B'rith Commission
on Continuing Jewish Education

Washington, D.C.
27 December 1991
20 Tevet 5752

Introduction

A quarter of a century has passed since B'nai B'rith published its *Great Books Series* that contained five influential volumes on Jewish history and thought: four volumes edited by Rabbi Simon Noveck and one by Dr. Abraham Ezra Millgram. Realizing this, Dr. Michael Neiditch, Director of Continuing Jewish Education for B'nai B'rith, had the excellent idea of adding to this important series by commissioning two new volumes, one dealing with *Thinkers* and one with *Concepts*, that would review and evaluate the developments of the last twenty-five years.

In designing these new works the Editor has sought both to chronicle the main issues that have been central to the Jewish agenda for the past three decades, for example, matters pertaining to the State of Israel, demographic trends, anti-semitism, and assimilation, as well as to focus needed attention on more recent concerns that promise to be consequential in the 1990's and beyond, for example, feminism, abortion, birth control, pluralism, nuclear war, and AIDS. In this way, the collection as a whole simultaneously points backwards to the recent past and forwards to the immediate future, and should thereby provide readers with the sort of historical and conceptual knowledge required for them to engage in serious *Jewish* reflection upon the complex matters here under analysis.

Given this goal the Editor invited contributions from authors who are both scholars of the tradition as well as active participants in the ongoing debates about which they write. Our ambition was to produce a book that while comprised of first rate scholarship also revealed the contemporary problematic, the deep, often anxious, questioning that the repercussive topics under review engendered for sensitive, caring, Jewishly committed individuals at the end of the twentieth century. As we approach the year 2000 of the Common Era, what does Judaism have to say that is genuinely interesting and persuasive about God, about the People Israel, about the salience of Jewish education, about war?

With this marked emphasis on the here and now the present volume, along with its companion *Interpreters of Judaism in the Late Twentieth Century,* truly fulfills its mandate to complement and bring forward the series which in its 1985 edition was aptly renamed *The B'nai B'rith History of the Jewish People.* These wonderful earlier anthologies had a heavy historical emphasis, covering the range of Jewish thinkers from the Prophets and Philo up to and including the early Mordecai Kaplan and the first wave of writings by R. Joseph Soloveitchik, i.e., up to and just beyond World War II. Even the volume dedicated to contemporary thought emphasized the strictly classical themes of *God, Torah and Israel,* as interpreted by recent authors. In contrast, the present volume, while feeling the obligation to re-examine several of these concepts, e.g. that of God or the Land of Israel, focuses on *new* subjects that have emerged uniquely in our time, such as AIDS and on issues that have taken radically original turns in the last few decades, such as the debate over Feminism, the negative spiral in Jewish population and its implications, and the dramatic consequences of assimilation on the one hand and religious pluralism on the other. Accordingly, the present volume is very much about today and tomorrow, not yesterday.

I have allowed each of our contributing authors the liberty of transliterating Hebrew words in the manner they prefer rather than imposing an artificial uniformity that would have made some of them uncomfortable.

In the creation, execution and production of this volume, I have incurred a number of debts. First of all, I would publicly like to thank the contributors to this collection who, on the whole, have made my job as Editor a relatively easy one. Secondly, I must thank Michael Neiditch who initiated this project, invited the Editor to undertake the work, and offered wise counsel whenever he was called upon to do so. Thirdly, the work of Ms. Trudie Calvert who expertly copy-edited the manuscripts is much appreciated.

Closer to home, I have benefitted greatly from the help of Mrs. Raihana Zaman and Mrs. Phyllis Emdee, both of the Department of Near Eastern Studies at Cornell University. Their constant willingness to lend a hand, always with a smile, is greatly appreciated. And lastly, and as always, I am indebted in countless ways to my wife Rebecca, and to my patient and loving children, Shira, Tamar and Yehuda.

STEVEN T. KATZ

Frontiers of Jewish Thought

The People Israel

EMIL L. FACKENHEIM

A Different People

Just before his death, the biblical Joshua performed an act, the consequences of which were to reverberate through the generations. Moses had not been permitted to enter the Promised Land so that his people could possess it. Having accomplished both, his successor did not consider his own work complete without a gathering of "all the tribes of Israel . . . , their elders, their heads, their judges, their officers" (Josh. 24:1). The gathering was meant to be solemn, comprehensive, and momentous. And all this it was.

Having assembled them all, Joshua delivered the last speech of his life. He began with a rehearsal of history. The people's ancestors once dwelled beyond the river, serving other gods. Then the Lord took Abraham, their father, led him into Canaan, and multiplied his seed. Centuries after He heard their descendants' cry as they groaned in Egyptian slavery and led them through trials and tribulations until at length they would return, as now was the case, to the long-promised land. Having said all this, Joshua at length came to the point of his rehearsal and, indeed, of the whole assembly: *he gave the people a choice*. The Lord had been faithful to them these many centuries; even so, they could now choose to abandon Him, whether to go back to the old gods beyond the river or forward to the new gods of the Canaanites. "As for me and my house"—thus Joshua completed his long exhortation—"we will serve the Lord." And when the people responded that they too would serve the Lord, Joshua uttered his climactic words: "Ye are witnesses against yourselves," and the people assented that witnesses, indeed, they were (Josh. 24:1–15, 22).

A choice was given to Abraham by Him who was to be called his God when He said unto him, "Get thee out of thy country, and from thy kindred, and from thy father's house, unto the land that I will show thee" (Gen. 12:1). A choice there was, for Abraham might have ignored or defied the divine command. A choice there was also when, centuries after, the whole people exclaimed at Sinai *"Na'asse ve'nishma"* (Exod. 24:7), "we shall do it and hear it," for this phrase is understood in the Midrash as a grandiose commitment because it is voluntary. (It is considered grandiose also because it is unconditional. There are other Midrashim, though, in which the choice is divinely forced on the people.) And now, in the assembly called by Joshua, they, the second generation, were given a choice once more. But—this is what makes Joshua's response to their response so momentous—*the choice given by Joshua to his generation was never given again.*

It is for this reason that the momentous words of Joshua and the no less momentous response of the people reverberated through the generations. They do so to this day: for this one need go no further than to the institution of *bar mitzvah*. A Christian youth is confirmed on being able to commit himself to the Christian faith. A Jewish boy may decide against a *bar mitzvah* ceremony; if rejecting Judaism in toto he may even be morally compelled: yet at age thirteen he becomes *bar mitzvah* regardless of his scruples or decisions. *Bar mitzvah* thus differs from confirmation. That it differs no less from a tribal initiation is proved by the very term. The boy becomes "son" of "mitzvah" (commandment), and the commandment is part of a covenant that, ever since Abraham, God made with his descendants; yet ever since Joshua these were not consulted.

Jews are, then, both a people and a people unlike any other. This is, of course, only what the Jewish tradition asserts. Whether at present it still must or even may be asserted is not self-evident. It is at least clear that what the tradition says about *bar mitzvah* is in no way altered by removing its "male chauvinism" from the institution. On the contrary, the new institution of *bat mitzvah* extends explicitly to both sexes of this people what implicitly has applied to both through the ages.

On Being Singled Out

The God of Abraham founds a tribe by initiating speech with Abraham. Yet in the biblical account this is no tribal deity: before this act, He is the God of all humanity and, subsequent to it, the God of all humanity He remains. Yet He is not a God of humanity in general who conveys to Abraham principles applicable to humanity in general. He wishes Abraham, and him alone, to get out of his country, his kindred, his father's house. This single human being is addressed, to be sure, by a radically universal God—but in his own no less radical singularity. What can be done neither by a tribal deity nor by a God of humanity in general is thus done by the God of the Jewish Bible: *He singles out.*

Within this book, to be singled out is a characteristic experience. It occurs to Amos, Jonah, Isaiah, Jeremiah, and indeed every prophet. Millennia later—from Soren Kierkegaard on—to be singled out is made central in the philosophy inspired by him. For existentialism, to be singled out is not confined to prophets. It applies to every human being. With regard to crucial decisions—though, of course, not with regard to trivial ones—no person is meant to be either a copy of someone else or a mere instance of humanity in general. Everyone *is meant* to be—is meant *to choose* to be—none but himself, a self irreplaceable and unique.

In the biblical account the whole Jewish people is singled out. But unlike Abraham, the prophets, the "individual" of Kierkegaard and of the existentialists, this people is singled out *as a people*—and, ever since Joshua's momentous assembly, with a choice no longer of *whether to accept* but only of *how to respond* to its singled-out condition.

It is therefore natural—nay, inevitable—that as constant a biblical theme as the covenant initiated with Abraham should be this people's wish *not* to be singled out, that is, to be like other nations. If to be singled out is the biblical theme of themes, this wish is the biblical countertheme of themes. To the minds of readers all too zealous in their "piety"—countless Jewish ones and all but a handful of Christian ones—this wish is rank ingratitude, impiety, apostasy. These should stop to consider, however, that, on an occasion as momentous as Joshua's assembly, the God of Abraham—now the God of Israel—shows Himself to be less of a zealot than all of them. The people have come to Samuel, wanting a king like all the nations. Horrified by such infidelity to *the* King, Samuel turns to God who is horrified also, but only initially. Subsequently He who is the King relents and does give them a king and thus also a state.

This divine act is no less momentous than the two human ones already discovered, both of which occurred in the assembly called by Joshua. What makes this divine act momentous is the recognition that these humans are not a group of individuals—*adult* individuals—who have chosen a holy life, say, in a monastery. This is a people composed of men, women, and children, who cannot live unless, if not a nation like all others, they are at least sufficiently like them to be able to survive among them. Whatever may be meant by the expression "kingdom of priests and holy people" (Exod. 19:6), it cannot mean obedience to "laws" by which such a people would "die" rather than "live" (Deut. 30:11–14, 19).

This People and Its City

In his *City of God* St. Augustine attempts to identify that "city" but succeeds only in divorcing it sharply from the "city of man." The first city is inhabited by prophets, saints, and monks absorbed in prayer and holy works. The second is marked (to use Franz Rosenzweig's expression) by the "murder and manslaughter" that Augustine witnessed when his own city of Hippo was besieged by the Vandals. (Shortly after his death, they conquered the city and destroyed it.)

The distinction between these two cities is alien to the Jewish Bible, in which history is all one, the "sacred" history of the covenant and the ordinary or "profane" history, which includes murder and manslaughter. This is well illustrated by what happens to the first king of Israel, whom Samuel anoints in the name of a God who has yielded to the request of His people. Saul is a king like others—but unlike them in that he is divinely appointed. There are two biblical accounts of what happens to Saul and his kingship. When, through disobedience, he fails the test of a God-appointed king, the kingship is taken from him: on this the two accounts agree. They disagree in their view of his subsequent fate. According to Chronicles Saul continues to sin; hence when he dies in battle the God who already has taken his kingship punishes him further by taking his life. In Samuel, however, for all his prior disobedience Saul is pictured as a hero rather than a sinner; and when, having lost in battle, he dies at his own hand his death is lamented as a tragedy (I Sam. chaps. 15, 31; I Chron. chap. 10).

To be sure, the more "pious" standpoints of the Chronicler is not his alone. His being the concluding book of the Jewish Bible, it is also the standpoint of the redactor of the Jewish Canon, and this in turn is the standpoint of a people that, having returned from their Babylonian exile to Jerusalem, find the divine Presence in history vindicated by their own experience. To the modern-minded reader, however, it is significant that of the two accounts, only that in Samuel is a literary masterpiece. And what ought to be significant to *any* reader—Christian as well as Jewish, the most extreme secularist among Jews no more than the most extreme among their pious—is that for all his piety it does not occur to the redactor to exclude the Samuel account from the canon or even to tamper with the text so as to make it more pious.

Exile without Foreseeable End

The standpoint of the canonizer is marked by the experience of the end of an exile. A new standpoint was made necessary with a new exile, if no sooner than when (with the loss of the Bar Kochba war) its end became unforeseeable. No Jewish state remained. No Jewish king remained. All that remained was the King of Kings.

But did even He remain? Had He not abandoned His people? No, He had not abandoned them, was the momentous response: it was they who had abandoned Him, and exile was divine punishment for their sins. Not even their gravest offenses could make Him abandon them. The sufferings of exile were therefore sufferings of love, sent to cause them to return unto Him. And He who now caused them to suffer would not let them suffer forever. With or without sufficient repentance on their part, He would end their exile. Indeed, the redemption to come would be final. The state restored would be a messianic state, governed by a messianic king. Whereas the end of exile was unforeseeable, it was sure to come. Nor was it meaningless while it lasted.

The tenth-century Gaon Saadia thus states correctly that Jews *are* a people only because of the Torah; and the eleventh-century poet-philosopher Yeduda Halevi says that they *remain* a people only through fidelity to the Torah. Both these thinkers may be wrong about this people's history as a whole. (Evidently this is the view of the present writer.) They are right, however, for the period of an exile whose end was unforeseeble. It was from the Torah that this people took its being singled-out by God, that the God who had done the singling out would never abandon them, and that therefore the exile would not last forever and was not meaningless while it lasted. Even as they kept the Torah, they were thus themselves kept by it.

This standpoint necessitated a reading of the Bible in a spirit more pious than that of the Bible itself. Of this Esther is the most striking example. In the biblical text a saving God may be implied but is not mentioned: the explicit saviors are Esther and Mordecai, aided by an astonishing series of coincidences. In the Purim prayers that commemorate that salvation, however, it is the divine Savior that is celebrated. It is His miracle that saved the people then, and it is His miracles that will keep on saving them until the advent of the great Salvation.

The theme of being divinely singled out had existed since Abraham. During the exile whose end was unforeseeable, it became the theme without which the people—stateless, kingless—could not have survived. Even so, however, what had all along been the countertheme of themes did not vanish altogether. In interpreting the divine law the exilic rabbis rarely forgot that a people composed of men, women, and children must be able to live rather than die by it. To go further, in times of persecution extreme enough to endanger the people's very survival, the countertheme was taken up even by pious rabbis. Thus the eighteenth-century Hasidic rabbi Levi Yitzhak of Berdiczev once interrupted the solemn Yom Kippur service—an unheard-of scandal—to protest that, whereas all nations had kings protecting them, His people were unprotected by the King of Kings. Thereafter, to be sure, having uttered his protest, he went on with the *Kaddish*, the sole theme of which is praise of God.

A lover of God, the protesting Levi Yitzhak never ceased to praise Him; yet a lover of his people also, he considered it entitled to its share of apostates. Walking in the street one Shabbat, he met a Jew who, smoking a cigarette, was brazen enough to boast to the rabbi of this breach of the Shabbat law.

Levi Yitzhak looked heavenward and exclaimed, "O God, how faithful is Your people Israel! They remember You even when they break Your laws!"

In tolerating apostates the eighteenth-century Hasidic rabbi had a predecessor in the second-century Rabbi Meir. His teacher Elisha ben Abuya had become an apostate. Perhaps he was dabbling in Greek philosophy or was in despair because of the catastrophes of the age. The rabbis condemned his apostasy. They no longer even mentioned his name. But rather than excommunicate him they kept hoping for his repentance. Rabbi Meir did not even shun his teacher but continued to associate with him and to honor him for his learning.

Modernity

"We consider ourselves no longer a nation," a group of Reform Rabbis wrote in 1885 in what came to be known as the Pittsburgh platform, "and therefore expect neither a return to Palestine . . . nor the restoration of any of the laws concerning the Jewish state." In making this statement, these men of the New World expressed in radical terms what was held less radically by many others—liberals, conservatives, and even some of the modern Orthodox—in this new age. A version of some such view was only natural. A Jew could hardly demand—let alone receive—emancipation in a free modern nation and also consider himself part of an exiled nation; nor could he—or so it seemed—demand equal rights in the modern state of his domicile and yet hope for a restoration of his own ancient state. Why then survive at all? The Pittsburgh rabbis went on to declare that they were a "religious community" and thus were obliged to survive because, whereas the modern world was progressing toward the "kingdom of truth, justice and peace" envisaged by the biblical prophets, to hasten that progress was the "mission of Israel."

It is easy to dismiss this naively optimistic nineteenth-century view in light of the grim twentieth century. Yet tribute should be paid to much high-minded work that was done—and continues to be done—by Jews in the name of the mission of Israel. There was, however, at least one jarring note in the whole conception from the start: no one is born a missionary.

Occasional attempts were made to get rid of this jarring note, the most characteristic of which was the replacement of *bar mitzvah* with a ceremony of confirmation. *Bar mitzvah*, however, won out. To this day it remains the great institutional nemesis of the modern Jewish attempt to get rid of Jewish peoplehood.

An external nemesis in the modern East corresponded to this internal one in the modern West. There was no emancipation for the Jewish masses of czarist Russia: being both masses and un-emancipated, they continued to be a people, with their own language, their own culture, and even fragments of a government. But affected by the spirit of modernity even if not benefiting from it politically, they began to question the covenantal tradition, especially taking issue with the view that they were not a nation like others but different, and this by a force not of their own making, call it God or fate or world history. If Western Jews may be said to have widely responded to modernity by fidelity to the Jewish God but abandonment of Jewish peoplehood, Eastern Jews may be said to have widely done the opposite: they remained faithful to Jewish peoplehood but abandoned the Jewish God. There arose a secular Jewish people.

This response to modernity, however, had an internal nemesis also. If Jews were no longer a divinely singled out people, why go beyond bemoaning such facts as assimilation, intermarriage, the weakening of what came to be called Jewish "culture"? Why consider all this a sin and a betrayal? Did Jews continue to be *b'ne mitzvah* (children of the commandment), even if there no longer was a *Metzave* (commander)?

The most striking response to this question was the Zionism of Ahad Ha-am (1856–1927). His core concern was the threatened dissolution of the Jewish people and the "creative" development of a "culture" that alone could save it. He saw no hope for such a salvation, however, except in a new cultural Jewish center in the ancient Jewish land.

A Zionism quite different from this Eastern version was advocated by Theodor Herzl (1860–1904), an assimilated Western Jew at home in modern Vienna. More assimilated still was Captain Alfred Dreyfus (1859–1935), for he was at home in modern Paris, the city that had once witnessed the storming of the Bastille. After the vicious anti-Semitism that victimized Dreyfus in the "Affair" named after him, Dreyfus himself may have remained at home in Paris. Herzl ceased to be at home in Vienna. He might have ignored the explosion of Jew-hatred in the citadel of liberty, equality, and fraternity. Alternatively, he might have belittled it as a temporary lapse, or fled into baptism, or into humanity in general or—most effectively of all—into joining the Jew-baiters. All this has been done and continues to be done. (For Herzl, assimilated Jew that he was, it would have been easy.) But he rejected it all as contrary to human dignity. "The enemy makes Jews a nation," he declared, "whether they like it or not." For Herzl, the enemy made into a naton at least those Jews compelled by self-respect to refuse to go, cap in hand, to governments, universities, the press, pleading that Jews too were human beings, and this not despite their Jewishness but, if anything, because of it. To survive by such pleas, and in states that boasted of their liberty, their equality, their fraternity, was simply not honorable. Hence, whereas Ahad Ha-am sought a center of Jewish culture in the ancient land, Herzl sought a Jewish state.

Modernity and Postmodernity

"The day the Bastille fell, the foundations were laid for the gas ovens of Auschwitz—and for the revival of the State of Israel." Thus writes the contemporary right-wing Israeli thinker Israel Eldad. This is, of course, an insane statement though it must at once be asked whether "sanity" after Auschwitz is not itself insane. Eldad goes on to explain that Napoleon offered Jews a choice between a "Jewish state in Palestine" and "complete assimilation." "What he could not tolerate (and rightly so) was the limbo of uncertainty, the Jews being neither here nor there."[1]

Of course, Eldad's explanation fails to justify his insane statement, for truly modern states—North America but also European democracies, including France herself—did in due course manage to "tolerate" the "limbo" of Jewish peoplehood. (In some cases they have even come to esteem it.) Even so, however, Eldad's explanation cannot simply be dismissed. When Jews could still flee from their Nazi enemies, their democratic friends failed to open their doors wide to them; and when Jews could flee no longer, these friends failed to bomb the railroads to Auschwitz.

A writer of sanity was Arthur Koestler. A man of his time, he wrote novels about the great issues of his time—the "failed god" communism, the Holocaust, and the armed Jewish struggle for a Jewish state. Having supported that struggle for most of his life, he saw it ended when the state at last had arrived. To Koestler this was the last event in a long history of Jewish abnormality. Jews now had a choice between two kinds of normality. One was to be a Jew in a state like all others. The other was dissolution of Jewishness through complete assimilation. This latter had been a possibility ever since the advent of modernity, and many Jews had chosen it. But in Koestler's view it had not been honorable for some Jews to choose it so long as others still suffered the fate of Jewish abnormality. With the advent of a Jewish state, however, assimilation became honorable.

Koestler may be viewed as the last Jew of modernity. The course he advocated in 1949 was first advocated by the first Jew of modernity, Baruch Spinoza (1632–77). Not accidentally Spinoza was a Jew who rejected the Jewish religion; and not accidentally Koestler used no Jewish symbol when calling for an end of Jewish abnormality. His 1949 advice ends: "Now that the mission of the Wandering Jew is completed, he must discard the knapsack and cease to be an accomplice in his own destruction. If not for his own sake, then for that of his children and his children's children. The fumes of the death chambers still linger over Europe; there must be an end to every calvary."[2]

Prospects

Forty years later—a biblical number—Koestler's advice is irrelevant. Within the Jewish state, Jews are divided into right and left as to how best to end their forty-year seige: without genuine peace theirs cannot be a state like others. Whether it should be such a state is the question that divides them into "religious" and "nonreligious." Normality, then, eludes Jews in the state within. It equally eludes them in the diaspora without. To be sure, there is plenty of "normality" among half- or wholly assimilated Jews. By the standards set by Koestler, however, assimilation is no more honorable after the advent of the Jewish state than before: if once would-be assimilating Jews owed solidarity to Jews still in exile, they owe solidarity now not only to these—Jewish exiles surviving in Syria and Ethiopia, Iran, and the Soviet Union—but also and above all to the besieged Jewish state. They owe it solidarity at least until the siege has yielded to the normality of peace.

What to Koestler was a possibility could conceivably become the Jewish actuality, if not now, then at some future time. For

Koestler, however, the "mission" of the Jewish people was simply to cease wandering, to achieve normality, and hence to reject with might and main all thoughts of being singled out for a special destiny. Consequently the Holocaust was for him but the worst in a history of disasters, caused, in the last analysis, by Jewish abnormality.

The Holocaust, however, was not just the worst; it was unique. Singled out since Abraham and Sinai, and since Joshua with a choice not of whether to accept being singled out but only how to respond, this people was singled out at Auschwitz. This time, however, it was not for blessing and life but for curse and death, and—except for the few able to choose resistance or martyrdom— its death and its curse were totally choiceless. On *Yom Ha-Shoah*, the Jewish people commemorates the heroes and martyrs of the Holocaust. But whereas it knows that it must remember also the choiceless victims—indeed, them above all—it does not yet know how.

The Holocaust has yet to penetrate fully the Jewish consciousness, both secular and religious, or that of the world. Until these processes have taken shape, little can be said of what the Jewish future will be or what it ought to be. The Jewish people once returned to Jerusalem from exile: the consequences of that return were world-historical. Now this people has returned a second time. But the consequences of the process now under way in our postmodern world are still clouded in mystery.

Notes

1. Israel Eldad, *The Jewish Revolution* (New York, 1971), pp 17 & 18
2. Arthur Koestler, *Promise and Fulfilment* (London, 1949), p. 335

FOR FURTHER READING

Avi-Yonah, M., *The Jews of Palestine* (Oxford, 1976). A ground-breaking work showing how, from the end of the Bar Kochba war to the Arab conquest, the political will of Palestinian Jewry remained alive, serving as a substitute for the destroyed state.

Ben Gurion, David, *Israel* (New York, 1971). The personal history by the chief architect of the reborn Jewish state.

Buber, Martin, *On Zion: The History of an Idea* (New York, 1973). An authoritative account by the man widely considered this century's greatest Jewish thinker who was also a life-long Zionist.

Fackenheim, Emil L., *The Jewish Bible After the Holocaust—A Re-reading* (Manchester and Bloomington, 1990). A re-reading, after the epoch-making events of this century, of the Book without which the Jews would not be a people—nay, would not be.

— , *The Jewish Return into History* (New York 1978). Essays seeking to show that, after a bi-millenial exilic existence at the margins of history, the Holocaust has made the Jewish return into history necessary, while return to Jewish statehood has made it possible.

— , *What is Judaism?* (New York, 1987, 1988). Written for the lay reader, this book expounds Judaism for the present age, in which Jewish faith is threatened by the Holocaust, even as it has become inseparable from a commitment to the survival and safety of the State of Israel.

Kaplan, Mordecai, *Judaism as a Civilization* (New York, 1957). The magnum opus by the thinker who sought to preserve the distinctiveness of Jewish peoplehood, while abandoning, boldly and forthrightly, the traditional doctrine of Jewish chosenness.

Yehudah Halevi, *The Kuzari* (London 1906). The classic medieval account of Jewish peoplehood and its religious foundations.

The Land of Israel: Its Contemporary Meaning

MICHAEL ROSENAK

Many observers are astonished that the land of Israel has meaning to most Jewishly identified contemporary Jews, that they care, contribute, visit, and worry with an intensity and involvement that is often lacking in other Jewish dimensions of their lives. One would expect that that feature of Jewishness and Jewish tradition which assumes and demands a special link to a particular and remote land would be among the most problematic and unsavory to the emancipated modern Jew who is now, for the most part, a citizen of one of the nation-states that is experienced as liberal, culturally enhancing, and pluralistic. The territorial connection of Judaism to Eretz Yisrael is in many ways incongruent with the world of that modern Jew. It suggests that Judaism has a specific geography, that its memories and myths have a particular and ongoing historical and cultural context, that Jews "have a land," and that they are a nation.

What the sacred sources of Judaism say about this "territory of Judaism" could plausibly be the least congenial aspect of the tradition. What have dwellers of comfortable suburbs to do with ancient desert tribes ready to call a tiny and arid place a pleasant and broad land flowing with milk and honey? Why should this somewhat elusive "portion" promised by God to the forefathers interest the well-situated descendants?

Yet Eretz Yisrael *is* important to Jews. They recognize it as relevant to their identity as Jews. They are proud, often concerned, sometimes deeply embarrassed. They feel that what happens in this land, what is said in it and about it, touches directly on their innermost being and on their public image. Those among them who take religion seriously see involvement with Eretz Yisrael as an inevitable part of the package; others, less pious or indifferent, see their involvement with Israel as secular religion. And those who care not at all about Israel have, in all but fringe groups, read themselves out of the community. This is astonishing.

That Israel has meaning for most Jews is not merely astonishing; it is ironic. The many Jews who turn first in their morning newspapers to news about Israel (news found in ludicrous abundance, in part because editors know their Jewish readers) have, generally speaking, no intention of going there to live; this applies too to the small minority who still, thrice daily, beseech God to return them to their land and to rebuild His Temple. Indeed, those who do live there are vaguely categorized as the (formerly) oppressed and homeless, or as victims of historical circumstances that led them East instead of West, or idiosyncratic idealists, people of commendable ideological stature but strange. The assumptions and doctrines of Zionism are not those of most diaspora Jews and yet, ironically, it is this movement that put the land of Israel near the center of the contemporary Jewish experience. The Zionists claim (when they dare) that they wish to end *Galut* (exile) and that Jews should proceed with the venture of "ingathering of exiles" without waiting for God to send His messianic redeemer. For the majority of Jews in the diaspora, *Galut* no longer exists; they are not in exile but voluntarily dispersed in blessed lands, and neither God nor man is invited to change that reality. Yet despite this profound disagreement between the ideological Israelis and almost everyone else, the Israel created by Zionism is generally considered to be, in some sense, a miracle, changing what it means to be a Jew and making belief in a provident God, even after the Holocaust, more cogent than it was.

We may say that all genuine Jewish interest in Israel is ironic because contemporary Jews are modern in consciousness—and what most characterized Jewish modernization in its more rigorous and systematic formulations was the need to put both the concrete halakah and the actual Eretz Yisrael in historical perspective, at a chronological and existential distance. The Zionists and the neo-Orthodox were mavericks of Jewish modernity, the former because they longed for Zion and the latter because they adhered to halakah. The classical Reform movement represented the modern tendency more consistently and, with regard to Eretz Yisrael, expressed it succinctly. Berlin, they said, is our Jerusalem. The lands of emancipation, as the Reform and the neo-Orthodox and all others who welcomed emancipation knew, were attractive, they appeared spiritually exciting, *and they demanded loyalty.* Conversely, the Jewish belief system in which a concrete and historically accessible Eretz Yisrael played a central role belonged to a world regulated by halakhic practices that were no longer authoritative for most Jews and to a messianic hope whose seeming "particularism" could not command their loyalty.

What did Eretz Yisrael mean before the Enlightenment and the emancipation undermined it? The sources of Judaism, in variegated texts and contexts, stated it clearly and elaborately: it was the land of covenant, imbued with holiness. The concept of Holy Land has an aspect of inherent specialness, leading poets to sing its praises and kiss its soil, but it should not be confused with the mythical idea of Holy Land, whose meaning is exhausted in pilgrimages and moments of awe associated with being "where God was" and walking in His footsteps. In Jewish Scripture, the status of the covenanted land derives not from God's bestowal of grace on the human soul but from his revelation of commandments to a people—and giving them a land within which to live in accordance with His will. Tradition has it that the Temple was built on Mount Moriah, not because God was uniquely *there* but because Abraham was prepared in that place to sacrifice his son in accord with the inexplicable divine command. The Bible declares the land of Israel holy because therein Israel was to live a holy life. If Israel keeps the covenant and carries out God's behest, He will bless them and the land, and His eye will be upon it, its people and produce, continually. Should they, however, do evil and walk in the idolatrous and immoral ways of the nations that preceded them, the land will "vomit them out" as it did the previous tenants who, too, had not understood that "all the earth is Mine" and that all peoples are His subjects. For having agreed to "hear" (that is, understand) this, Israel was given the land of Canaan, named for the most ignoble of Noah's descendants, now designated through Israel and Torah as worthy of becoming the throne and the sanctuary of the King.

After the exile from Eretz Yisrael, Jews, carrying the Torah with them, remembered the land primarily in this religious dimension, which was its essence, which made it unforgettable as long as there was Judaism and a covenant. And with religious memory came theological anticipation. Maimonides, in describing the days of the Messiah, gave a classic description of the hope and the expectation, elevated to doctrine:

> King Messiah will arise and restore the kingdom of David to its former state and original sovereignty. He will rebuild the sanctuary and gather the dispersed of Israel. All the ancient laws will be reinstituted in his days; sacrifices will again be offered; the Sabbatical and Jubilee years will again be observed in accordance with the commandments set forth in the Torah.
>
> He who does not believe in a restoration or does not look forward to the coming of the Messiah denies not only the teachings of the prophets but also those of the Torah and Moses our Teacher, for Scripture affirms the rehabilitation of Israel, as it is said, "Then the Lord your God will turn your captivity and have compassion upon you and will return and gather you . . . and the Lord your God will bring you into the land which your forefathers possessed. (Deut. 30:3–5).[1]

Only a small minority of contemporary Jews "remember" this anticipation or could be aroused to guilt by their forgetfulness, though the traditional prayerbook, like the Bible and Talmud, faithfully records it and persistently calls for its liturgical reenactment. One is expected to pray for rain on the last day of the *Succot* season (*Shmini Atzeret*), for that is the beginning of the rainy season in Eretz Yisrael, and to ask for dew on Passover—the beginning of the long dry summer. After every meal, the *Siddur* expects the Jew to pray for the restoration of Jerusalem; a plea for the rebuilding of Zion is also incorporated into each of the daily prayers. No wedding ceremony may delete the longing for the rebuilt cities of Zion, and mourners are consoled with the prayer that God will comfort them "together with all the other mourners for Zion and Jerusalem." The drama of remembering reaches its dramatic peak during the *Mussaf* service of Yom Kippur in which the sacrificial service of the high priest on this holiest of days is recited, followed by liturgical poetry which compares the appearance of the high priest after the service to, among other glories, the radiance of the morning star and the splendor of the rainbow. The poetic remembering of the exaltation and solemnity of the

Day of Atonement in Jerusalem concludes with the refrain, "Happy is the eye that saw all of these," a dramatic turning point in the religious drama of the liturgy, for it is followed by a dirge, recalling the catastrophes that befell our ancestors "for because of our sins and those of our fathers all these have been taken from us." This moment in the liturgical calendar, the *Ávodah*, that is, the recitation of the service, was traditionally a highlight of Jewish experience, a veritable "happening." The *Ávodah* is largely a technical description of sacrificing, garment changing, and discharging of the scapegoat into the desert, but it is interspersed with dramatic prostrations, prayers for atonement and reconciliation, and proclamations of God's kingdom. The recitation ends most fittingly yet incomprehensibly for many modern Jews with the joyful cry: 'Happy is the people whose lot is thus, happy the people whose God is the Lord."

I have expanded on this feature of remembering "when Israel dwelt in its land" to highlight the problematic character of traditional meanings of Eretz Yisrael for contemporary Jews. Who can be an Englishman—not merely a sojourner in England for a couple of centuries—and pray for rain? Who, being Argentinian or Australian, can pray for a good winter in October? When Jerusalem has been rebuilt, as it has been, who rightfully and honestly prays for its rebuilding? (This problem is most acute for observant Israeli Jews who speak these words in their vernacular and understand exactly what they are saying.) Who awaits a Messiah bent on restoring the sacrificial order and authorized to ensure the faithful observance of the Torah upon all? Is the running to and fro of the high priest, preoccupied with burnt offerings no less than with prayer, what we appropriately anticipate? If we do, why? What do modern people who still recite this liturgy with high emotion mean? The Mishnah[2] declares Eretz Yisrael to be the holiest of lands because of the commandments to be observed only therein; Jerusalem, the Temple, and the Holy of Holies are more sacred still for the same reason. What meaning can this convey to those estranged from commandments and perhaps particularly uncomfortable with those commandments "that can be observed only in Eretz Yisrael"?

My point, I hope, is clear. The significance of Eretz Yisrael was intrinsically bound up with the significance of biblical and talmudic Judaism. It was undermined by a modern culture, which called into question the plausibility and worth of Judaism's norms, hopes, and cultural gestures. Eretz Yisrael had meaning when the Sabbatical year, the pascal lamb, and the Sanhedrin deciding the beginning of each new month had meaning.

And here we return to the astonishment and irony with which we began. For it was Zionism, a largely secular movement, that restored Eretz Yisrael to the consciousness of Jews who did not wish to live under talmudic law, had no desire to see the Temple rebuilt, and anticipated no Messiah. The Zionists, indeed, had pious precursors, men such as Rabbis Alkalai and Kalischer, who drew traditional historiosophic conclusions about an imminent return and possible redemption from the momentous developments they perceived in modern history. These precursors had, in a sense, never left home. The traditional texts and liturgy spoke to them convincingly, without mediation, and they looked out of the window at modern history to see when the way had been cleared for the Messiah.

Unlike them, their secular Zionist heirs, men such as Pinsker, Herzl, and, in his own way, Ahad Ha-am, had been changed by history. Jewishness was a problem for them. They were concerned with reshaping the materials of Judaism—Torah, messianism, and Eretz Yisrael—to solve that problem. Many of them had been emancipated, and the emancipation had failed them. Many were impressed by national movements around them and hoped for something similar that could be historically continuous with Jewish memories and culture. Their concern, like that of other modern Jews, was not primarily covenant and obedience to God through the commandments of the Torah but a secure identity thoughtful connectedness to their own past, and a safe and dignified interaction with present-day humanity.

The concern for a firm and untroubled Jewish identity, so characteristic of modern Jews, was a hallmark of Zionism as of the other, competing, movements of modern Judaism. The very question of Jewish identity perceived as a problem marked Zionists like other modern ideologies, as rebellious and unfaithful. (Had God not called Israel by name? Was there a more magnificent and stable identity than that?) The ultratraditional faithful saw that almost immediately and condemned Zionism as heresy.

A more empathetic way of stating it would be that Zionism, like all modern Jewish movements, was born of crisis and that it was constructed, like all other modern Jewish ideologies, of broken vessels, which the builders refused to abandon. Therefore, it sought to make what had been a holy tongue into a vernacular; what Jews had revered as a sacred tradition, it extolled as a national culture. And it wished to transform the Holy Land into a Jewish homeland, like any other, only different because Jewish culture was different. Jacob Klatzkin, one of Zionism's more radical spokesmen, noted caustically that those who could still maintain allegiance to the halakah and its theological assumptions would not need Zionism because the law and its institutions provided them with a homeland. Nor would those who wished to assimilate and succeeded in so doing have recourse to contemporary Jewish nationalism. Berl Katznelson, a key socialist Zionist, pleaded with the youth not to deride tradition because it was not a cultured thing to do: "If a people possesses something old and profound, which can educate man and train him for his future, is it truly revolutionary to despise it and become estranged from it?"[3] Martin Buber reminded his readers that a living tradition must meet challenges: a tradition that was unchanging and static was fit only for exhibitions in museums. Herzl was prepared to take the Jews to Uganda because it was apparently available. He was able to mobilize the support of some religious Zionists (the mavericks of that movement, who wished to be both radical and traditional) because Eretz Yisrael was too holy for what Zionism had in mind. Zionism, as far as they were concerned, was designed to solve the prosaic "problem of the Jews," not to rewrite Judaism's redemptive philosophy of history.

No wonder that the ultratraditionalists would have none of this. For them, the meaning of Eretz Yisrael was what it had always been because their Judaism was (ostensibly) what it had always been. Eretz Yisrael meant a sacred remembered past and a glorious redemptive future. The present was the dark gray of *Galut*, not theologically significant. No wonder, too, that the assimilationists considered Zionism a regressive romanticism. The ultratraditionalists wanted (or rather, had) to be Jewish but considered this incompatible with modernity; the latter thought that being modern required relinquishing Judaism (or rather, Jewish identity).

Zionism's unique contribution to modern Jewish life was that it suggested a meaning to the land of Israel for Jews that drew on the tradition but was fully compatible with modernity. Zionists envisioned a holy life in Eretz Yisrael, but prophets of socialism were enlisted to supply substance to that holiness. In the new Eretz Yisrael, there would be a sublime value and norm of *avodah*, but it had only a semantic connection with what the high priest did on Yom Kippur, or, for that matter, what was done in the Temple every day. *Avodah* was work, pure and simple, and dignified (unlike what Jews allegedly were doing in *Galut*). Even the religious Zionists accepted this new understanding of *avodah*, for the socialists among them marched under the banner of *Torah v'avodah*, that is, "religion" in addition to work. And a new ideal type was added to Jewish life—the *chalutz*, the pioneer, who was expected to stand head and shoulders (literally) above the bent-over scholar, the pietist, the saint.

Zionism, even among modern Jews, that is, those who were not ultratraditional or assimilationist, was hardly popular. Jewish socialists in Eastern Europe considered it a romantic conceit of the literary-minded bourgeois who snobbishly preferred Hebrew to Yiddish. Reform Jews saw it as a fixation on a prior epoch in the development of Judaism; the neo-Orthodox saw it as heretical for it did not demand halakhic observance. And gentiles had trouble understanding it. Did Jews who had been accepted in liberal societies as a religious "persuasion" intend to return to the old Jewish nationalism (or "tribalism")? Could Jews return to the Holy Land before the Second Coming? What would happen to the Holy Land? If Jews stopped being a symbol in Western society and became real, might not the land of myth become distressingly concrete? And what about dual loyalty? Some gentile romantics were impressed by Zionism, but many others were worried, and that was of concern to Jews, for their identity as modern Jews was closely linked with what gentiles thought of them, not merely as in the past with how they treated them.

And yet Zionism has a larger measure of success than its opponents and many of its devotees expected. It created an ethos that gave new vistas to Jewish life, it changed the map of Eretz Yisrael, and it brought a Jewish commonwealth into being. The *Yishuv* had to make do, in this enterprise, with far fewer Jews than emigrated from Russia to the United States; moreover, most of the potential citizens of the new Jewish state were killed in the Holocaust. Its territory was minute, and its neighbors had no intention of living in peace with it. Most of those who did come to live in Israel in the early years of mass aliyah knew little of the European Jewish experience and of the Zionist ideology it produced. Yet it was on the map, its creation was widely considered as one of the astounding events of world history, and, in a seemingly miraculous and definitely paradoxical manner, it restored a measure of credibility to the theological historiosophy of traditional Judaism. Maurice Samuel, reflecting on the Jewish national rebirth, once wrote that many motherlands create colonies but colonies rarely create motherlands. The Jews did it after the Babylonian exile and now, some eighteen hundred years into the Roman exile, they were doing it again. "Once," remarks Samuel, "is an accident; twice is a habit." What does one do with such persistence, with an affinity for a land that can survive even the belief system that nurtured it? Samuel recalls: "Mobs attacking the Jews incited themselves with the cry: *Hep! Hep!* The syllable, some say, is made up of the first three letters of the words: *Hieroselyma est perdita!* Jerusalem is lost. My father heard that cry in Roumania, in his boyhood. . . . Why should Roumanian peasants taunt the Jews with the destruction of Jerusalem, if Jerusalem was nothing to the Jews? But the truth is that the rioters really doubted what they said. Jerusalem was not lost: only its people had been mislaid."[4] This state changed Jewish existence everywhere, if only because it provided a new collective focus for Jewish identity. It also provided a new and highly visible target for the enmity of Jew haters, who discovered the promulgated the idea that "Zionism is racism." But for some among the nations, as among Jews, there was also awe and joy. The Israeli philosopher Samuel Hugo Bergman relates that he was in Sweden at the time of the establishment of the state of Israel and that he witnessed rejoicing and a feeling at large that the rise of Israel was an event relevant to the whole world. He cites the scholar Pierre Van Passen, who wrote then: "In Israel there will live a prophetic people. . . . The history of the people of Israel is the history of mankind. The State of Israel is the laboratory of mankind, a laboratory where the problems of society will, at least in principle, be solved, with toil and sorrow, and at the same time, with the joy of faith."[5]

Van Passen, a fervent lover of the Jewish people, expressed, in a touching way, what Holy Land, land of covenant, implies in the Jewish tradition. The partially secularized formulation of an ancient religious doctrine would have met with the enthusiastic approval of Ahad Ha-am and all those who posited that, in the return to the land, the Jewish people would move smoothly back into the theological mold of the deepest meaning of Eretz Yisrael.

But as Yehezkiel Kaufmann had pointed out, the crisis of faith could not be whisked away simply by settling the land; without the faith of Judaism, Jews would have no valuative reason to return.[6] (He might have added that, without such valuative reasons, grounded in Judaism, they would leave the land when other countries became accessible and attractive.) Kaufmann did not foresee a smooth renaissance of "Jewish moral culture" such as that envisioned by Ahad Ha-am. He believed that faith was the key to the culture of Judaism; secular nationalism was no substitute and could engender no "prophetic people" simply by transplanting Jews to the landscape of the prophets. One could only hope that in Eretz Yisrael, as elsewhere, Jews would, through common experience, look for meanings and discover them, but they dared not assume them. They had to reembark on a search for wholeness.

If we wish to state this less somberly, we may say that, despite their having a state in Eretz Yisrael, Jews have not ceased being modern Jews, struggling with their identity as Jews. The restoration of Eretz Yisrael to a prominent place in Jewish life actually makes the struggle and the search more complex and even frustrating, but, for those who persevere, more interesting and promising.

I should like to try briefly to explain this point, suggesting that the contemporary search for a meaningful Jewish identity deals with a delineation and understanding of the Jewish self vis-à-vis others (i.e., those having different identities) on three levels, involving three relationships to peoples and cultures. They are the Jew's relationship to Jewish tradition, the relationship to the nations of the world, and the relationship of Jews to one another.

The first issue raises not only questions about the tradition's normativeness, authority, and value but, especially through the prism of Israel, about its fundamental character. What kind of tradition is it? Should it be defined and viewed primarily as religious or as national? Or both? Or neither? (And how shall we explain the nature of this tradition to others?) Through Israel, questions of norms and values are also sharpened, for we argue about whether we want Jewish law in the Jewish state and whether we want religiously based legislation in a largely secular society. Can such a law be imposed, or should it be considered a historical relic, or perhaps as a valuable resource from which to select judiciously? What—if any—conditions and orientations of conviction and flexibility will make it viable for a Jewish *society,* possibly opening new vistas for the development of the oral tradition of Judaism? Finally, since Israel, by its very existence, stakes a claim for Jewishness as (some kind of) nationality, it raises questions and possibilities of identity for Jews living in communities that have, since the emancipation, been defined as religious communities. What are the options for Jewish belonging that are brought into view by a Jewish commonwealth for those who cannot be religious in any communal or conventional sense?

The second issue, of how Jews seeking an identity and expressing themselves Jewishly in the circumstances of our time shall relate to the nations of the world and to their cultures, is likewise accentuated by *Medinat Yisrael* (the State of Israel) in Eretz Yisrael. Israel has made the dimension of polity in Jewish life more weighty in Jewish life everywhere, for it represents collective Jewish existence in the public domain of humanity and serves as a model for Jewish communities defined consensually rather than normatively.[7] One could illustrate this with the pride of Jews in Entebbe or with the new status of federations in Jewish communities or with the new self-assurance of Jewish spokesmen when they speak to statesmen and popes. Israel, as a friend returning from a trip to Poland recently explained, has made it possible for Jews, waiting at the Warsaw airport for their plane to Israel or the United States, to daven *Minchah*. When there were 3 million Jews in Poland, it would have been unthinkable; today, though they killed so many of us, we are here. "Israel," he said, "means we are here and it affects everything. Now, even a non-Orthodox Jew like myself can 'make a minyan' in that public Polish place."

The emotion my friend was expressing was pride, but the issue of "Israel and the nations" creates perplexities and confusions and embarrassment as well. In synagogues throughout the world Jews pray for the welfare of "our country" and its leaders and ask God to protect the soldiers of the Israel Defense Force "who stand guard over our country from the borders of Lebanon to the desert of Egypt." The incongruence is one some people live with comfortably, others ignore or are disgruntled with, and some draw conclusions about their Jewish identity that make them less—or more—definable than they thought. (A former president of the World Zionist Organization once related that he became a Zionist as a child, one *Shmini Atzeret,* in Mexico City, after the prayer for rain had been recited in the synagogue. Looking at the downpour outside, he asked his father why they were praying for rain, since it was raining so much. His father replied simply: "You don't understand. This is not *our* rain." Then he decided to live where he could see his own rain, that which he prayed for.)

The third issue, of a common Jewish identity at a time when Jews are so different from one another, is brought into sharp focus by Israel, which seems to claim that in a nonreligious age, it can be a new "common ground" and basis for unity. This claim is not only thoroughly resented by traditionally religious Jews but ignores the fact that in Israel-diaspora relations there is animosity and distrust as well as love and mutual responsibility.

Why animosity? Because Herzl and his colleagues wished for the Jews to be a nation among nations—definable and comprehensible at last—but Will Herberg and others celebrate the status of Jews as a religion among religions. Both are projects of normalization, *and each is undermined by the significant presence of the other.* The viable life of the diaspora undermines the Israeli "normalization of the Jews" just as the partial "ingathering of the exiles" in Eretz Yisrael "abnormalizes" Jewish diaspora life as the life of a religious entity. That is, with an interlinked Israel and diaspora, neither "the world" nor Jews themselves will believe that the House of Israel is either a normal religion or a normal nation unless, perhaps, Israel and the diaspora dissociate themselves from each other. This situation engenders anger. Israel, despite its best intentions, cannot be like the other nations, and the diaspora cannot be like other religious communities, at least partly because of the other.

And yet, because of the love and mutual responsibility created by common memories of covenant, a common fate, and the gentile world's relationship to Jews, the "normalizing" dissociation of Israel and the diaspora from each other is categorically repudiated as an option except for fringe groups of "Canaanites" (in Israel) and varieties of the American Council for Judaism (in the diaspora). Despite ideological and existential competition and friction, Jewish identity is now almost universally recognized as encompassing all Jews, as transcending, therefore, all modern Jewish ideologies which implied the exclusion of some of them. The Jewish people, for reasons intuited to have some connection to the religious-national covenant, is more important than the national or religious self-definitions that merely attempted to make us (to ourselves and others) more comprehensible. Yet the frictions persist, especially about the meaning of Eretz Yisrael. (Is it "home"? A "resource" for Jewish life everywhere? Is it heroic to be a good Jew in a gentile society and should Israel appreciate that and support it? Are Israeli wars Jewish ones and, if so, why should Israelis have to fight them alone?) We have not dealt with the schism between East and West, between "Oriental" and Ashkenazic Jews, which will not simply go away and, in recent years, has taken on a new, political dimension on the Israeli parliamentary scene. Clearly, that is another aspect of the general question, What shall be our common Jewish identity when the rabbinic tradition of halakah and doctrine can no longer be assumed?

There is, thus, a clear Eretz Yisrael dimension in the search for Jewish identity. Eretz Yisrael is still a holy place for Jews insofar as they bring to it that which is holy to them, that in which they have made an investment. They bring what is holy to it and seek it out, hoping to be enhanced, through the land, by a clearer and more coherent vision. Since they no longer agree about a single identity, they bring and look for different things, have diverse anticipations, and find different meanings.

We suggest that there are six recognizable types of Jews who have a Jewish identity base that enables them to articulate Jewishness and to look for diverse meanings in the land of Israel today. All must relate to the three issues briefly discussed above, but they relate differently. As "pure types" we shall refer to them as ultratraditional, halakhic neotraditional, cultural, ideational, secular-national, and existential modes of Jewish identity and identification.

The ultratraditionalist lives in communities in which it is affirmed that nothing in the sacred system of Judaism should change or has changed. The defection of the majority from the truth testifies not to problems of the Jewish tradition vis-à-vis the world but to the sinfulness of Jews who have succumbed to "the world" (i.e., gentile culture). For this group, the meaning of the land is ostensibly what it has always been; thus Zionism and the meanings it suggests are rank heresy, false messianism, perhaps even a cosmic catastrophe impeding the awaited Redemption. The issues of identity—tradition, the nations, inter-Jewish understanding—are concoctions of infidels. The tradition, in its pristine authority and clarity, determines how Jews should relate and who they are. In a sense, the ideological task is to hold the fort against the pseudo-meanings of the Zionist heretics and their admitted or disguised cohorts—all other modern Jews.

The halakhic neotraditional Jew is a modern person, who knows that participation in modern life requires encounter and negotiation with its cultural goods and even with its spiritual life. In the cognitive negotiation with modern culture these Jews have given up isolation in return for the right to maintain "Judaism in its essence," which they define in halakhic terms of observance and adherence to those doctrines which make such observance feasible. They see the meaning of Eretz Yisrael, generally speaking, through a religious-Zionist perspective: they hope it will be a "Torah state" that will justify itself as the consummation of the traditional messianic hope to which they subscribe, though often with (unarticulated) reservations. Pluralism, which is acceptable and desirable in the diaspora, is problematic in Israel, for it militates against the meaning of Israel, yet the neotraditionalist is grudgingly committed to it in Israel too, though hard-pressed to find legitimation for it in the sources. The diaspora neotraditionalist, unlike most other Jews, feels ill at ease for having decided not to live in Israel, "the beginning of our redemption," and, in principle, contemplates aliyah. Yet the paradoxes in his situation, especially his relationship to nontraditional Jews in a Jewish state (his relationship to gentile society is far less complex), often lead him or her in the opposite direction. In a sense, for this person, *because* of the abundance of Jewish meaning in Eretz Yisrael, "it is easier to be a Jew in *chutz l'aretz*."

The third group believes, with Ahad Ha-am and his disciples, that Judaism is a national culture, possessed of a special moral and even "prophetic" character that is not inherently bound to religion and, for moderns, certainly need not be. They see in Eretz Yisrael the locale in which the real meaning of Judaism for contemporary Jews can be fully realized and in a contemporary idiom. Their motto is "Only in Israel." Only in Israel is Hebrew the national language, the Bible a core subject in the school curriculum, the calendar and festivals Jewish, the streets named for *our* great personalities and memories. Eretz Yisrael is not only the only habitat of Judaism, as interpreted by cultural Zionism, it is also the only place in which it can outgrow the authoritarian religious mode that preserved it in *Galut*. The cultural Jew may not live in Israel, but for his or her Judaism, Israel is home, to which he constantly returns and where his or her children, through courses and tours, will "catch" their Judaism. Climbing Massada, studying at an Israeli university, the Shabbat atmosphere of Jerusalem—these are the staples of contemporary Judaism and its pedagogy.

The ideational Jew is, as his or her name suggests, one for whom Judaism is primarily a worldview, a set of ideas, which has been translated by the Jewish people throughout its history into values and norms. Eretz Yisrael was, in the ancient past, and may be again today, the laboratory for the ideas of Judaism in action, a "light unto the nations," demonstrating benign nationalism, building new social forms that reflect the idea of mankind in God's image and the moral demands made on society by moral monotheism. The ideational Jew points with pride at the kibbutz, seeks evidence that the Israeli army is different from others, was happy about Israeli assistance to underdeveloped African states. He is also easily disillusioned. As an Israeli, he or she is likely to be in the ranks of social and political activists on the left of the political spectrum, yet in the diaspora ideational Jews may demand of Israel what they demand or expect from no other society, their own included. In such a case, the meaning of Israel may become negative, expressed with a "God-that-failed" enmity.

The secular-national Jews seek in Eretz Yisrael the same meaning that members of other nations find in their homelands. For all their land is the natural landscape in which people bound by history, a common language and culture, and mutual problems and challenges live, express themselves and solve their problems, even as they meet the challenges inherent in social and individual life. The traditional religious meaning of Eretz Yisrael is of historic interest, as is the religious past of all civilized groups, but at present, the persistence of religious-theological forces in Jewish-Israeli society is a vexing problem that threatens the proper development of modern Jewish national life. Metaphysical meanings, whether of the ultra-Orthodox, neotraditional, or culture species, are pretentious illusions. Normal, certainly liberal, nations do not expect their lands to "mean" anything: they are environments, often endearing or even beloved, but neither sacred nor intrinsically significant. The secular-national Jew lives "naturally" in Israel, though diaspora Jews who have adopted the consensual polity model of Jewish life are close relations.

Finally, there are the "existential" Jews, individuals whose basic relationship to Jewishness is that, on grounds of authenticity, *they will never deny it*. No anti-Semite will frighten them out of Jewish self-affirmation, though they are little interested in Jewish modes, national or religious, that provide others with avenues of Jewish identification. Their Jewishness is evident whenever they are asked, by Jew-hating thugs or by nine Jews seeking a tenth for a minyan, whether they are Jewish; their answer is yes. They refuse to be burdened with metaphysical or ideational assumptions or religious-national obligations. Jewish is what they were born, are, accept. Eretz Yisrael has no special meaning for them, except through *Medinat Yisrael*. For now and here, Israel means that they can say yes to their Jewishness simply by being Israelis, leaving them free to proceed to the exploration and cultivation of their own lives, in accordance with their own dispositions and desires. As Israelis, they have, once and for all, affirmed their Jewishness, and they need discuss it no further.

What, then, with regard to common meanings for the land of Israel, something that can attract and even oblige all? Neither Maimonides nor the liturgy can create a united focus for all Jews today, but Eretz Yisrael does give them, I believe, something in common.

First, though Jews bring varying significances to Israel, *their bringing them to this land testifies to its status as a holy place*. Yet the Jewish commonwealth in the land of Israel, which has made it dramatically focal and accessible in a self-understood manner, as the place of Judaism as a collective presence in contemporary history, is still being challenged, its existence still a matter for dispute and strife. Whether this challenge should be met with more conciliatory or with uncompromising positions is a matter of debate among Jews and not our subject here. But whatever positions Jews take on the question of how to meet the challenge, all but the ultratraditionalists agree (and their implicit views may be somewhat different from their explicit pronouncements) that no search for the meanings of Eretz Yisrael in contemporary Judaism can be undertaken without that which Zionism and its allied forces in the Jewish world have achieved. Eretz Yisrael today means the Knesset, kibbutz, Hebrew, the blue and white flag of Israel, even Egged and Dizengoff Square—no matter what else it also means. In the Israeli army, no one is disqualified because he ascribes different meanings to Israel than others do—or no meanings at all. Almost all Jews agree that the meaning of Eretz Yisrael is tied up with the existence of *Medinat Yisrael,* and Jews deliberating on dangers to its existence, not all of which are military or external, need not be theologians or philosophers to participate usefully.

Second, the variety of modern Jewish identities, or what may be termed "the languages of Jewishness," seems to be part of the meaning that Jews come to Eretz Yisrael to see. For here all the languages of Jewishness are present, jostling for position and attention. Their presence, insistent and sometimes boisterous, shows Eretz Yisrael to be the *axis mundi* of the Jewish world, a focus of search, a soil carrying perhaps the seed of a revitalized tradition in which Judaism and Eretz Yisrael may be seen whole. Here is the world of the Yeshiva, non-Zionist, yet paradoxically nowhere at ease as in Jerusalem, the capital of Israel.[8] There are *datiim* and secular nationalists and Jews who see no reason to apologize for thinking of abstract art when they think of culture. There are idealists who strive to change development towns and Jews who seek social justice or God or peace in the desert. It may all look like anarchy or disintegration, but it may also be the harbinger of a great richness yet to come out of Zion, a richness that, in a mysterious and meandering way, will be within the tradition through which God is said to bestow responsibility and meaning upon Jews. It is a tradition of a land as well as a book. This land, like the book, has a way of not falling out of view. Even if it is hardly seen on the map, it is clearly heard.

Notes

1. Maimonides, *Mishneh Torah, Hilchot Milachim,* 11:1 (as found in Isadore Twersky, *Maimonides Reader,* (New York, 1972), p. 222).
2. *Kelim,* 1:6–9.
3. Berl Katzenelson, "Revolution and Tradition," in Arthur Hertzberg, ed. *The Zionist Idea* (New York, 1959), p. 393.
4. Maurice Samuel, *Harvest in the Desert* (Philadelphia, 1948), p. 17.

5. Samuel Hugo Bergman, "The Spirit of Israel in the Land of Israel," in *The Quality of Faith* (Jerusalem, 1970), p. 49.
6. See Yehezkiel Kaufmann, "The National Will to Survive," in David Harden, ed., *Source of Contemporary Jewish Thought*, vol. 2 (Jerusalem, 1971), pp. 83–121.
7. Normative models of identity, of course, posit authority and obligation. Consensual communities are based, in Arnold Eisen's words, "upon a shared definition of what is Jewish. If the definition is authentic, its values will come from a prominent tendency in the history of Jews and Judaism" ("How Can We Speak of Jewish 'Values' Today?" *Forum*, no. 42–43 [Winter 1981], p. 76).
8. See the discussion by Janet Aviad, *Return to Judaism: Religious Renewal in Israel* (Chicago, 1983), chap. 2.

FOR FURTHER READING

Hertzberg, Arthur (editor), *The Zionist Idea* (Garden City, 1959). An excellent and comprehensive selection of essays by the classic Zionist thinkers and statesmen of all political and spiritual persuasions. The essays usually relate historical patterns and contemporary dilemmas of Judaism to the issues involved in the return to Zion. The lengthy introductory essay by the editor remains one of the impressive monographs on the subject.

Schweid, Eliezer, *The Land of Israel* (London and Toronto, 1985). The author carefully examines ideational approaches to Eretz Yisrael from the Bible to modern thought. He places Eretz Yisrael within the context of comprehensive theologies within Judaism. Schweid is critical of some national ideological writings which posit an attachment to the land of Israel while removing it from the cultural context of a religious tradition.

Herzog, Yaakov, *A People That Dwells Alone*, edited by Misha Louvish (New York, 1975). Articles, studies and lectures of the renowned diplomat-scholar who is best known for his debate with Arnold Toynbee on Jewish destiny and the legitimacy of Israel. Herzog addresses such questions as "The Meaning of Israel's Resurgence" and Israel-Diaspora relations. He also writes about various historical and theological themes that he finds running through the perennial Jewish experience. A reflective yet deeply involved man examines the significance of his identity and his times against the backdrop of the renaissance in Eretz Yisrael.

Heschel, Abraham Joshua, *Israel: An Echo of Eternity* (New York, 1967). The renowned American-Jewish thinker discusses the meaning of Israel, in the aftermath of the six day war of 1967. He considers Israel to be a miraculous (thus, for some, scandalous) embodiment of central Biblical assumptions and aspirations. Israel represents the religious significance of history, it bespeaks Judaism's demand that body and soul be linked—and it must be seen within the framework of Judaism's anticipation of redemption. Thus Israel must also be viewed as intrinsically connected to Biblical demands for social concern and justice. Heschel's style, here as always, is evocative and poetic; often more suggestive than descriptive.

Samuel, Maurice, *Harvest in the Desert* (Philadelphia, 1948). Samuel's description of the "waves" of return, from the days of the Bilu settlers until 1939, remains a singular work, both truthful and loving. Samuel's descriptions of what Eretz Yisrael meant in Jewish tradition and how modern Zionism sought to build boldly on this tradition is moving yet realistic. The chapters are useful as individual essays and can readily be used in study groups, though they do form a continuous narrative.

The State of Israel

SHLOMO AVINERI

The establishment of the State of Israel in 1948 has undoubtedly been the most revolutionary development in modern Jewish history. Although the Holocaust was the most traumatic modern experience in Jewish life, it does not—in a most profound way—form part of Jewish history proper. If history is the story of the actions of a group or a people, the Holocaust is what others have done to the Jews; horrible as it is, it is part of European history, much less of Jewish history. With the establishment of the State of Israel, the Jewish people have become again an actor on the historical scene, not a mere passive object of the actions—whether murderous or benevolent—of others. This is the meaning of the Zionist revolution.

Zionism as a political movement was both a revolt against the Jewish tradition and a return to Jewish self-consciousness. Nurtured by the ideas of national liberation and the revolution in political consciousness that spread through Europe in the wake of the Enlightenment and the French Revolution, Zionism integrated the ideas of secular political action into its program and thus was a most radical break with the Jewish tradition of passivity and quietistic waiting for an otherworldly messianic redemption. Zionism, however, and its product, Israel, was a return to the land, the language, the political sovereignty, and the culture of the historical Jewish people.

Viewed against the maximalist claims of Zionism—that *all* Jews should come to Israel—Israel has failed to inspire massive Jewish immigration from Western, open societies. Most immigrants to Israel came and continue to come from countries in which Jews are persecuted or Jewish life is endangered: Eastern Europe (with its twin traditions of nationalist anti-Semitism and communist suppression of Jewish life), Middle Eastern countries, and some areas in Latin America. But viewed from the cultural perspective of Jewish identity and self-consciousness, Israel has radically transformed the Jewish landscape around the world.

Not only have the various forces—be they religious or secular—that initially opposed Zionism on ideological grounds been almost completely marginalized: both Israel's struggles and successes, as well as the Holocaust, made ideological opposition to the Jewish state, as once expressed by radical Reform or the Bund, or extreme Orthodoxy basically irrelevant or even obscene. But Israel succeeded in becoming the focus of Jewish identity the world over in a novel and revolutionary way that was never predicted by most Zionist thinkers: Israel has become, existentially, the broadest common denominator of Jewish identity in the Diaspora, encompassing members of various streams of religious Jewish expression (Orthodox, Conservative, and Reform), as well as a multiplicity of secular and cultural identifications with the Jewish state.

No other Jewish symbol or norm brings together under one normative umbrella such a variety of Jewish persons and organizations as does activity on behalf of Israel. Fund-raising organizations for Israel are the most inclusive Jewish arenas of activity in many communities, and raising funds for Israel, as shown by the United Jewish Appeal in the United States, has also become the most effective vehicle for raising funds for local community activities. Political activity on behalf of Israel bridges the gaps between various religious and secular organizations (as in the case of the Conference of Presidents of Major Jewish Organizations and various AIPAC-related activities). The atmosphere surrounding the Six-Day War in 1967, the Yom Kippur War in 1973, and the campaign against the United Nations condemnation of Zionism in the mid-1970s has shown how central is Israel to Jewish identity all over the world and how world Jewish opinion can be mobilized on behalf of Israel more than on behalf of any other issue on the Jewish agenda. Even the campaign for Soviet Jewry was to a large extent premised on the struggle for their right to emigrate to Israel and was built organizationally on the infrastructure of pro-Israel institutional activities in the various communities.

The reasons for the emergence of Israel as the normative center for Jewish identity and public activity are multiple and complex: an enhanced feeling of the need for a secure political haven in the wake of the Holocaust, coupled with a reawakened feeling of collective identity and sometimes guilt evoked by it; pride in having a public, political expression of normative Jewish existence; in the American pluralistic and multiethnic context, the emergence of Israel as a substitute for the "old country"—a Jewish Ireland or Italy; a convenient umbrella for overcoming deep differences within Jewish communities in the Diaspora; an effective consensual vehicle for communitywide fund-raising; a projection of Israel onto the world screen as a model society expressing Jewish ethical values; religious beliefs in seeing Israel as "the beginning of our redemption"; identification with Israel's erstwhile pioneering and socialist values; and a genuine feeling that despite all the relative security and prosperity of Jewish life in the democratic West, a viable symbol of Jewish sovereignty may ensure Jewish survival and security more than any institutional guarantee in the Diaspora.

The real or presumed identification of Jews with Israel and their allegiance to it, however, have more than once complicated Jewish life in the Diaspora (in the Soviet Union and other communist countries, as well as in Syria and Islamic Iran). Also in the West, when local *raison d'etat* clashed with Israeli actions or interests, Jewish leaders and communities occasionally felt uneasy about a possible conflict of interest between their political loyalty to the country of which they are equal citizens and their allegiance to Israel (for example, French Jewry after de Gaulle's famous anti-Israel diatribe in 1967 and some U.S. Jewish organizations in the wake of the Pollard affair).

The complex relations of state and religion and the virtual monopoly of Orthodox Jewry over public religious services in Israel have created, on numerous occasions, friction between various sectors of Diaspora Jewry and Israel (for example, the question of the official status of Conservative and Reform rabbis in Israel and the "Who is a Jew" question).

Yet the major dilemma facing Israel in its internal development as well as a focus of universal Jewish identification with it stems today from the conditions of its relationship to its immediate surroundings. Before 1967 the question was Israel's survival and was basically an issue of external politics; since 1967, it has become an internal problem of how to deal with the question of Israel's relationship to the Palestinians and its control over almost 1.5 million Arabs in the territories ruled by Israel since the Six-Days War.

When Herzl envisaged a Jewish state emerging in the Land of Israel he saw it as a neutral, virtually demilitarized country, almost a Middle Eastern Switzerland. He conceived its emergence as dependent upon an international agreement of the major European powers and expected its establishment to proceed peacefully so it would have no enemies and would not need to maintain an army.

Few of the visionaries of Zionism imagined that the establishment of a Jewish state would be accompanied by a war in which 1 percent of inhabitants would be killed and hundreds of thousands of Arabs would be uprooted. Even when this happened in 1948–49, the conventional wisdom of the period was that sooner or later the neighboring Arab countries would resign themselves to the existence of Israel. The armistice agreements of 1949, signed between Israel and the main Arab belligerents (Egypt, Jordan, Lebanon, and Syria) were premised on a stipulation of forthcoming negotiations for a settlement of the dispute. Consequently, the prevalent view after the War of Independence was that within a year or two the technicalities would be worked out (borders, recognition, demilitarized zones, compensation for refugees, and so on). Nobody expected a protracted and ever-intensifying conflict of forty years duration.

The Six-Day War of 1967 invested Israel–and the Jewish community all over the world—with a larger-than-life stature, coupled with a belief that the future of the territories gained in the war, especially the West Bank and Gaza, would be worked out within a relatively short period, surely no more than a few years. Most of Israel viewed the territories—with the exception of east Jerusalem—as trump cards in the negotiation process, not as objects for territorial claims. It is fair to guess that if the Arabs had accepted Israel's offer for negotiations in 1967, rather than issuing the Khartoum declaration of no peace, no recognition, and no negotiations with Israel, Israel would have ceded practically all the territories gained, including the West Bank and Gaza (minus Jerusalem) in return for a peace treaty. Nobody thought at that time of a prolonged deadlock of twenty years, during which Israel would continue to control on a temporary basis an occupied population of more than 1 million Palestinians.

When Anwar Sadat came to Jerusalem in 1977, hopes were raised for an immediate solution. When the Camp David accords were signed, few thought that ten years later Israel would still control the West Bank and Gaza and that a solution to the Palestinian problem would be as distant as ever.

As a consequence of all these dashed hopes, as well as increasing frustration and radicalization on all sides, Israel is today a very different country from the one that went, David-like, to war in 1967 to defend its existence against an aggressive Arab nationalism as expressed by Gamal Abdel Nasser's Pan-Arab ideology. No longer an underdog, Israel today—though still threatened—has for over twenty years held power over the life and destiny of 1.5 million Palestinian Arabs in the West Bank and Gaza, and the conflict between Israel as a state and the surrounding Arab countries has, to an extent, reverted to what it was before 1948—a struggle between two communities for control over a territory claimed by both as their homeland. The settling of about fifty thousand Jewish settlers, most of them right-wingers, in the territories has, especially since 1977, exacerbated this changed nature of the conflict.

The Palestinians' stunned acceptance of the Arab defeat in 1967 gave way gradually to a sullen enmity accompanied by bloody terrorism against civilians instigated by the Palestine Liberation Organization and its affiliates, directed and operating from outside the territories. But since December 1987, the twenty years of Israeli occupation has spawned a widespread civilian uprising in the territories, the *intifada*, against which the entire might of the Israeli army appears to be basically impotent. With thousands of Palestinians in detention—many of them under administrative detention, hence not convicted of any specified charges—Israel has begun to learn that though an army can beat an army—and Israel's army has until now been able to beat any coalition of Arab armies—an army cannot beat a people. Nor can it comfortably sit on bayonets. The lesson the United States learned in Vietnam and the Soviet Union learned in Afghanistan, Israel is now painfully learning in Nablus, Ramallah, Hebron, and Gaza.

The changing climate of opinion in Israel since 1967 has also greatly strengthened the nationalistic political right wing-the

Likud party—at the expense of the traditional social-democratic Labour party that had led Israel since 1948. The rise of the Likud has complex social, ethnic, and cultural causes, but it was undoubtedly strengthened by the clear-cut Likud message, "The Land of Israel belongs to the People of Israel," calling for the retention of Judea, Samaria, and Gaza. The sometimes convoluted diplomatic and demographical considerations of Labour and its allies are much less pithy and are hard to encapsulate in similar catchy slogans.

Parallel to this military situation, a religious messianism, viewing Judea and Samaria as an inalienable part of a holy patrimony of the Jewish people, has been wedded to a secular, militant nationalism always present in the Zionist movement and in Israel but before 1967 relegated to the political periphery. It has now become part of the mainstream of Israel's political life and the more humanistic, universalistic ideas of liberal and Labour Zionism are becoming increasingly attenuated. The inability of Labour to win any election since 1973 is an expression of this fundamental change in Israeli society.

Labour's weakness poses a double dilemma—for Israel and for the Diaspora. In Israel, the political debate since 1967 has focused almost exclusively on issues dealing with the Israeli-Palestinian conflict, and questions of social structure, welfare policies, education, and nation building have been relegated to the bottom of the national agenda. Israel will have to choose in the next few years what kind of society it would like to be: one that views territorial aggrandizement as a paramount national goal, to the detriment of its democratic and liberal character and institutions as well as to its nature as a Jewish homeland with a built-in Jewish majority; or one that is willing to take risks for peace as it has taken risks for war and be ready to make painful concessions to save its character—and its soul—as a Jewish and democratic society. Can one build Zionism while crushing Palestinian self-determination—or can Zionism be achieved only on the basis of striving—even if unsuccessfully—for an accommodation and compromise with the Palestinians' will for national self-expression.

For Diaspora Jews, their dilemmas facing Israel are reflected and will continue to be reflected ever more agonizingly in the future in having to redefine their relationship with the Jewish state. As long as Israel was the threatened David in the Middle Eastern power equation and could be viewed—for all its blemishes and imperfections—as an expression of a noble striving after a model society—identification with Israel was morally rewarding and quite easy, as when Israel was winning stunning victories against tremendous odds in what were almost universally perceived as just wars of defense.

But when Israel is torn from within and its image—and reality—become tainted with politics that appear to be increasingly in contrast with liberal values and with its own professed self-image, a cognitive dissonance is to be felt among many Diaspora Jews. No longer can virtually automatic support for the policies of the Israeli government of the day serve as a self-evident compass for Jewish politics. Though public criticism of Israel is—and will probably remain for a considerable time—muted, a feeling of anguish has replaced the outburst of pride traditionally connected with Israel. Many Jews, no doubt, will continue to support Israel whatever it does, expressing a centuries-old Diaspora mentality of not speaking evil of Jews in front of the gentile world. But with the pride gone or diminished, it will become increasingly more difficult to recruit added active support—political or economic—for a government of a country about which there will be privately more ambivalent feelings than the public expression of organized Jewish life will allow itself to utter. It will also become more difficult to get younger generations of Jews, usually better educated than their parents and in many cases less ethnocentric, to identify with a country whose image no longer evokes the memories of either the Holocaust or 1967, but whose spokesman will have to spend increasingly more time in explaining why the situation in Israel is *not* analogous to that in South Africa (it is not; but when it has to be explained, it is no longer self-evident). The image of a model society will be replaced by that of one responding to problems of how to wield power as in any other society. This may not be reprehensible, but the glamour will be gone.

Perhaps judging Israel by such lofty ideas is unfair, and the application of double standards to Israel is a legitimate complaint. But does Israel really want to be compared to Syria and then be praised on the basis of such a comparison? The tension as to whether Israel should be "a light unto the nations" or just like all other nations becomes even more agonizing when one has to make such decisions while trying to quell an uprising of 1.5 million people whom one is occupying. But until Israel sorts out this dilemma and decides what kind of country it would like to be, it will be impossible not to ask these questions, both in Israel and in the Diaspora. It is, no doubt, much more difficult for Diaspora Jews, who do not bear the burden and the agony of the decisions involved, to articulate these questions publicly, but there is no way to prevent them from feeling torn by the context they present.

It is these questions, with their mix of national, religious, strategic, and humanistic criteria all thrown together into a culture that still has to define itself vis-à-vis its immediate surroundings, that will make all other issues (state and religion, the future of the welfare state) pale in relation to this primary, existential issue. This issue will ultimately decide the future of the Zionist enterprise, its place in Jewish history, and the Jewish people's relationship to it.

FOR FURTHER READING

Avineri, Shlomo, *The Making of Modern Zionism*. New York, 1981. An account of the ideas of the central Zionist thinkers in the nineteenth and twentieth centuries.

Davis, Moshe, *World Jewry and the State of Israel*. New York, 1977. A survey of different attitudes toward Israel and Middle Eastern politics as expressed in the public activities and publications of Jewish communities the world over.

Fein, Leonard, *Israel—Politics and People*. Boston, 1968. A survey of the political institutions and parties of Israel in its first decades.

—— *Where Are We?* New York, 1988. An original and controversial treatise about the present state of American Jewry and its relationship to Israel.

Halpen, Ben, *The Idea of the Jewish State*. Cambridge, Mass., 1961. An account of the political and ideological struggle, focusing mainly on the United States, of how the idea of the Jewish state became legitimized and accepted in the Jewish community and on the level of power politics.

Hertzberg, Arthur, *The Zionist Idea*. New York, 1969. A most useful and extensive anthology of the most important Zionist thinkers, accompanied by an extensive introductory essay on Jewish life and thought following the Enlightenment and giving rise to Zionism.

Horowitz, Dan, and Lissak, Moshe, *The Making of the Israeli Polity*. Chicago, 1978. A study of the institutions of the Jewish community in Palestine and the structures of various Zionist organizations and parties and their contribution to the emergence of Israeli parliamentary democracy and the contemporary political culture of Israel.

Vital, David, *The Origins of Zionism*. Oxford, 1975. A detailed historical account of the intellectual and organizational origins of Zionism.

God: The Present Status of the Discussion

NORBERT M. SAMUELSON

In general, discussions of "God" in the three Abrahamic faiths—Judaism, Christianity, and Islam—fall under three general headings: (1) How is it possible to speak about God? (2) Does God exist? (3) How is God related to the world? The three are obviously interrelated. Just what it means (2) to prove that God exists depends on (1) what kind of God we are discussing. At the same time, (1) what kind of God we affirm depends on (2) what kind of deity we believe can exist. The same is true of any proposed solution to (3) the problem of divine providence. Furthermore, the three Abrahamic faiths share the same tradition of speech about and faith in God, and historically their discussions of this dogma never have been independent. Hence, to a great extent any discussion of what one of these religions says about God in isolation from the other two is myopic. All contemporary discussions of God do not take place in a vacuum. They are deeply influenced by the medieval theological development of God concepts by Muslims, Jews, and Christians in interaction with each other, who determined the parameters for contemporary Jewish and Christian discussions of God.

Contemporary Jewish and Christian philosophy has developed in two distinct directions out of its modern sources in Continental Rationalists and British Empiricists. The English-language tradition of philosophy has contributed most to the discussion of proofs of the existence of God, and the Continental German- and French-language traditions of philosophy have contributed most to the discussion of the nature of God. Furthermore, since the dominant tradition of contemporary theology is more rooted in the Continent, particularly through the writings of late nineteenth- and early twentieth-century German Jewish theologians Hermann Cohen, Martin Buber, and Franz Rosenzweig, Jewish thought has paid more attention to what we can say about God than how we can prove that God exists.

Divine Attributes

The word *God* has been used throughout Jewish history to name that entity who is most worthy of worship, yet it is far from clear that the entity named in each case is the same. Clearly Jews have said radically different things about God, and there is no simple way to determine what their difference is. One possibility is that they are talking about the same entity, in which case they differ in their description of him. Even the use of the word *him* with reference to God is problematic, for at present there is a major controversy over the convention of using masculine pronouns to refer to God.[1] A second, even more serious possibility is that these Jews are talking about different entities. In the former case, if we assume that the deity described is the God of Israel, at worst someone who is wrong is a heretic, but in the latter case someone who is wrong is guilty of idolatry, the most serious of all crimes from the perspective of both the Hebrew Scriptures and rabbinic tradition.

Traditionally the God of the faith of Israel has been called both "Adonai" and "Elohim" and referred to both as the deity of Abraham, Isaac, and Jacob and as the creator of the world. Again, traditionally these two names and two references have been identified, that is, Adonai is Elohim, who is both the creator of the universe and the deity of the Bible's patriarchs and matriarchs. This identity, however, is not self-evident. If we exclude the authority of the arguments of medieval Aristotelian philosophers who were committed Muslims, Jews, or Christians, it could be the case that they are not the same or that one but not the other or neither of them exists.

For the sole purpose of simplicity in this essay, I will reserve the term *Elohim* for the purported creator of the universe and *Adonai* for the deity associated by Scripture with the patriarchs and matriarchs. The claim that both exist and are one requires three distinct lines of demonstration. Although most modern Jewish thinkers have made these three traditional claims with or without demonstration, not all of them have, and some of the most interesting ones have not. Spinoza would affirm the existence of Elohim as the one absolutely infinite substance but not the existence of Adonai. Conversely, Buber speaks of Adonai, to the exclusion of Elohim, as the Eternal-Thou. In this context it is of interest that whereas Buber's colleague Franz Rosenzweig focused his attention primarily on creation, revelation, and redemption (redemption expressing how man relates to the world; creation and revelation expressing God's relationship respectively to the world and man), and Buber deals extensively with redemption and revelation, Buber says nothing about creation. Creation has to do with how God relates to the world of objects, what in Buber's language are instances of the I-It relationship; but Buber's deity is always *thou*, an entity who in principle does not and cannot relate to objects. Consequently, in the language adopted for this essay, Buber clearly dissociates Elohim from Adonai and affirms faith only in Adonai. Finally, Mordecai Kaplan, the single most influential American Jewish religious thinker, identifies Elohim and Adonai, but he does not give this deity's existence a central role in Jewish belief. Its importance is solely that it is useful for preserving the Jewish people. In this most radically heterodox of theological positions, Kaplan's agnosticism probably is most representative of the majority of self-identifying Jews in the contemporary world.

In any case, to ask if Elohim and Adonai exist and are the same referent presupposes some prior concept of what they are. In the case of Adonai this is a fairly easy question to answer. He is the author of the Torah. How he did so, for our present purposes, is unimportant.[2] It may be, as most contemporary Orthodox Jews believe, that the Torah that we possess today is the sole creation of that deity, and he may have transmitted it to Moses at Sinai some four thousand years ago. Or it may be, as many liberal religious Jews believe, that Adonai is a force that guided some or all of the Jewish people, who through his influence composed our Torah and attributed it to him. These questions of authorship are of great importance, but again, they lie outside the scope of this essay. Our question is not, How did Adonai author the Torah; it is instead, Who is its author?

Our question about Adonai is similar to asking who could write Shakespeare's plays rather than asking how Shakespeare's plays were written. The answer to the latter question could be that there was a single producer and director who composed all of the plays that his London company gave, or it could be that every play presented by the company had a different author but all were called "Shakespeare's" because he was their producer. In contrast, an answer to the former question could be someone loyal to Queen Elizabeth who had a Thomistic view of the heavens and enjoyed slapstick comedy. In this sense, Adonai is a person with a flexible body. He is a person in that he can be the subject of mental acts and can will actions. And his body is flexible in that he can appear in, at or through different physical objects and that there are no limitations on the physical forms that are associated with him, even though the ones that Scripture tends to mention involve fire and light in one way or another. Furthermore, he exhibits many characteristics that, though they need not be identical with human characteristics, are in a significant way similar to human qualities, such as loving and judging. Furthermore, whatever is the precise meaning of saying that Adonai loves and judges, he loves and judges different species of individual living things and different nations of human beings in different ways. In this vague sense it can be said that Adonai loves the nation of the people of Israel and he promises to preserve and prosper it. Furthermore, any entity of whom the above statements are not true is not the author of the Torah. This denial is logically comparable to saying that any person or persons who did not hold the views and did not have the artistic style of the author of Shakespeare's plays is not Shakespeare, no matter who Shakespeare was.

To ask who Elohim is is more difficult. In this case, there is no single answer. Who Adonai is is defined by his relation to the Torah. Although contemporary Jews disagree about how the Torah was written, there is no comparable problem in identifying the Torah. It is a certain, commonly accepted set of writings in a form over which there is relatively minimal disagreement. Conversely, who Elohim is is defined by his relation to the universe, and it is far less clear what the world is. There are as many different views of the universe as there are systems of contemporary philosophy and physics. How Elohim is described differs radically depending on what kind of world we are discussing. Historically the tradition of classical Jewish and Christian philosophy that contemporary theologians have inherited synthesizes the philosophies of Plato and Aristotle, but these two philosophers proposed significantly different worldviews. The Platonic universe is a world of perfect ideals that have absolute existence, that are related by some theory of imitation to less perfect entities, which are subject to different degrees of existence/reality, depending on their different degrees of perfection. Conversely, the Aristotelian universe is a world of general forms, whose existence is mental and that inhere in material entities that occupy three-dimensional space. At the same time, Newtonian physics posits an atomist universe of simple quantities that occupy multidimensional space.[3] Nor are these the only options. Modern philosophers have constructed many different ontologies, and many of them have had an important impact on contemporary Jewish theology. For Rosenzweig the influence is the ontology of Friedrich Wilhelm Joseph von Schelling; for Kaplan the influence is the process philosophy of Alfred North Whitehead; and for Europe's foremost contemporary Jewish thinker, the French philosopher Emmanuel Levinas, the dominant influence is the ontology of the existentialist Martin Heidegger. All other factors being equal, each of these different worldviews requires radically different ways to speak about Elohim as the creator of the universe. Furthermore, there will be as many additional ways of talking about him as there are possible ways to combine each of these distinct worldviews into a single concept of the universe.

In general, rabbinic tradition (which includes the writings of both philosophers and Kabbalists) affirmed cosmologies in which Elohim is (a) something no greater than which can be conceived, (b) unlimited, (c) something whose existence and nonexistence is mot merely logically possible, and (d) something that can neither come into existence nor cease to exist but (e) necessarily exists. What these claims mean is not self-evident. Maimonides—Jewish tradition's most influential exponent of negative theology—made the most extreme claim. What any descriptive term means when it is applied to the creator is completely different from what that term means when it is applied to any creature. Furthermore, since our understanding of all language ultimately depends on reference to creatures, statements about God can have no positive descriptive content whatsoever. Gersonides adopted a more moderate position. Any predicate that can be affirmed of God applies primarily to God in an absolute sense and derivatively to anything else in a less than absolute sense that admits of degrees of perfection. For example, God knows himself in a single act of knowledge that is identical with God, and in knowing himself he know everything as its cause. In contrast, we know something through multiple acts as an effect of what exists through God's causation. Furthermore, in our case the following are all distinct—each of us as the subject of the act of knowing, our acts of knowing themselves, and the objects of our knowledge. In these ways our knowledge is both dependent upon and inferior to God's knowledge.

These two primary interpretations of divine attributes in classical rabbinic theology need not be viewed as mutually exclusive. Zevi Diesendruck, following in the philosophical tradition of Hermann Cohen, interpreted Maimonides' theory of negative attributes as an instance of Kantian infinite judgments. The sense in which the statement that an infinite series of individual acts of negation can express something positive turns on Cohen's application of the infinitesimal calculus to theology. The model employed is that of asymptotic functions with a finite limit. Every formally descriptive statement about God is rooted in the dictum, "You shall be holy as I the Lord your God am holy." To affirm some property of God is to command humanity to become it. Hence every descriptive statement about God commands a general function. It is an asymptote because to be whatever that property affirms lies beyond human capability. At best in this world we approximate this ideal by avoiding each of the infinite number of its contraries that are not true of God. In this life this moral guide is how we relate to God.

Gersonides would agree with Maimonides that every predicate attributed to God is part of an equivocal expression that affirms an absolute moral ideal for human behavior. Cohen's identification of theology and ethics is well rooted in this classical tradition of Jewish philosophy. The sole significant difference between Maimonides and Gersonides has to do with just how little we know about God. According to Maimonides, we know something about ethics but absolutely nothing about God; according to Gersonides, moral and theological statements mutually entail each other so that the very moral commandments we do know are in themselves knowledge of God. We can differentiate between how we and God know and affirm that God's way of knowing is superior as an ideal that we, in fulfilling the moral obligation to gain knowledge, constantly attempt to approximate. The former, Maimonidean thesis has its greatest impact on contemporary theologians whose proximate Jewish source is Jewish mysticism. The latter, Gersonidean thesis has its greatest impact on contemporary theologians whose proximate Jewish source is Jewish philosophy.

The Existence of God

In general the different forms of arguments proposed over the centuries to demonstrate that God exists can be classified as ontological, cosmological, or teleological. The teleological argument is the easiest to understand and is most widely used. It is the one form of argument explicitly found in the Hebrew Scriptures.[4] All of the versions of the cosmological argument go back at least to the writings of Aristotle,[5] and were used in almost identical forms by Muslims, Jews, and Christians. The ontological argument, developed by Anselm, is unique. First, it is the most difficult form of demonstration of God's existence to understand and consequently is the least compelling version. Second, it was unknown to both the Muslims and Jews until they had contact with Christian civilization after the thirteenth century C.E. Once Christians like Thomas Aquinas absorbed the then more advanced Muslim-Jewish civilization, they used the cosmological and teleological arguments but rejected the ontological one. It was not until modern times that Jews such as Spinoza[6] and Mendelssohn[7] began to treat this form of argument with the seriousness it deserves. Furthermore, even after Hume and Kant attempted to disprove it, based on the considerable attention given to it in contemporary journals of philosophy, most philosophers of religion seem to consider the ontological argument to be the best possible attempt to demonstrate God's existence.

The classical version of the ontological was formulated by Anselm.[8] It is widely accepted that David Hume and Immanuel Kant definitively disproved it.[9] Almost all Jewish thinkers have taken it for granted that Hume and Kant settled the issue. There are a significant minority of Jewish thinkers, however, of which I am one,[10] who believe that Anselm's argument has sufficiently been defended by the contemporary American philosophers

Charles Harthshorne and Norman Malcolm, and the issue of the validity of the argument is again open to scrutiny.[11] I would argue that the argument is valid within a limited range, viz., that is proves that this Elohim must exist in a Platonic world, and that it may but need not be true in any other universe. For Anselm this was no problem because he was convinced that his world was the only possible one. We do not share his conviction. What is at stake here is neither theology nor logic. Rather, the issue involves ontology and physics. We know with certainty what can be said about any deity who creates a Platonic universe. Here *to create* means *to be a perfect instantiation.* Furthermore, we know with certainty that if a Platonic universe exists, then that deity no greater than which can be conceived exists. The only qualification is that we do not know if the universe is in any sense a Platonic one; most people are inclined to think that it is not.

The classical version of the cosmological argument was presented by Abraham ibn Daud in Book One, chapters 4–5 of his *Exalted Faith.* Maimonides reformulated this argument into five versions in his *Guide of the Perplexed* that Thomas Aquinas reproduced in his *Summa Theologica.* Over the objections of Hume, Kant, and their followers, the Thomistic statement of this argument has been reconsidered by contemporary philosophers such as John Hick and Alvin Plantinga.[12] Jewish philosophers have paid little attention to this current debate. I would argue that, as in the case of Anselm's ontological argument, ibn Daud's cosmological argument has limited validity. Although it did not demonstrate that Elohim must exist in any possible world, it shows that Elohim must exist in an Aristotelian universe whose basic principles of motion are form and matter, which excludes the possibility of infinity because Euclidian geometry describes reality. For ibn Daud this was no problem because he was convinced that his world was the only one possible. We do not share his conviction. Again, what is at stake is neither theology nor logic; rather, the issue involves mathematics, ontology, and physics. Within the limited range in which this proof is valid, we can claim with certainty that if an Aristotelian universe exists, that deity who is its first mover exists. In this case "to be a first mover" is what Jewish tradition means by *to create.* Such a deity would be something without potential that is in every respect actual, that moves but is unmoved, that affects but cannot be affected, and that has a single function with which it is identical that has neither beginning nor end.

Classical versions of the argument from design can be found in Maimonides' *Guide of the Perplexed* and Thomas Aquinas' *Summa Theologica* as their fifth arguments for God's existence. I would contend that the most rigorous version of this argument was presented by Saadia in his *Book of Beliefs and Opinions*.[13] Although this form of argument continues to enjoy some popularity in nontechnical literature, almost all philosophers agree that it is invalid. It is nothing more than a weak analogy between the world and human artifacts that, without any evidence, presupposes that there is need to find a mental in addition to a natural order to events. At least one attempt has been made by a Christian and a Jewish philosopher to claim that the argument has a cumulative effect to favor a supernatural over a natural account of the universe.[14] Neither Tennant nor Fackenheim would claim that this argument demonstrates that Elohim must exist in any world, including an atomist one. Rather, the argument shows that the existence of Elohim is the most reasonable hypothesis in an atomist universe whose quantitative/mathematical way of schematizing empirical data leaves room for no causal principles other than statistical, chance probability, and acts of will. Again, what is at stake here is neither theology nor logic. Rather, the issue involves mathematics and physics. In this case we do not even know with certainty what can be said about any deity who creates an atomist cosmos. We can only say that the assumption that Elohim exists is more reasonable than either the assumption that he does not or the assumption that we can make no assumptions. Here "to create" means "to be that force who initiates and directs the energy of the cosmos." Therefore, what can be said about Elohim depends on what mathematics and modern physics say about energy and force.

Divine Providence

Contemporary reflections on the relationship between God and the world in all Jewish thought and much Christian theology are marked in some significant way by two events—the Holocaust and the creation of the modern state of Israel. It is the attempt to appropriate these events into an adequate conception of divine providence that most distinguishes contemporary Jewish thought from earlier modern as well as classical Jewish theology.

Maimonides' thirteen principles in his commentary on the Mishnah are as close as traditional Judaism comes to a statement of dogma in the sense that any responsible formulation of Jewish belief will deal with it.[15] But it is not dogma in the sense that it compels consent. On the contrary, whereas practically every rabbinic authority has dealt with these principles, few have agreed with everything that Maimonides says about them.[16] In general the claim is that there exists a creator of the universe who is in himself perfect and the ultimate cause of everything else that exists (first foundation); he knows everything (tenth foundation), and he both rewards those who obey his commandments and punishes those who disobey them (eleventh foundation).

It is not possible in a single essay to deal with every significant attempt to understand the relationship between God and the world.[17] Instead, I will limit my attention to a summary of only two discussions—those of Emil Fackenheim and Harold Schulweis. They are of particular interest because they reflect two radically different Jewish approaches to the question. Both thinkers are actively involved in contemporary Jewish life, and both root their thinking in classical Jewish sources, but they reach conclusions that in significant ways break with pre-twentieth-century Jewish religious thought. The significant factor in accounting for their differences is their philosophical, intellectual sources. Emil Fackenheim, is rooted in German existentialism. Harold Schulweis, draws upon his absorption of American process philosophy.

Fackenheim's theology calls into question Maimonides' entire formulation of Jewish faith and, in particular, radically alters the meaning of his eleventh foundation. From Fackenheim's perspective, the principles of Maimonides are part of a set of general schemata developed in Western civilization to make intelligible all past human history in the hope that it will continue to make intelligible the future as well. Certain events, however, defy any such categorization. Their uniqueness is so radical that it demands that we rethink our previous ways of understanding everything. Such historical singularities are called "epoch-making events." Traditional Judaism counts the exodus from Egypt, the theophany at Sinai, and the destruction of the first two temples as such events. Traditional Christianity lists the covenant with Abraham, the theophany at Sinai, and the crucifixion and resurrection of Jesus. Fackenheim argues that the Holocaust is an epoch-making event and, as such, it makes new moral demands on all humanity.[18] Specifically with reference to the Jewish people, the new moral demand is the "614th Commandment," viz., an "authentic Jew of today is forbidden to hand Hitler yet another, posthumous victory.[19]

Maimonides' first and tenth principles presuppose a harmony between the conclusions of correct human reasoning and the demands of divine revelation. This assumed harmony entails that human reason provides a tool by which we can judge what prophets and their disciples claim to be the content of revelation. In contrast, Fackkenheim claims that the Holocaust reverses this relationship. The tradition of Western civilization culminates in the philosophy of Martin Heidegger, and Heidegger was a Nazi. At worst, his immorality was a necessary consequence of his philosophy. In this case the events of the Holocaust and Heidegger's complicity in them entitle us, from the vantage point of the Jewish tradition of biblical prophecy, to condemn all of philosophy as immoral and therefore, as false. At best, Heidegger's immorality was independent of his philosophy. In this case, the events of the Holocaust and Heidegger's complicity in them entitle us, again from the vantage point of the Jewish tradition of biblical prophecy, to condemn all of philosophy as irrelevant to lived life in human society. Fackenheim's claim is not that philosophy is dead. Rather, his judgment is that after the Holocaust philosophy has lost its privileged place as the judge of prophetic faith. Philosophy should continue, that is, human beings should continue to struggle to formulate new schemata that will be able to make intelligible the course of human history. In the future, however, Judaism will judge the validity of the schemata.

Furthermore, Maimonides' eleventh foundation presupposes that God's demands are a fixed given. God revealed once and for all what He requires from humanity to Moses at Sinai, and the tradition of rabbinic interpretation is the means by which God's word is to be clarified. The focus of human attention is to be given to the text of the Hebrew Scriptures and the interpretations of the rabbis. The human experience of reward and punishment plays a secondary role in Maimonides' schema. The schema, itself revealed by God, is the absolute by which human events are interpreted as reward and punishment. Fackenheim also reverses this order. Reward and (more important) punishment become the given through which both previous revelation is interpreted and new commandments are formulated.

Fackenheim's implicit understanding of divine providence is a more dynamic view than the one explicit in Maimonides' classical formulation of Jewish belief. For Maimonides, the laws that serve as the standard for interpreting reward and punishment are eternal; for Fackenheim, the lived experience of reward and punishment changes the very nature of the commandments. In Maimonides' case, God, in a single, timeless self-revelation, gave an absolute truth that human beings in time and space struggle to approximate. In Fackenheim's case, there is no absolute standard beyond the unquestionable faith that God commands the perpetual existence of the Jewish people.

The three classical pillars of Jewish theology are God, Torah, and Israel. Fackenheim's theology, influenced by Rosenzweig, radically alters the classical understanding of revelation. His Torah has no set content. Rather, it simply expresses the dynamic relationship (as act of love) between the two related terms, God (the lover) and Israel (the beloved). In contrast, Schulweis's theology preserves a more classical understanding of Torah, although it radically alters the conception of God.

Schulweis argues that the Holocaust does not raise any new issues about the traditional belief in divine providence, but it does make the problems more apparent. The problem of theodicy arises from three irreconcilable premises—God is omnipotent, God is all good, and evil exists. Classical Jewish and Christian theologians have traditionally denied the third premise by claiming that the evil of some events is only apparent. If we knew what God knows we would understand why what happens must happen. In other words, classical theologians deny the existence of anything that is fundamentally or radically evil. The Holocaust is an obvious candidate for this status. To deny that it was evil defies reason and borders on obscenity. Drawing upon his careful reading of the contemporary theological writings of Charles Hartshorne, Henry Nelson Wieman, and Paul Tillich, Schulweis argues that the better choice is to deny the first premise.

The premise that God is omnipotent, like Maimonides' first foundation, treats the term *God* as a subject of predicates. Schulweis proposes that it would be better to use this term as a predicate. Instead of naming a substance, the term expresses a set of functions in relationship to humanity. In this context, what the proclamation of God's unity (the *Shma*) expresses is the shared commonality of all divine qualities. In other words, God expresses a combined whole that constitutes goodness while affirming that none of these qualities are isolated from each other.

Conclusion

I am far from satisfied with any of the contemporary formulations of theology discussed above. The biblical text that Maimonides cites to support his assertion of divine reward and punishment is Exod. 32:32–33. In this passage Moses says to God, with reference to the sin of the Golden Calf, "Now, if you forgive their sin, (fine,) but if not, then please blot me (as well) out of Your book that you have written," and God responds, "Now, go forth (and) lead the people to the place about which I spoke to you. My messenger will go before you. However, in the day of my visitation I will visit upon them their sin." In the next verse we are told that "the Lord smote the people because they made the calf that Aaron made."

Presumably Maimonides chose this passage because it supports his claim that God rewards obedience and punishes disobedience. The biblical selection is troublesome, however. One would have expected Maimonides to choose Deuteronomy 1:13–21 for two obvious reasons. First, it states explicitly in the most direct terms Maimonides' thesis: "If you keep My commandments . . . then I will give your land the former and latter rain in its (proper) season so that you may gather in your grain, wine and oil, and I will give your cattle grass in your field so that you may eat and be satisfied. . . . (However, if you do not keep the commandments, then) the sky will be closed, so that there will be no rain, so that the land will not give forth its produce, and you will perish." No causal connection between obedience/disobedience and prosperity/failure could be more direct. Second, the passage would be familiar to every Jew because it directly follows the recitation of God's oneness (the *Shma*) in every worship service. By contrast, the passage Maimonides does select has neither of these virtues. In fact, it is not altogether clear what its point is. Moses asks that the people not be punished, and God says that he will grant Moses' request for the short run so that the people may continue on their pilgrimage to Canaan. In the end, however, they will and do pay for what they did. It would seem that Maimonides intentionally avoided the obvious passage and chose this more oblique one as a way of saying, "Don't think that there is a simplistic, automatic connection between what you do and what you receive. God's providence is far more complex than that. In the end the scales of justice will be balanced, but only in the end."

Jewish thinkers have always affirmed that there exists one God who created the universe in the most perfect way possible, that the universe is constantly moving toward an end that is identified as the World to Come and all human beings are divine creatures who play a special role in bringing about this messianic end, that Jewish law specifies guidelines for individual human morality, that what occurs in the universe is subject to moral judgment, and that the moral judgment of what happens to human beings is causally connected with their moral behavior. There is more than one way to explain these claims.

The Hebrew Scriptures make no claim that God is all-knowing, all-powerful, or perfectly good. In general, the Hebrew Scriptures neither affirm nor deny these attributions of absoluteness. It is a category of judgment that does not seem to have a place in the Bible's language. Rather, the claim is made that He is the deity who is most worthy of obedience because He is better and has more knowledge and power than any other person in the universe. To justify this assertion the prophets appeal to the course of history, from the creation of the world through the destruction of the Israelite commonwealth. The Lord is most knowing, for only through his revelation can we know the course of events before the beginning of human history, from creation to the period of the universal flood. The Lord is most powerful, for only this deity has the capacity to enable a small nation of slaves (the Israelites) to humble the most powerful nation in the world (Egypt). Finally, He is the best of persons because only through obedience to his will can human beings maximize their potential for national prosperity.

Notes

*I wish to express my thanks to my colleague Thomas Dean at Temple University for his valuable suggestions for improving an earlier version of this essay.

1. I believe that the issue is important, but I have as yet nothing to contribute to this part of the discussion of theology. If I could find an easy way to avoid masculine references I would do so, but I cannot. The use of the feminine does not seem to me to be preferable, and the use of the plural with reference to God clearly is worse. Similarly, to say *it* rather than *he* or *she* or *him* or *her* is worse because the usage implies that God is not a person. In any case, the problem is the limitation of the English language that provides no genderless term to refer to a person. No serious religious thinker believes that gender is appropriate with respect to God.

2. The answer to this question depends on the developed doctrine of revelation.

3. On Einstein's model, space has four dimensions–length, width, depth, and time. More contemporary physical theories that attempt to reconcile Newtonian physics with quantum mechanics project mathematical models that involve many more dimensions than four.

4. E.g., Isa. 40:21–26.

5. E.g., *Physics* 7:1 and *Metaphysics* 12.

6. In his *Ethics*.

7. In his *Morgenstunden (Morning Hours, or Lectures on the Existence of God)*.

8. See Anselm, *Proslogium*, trans. Sidney North Dean (LaSalle, Ill., 1903).

9. See David Hume, *Dialogues Concerning Natural Religion* (1779), Critical ed. by N. Kemp Smith (New York, 1947); Immanuel Kant, *Critique of Practical Reason*, trans. L. W. Beck (New York, 1956), ii, 2.

10. See Norbert M. Samuelson, "On Proving God's Existence," *Judaism*, Vol. 16, No. 1 (Winter 1967), ii, 21–36 and "That the God of the Philosophers Is Not the God of Abraham, Isaac and Jacob," *Harvard Theological Review*, Vol. 65, No. 1, (January, 1972), pp 1–27.

11. See Charles Hartshorne, *The Logic of Perfection* (La Salle, Ill., 1962), and *Man's Vision of God* (New York, 1941); Norman Malcolm, *Knowledge and Certainty* (Englewood Cliffs, N.J., 1965).

12. See John Hick, *Arguments for the Existence of God* (New York, 1970), and *The Existence of God* (New York, 1964); Alvin Plantinga, *God and Other Minds* (Ithaca, 1967).

13. See Norbert Samuelson, "Medieval Jewish Philosophy," in Barry W. Holtz, ed., *Back to the Sources* (New York, 1984), pp. 288–92.

14. F. R. Tennant in *Philosophical Theology*, Vol. 2 (Cambridge, 1930); Emil Fackenheim, *Paths to Jewish Belief* (New York, 1962).

15. Rabbi Joseph Kafich, ed. and trans., *Mishnah im Perush Rabbenu Moshe ben Maimon* (Jerusalem, 1963). The principles are presented in his commentary on *Perek Chelek*, the tenth chapter of the Tractate Sanhedrin of the Mishnah.

16. See Menachem Kellner, *Dogma in Medieval Jewish Thought: From Maimonides to Abravanel* (Oxford, 1986).

17. Of the books listed below under "Works Consulted" the studies most revelent to this discussion are those of Berkovits, Katz, Riemer, Rosenfeld, and Rubenstein.

18. Although Fackenheim's statements in this regard are ambiguous, he probably would include the subsequent creation of the modern state of Israel as part of the event.

19. See *Judaism*, Vol. 16 (Summer, 1967), pp. 269–73. Emil Fackenheim's contribution to the symposium entitled "Jewish Values in the Post-Holocaust Future." (No contribution has a title of its own).

FOR FURTHER READING

The books listed here, relevant to the content of this essay, are for readers to consider as a next step in learning about the contemporary discussion of God
from the perspective of Jewish tradition. The list presupposes minimal
technical background in either philosophy or Jewish studies. The books are
listed in a logical sequence rather than alphabetically by author.

Hick, John, *Arguments for the Existence of God* (New York, 1970). This book is
the single most influential current textbook in undergraduate courses in
philosophical theology. Its major defect for our purposes is that its author's
understanding of religion is limited to a Protestant perspective.

Davies, Paul C. W., *God and the New Physics* (New York, 1983). In my judgment
this is the best of the recently published studies that deal with the significance of contemporary physics for religious thought. Its major defect for
our purposes is that its author's understanding of religion is limited to an
Anglican perspective.

Borowitz, Eugene R., *Choices in Modern Jewish Thought: A Partisan Guide* (New
York, 1983). Borowitz is one of American's leading Jewish theologians.
This book is an excellent overview of the major claims of the giants of mod-
ern Jewish thought.

Samuelson, Norbert, *An Introduction to Modern Jewish Philosophy* (Albany, 1989),
is what its title says: a comprehensive introduction to modern Jewish philosophy. Particular emphasis is given to the writings of Spinoza, Cohen,
Buber, Rosenzweig, and Kaplan.

Wetlesen, Jon, *The Sage and the Way: Spinoza's Ethics of Freedom* (Assen, the
Netherlands, 1979). Spinoza's *Ethics* set the agenda for all subsequent modern religious thought. In my judgment, Wetlesen's book is the most useful
introduction to it. If the reader wants to look at Spinoza directly in English
translation, I would recommend Spinoza, Baruch, *Ethics and Selected Letters*. English trans. Samuel Shirley. (Indianapolis, 1982).

Cohen, Hermann, *Religion of Reason out of the Sources of Judaism*, English trans.
Simon Kaplan (New York, 1972). This is Cohen's major work in Jewish
philosophy. In many ways it set the agenda for the thought of his students
Franz Rosenzweig and Martin Buber.

Diamond, Malcolm, *Martin Buber: Jewish Existentialist* (New York, 1960).
Buber's *I and Thou* set the agenda for all subsequent Jewish theology. In my
judgment Diamond's book is the best introduction to it. If the reader wants
to look at Buber directly in English translation, I would recommend Buber,
Martin, *I and Thou*, English trans. Walter Kaufmann (New York, 1970).

Rahel-Freund, Else, *Franz Rosenzweig's Philosophy of Existence: An Analysis of the
Star of Redemption* (The Hague, 1979). Rosenzweig's *Star of Redemption*
English trans. William Hallo, (Boston, 1971) is his major work in religious

philosophy that influenced all subsequent Jewish philosophy. In my judgment Rahel-Freund's book is one of the better introductions to Rosenzweig's thought that currently exists in print in the English language.

Kaplan, Mordecai, *The Meaning of God in Modern Jewish Religion* (New York, 1937), is the classic attempt by America's most influential religious thinker to apply the schemata of the American tradition of philosophy to understanding the place of God in Judaism.

Katz, Steven T., *Post-Holocaust Dialogues: Critical Studies in Modern Jewish Thought* (New York, 1983). This collection contains a broad range of reflections on the significance of the Holocaust by many of the more important contemporary Jewish theologians.

— , *Historicism, the Holocaust, and Zionism: Critical Studies in Modern Jewish Thought and History* (New York, 1992). A second, wide-ranging, collection of important essays by Katz on contemporary Jewish thought.

Fackenheim, Emil L., *To Mend the World* (New York, 1982). Any study of contemporary Jewish thought must include Fackenheim's work. If I would have to pick a single book, this is it. This book, however, is best read in connection with Fackenheim's earlier works that set the scene for his discussion here of theology in the light of Spinoza, Rosenzweig, the Holocaust, and the modern state of Israel. Of the earlier books, the important ones are *Encounters between Judaism and Modern Philosophy* (New York, 1973), *God's Presence in History* (New York, 1970), and *The Jewish Return into History: Reflections in the Age of Auschwitz and a New Jerusalem* (New York, 1978).

Schulweis, Harold M., *Evil and the Morality of God* (Cincinnati, 1984). Schulweis is one of America's most creative and influential religious thinkers. This book is one of the few serious attempts to apply the American tradition of process philosophy to understanding Jewish theology.

Feminism

SUSANNAH HESCHEL

Pinpointing the beginnings of the Jewish feminist movement generally leads us back to the beginnings of the modern period in Jewish history, in Europe, Russia, and the United States during the late eighteenth and nineteenth centuries. The advent of modern secularism and movements of religious reform caused a weakening of the traditional rabbinic authority structure governing the semi-autonomous Jewish communities.[1] That authority structure and the rabbinic texts through which it both made religious decisions and received its theological approbation were entirely male.[2] Some women received Jewish educations, but they were rare, and whatever their education, rabbinic ordination and the power it brought were always limited to men.

Although modernity did not immediately bring about many changes in community structure and religious practices affecting women, it did bring the possibility of women and men eluding rabbinic strictures. New, non-Orthodox modes of Jewish identity emerged: the Reform and Conservative denominations; political affiliations such as Jewish socialism and Zionism; and literary movements as part of the creation of modern Hebrew and Yiddish belles lettres.[3] Increasing numbers of Jewish women were able to seek secular educations and professions, and many took active roles in movments for social change—for example, in the Bund in Eastern Europe, in the American anarchist movement, and in the revolutionary movements in Russia.[4]

But at the same time, modernity brought disadvantages for women. The move from rural to urban centers and the rise of industrialization meant that family finances became the responsibility solely of the husband, who worked outside the home. Previously, husband and wife had shared responsibilities, whether in agriculture or running a small shop. Often, particularly in the small, pious communities of eastern Europe, women took full responsibility for the family finances while the men studied religious texts. Now, with modernization, women were increasingly confined to household duties and isolated from the community. Segregation of the sexes in Jewish life actually increased. Communal affairs, heretofore handled informally by the women of the local village or town, now became the responsibility of formal organizations, run by men. The new, middle-class Jewish housewife seems to have lost power even while gaining the cultural and economic benefits of living in a city.[5]

By the end of the nineteenth century, in poetry, fiction, and essays and through communal organizations, the position of women in Jewish life was challenged. The early writers of secular Hebrew and Yiddish literature, nearly all East European Jews, described the unhappiness of women in arranged marriages, in their limited educations, and in their lack of control over their own lives.[6] Usually these protests were directed against Jewish tradition and rabbinic leaders, with the implication that religious reform and secularization would prove the solution to women's secondary status. Sexism was equated with religion; the answer was to be found in secularism or socialism. Clearly, the approach was greatly influenced by the emerging socialist and feminist movements in Russia in the mid- to late nineteenth century. In central Europe and in the United States, Jewish women formed organizations to promote their interests, and these women became important forces for social change in their communities, although they tended to shy away from religious issues. Synagogue reform, which began in Europe and was carried over to the United States, was undertaken by rabbinic and lay leaders not out of feminist considerations to make the position of women equal to that of men but to equalize the position of Jewish women with that of non-Jewish women. In that way, Jewish women's disabilities were twofold: as women and as Jews. For example, the enfranchisement of Jews in Germany applied to men only; Jewish women had to wait until German women were enfranchised. And then they had to fight for enfranchisement within the Jewish communal structure.[7]

Beginning in the early 1970s in the United States Jewish feminism assumed a new posture.[8] Rather than breaking away from the religious community to achieve equality, American Jewish women in the last fifteen years have been struggling to become full members of the community. Conferences of Jewish women were convened in the 1970s to discuss what appeared to be the central stumbling block: Jewish religious observance, halakhah. Some feminists called for change within the halakhic system; others called for change of the system. Yet the primary issues were the same: rabbinical ordination and equal participation in synagogue and observances such as being counted in the minyan, the prayer quorum, and being called to the Torah for an aliyah. In addition, Jewish marriage and divorce laws and their attendant ceremonies were scrutinized and a total overhaul was called for. Change came quickly: women began to be ordained rabbis in the Reform and Reconstructionist movements; the Conservative movement announced a decision (which could be adopted or rejected by each member synagogue) to include women in the minyan; and various proposals for equalizing divorce proceedings were put forward by rabbinic leaders.

The desire for official change in the religious institutions was the common platform in the early years of the 1970s. The first articles on Jewish feminism, which began to appear in journals during those years, expressed an optimism that change would come and resolve the conflicts. The tone of those first publications suggests a bargain: ordain me a rabbi and I won't complain about your sexist liturgy; give me a greater role in the synagogue and I will devote myself with even greater intensity to raising Jewish children.

By the end of the decade, however, that tone changed. Bargaining for change seemed to bring about an even deeper sense of alienation. The process of fighting for changes in the synagogue evoked such strong resistance that, despite many gains, feminists became increasingly aware of their exclusion from the formulation of Jewish law, tradition, interpretation, and application. We were told, for example, that women could not be called to the Torah for an aliyah because, in the words of the Talmud, "of the honor of the congregation." For years we argued about the term *honor*—does it really constitute a dishonor to men, in this day and age, if women demonstrate superior or at least equal religious knowledge and devotion? Yet eventually, we came to the painful realization that the concept of congregation refers exclusively to male Jews. Whose honor is at stake? Certainly, in the traditional framework, not women's. Further and deeper study of Judaism brought feminists to the conclusion that the problem is not individual prayers but the entire liturgy; not particular rituals but the entire symbol system; not today's community but the entire course of history. However pleased we were with the changes made by Jewish leaders, such as ordaining women rabbis, we realized that the problem ran far deeper.[9]

Increasingly, articles were published expressing anger over women's traditional role in Judaism, and most expressed frustration over the lack of alternatives. More and more, women began experimenting with creating new forms of Jewish expression— rituals that combined Jewish symbols while putting them in a new, feminist context. For example, feminist Passover Haggadot (liturgies for the Passover Seder) were written which turned the holiday into a feminist celebration.[10] In the traditional observance of Passover, each person must experience the exodus from Egypt as if he or she personally went forth from Egypt. In some feminist Haggadot, the exodus from Egypt is interpreted as a movement for women's liberation from Judaism. In other cases, the going forth from Egypt, through the waters of the sea, born as a people, is interpreted as quintessentially women's experience: God our Mother giving birth to Her people, who must rush hurriedly through the birth canal of the Red Sea. The opening chapters of Exodus, with their stories of birth and midwives, seem to strengthen that interpretation. Other rituals included celebrating Rosh Hodesh, the new moon, as a women's holiday, an old tradition mentioned in rabbinic literature but long forgotten.[11] In recent years, groups of Jewish women through the United States have met each month for discussions, rituals, singing, and prayer to explore the connections between the Hebrew lunar calendar and women's ancient and forgotten rhythms.

The awareness of the depth of sexism in Judaism led feminists increasingly to a concern with the theological underpinnings of Judaism and to develop a feminist theological perspective. Today's Jewish feminists, in contrast to those ten or fifteen years ago, are no longer primarily concerned with justifying feminism to a Jewish audience but with explaining to a feminist audience why they remain committed to Judaism. Clearly, these feminists do not seriously consider ceasing remaining Jewish; Judaism is not the only phenomenon of sexism in the world. To abandon Judaism in the hope of escaping patriarchy is absurd and impossible. Most Jewish feminists remain in close contact with Christian feminists, sharing modes of critical analysis and constructive theology and commiserating over similar dilemmas. Christian feminists, who have developed a broad theological literature, face similar conflicts in coping with a male-dominated religious tradition.

The problem for Jewish feminists involves creating a theology that would account for the sexism of Judaism and supporting a new, feminist Judaism. The implications of the sexism in Judaism go to the heart of traditional Jewish beliefs concerning God, revelation, and Torah. For example, if the Torah holds women in positions of subservience or contempt, contradicting women's self-understanding, then, feminists conclude, either the God who has revealed the Torah is a malevolent deity or the Torah is not God's revelation but merely the projection of patriarchal society intent on preserving its status quo.

In a sense, the feminist challenge to Judaism can be compared in magnitude to other major crises in Judaism such as the destruction of the Jerusalem Temple, which necessitated the shift from sacrificial to liturgical worship. Such a comparison is encouraging to feminists because it concedes the possibility of radical change in Jewish religious and political life without losing the continuity with previous history and with Jewish peoplehood. The Holocaust was another important historical crisis in Jewish life. The destruction of European Jews and the Jewish civilization they created raised both a theological and a social challenge. The religious despair engendered by the Holocaust has been accompanied by social despair at the abandonment of the Jews by the non-Jewish world. But the Holocaust also emphasized the importance of rebuilding Judaism and strengthening the surviving Jewish community by creating new forms of Jewish religious expression. For feminists, a particular tragedy of the Holocaust was the loss of women's traditions, transmitted orally through the generations. The special prayers, meditations, customs, and rituals of women from earlier periods were rarely written down and now are lost.

The modern Zionist movement and the establishment of the State of Israel also have special meaning for feminists. Structurally, Zionism has many of the same internal dilemmas as feminism. Even while negating the diaspora, Zionism developed within the diaspora and is in many ways an outgrowth of it. Similarly, feminism, even while negating traditional Judaism, grew up within it. The Israeli state represents to feminists an important vehicle for developing new forms of Jewish expression outside the rubrics of religious thought and practice. At the same time, Israeli feminists are faced with their own agenda of cultural and political sexism.[12]

The specific theological formulations of Jewish feminists vary and are continually in process. One of the earliest and most popular approaches to Jewish feminist theology argues that the sexism in Judaism is not intrinsic but incidental to Jewish belief. Cynthia Ozick has articulated this position by arguing that Torah itself, though lacking a commandment stating, "Thou shalt not lessen the humanity of women," nonetheless contains the basis for a non-sexist Judaism in the proclamation of justice as an absolute requirement.[13] Yet her argument fails to address the problem of how a teaching that claims to be divinely revealed can legislate practices that are in total opposition to its self-proclaimed goal of justice. In other words, she fails to account for the sexism in Judaism. If Torah is the revealed word of God, how can it be other than just and right in all its aspects? Moreover, how can we even claim knowledge of what is just and right without that divine source of knowledge? Once we step outside the "sacred canopy," religious truth cannot be so superficially reaffirmed.[14] Finally, Ozick's argument shares with those of other Jewish theologians the seemingly insoluble quandary of determining what constitutes the revealed, immutable essence of Judaism and what should be viewed as merely a temporal, human invention.

In recent years, Jewish feminists have sought new approaches to Judaism by attempting to redefine both feminism and Judaism. The starting point for this newly emerging Jewish feminism is the application of the classic formulations of feminist thought to Jewish texts, beliefs, and practices. Classic feminist theorists such as Mary Daly and Simone de Beauvoir define patriarchy as the situation in which men's experiences and expressions of them are equated with normative human nature and behavior.[15] Men are the subjects, the humans, while women stand as "other," outsiders,

fact it will make little difference in the holiness and joy of the celebration.

b) Naming a baby girl in the synagogue is not new. Although tradition established no formal covenantal ceremony, it instituted long ago the custom of naming baby girls in *shul* at the time of Torah reading. For reasons which remain unexplained, this naming did not take place at the central communal Torah reading—on Shabbat morning—but rather at a Monday or Thursday *shakharit* (morning) or Shabbat *minkha* (afternoon) Torah reading, with a much smaller community presence. But that too is changing. In many modern Orthodox shuls, baby girls are now often named at the central liturgical moment of Torah reading—on Shabbat morning immediately preceding the *mussaf.*

c) Giving a Jewish name is a matter of great significance. From earliest times (and, as the Rabbis[2] teach, from the very first sojourn in Egypt) no matter what host culture or country, no matter what the conditions of their lives, Jews declared their identity by giving Jewish names and holding fast to them. Traditionally, a Jewish name was composed of a Hebrew name plus the given Hebrew name of the father which became the surname of the child. For example, Benjy Weiss's Jewish name was Binyamin *ben* (son of) Avraham. His sister's name was Dinah *bat* (daughter of) Avraham. In very special circumstances, such as when a special prayer for healing was made, the mother's name was used: Binyamin *ben* Sarah or Dinah *bat* Sarah. But otherwise, at the moment of giving the name and in all other formal usage, only the father's name was appended as surname.

During this last decade, however, at a baby naming in shul or at a *simkhat bat* ceremony, and even at an occasional *brit*, both parents names have been added as surname, as in Binyamin ben Avraham V'Sarah. Women called up to the Torah in women's *tefila* also use the Hebrew names of both parents. Thus far, I have not heard of a bar mitzvah boy being called up to the Torah for his first *aliyah* with his mother's name included, but I suspect that day is not far off.

d) The Jewish "infant formula" was a not so subtle indicator of community expectations. For baby boys, the custom was to recite the formula of greeting at a *brit:* "May he grow to [a life of] Torah, the wedding canopy, and good deeds." For a baby girl, the traditional greeting (recited at her naming) was: "May she grow to the wedding canopy and to good deeds." During the past decade, one hears the words, "to Torah" inserted into her blessing as well. In most Orthodox shuls, it is now the standard formula.

B. *Bat Mitzvah.* The celebration of *bar mitzvah*—a boy becoming an adult Jew under the canopy of Torah—is a relatively late custom in Judaism, only several hundred years old. But the celebration of *bat mitzvah* began only yesterday, as Jews count time. It was an innovation of liberal Jews in the early part of this century. In fact, up until a score of years ago, *bat mitzvah* celebration evoked suspicion and derision within Orthodoxy.

Not so any longer. As Jewish education spreads increasingly to young women, as the feminist notion of openly celebrating women's experience has gained strength, the rabbinic definition of Jewish female adulthood—at age 12—is affirmed in a public context.

Bat mitzvah celebrations within the Orthodox community are even less standardized than *simkhat bat* ceremonies. The settings run the gamut. For example: a *kiddush* in the home, accompanied by speeches and *divrei* Torah; a celebration at the *yeshiva* day school; family and friends spending Shabbat at a hotel to extend the honor of the event; marking the event in *shul* with rituals such as the father of the girl called up for an *aliyah* and/or reading the Torah, the rabbi of the congregation calling upon the girl and her mother to stand in their pews as he addresses the *bat-mitzvah;* the presentation by the young woman of a *d'var* Torah before the entire congregation gathered for *shaleshudos* (the third Sabbath meal) in the synagogue vestry between *mincha* and *maariv* prayer services; the presentation of a *d'var* Torah by the *bat mitzvah* from the *bimah* to the entire congregation, following Shabbat morning services; the celebration of a *siyyum* Mishnah, the conclusion of a tractate which she had studied during the entire year as preparation for becoming *bat mitzvah.*

Another significant celebration of bat mitzvah has been that which takes place in the women's *tefila* groups. During the first half of the dozen years of existence of the Riverdale Women's *Tefila*, the number of 12-year-old girls who celebrated their *bat mitzvah* in this sub-community could be counted on one hand. But during the last six years, there have been a handful each year. The young woman will read her portion of the Torah and *haftorah*, deliver a *d'var* Torah, lead the prayers. She may do all of the above, or enlist family and friends to share some of these roles. At the most recent celebration, the girl's mother lead the warm-up and *shakharit* prayers, a friend read the haftorah, and the *bat mitzvah* girl read from the Torah, delivered a d'var Torah, and lead the *mussaf.* After *aleinu,* a dozen little girls came up to the bimah and led the concluding prayers.

The *bat mitzvah* girl is called up for an *aliyah* and is given a special blessing by the *gabbait.* Everything is connected to her identity with Torah. All of this is followed by a *kiddush* or luncheon in her honor. No more the shy 12-year-old sliding silently into Jewish adulthood.

Two other unique *bat mitzvah* celebrations stand out in my mind, one of a decade ago, the other of recent vintage. The first was a Tu Bi'Shvat *seder.* The young girl spent a year with a special teacher studying the traditional sources on all that had to do with trees and fruits of *the land of Israel.* Her texts were primarily Talmud and Midrash. She and her family compiled a Tu Bi'Shvat *haggadah* which was given to each guest at the feast, at which foods and fruits of the Holy Land were served. She read and taught from the *haggadah* while the guests followed along in their texts. It was a unique Torah learning experience for all.

On Purim of 5751 (1991), another first in Jewish history (of the Orthodox community) took place. To celebrate this day in her life the *bat mitzvah* girl read the Purim *megillah.* She read it for the entire congregation, male and female guests alike, in the main sanctuary of the *shul.* According to the tradition, the *megillah* reading is the one Torah reading where a woman reader may fulfill a man's obligation to hear the *megillah* as well as her own. This young woman read all ten chapters, alternating voices from deep stentorian tones for King Ahasuerus, to gravelly ones for Haman, to a sweet soprano for Esther. *Divrei Torah* followed: her own, family members and guests including several Orthodox rabbis (among them her uncle and grandfather). The liturgical feast was followed by a culinary one. As I participated with great joy, I thought of the wonderful memories that she will carry with her for the next fifty years of her life. What a contrast to the Orthodox women of my generation, who can recall their sweet sixteen parties but not the day of their *bat mitzvah*—because there was nothing to remember.

C. Marriage. In the traditional Jewish wedding ceremony, the bride and female guests have few vocalized roles. The bride is covered with the veil by her husband (*bedeken*); she walks seven times around her husband under the wedding canopy;[3] she hears the marriage declaration and accepts the ring on her index finger; she acquires the *ketubah* (the marriage contract). But traditionally, she recites no words. Nor do any of the women guests participate in any of the special honors associated with the wedding ceremony.

Now I am certain that brides of the past did not take umbrage or slight at the beautiful traditional wedding ceremony. The reality was that no matter how little formal ritual participation, the traditional Jewish bride, as brides in every culture, was still the center of the universe.

Nevertheless, some brides now want to have their female friends share in the ritual; and some want to have a more expressive role themselves. Here are several of the new customs that have grown during this last score of years:

ITEM. One of the most beautiful pre-ceremony customs is the *bedeken*, the veil covering ritual. The groom, accompanied in song and dance by a male entourage, approaches his bride and gently draws the veil over her face. Just before that moment of veiling, a most poignant custom takes place: the father of the bride places his hands over her head and blesses her. The father of the groom follows suit. In very recent times, some mothers have also joined in blessing the bride.

ITEM. One Orthodox rabbi lately instructs the bride to present the groom with a *tallit* at the time of the *bedeken*.

ITEM. Women hold up the poles of a portable *huppah* (the marriage canopy).

ITEM. A female guest reads the *ketubah* (marriage contract) during the ceremony. Some rabbis will allow a woman to read only the English translation of the Aramaic *ketubah*, but there are other Orthodox weddings where a woman has read the *ketubah* in the original.

ITEM. A bride recites under the *huppah* some words of love, usually taken from Song of Songs. In such instances, this is done after the marriage ceremony has technically and formally been completed (by the groom's recitation of the marriage formula, "Behold, with this ring you are consecrated unto me according to the laws of Moses and Israel.") Oftentimes, the bride will recite her words after the *ketubah* has been read or after the *sheva berakhot*, so as to distinguish her words from the traditional marriage ritual. Similarly, where a bride wishes to give her husband a ring, she will do it in a manner that does not confuse it with a double ring ceremony. Some Orthodox rabbis will not permit a bride to give a ring under the *huppah* altogether, but others who do are careful to point out what is tradition and what is not.

ITEM. At a recent Orthodox wedding, at the conclusion of the ceremony but before the breaking of the glass, seven women were called up to the *huppah*, one at a time. Each recited words of blessing, corresponding to the *sheva berakhot*, the seven traditional wedding blessings that, moments earlier, had been recited by seven male guests.

ITEM. At the *sheva berakhot* celebrations that take place during the week following the wedding, the seven blessings are again recited each night. On occasion, women have been invited to recite the individual blessings.

Several of the pre-ceremony customs have also been adapted to include:

ITEM. At the traditional *aufruf*, which usually takes place on a Shabbat preceding the wedding, the groom is called up to the Torah for an *aliyah*. Oftentimes a *kiddush* following the services celebrates the *aufruf*. Very recently, at women's *tefila* services, a bride's *aufruf* is celebrated. She is called up to the Torah for an *aliyah*, reads her Torah portion if she is able or gives a *d'var Torah*. A *kiddush* is celebrated in her honor.

ITEM. Another variation on this theme has been grafted onto the Shabbat *kallah*, the bride's Sabbath before the wedding. This is typically a time when the bride's family and close friends will keep her company and attend to her. Recently, the Shabbat *kallah* also includes a *shiur* (the studying sacred texts) which her friends will have prepared in her honor.

ITEM. The *kallah's tish* is derived from the custom of *chattan's tish*, (groom's table), the pre-ceremony gathering of men (around a table set with light fare) where the groom will recite words of Torah. At the first *kallah's tish* that I attended several years ago, the *d'var Torah* was presented by the bride's sister, a teacher of Talmud.

D. Death. In this complex, highly emotional and acutely sensitive area, we can observe the interplay of several forces:

    1. Because of its associated mystery and taboo, death has tended to sharpen the divide between the sexes. One example of this

is women's participation in burial rites. In certain cemeteries run by the more right-wing *hevra kadisha* (holy burial) societies, women may not enter the cemetery but must remain at the entrance gate. (In some extreme instances, this includes the female mourner as well.)

2. Yet, because of the intense grief and need to be comforted, it was logical that the impulse of lovingkindness and consolation would bridge the separation. Thus, for example, at many Orthodox funerals, male and female visitors will be seated separately in the funeral parlor, but the family of mourners will sit together, undivided by gender.

3. On the other hand, the domino effect of one aspect of tradition upon the other—in this case, women's more circumscribed liturgical role—mutes a woman's natural inclination to participate in rituals of mourning. In the absence of obligation upon them to be part of the *minyan*, women mourners typically do not recite the mourner's *kaddish* (recited in the presence of a *minyan* in the mourner's home) even though they recite all other parts of the service, such as the *kedusha* or the *borchu* which may also be recited only in a *minyan*.

4. Because of the vulnerability of the moment, decisions rendered on the spot by others are unquestioned and unchallenged. Occasionally, women will describe a sense of bewilderment at being told, "no" to that which they would instinctively want to give expression. For example: at the moment that a female relative or friend she feels the urge to join others at the cemetery who, one by one, have taken up a shovel to heave a bit of earth on the coffin, a sign of honor and closeness to the deceased, she is told that "only men may do so." At that moment a woman would not think of creating a stir. Or at times, women mourners are banished to the kitchen or hallway during the services and consequently miss the learning segment where a guest also speaks of the character of the deceased. Only after the fact do some women articulate their heightened sense of loss at not being able to honor the dead or accept consolation in the same manner as male family and friends.

But the new sense of self and of emotional entitlement has impacted on all of the above.

Kaddish is one area where this can be seen. *Kaddish* is a most powerful healing ritual. Recited daily at the communal prayer services during the eleven months following the death of a parent (or thirty days for other members of the immediate family), the *kaddish* helps a mourner knit together in the framework of a loving community. Some few women (far fewer than in the liberal denominations where many women recite the daily *kaddish*) have taken upon themselves the daily *kaddish*. Several have described the spiritual experience, the psychological and emotional value, as well as the gradual process of their integration into the healing community.

Regarding the latter, the process usually runs something like this: during the first few mornings, the regulars of an Orthodox *minyan* are somewhat uncomfortable as a woman appears, and everyone shifts around a bit uneasily. Since the weekday services are attended only by men, and in fewer numbers than on a Shabbat, these services are often held in a small room or chapel of the synagogue, where there is no *mechitza* (partition screen or curtain separating men and women). Therefore, for the first few mornings, a woman usually recites prayers and *kaddish* from the hall. Within a very few days, a special section is created for her by a *mechitza*, so that she need not remain out in the hall. Little by little, she becomes part of the group of regular "*minyanaires*," though services will never begin until ten men have assembled.

Few of the women who have described their experience over the course of a year have ever reported a continuing hostility towards them. On the contrary, after the initial hesitation and suspicion, a woman is generally treated with graciousness and welcome. By the time the eleventh month rolls around, she has become such a regular feature of the group that the men are sorry to see her leave, which inevitably she does. So far.

Altogether new is a woman offering a *d'var Torah* at a *shiva minyan*. *Shiva* is the seven-day mourning period following burial. During these seven days, the mourners stay at home, sit on low wooden stools, and are visited by family and friends who come to comfort, distract, help, listen. . . . A *minyan* is held at the home of the mourners so that the *kaddish* can be recited during the morning, afternoon, and evening prayers. In order for an additional *kaddish* to be recited, and in order to create a demarcation between the afternoon and evening prayers which are usually held in tandem, five to ten minutes of study are inserted between the two. Usually, one of the visitors will teach a few verses from the Mishnah and then relate its context to the life of the deceased.

At one particular *kaddish minyan* not long ago, it was the granddaughter and granddaughter-in-law who taught the *mishnayot* between the afternoon and evening prayers. I am quite certain that this was the first time in Jewish history that such a thing was done. How did it come to be? As for most "firsts," there's a story behind it.

Both granddaughters live simultaneously in the Orthodox community and in the modern world. Both are well educated. One is also a strong feminist. Both were trained to show great respect for their grandparents. And because they loved their grandfather very much and were unusually close to him—they wanted to have some special part in this period of mourning.

Now the father/father-in-law of these two young women was not quite comfortable, with their request, although his wife was altogether for it. In fact, had someone other than his children asked the question, he would surely have said "No," not to be recalcitrant but simply because it had never been done before and then as is common, the arguments are lined up around that position. But here it was his own children, and he heard their plea. Yes, they would teach the *mishnayot*.

However, reciting *kaddish* after a woman's learning was more than he could handle. His compromise was that after the two women finished teaching the Mishnah, one male guest would read a single verse from the text and then the *kaddish* could be recited. Perhaps in a few years, or perhaps now at some *kaddish minyan* elsewhere in this country, a woman will teach the Mishnah and those assembled will recite the *kaddish* immediately following.

6. **Learning.** Search for the focus of feminist values in a particular denomination and you will find it in a different place in each one. In Orthodoxy, it is in the study of sacred texts that feminism has most powerfully taken root. One example that points up the difference is the reclaiming of *Rosh Hodesh* as a woman's holiday. While a host of monthly rituals and worship have been introduced by religious feminists of other denominations, Orthodox women have tended to mark the new month with special learning groups. In my community, during the past few years the local Amit and

Emunah women's groups have scheduled *Rosh Hodesh sheurim* (learning texts).

We are witnessing a virtual explosion of women's learning in the Orthodox community, modern and fundamentalist alike. Some would demur, saying that feminist values have had nothing to do with it but I believe the timing is more than mere coincidence.

The Orthodox community has always emphasized Talmud Torah, with particular attention to the study of Talmud. High value was placed on its learning, and great status was conferred upon the learned. Women, however, were simply not part of this exalted enterprise. My two sisters and I grew up in a home in which primary emphasis was placed on our Jewish education. My parents uprooted themselves and moved across the continent in search of the best Jewish schooling that could be had. But neither my sisters nor I ever were ever introduced to a page of the Talmud in all of our years of elementary, high school and college education. By contrast, male cousins and friends had many pages of Talmud behind them by the time they were thirteen.

That has changed. Today, young women in *yeshiva* day schools are taught Talmud at an early age, at the very same ages as their brothers. Women fill the Honors Talmud class in high schools such as Ramaz. Institutions of higher Jewish traditional learning such as Drisha in New York, and Matan, Machon Lindenbaum, and Nishmat in Israel have been created specifically for women. These academies are outstanding in the level and intensity of learning, the caliber of faculty and students and the scope of texts taught. Before these new institutions were created several fine institutions of higher learning had already begun to introduce the subject of Talmud to women. Yeshiva University's Revel Graduate School and Stern College for Women pioneered in this area as far back as the late 1960's. Whereas for the better part of Jewish history the study of Talmud was largely out of bounds for women, it is now well if not yet widely accepted.

There are all kinds of encouragement for women to develop themselves in areas of Jewish learning. In their local communities, women study Torah, Talmud and other serious texts; but of equal significance, they manage to carve out the time for regular learning and *shiurim*. A once uncommon sight is now almost taken for granted: women walking through the streets on a Shabbat afternoon—in communities where there is an *eruv*—with a tractate of

Mishnah or Talmud tucked under the arm as they wend their way to class.

As the pool of women who learn enlarges, so does the number of those who commit themselves seriously to long-term study of religious texts; so, too, does the number of women who become teachers in the community, including teachers of Talmud and halakha. Remarkably, there are now a dozen or so Orthodox women around the world who have spent the last decade concentrating on this field of study. And there are dozens more coming up through the pipeline.

7. **Leadership.** All of this discussion about learning brings us round to the subject of leadership, because learning and leadership are inextricably linked in Orthodox Judaism. It seems not at all unreasonable, therefore, to make the following prediction: that in the not too distant future, women in the Orthodox community will also hold the title of rabbi. The meshing of two forces—on the one hand, the explosion of women's learning, and on the other, the very powerful model of women rabbis in the liberal denominations—is surely going to create that fact. Initially, it seems unlikely that Orthodox women will serve as pulpit rabbis, for the community probably will not be ready for that step. But that is not of concern to us now. The first step will be the ordination of women based on their mastery of texts. We will witness this in our time because we are charted along an irreversible course and because women, in significant numbers, will become proficient in all that qualify them for ordination.

Meanwhile, we can also take note of the fact that so many women have assumed lay leadership roles. Women now serve as officers of Orthodox synagogues, up to and including the office of president; a broad leap from their status of a generation ago when women were not even entitled to vote as members of an Orthodox *shul*.

Currently, several women serve as executive directors of Orthodox synagogues. Women sit on rabbinic search committees and some who do exercise the opportunity to query a rabbinic candidate on attitudes towards women's issues. Women serve as chairpersons and as guests of honor at *yeshiva* dinners. The all male dais can now be found only in the right wing *yeshiva* world. And in Israel, women have been elected to town rabbinic councils following the landmark Leah Shakdiel case.

IV

Above, I stated that in the Orthodox community, feminism is not systematically used as a valid criterion to redefine the law. But one can easily see that it has greatly influenced change. Everything described above is a clear departure from the past. Yet each new phenomenon is now considered halakhically acceptable by some segment of the Orthodox community.

But what of it? At the outset of this essay, I made the claim that much has happened. Yet surely some readers are still waiting to hear a bit of hard news, an item to be surprised by. To one who comes from outside of Orthodoxy it might all seem totally inconsequential, or worse—laughable! So what if women recite a bit of Torah in public? So what if a girl stands in the women's section and the rabbi recognizes her on her bat mitzvah day? So what if a Jewish lout must still be shamed into giving his wife a *get?* What is so remarkable about the fact that a Jewish child finally carries both mother's and father's names?

Moreover, the reader would be altogether correct in pointing out that some examples cited were nothing more than one-time episodes, mere happenstance. What could I be talking about when I say a lot has happened? In the course of hoping and longing, have I become totally disconnected from reality?

But I believe these changes are highly significant, in fact, nothing short of revolutionary. There are two reasons to explain why:

1. Taken item by item, none are earth shaking. But all together, they add up to a matter of great significance: the redefinition of women's role in the liturgical, spiritual, and intellectual life of the community. This redefinition has two components to it. One incorporates issues of equality, dignity, and access. The other is the fundamental shift from private to public roles, from the classic assumption that women's basic dignity—"the honor of the king's daughter"—is in the home and, by extension, her religious life and expression is contained therein as well.

That is why I call the impact of feminism upon Orthodoxy a "revolution of small signs." All these small steps reflect new spiritual expectations of and by Orthodox women. Each act proclaims the growing acceptance of women in public roles in Jewish life. The presumption today is that women will locate themselves in academy and synagogue, as well as in home and *mikvah.* Slowly but surely, a woman's presence in sacred settings is becoming normal, natural, familiar, everyday. The taboos against seeing her and hearing her in the performance of communal acts of holiness are being lifted.

One independent confirmation comes from a surprising place, the *eruv*. The Shabbat *eruv* (mixing together) is a rabbinic institution that transforms the nature of real property. It addresses the proscription against transporting items on Shabbat through the public domain. In some communities, this proscription limited mobility and comfort on Shabbat. The Rabbis of the Talmud ingeniously created the concept of *eruv* to enhance oneg Shabbat, the joy of the day. The *eruv* "mixed" together public and private domains. Through this legal fiction, the public domain becomes an extension of the private and thus, one may carry through it.

Legal fiction alone, however, cannot transform the domain. The Rabbis mandated a physical bridging of the areas.

Today, connected telephone poles, fences, wires, ropes, etc., create a circumference that encircles and links together public and private domains. It takes a considerable amount of effort, ingenuity and expense to erect and maintain an *eruv* that encloses an entire neighborhood. This explains why, for the better part of American Jewish history, few Orthodox communities had one. (The liberal denominations do not accept as binding the injunction not to carry on the Sabbath.)

It was mothers of the young, who could not "transport" an infant or carriage who were most affected by lack of an *eruv*. Oftentimes, mothers of very young children did not see the inside of a synagogue on the Sabbath for months at a time. What is more, no one questioned their absence. Now that I live in a community that has an *eruv*, it seems almost strange; but that is the way it was for young families during all the years when our children were babies. Occasionally, I hired a baby-sitter; but more often I simply did not go.

During the past fifteen years, there has been a tremendous expansion of *eruvin* (pl.) in the U.S.—wherever there are concentrations of young Orthodox families. On Sabbath morning, one can see a plethora of strollers lined up outside of *shul*, testimony to the presence of young mothers whose own mothers and grandmothers minded their children at home on Sabbath mornings. Today, a self-respecting couple of child-bearing age would think twice about

moving to an "eruvless" neighborhood; prospective home buyers make it their first question; even real estate brokers in Jewish neighborhoods put the word "*eruv*" into their ads. Women's presence in shul on Shabbat is anticipated!

2. The second reason these small signs and are so important is that this is a community that lives by precedent. Each individual experience,—previously untried but now deemed to be not contrary to halakha—expands the art of the possible. Each "kosher" precedent, legitimate in one halakha-abiding community or family, can be replicated by others. Of course, there are those who would quarrel with the idea of a woman reading the *ketubah* at a wedding. But there are others who would say, "Well, if it was permissible at that wedding, performed by Rabbi X, then perhaps we can do the same at our wedding." Or procedurally more correct, "Let us ask Rabbi X if we may introduce that at our wedding."

The power of a model is far greater than impassioned argument. You can have a thousand discussions on what women may or may not do, but if you have one live case that has passed halakhic muster, the argument is over—better yet, never engaged.

Of course, it is a far slower process, these small signs, cranking it out inch by inch. There is much to recommend against so slow and cautious a pace. Is there anything at all to be said in its favor?

I believe so. One is the phenomenology of the vertical chain. If you take incremental steps, as opposed to giant ones, you feel more joined to the tradition, continuous with it. A sense of continuity is more than legal; it must also be psychological. When there is organic change, everything seems to fit; novelty is experienced not as novelty; change is perceived as being not in tension with what went before but rather as flowing forward smoothly through time, history, and community. This sense of connectedness is one of the great strengths of Orthodoxy.

Similarly, the dilatory response of Orthodoxy has uniquely enabled us to monitor a broader issue: the effects of a new social ideology upon a normative monotheism. Modern Jews still do not know how to answer the vital question: to what extent and at what pace can you change from what was, yet continue to feel tied to Revelation. Introducing change can both enhance and diminish the ability to hear the Commanding Voice. The question is: what is the cut-off point that reverses direction downwards? Orthodoxy offers a model of a community that, remarkably, has maintained

both the authority and the sense of Revelation through all the in-
tervening years since Sinai. Of feminism and Orthodoxy it ultimately might be said: there are two ways to get to the revolution.

A second thought about the benefits accruing from the marriage
of feminism and a slow moving Orthodoxy: all of the answers
about equality of roles are not yet in. Why should gender distinctive roles automatically and categorically be equated with inequity?
Who knows but that a blurring of all the lines, and at rapid pace,
might not be a blueprint for great confusion ahead? A (de facto)
feminist definition of equality-as-identicality, seems not quite adequate to the human condition; certainly not as fitting or felicitous
as one that allows for distinctive roles beyond pure biological ones.

To be sure, the very broad role distinctions in Judaism for male
and female that we have inherited and that have limited women's
access (e.g., men—learning and leadership, women—family and
home) certainly will have to go. Much of it has already fallen away.
But doing away with global distinctions does not mean that there is
no room for maintaining and creating some very specific, well defined roles and rituals for each gender.

Why ritual? Because one you acknowledge that there is value to
retaining gender definitions beyond biology, once you affirm that
it is possible to hold in harmony equality and gender distinctiveness, then finely detailed ritual is a warm spirited, non-
selfcentered way to differentiate. Ultimately, it is ritual that has the
capacity to take differences beyond the immediacy of interpersonal relationships to a transcendent place.

A tradition that moves with greater caution in redefining male
and female roles serves not only as recorder and anchor for Jews
but also carries a message of value for all of contemporary society.

V

Having said that I must say the other, lest anyone confuse my defense of a measured response with legitimation of reflexive nay-
saying, my affirmation of distinctiveness with an excuse for
freezing the status quo. We still have a long way to go in Orthodoxy. We still have much to learn from the other denominations.
We still have to open our ears and hear what society's new message
is all about. Inequity in divorce is outright inequity, not distinctiveness. The problem must be resolved, swiftly and in total good

faith. Prayer groups deserve a better hearing. If open welcome and praise be beyond the current communal reach, then at the very least, there must be a moratorium on suspicion and scorn.

The formalization of rituals that affirm the covenantal experiences of girls and of women; religious expression given to events and sensations that are unique to women; the broader realization of women's aspirations to religious leadership—all of this lies ahead.

VI

Given that reality, why write in so sanguine a manner about the small signs? Some would argue that Orthodoxy has so great a distance to go on women's issues that to say anything positive is akin to Uncle Tomism. At the very least, it is a premature pat on the back. And I know the facts. Only yesterday was my reverie shattered in a conversation with one of the dozen women I cited above as future Talmud scholars. After ten years of intensive Talmud study, she is switching fields. "An uphill battle for acceptance and legitimacy in the world of yeshiva learning . . . , a professional dead end. . ." As I stood on the corner listening to her, I couldn't help but think, with all that talent scholarship and talent turned away, the heavens must be weeping.

Still, I believe there is value to singing the partial praises of feminism-in-Orthodoxy. There are many reasons and one of them is the truth. That means telling the whole story. Once you stop believing that, once you take the slippery slope of half truths, you fall easily into exaggeration, rhetoric, and even lying.

Secondly, it is crucial for those who fear change will destroy the whole system to be able to see that it is simply not so. Such a fear is groundless and a look at the new realities can only help to dispel their panic. Orthodoxy is flourishing with the greater spiritual energy and intellect of women. To detail and to ungrudgingly applaud the new signs is a way of encouraging and inviting in.

Moreover, a clear sighted look at the way Orthodox feminists have gone about their business should reassure even the most implacable opponent of change. Everything has been done with total fidelity to tradition and its authority. The halakha remains binding as ever upon women, including those who innovate. Even agunot, who could end their personal misery by finding recourse elsewhere, do not bolt. Their faithfulness is unfathomable. Similarly, those who stall often do so not only out of a legitimate desire to protect the tradition but also because they believe that feminism has destroyed the family. True, the Jewish family is under siege. True, some aspects of feminism have contributed to its erosion. But not because of women's heightened participation in ritual, not because of women's immersion in the teachings of the Rabbis, not because of women's tefila groups where young children see their mothers daven and rejoice in Yiddishkeit, not because of pressure for equality in divorce law which restores glory to a just religion. All of this heightens commitment and identity which in turn strengthens the family. Besides, the larger picture is that equality in status, ritual and role generate a sense of equality in the relationship; that, and not hierarchy, is what contributes to a healthy stable family in our times.

VII

Which brings us to the very last point. How will all of this move ahead? I believe that it will happen largely to the extent that women in the Orthodox community will desire. At this moment in time, the majority of women in the Orthodox community are more oriented to preserving the status quo on many of these issues. That largely explains why the whole community has moved very cautiously and why the rabbinic leaders have not used the powers of interpretation given into their hands.

But to say that change will occur precisely in relationship to the growing and future readiness of Orthodox women is to say something glorious about the whole system. It is not a closed system as some would think, but rather a dynamic one, one that can blend tradition and contemporary values; one that can accommodate individual and group needs within the larger unity and with integrity to the faith system.

As feminism increasingly acts upon the lives of women in the Orthodox community, the process will move forward, the halakha will again open to interpretation, and we will see within it a definition of equality and distinctiveness of the sexes that will carry us faithfully forward into the next four thousand years of Jewish life.

Notes

1. This is the widely held view of the way things always were, despite the fact that several contemporary scholars have offered ample proof that other communal liturgical traditions existed in Jewish history. See for example, Bernadette Brooten's fine work, *Women Leaders of the Ancient Synagogue*, Scholars Press, 1982.

2. When the generic word "rabbis" is capitalized, it refers specifically to the Rabbis of the Talmud.

3. Some think this is a sexist custom, the groom standing in the middle and his bride and mother and mother-in-law circling about him: he is the center of the relationship, a Jewish prince. While any given act can be interpreted on multiple levels, I believe the sexist interpretation is forced. It is not consistent with the basic thrust of the ceremony—a sanctification of the union—nor with the contents of the *ketubah*—which focus primarily on his obligations to her and not vice versa. Moreover, the act itself evokes the symbolism of messianic times, as the prophet Jeremiah says, "The female will encircle the male", i.e. there will be an end to the stereotypes of passive female role (post Eden) and a restoration of the equality of the original Garden of Eden.

FOR FURTHER READING

Berkovits, Eliezer, *Jewish Women in Time and Torah*, New York: 1990. Berkovits examines critically and with great honesty the status of women in halakhah. He offers creative suggestions from the tradition to improve that status, particularly in the areas of divorce and ritual participation. Berkovits contends that adequate halakhic justification exists for women to join in the men's Grace after Meals, wear tefillin, and establish their own prayer groups. 143 pp, glossary, index.

Biale, Rachel, *Women and Jewish Law*, New York, 1984. Biale provides a scholarly survey of the sources on issues such as marriage, divorce, birth control, abortion, lesbianism and communal worship. Particularly striking is her chapter on rape, tracing it, as she does every issue, through biblical, talmudic and posttalmudic rabbinic sources. While she finds flexibility in the sources that can be applied today, she also attempts to understand the rationale behind those sources with which she disagrees.

Ellinson, Getsel, *Women and the Mizvot* (Hebrew). Jerusalem, 1974. Ellinson provides a basic primer for anyone who wants to study issues of women and halakha. He cites and explains the primary and pivotal sources on Jewish women's role in *mitzvot*. He covers women's special obligations, the areas of exemption for women, women and prayer, women and ritual, etc. This is the best introductory book to the sources and should be translated into English..

Frankiel, Tamar, *The Voice of Sarah*, San Francisco, 1990. In her interesting preface, Frankiel describes her spiritual journey to Orthodoxy and how feminism impacted on that journey. Using as models the central female figures of Jewish tradition, she shows how the tradition affirms a distinctly feminine approach to religious experience.

Greenberg, Blu, *On Women and Judaism*, Philadelphia, 1981. The author attempts to reconcile the claims of feminism with faithfulness to Jewish law. She explores the history of women's halakhic status in Judaism and shows how in every era the tradition responded to human needs. Building on her personal experience and on a theoretical framework, she outlines an agenda of dignity for traditional Jewish women in areas such as prayer, *mikvah*, abortion and divorce.

Heschel, Susannah, *On Being a Jewish Feminist*. New York, 1983. Heschel's collection of essays covers areas such as Jewish women in liturgy, myth, history, religion and contemporary Jewish life. The book is worth its entire value alone if only for Cynthia Ozick's extraordinary essay, "Notes Towards Finding the Right Question." Other seminal articles are Rachel Adler's and Heschel's (the introduction) in which both point to the deep and pervasive inequity residing in the tradition.

Schneider, Susan Weidman, *Jewish and Female, Choices and Changes in Our Lives Today*. New York, 1984. Schneider offers a fine summary of the impact of feminism across the board on the Jewish community. She describes the lives of Jewish women intellectually, spiritually, sexually, socially, in family relationship, and in the power and politics of Jewish communal life.

Wegner, Judith Romney, *Chattel or Person? The Status of Women in the Mishnah*, New York, 1990. With painstaking and in-depth scholarly research, Wegner raises probing and sometime uncomfortable questions regarding women's status in rabbinic Judaism. Questions of property, sexuality, autonomy, marital status—these are but a few of the areas she analyzes. She brings her own insights to mishnaic literature and explicates the most complex material, thereby making the Mishnah accessible to all who would want to study the matter further.

Weiss, Avraham, *Women at Prayer*, Hoboken, 1990. Rabbi Avi Weiss, dean of women's *tefila* groups, answers the halakhic criticism leveled against such assemblies. In doing so, he offers halakhic legitimation of women's *tefila* and he shows the importance of distinguishing between halakhah and public policy. He deals with many pertinent issues, such as that of women reading from the Torah scroll, and the non-halakhic basis of the taboo against handling the Torah during menses.

A shorter version of this essay has appeared in *Divisions Between Traditionalism and Liberalism in the American Jewish Community*, edited by Michael Shapiro (Edwin Mellen Press, 1992).

Women Today—A Non-Orthodox View

RELA GEFFEN MONSON

Although the contemporary feminist movement in the United States is usually traced to the early 1960s, specifically 1963, with the publication of and reaction to Betty Friedan's *Feminine Mystique*, and 1966, with the founding of the National Organization for Women, the Jewish women's movement was not born until 1972, when *Ezrat Nashim*, the fledgling Jewish women's study group turned consciousness-raising group became activist in its orientation.[1] The group grew out of the Conservative movement, but it became part of a larger push within non-Orthodox religious circles to include women in the mainstream of public Jewish life, which included the communal-organizational as well as the religious domain.

Although there had been some movements toward the inclusion of women in ritual and communal life before that time (such as the 1956 *responsum* of the Conservative Rabbinical Assembly Law Committee by Rabbi Aaron Blumenthal permitting the calling of women to the Torah and the beginning of the institutionalization of the *bat mitzvah*, albeit on Friday night), clearly it was involvement in and exposure to the civil rights movement and the American feminist movement that led to the growth of an organized Jewish feminist movement.

Until the decade of the 1970s, Jewish women's participation in religious life was primarily through the creation of high-quality Jewish home life. Thus in the home, women were responsible for the maintenance of the dietary laws (to the degree that they were kept), creating Sabbath and holiday atmosphere, educating young children into a strong Jewish identity, and making sure that children took religious school seriously. These activities were often supplemented by attendance at religious services and support of synagogue schools through parent-teacher associations as well as sisterhood activities, which supported Reform and Conservative synagogues more generally. Some women also taught in Sunday and afternoon schools and worked as youth leaders. Because in twentieth-century American suburban life many fathers commute to work and most mothers work outside the home for pay on a part-time basis, if at all, the mothers usually makes Judaism a living religion for their children and often for their husbands as well.

Though women were central to Jewish home life, their participation in public and even in home ritual or ceremonial life was usually limited to the role of facilitator or onlooker. This situation was almost as prevalent in the Reform and Conservative as the Orthodox community because such a division of labor reflected the structure of American familial and community life as a whole. Thus though the woman made the meal, the husband made *kiddush*, though she arranged the *bar mitzvah*, she did not receive a religious honor at the service; though she had the baby, she often spent the time of the *Brit Milah* in another room.

The ceremony of *bat mitzvah* was introduced in the 1920s by Mordecai M. Kaplan, but it was often different and more limited than that for boys and was far from normative. In Conservative synagogues it was an optional Friday night ceremony which was integrated into the late Friday evening service and might consist of the girl leading English responsive readings and perhaps chanting the next morning's prophetic portion without the benedictions. The family would then sponsor the congregational *Oneg Shabbat* in her honor. In Reform temples, it became more prevalent as *bar mitzvah* was reintroduced, but Confirmation remained the central rite of passage for boys and girls.

On the communal-organizational front, women were and continue to be the backbone of Jewish activities in North America, though some disillusionment with this role has recently become evident.[2] In addition to the role of sisterhoods of synagogues of all movements in maintaining physical plants, educational activities, and religious schools, women worked as volunteers for causes ranging from Israel to child care, Soviet Jewry, and mental and physical health services. Women's organizations such as Hadassah, ORT, and National Council of Jewish Women published magazines, sponsored youth movements and summer camps, and were actively involved in support of Israel and defense of needy Jews everywhere. In addition to participation in all-women's groups, women were active in national Jewish organization such as the American Jewish Committee, B'nai B'rith, the American Jewish Congress, and Jewish Community Relations Councils. Finally, women were active in support of federations of Jewish agencies and the United Jewish Appeal in local communities and nationally.

Until recently, women often performed these volunteer services without receiving the same rewards from the communal power structure that were given to some male volunteers. They were seldom officers of synagogues, members of agency boards, or public representatives of organizations to the community at large. Since the early 1970s expansion of these public roles has increased because of organized pressure on the religious and civic fronts.

The Early Years: The Decade of the 1970s

Partially as a result of the awareness of their own potential resulting from activities in the societal feminist movement, women created new groups in the early 1970s to consider the role of women in Judaism and to promote study and fuller participation of women in ritual and communal activities. The impetus for such groups came not only from the general women's movement but from the greater knowledge of their own tradition that women were able to acquire to some degree at secular universities such as Columbia and Brandeis. Even more crucial was their immersion in higher Jewish learning at religious seminaries such as the Hebrew Union College–Jewish Institute of Religion, later on at the Reconstructionist Rabbinical College, and most particularly at the Jewish Theological Seminary (JTS).

It was around the Columbia-JTS nexus and particularly as an offshoot of the New York *Havurah* that a women's study group was formed in 1971. This group was principally made up of women who were products of the Conservative movement and its institutions such as Camp Ramah, Leader's Training Fellowship, and the Jewish Theological Seminary. They were both learned and traditionally observant, and they decided to study the tractates pertaining to women in the Talmud once a week under the aegis of the first woman studying for a Ph.D. in Talmud at the Jewish Theological Seminary. They gave themselves the name *Ezrat Nashim* (literally "the help of women" and traditionally the name for the women's section in the synagogue). By the end of a year of study, they had become radicalized and determined to fight for change within the Conservative movement. After all, they reasoned, they were the "best and the brightest" that the movement had produced; how could it reject them?

The early 1970s were the heady days of women's consciousness-raising. These women felt an exhiliration in anticipating decompartmentalizing and reintegrating their religious and secular lives. As Paula Hyman noted in an interview with the *New York Post* in 1972, professors and students at Columbia were continually asking her why she changed into a different person on shabbat, who did not ask the same questions of the Jewish community that she relentlessly posed to the general American society all the rest of the week.[3] In preparation for confronting the Conservative Rabbinical Assembly at its annual meeting at the Concord Hotel in upstate New York in the spring of 1972, the members of Ezrat Nashim prepared a manifesto entitled "Jewish Women Call For Change." In it they said:

> It is not enough to say that Judaism views women as separate but equal, nor to point to Judaism's past superiority over other cultures in its treatment of women. We've had enough of apologetics, enough of Bruria, Devorah, and Esther—enough of Eshet Hayil! . . . It is time that:
>   women be granted membership in synagogues
>   women be counted in the minyan
>   women be allowed full participation in religious observances
>   women be recognized as witnesses before Jewish law
>   women be allowed to initiate divorce
>   women be permitted and encouraged to attend rabbinical and
>   cantorial schools and to perform these functions in synagogues
>   women be encouraged to join decision-making bodies and to assume
>   professional leadership roles, in synagogues and in the general
>   Jewish community
>   women be considered as bound to fulfill all mitzvot equally with men
> For three thousand years, one-half of the Jewish people have been excluded from full participation in Jewish communal life. We call for an end to the second-class status of women in Jewish life.

Since this manifesto was issued many of their demands have been met within the frameworks of the Reform, Reconstructionist, and Conservative movements at which the document was aimed. It is now taken for granted that women are members of synagogues, are eligible to be elected to boards of directors and to be officers of congregations, are allowed close to full participation in religious observances, are permitted to attend rabbinical and cantorial schools (though there is still debate and ambivalence about this), and are encouraged to join decision-making bodies and to assume a variety of leadership roles in the community. The other demands—the ability to be witnesses, to be allowed to initiate divorce, and, most important, that women be considered as bound to fulfill all time-bound mitzvot equally with men—are still problematic in the Conservative movement.

Bat Kol, Neshay Hayi, and other clones of Ezrat Nashim, established after the first women's conference organized by Network in New York in 1973, remained active intermittently until the late 1970s. All went through transformations from study groups to consciousness-raising to social action. They organized conferences, ran lecture bureaus, collected materials to make available library resources on Jewish women, and wrote nonsexist Jewish children's stories, birth ceremonies for baby girls, and nonsexist curricular for Jewish schools. Many gave lectures and debated rabbis and lay leaders considering changes in the status of women in ritual in their own congregations. The Jewish feminist magazine *Lilith* began at that time as did the issue of *Response* magazine on women (which was later published by Schocken as the first sourcebook of articles on the movement under the title *The Jewish Woman*) edited by Ezrat Nashim member Elizabeth Koltun.[4]

The growth of the *havurah* movement which preceded and then paralleled that of the Jewish feminist movement was also a catalyst and experimental training ground for it. Within the burgeoning *havurot*, both independent and connected to synagogues, egalitarian services became the norm. As the decade of the 1970s drew to a close, the goals of the first consciousness-raising groups were quickly accepted by the Reform, Reconstructionist (which began as egalitarian), and even Conservative movements. As a result, justification for the continued existence of these groups became muted. Their cause had been "mainstreamed" as it became fashionable to say in the lingo of the period. Similarly, the conscious-

ness-raising groups of the general women's movement disappeared as most charismatic cells became routinized into more traditional forms of organization.[5]

As one moves on to these new forms and challenges it is crucial
to recall those early activist women and the task they undertook.
Though their revolution was facilitated by general societal readiness for changes in the role of women, their effort and impact
were and are incalculable. Today, many of the women who were
members of these small groups are professors of Jewish studies,
editors of magazines, day school principals, and lay leaders of the
community.

Institutionalization of an Idea: The Decade of the 1980s

Participation in ritual is one index of full citizenship in a group.
Whether it be registering to vote, pledging allegience to the flag,
leading a prayer for the congregation, or carrying the Torah in
procession, performing a public ritual act often symbolizes the status of the individual. Exclusion may signify nonmembership or
probationary or neophyte status. Classes of membership may be
the result of temporary punishment for infractions of norms. Thus
a prisoner may not vote while incarcerated for a felony, a probationary nun wears a different habit from one who has taken vows,
and a twelve-year-old boy may not be called to the Torah.

The participation of women in positive time-bound commandments and the communal rituals surrounding them became the
central issue around which the dreams of the members of Ezrat
Nashim became institutionalized in the broader community in the
decade of the 1980s. This focus on ritual, even for women who
were not observant, occurred precisely because the leaders knew
and the followers sensed that by their presence on the *bimah* (ros-
trum) of the synagogue they would stake their claim to full citizenship in the Jewish community. Secondary foci were the creation of
new life cycle rituals and the modification of traditional ones to include women, a push toward power in the secular communal structure, and a new thrust toward a reconsideration of the language of
prayer and, more radically, the theology that language represented.

Analysis of the literature that has appeared considering the impact of feminism on American Judaism substantiates the statement
that the movement has been dominated by debate over expanded

synagogue ritual roles, with the ordination of women as rabbis and cantors as the apogee of the discussion.[6]

Within the Reform movement, halakah, Jewish law, was not a factor holding back the implementation of equality between men and women, yet distinctions in ritual participation persisted through the 1970s. The force of Jewish social custom reinforced by similar norms prevalent in the non-Jewish community yielded an "orthodoxy" potentially as inflexible as that grounded in Jewish law. The Reform movement, though sensitive from its inception to the idea of equal education for boys and girls, did not make the logical extension from this educational policy to equal participation in ritual roles. Actually, ritual roles were taken by professionals for the most part, and neither lay men or women had many opportunities for religious roles in the service.

Historically the halakic exclusion of women from ritual roles in traditional Judaism led to their being barred from organizational leadership and public communal roles of all types. If a woman could not read *Maftir Yonah* (the prophetic portion read on the afternoon of the Day of Atonement), carry a Torah, open the ark, or sit on the *Bimah* during the service as officers of the congregation traditionally did, then ipso facto she could not be an officer of the congregation.

Thus exclusion from ritual roles led to exclusion from secular leadership roles as well within the congregational structure and transferred from there to other communal spheres. Consequently, women were not accustomed or allowed to represent the congregation in public roles even if these roles were divorced from the religious sphere. Even in Reform temples women did not attain positions of power in administration or in ritual roles. For them to do so did not "feel right" to the men and the women of the congregation.

When the women's movement began to gain strength in the United States, leaders of the Reform movement quickly moved to institute the logical extension of their educational philosophy to female participation in public roles. Despite this theoretical openness, many women found that breaking through a barrier of social custom was at least as difficult as piercing one of law. There is an old Yiddish expression, "*a minhag brecht a din*"—a custom breaks a law—which many women in the Reform movement found to be an apt adage for their dilemma.[7]

A great shift in the role of women in synagogue ritual has taken place in the Conservative movement. In 1955 the Law Committee of the Rabbinical Assembly published a halakhic opinion authored by Rabbi Aaron Blumenthal permitting *Torah* honors for women. By the end of the 1960s a handful of Conservative congregations actually granted the right of aliyot to adult women with no restrictions. By the early 1970s 7 percent of rabbis responding to a survey on this matter in the Rabbinical Assembly newsletter reported that women received Torah honors regularly in their congregations, though another 17 percent said that they received them only on special occasions.[8] Even fewer said that they counted women in the *minyan* (quorum for prayer), 11 percent noted that women were allowed to read from the Torah scroll, and one-third reported that adult women could read the weekly prophetic portion from the Bible.[9]

Measured against these early figures the extent of change within the Conservative movement stands out starkly. A 1987 survey of Conservative congregations conducted by the Women's League for Conservative Judaism led to the following figures. Of the 705 affiliated sisterhoods reporting, women were counted in the *minyan* in 60 percent (450) and given aliyot on all occasions in 61 percent (460) and on special occasions in an additional 61 congregations.[10] This is an extraordinary change from the perspective of social science, which would view a 15 to 20 percent shift in fifteen years as significant. In each case, changes of more than 50 percent have taken place.

To be sure, these changes did not occur without reverberations. The debate over the status of women, especially over their ordination as rabbis, sparked a backlash in the formation of the Union for Traditional Conservative Judaism (UTCJ). This group is centered about the senior Talmud faculty of the Jewish Theological Seminary, about 10 percent of the membership of the Rabbinical Assembly, and some wealthy and influential lay leaders. This group has championed the cause of traditional roles for women within the Conservative movement. Although individual observance of kashrut and shabbat have also been foci of the organization, it was conceived and organized around opposition to what was clearly a fast-growing consensus on egalitarianism which they felt threatened to "read out" the right wing of the movement. The actual power and influence of this group is not yet known because it is so new. It has a full-time national director, a halakhic panel or law committee which regularly issues responsa, an annual convention, a newsletter, a kashrut hotline and has announced plans to open a rabbinical seminary.

By late 1985 the focus of the group had shifted somewhat to issues such as patrilineal descent and the legitimacy of the new Rabbinical Assembly prayerbook, but the decision in 1986 by the chancellor of the seminary to ordain women as cantors reopened the women's issue. The UTCJ has allied itself in this matter with the Conservative Cantor's Assembly, which voted in 1988 not to admit female Cantor's Institute graduates to membership in its professional organization and not to place women cantors through its placement service. Thus the seminary has had to open a separate placement service for its female graduates. In addition, the rabbinical school of the Masorti (Conservative) movement in Israel does not admit women for ordination. The Israeli Rabbinical Assembly, which has more than one hundred members, has not yet faced the issue of whether to admit as a member of its region a woman graduate of the seminary in New York.

In sum, the Conservative movement has experienced extraordinary changes in a fifteen-year period culminating in the emergence of a new consensus on the issue of the role of women in Judaism. This symbolic peak of change occurred in October 1983 with the decision by the faculty of the rabbinical school of the Jewish Theological Seminary to admit women for ordination.[11]

In some areas of Jewish law, however, that consensus is far from harmonious or complete. Clearly, the period of transition is not over as the issue of *hiyyuv*, the obligation of women to perform positive time-bound commandments, is tackled head-on for the first time.[12] This issue is at the core of the legal dilemmas that remain such as women serving as witnesses and judges for marriages and divorces and enabling the masses of women formally to take on obligations and have them be binding in Jewish law so that they may lead their congregations in prayer.

In sum, though the ideology of the Conservative movement contains the seeds of an egalitarianism that could reach beyond the removal of the *mechitsa* (barrier between men and women during prayer), changing the text of the morning benediction from thanking God "that He has not made me a woman" to thanking God for creating human beings in the divine image, and the institutionalization of the *bat mitzvah*, this potential was not activated until the American feminist movement emerged as a catalyst.

As in the Reform movement, although equal access to Jewish education was provided, the logical extension of this philosophy was not followed. Moreover, American societal norms were not supportive of an expanded public role for women. There was no push from within and no support from without. Generally, social change requires some jolt from the outside or some radical group from the inside to initiate a movement. Most people are comfortable with the status quo, and the suburban Reform and Conservative synagogues that were built after World War II and flourished in the era of the "feminine mystique" were so successful that tampering with the delicate balance of power within them was unthinkable for two decades. This conservatism makes the changes that did occur in a fifteen-year period all the more remarkable.

A Typological Overview

To synthesize the data presented thus far and view the impact of the Jewish feminist movement in another way one can use a typology of ritual based on two dichotomous dimensions. Rituals may be traditionally performed or newly formulated. They may be performed personally or in the community. Table 1 shows how commonly practiced rituals now performed by women can be placed in such a typology. With few exceptions, the focus of the struggle for women's participation in ritual has been around the Type I and Type III rituals. They are the most visible and most significant indexes of power and prestige in the community.

Table 1 *Typology of Ritual*

	Traditional	Innovative or Reformulated
Communal	Type I Traditional/Communal Leading worship Counting in minyan Torah honors	Type II New Communal Women's minyan or Tefila group Birth ceremonies for girls Bat mitzvah
Personal	Type III Traditional/Individual Wearing a tallit Wearing tefillin Saying kaddish	Type IV New/Individual Mikva for single women Beraha for menstruation New prayer garment for women

From the halakhic perspective, Type III rituals such as wearing a tallit (prayer shawl) or tefillin (phylachteries) are permitted though not mandated for women. Therefore, their performance has not provided major grounds for contention, though women sometimes make themselves self-conscious and others uneasy when they first take them on.

New, personal rituals (Type IV) have been embraced by a small minority of women and are privately performed. They have neither been bones of contention nor become popular. It is the rituals in Type I, which are both traditional and communal, that have been the principal locus of the struggle of the Jewish feminist movement. For Orthodox women, it is the Type II reformulated public rituals such as the women's *tefila* (prayer) groups that have generated controversy whether meeting just on the new moon or more often. The new rituals welcoming Jewish baby girls into the world, on the other hand, have been received with enthusiasm by nearly all segments of the community.[13]

Public ritual and secular leadership roles are related so a look at the secondary focus of the Jewish feminist movement, that of increased power in the secular organizational sphere, will briefly be considered. Spheres of leadership, like rituals, may be divided into four types along the dimensions of lay or professional and secular or religious (see Table 2). All these leadership roles are communal and therefore have the appeal of being public ritual indicators of citizenship, power, and belonging. Table 2 shows that the first type of role is both lay and secular such as president of a federation

Table 2 *Typology of Leadership Roles and Spheres*

Institutional Sphere	Lay Roles	Professional Roles
Secular	Type 1 President of Jewish Community Relations Council President of Federation	Type II Executive director of federation or Jewish Community Relations Council
Religious	Type III President of synagogue Chair, ritual committee	Type IV Rabbi Cantor

or Zionist organization. The second is secular and professional such as executive director of a community center or federation. The third is lay and religious such as president of a synagogue or chair of a ritual committee. The fourth is professional and religious as exemplified in the roles of rabbi and cantor.

The progress made by Jewish women varies from sphere to sphere. Within moderate Orthodoxy, for instance, there is a tendency to move toward permitting women to lead the community in lay and secular functions. But because Orthodoxy defines most of life as religious, it is highly unlikely that even lay religious roles would be found appropriate for women. Indeed, the farther right in the Orthodox camp one moves, the less likely one would be to find it acceptable for women to occupy even secular lay leadership roles unless the organization was made up only of women. Thus one might find women Jewish leaders, but they would be principals of girls' schools, presidents of womens' organizations, and the like.

What is more striking is the continuing scarcity of women in lay secular leadership roles in the non-Orthodox community. An explanation of this may be that one key to rising in the system is affluence. Not enough women have yet amassed the wealth or professional prestige to rise to the top ranks of federation leadership unless they are married to wealthy men. Moreover, the young leadership cadre has only had a decade in which to begin the climb to top leadership roles. This process often takes much longer even for qualified men, who are more readily accepted into the system at all levels. Therefore, we should expect that a significant number of women would have risen only to middle-range leadership roles by this time.

A number of communities have by now had women presidents of federation as well as of community agencies such as Jewish community centers and day school boards. In the last few years, women have chaired the Jewish Welfare Board and the Council of Jewish Federations for the first time. As women gain in wealth, experience, professional expertise, and contacts, their numbers in top national leadership roles should continue to grow.

The greatest scarcity of women in leadership roles is found in Type II, the secular professional roles. Rare indeed is the female executive director of a national Jewish organization, a mid- to large size federation, or even a federation agency in a mid- to large size city. Many more cities have had a woman president than executive director of the federation. More women chair boards of day schools and centers than are principals or executive directors. Ironically, once entry into rabbinical school is achieved, the path into congregations, Hillel foundations, and educational directorships of synagogues is fairly open. In contrast to this the woman with a master of social work, however, faces the same problems all women do climbing to managerial positions in welfare agencies in the general job market, which are not alleviated when religious barriers are removed. Thus, their upward climb is quite slow.

It is within Type II that the barriers are least Jewish and most societal. Women have not been seen as top-notch fund-raisers, money managers, or supervisors of large staffs. When employees are considered for promotion from within, women are often not candidates for moving up the organizational ladder. Moreover, they tend to have degrees that enable them to work with others but lack training in business and fiscal management. Yet men in this category are viewed as trainable but women usually are not. In addition, there is still a fear that some men will not work for a woman supervisor. All the prejudices prevalent in the general society works against women in secular professional roles, and there is no ideological or religious fervor to the quest for attaining them.

Since 1985, professional associations of communal workers, administrations of schools that train Jewish communal service workers, private foundations, and the Council of Jewish Federations have been looking into these problems. All agree that is in the interest of the community that excellent professionals, both women and men, be recruited and retained in Jewish agencies. This issue is now high on the strategic planning agenda of the community, and progress for women in this sphere should occur in the next decade.

Looking to the Future

It has been the thesis of this essay that the Jewish feminist movement of the 1970s and 1980s has been more than a modest success measured by its own goals of 1972. A remarkable amount of what the members of Ezrat Nashim saw as an ideal and a dream in their manifesto has been achieved. The egalitarian vision in the synagogue has been completely realized in the Reform and Reconstructionist and *Havurah* movements and to a large extent in the Conservative movement as well. Many of the ideas of the early 1970s have become normative in the 1980s. What will the issues be for the 1990s for women outside of the Orthodox camp and to some extent for them as well?

First, there are the large legal issues surrounding *hiyyuv.* This will be an important focus in the Conservative movement. Second, there will be a continuing drive to achieve parity in the lay organizational power structure. Third, there will be a major push for women to achieve professional positions of power within the community. Fourth, a small cadre of women will become very involved with feminist theology within Judaism. This group will emerge from among academics and perhaps at the Reconstructionist Rabbinical College. Fifth, there will be a growing concern with the status of Jewish women in the rest of the world, which will serve as a focus of Israel-diaspora relationships, particularly along with dialogue and coalition building with Israeli Jewish feminists.

Sixth, along with global, communal, and spiritual concerns, there will be a focus on strengthening the Jewish family and parenting while playing down careerism without returning to paternalistic models. Finally, the problems of developing positive relationships between Jewish men and women in a transitional generation will be tackled. This will include combating negative stereotypes. The building of a nonsexist Jewish community will be seen as a cooperative and crucial task of women and men.

Notes

1. Virginia Sapiro, *Women in American Society* (Palo Alto, 1986), pp. 460–465.
2. My study *Jewish Women on the Way Up* (New York, 1987) documents a changing attitude, particularly among single women.
3. "Ten Jewish Feminists Confront the Rabbis," *New York Post,* March 14, 1972. Hyman is quoted as saying, "And then a professor said to me, 'What do you do the 24 hours from Friday night to Saturday night? Do you forget you're a feminist?' "
4. Elizabeth Koltun, ed., *The Jewish Woman, New Perspectives* (New York, 1978).
5. One result of such mainstreaming is that the groups that do remain may be focused on more radical issues and dominated by fringe or one-issue groups. This has been the case with the issue of gay/lesbian rights in the general feminist movement in the small consciousness-raising groups that remain.
6. The best review of this phenomenon for the 1970s is found in Anne Lapidus Lerner, "Who Has Not Made Me a Man," *American Jewish Year Book* (New York, 1977). See also Rachel Adler, "The Jew Who Wasn't There: Halacha and the Jewish Woman,"

Response, Vol. 7 no. 2 (Summer 1973), pp. 77–82; and Paula Hyman, "The Other Half: Women in the Jewish Tradition," *Conservative Judaism,* (Summer 1972).

7. In speaking of this dilemma, Annette Daum, a leader in the Reform movement, told me of her experience as one of the first women presidents of a temple in the late 1970s. At a Union of American Hebrew Congregations Biennial Convention, when she came to the head of the line of those waiting for synagogue president's badges, she was told by the woman distributing regalia that she was in the wrong line; sisterhood presidents were at another station.

8. Rela Geffen Monson, unpublished survey of Rabbinical Assembly members, sponsored by Ezrat Nashim through the Rabbinical Assembly newsletter in 1972.

9. The 1955 decision of the Law Committee was not implemented globally until the Jewish feminist movement blossomed in the 1970s. In the mid-1970s one common response in Conservative congregations to the later decision to permit counting women in the minyan was to grant them Torah honors instead, varying from opening the ark in more right-wing congregations to full participation in more liberal ones.

10. Reported in "Focus On: Women," *Outlook* 59 (Fall 1988), pp. 17–18. The article following the survey results is entitled "Women in the Rabbinate—No Longer on the Fringe," by Judith Hauptman, a member of Ezrat Nashim, and the first woman Ph.D. in Talmud, who is now a tenured member of the rabbinics faculty of the Jewish Theological Seminary.

11. The admission of women to the Reform and Conservative rabbinical schools was not without strife. Admission and social and intellectual acceptance are different stages. Early students at Hebrew Union College reported hostility from some professors and at JTS several faculty members left or remained and declined to teach in specific rabbinical school classes. One even sued the seminary for breach of contract. The less obvious fallout was in the lack of amity among faculty who had disagreed on or voted against the decision and who felt that those who had supported it (particularly at JTS) received more favorable treatment from the administration of the school. Since the decision, JTS has tenured a woman faculty member and has a female dean of the undergraduate college. Hebrew Union College in Cincinnati does not have a single woman faculty member.

12. "A faculty committee recommended and it has been accepted that all women who wish to be considered as candidates for ordination voluntarily accept all the obligations of the Torah without regard to sex. (*Ometz Shaliach,* Winter 1984, page 1) "In other words, even those positive commandments from which women are traditionally absolved would have to be voluntarily accepted by a woman rabbinic candidate." In this same article, the then chancellor, Gerson D. Cohen, stated that "the decision to admit women to the Rabbinical School is not a concession to feminism. It is a watershed in our religious history. You don't open floodgates without dikes that control the flow. I am not going to make the laws of the Torah easier for anyone." Thus Cohen suggested that he was expanding commitment and obligation rather than pandering to outside forces through the initiation of this change.

13. For a strong objection to such ceremonies see Moshe Meiselman's book *Jewish Women in Jewish Law* (New York, 1978).

FOR FURTHER READING

Biale, Rachel, *Women and Jewish Law*, New York, 1984. The best single book on all of the Jewish legal issues affecting women, with the classical sources cited and explicated.

Henry, Sondra, and Emily Taitz, *Written out of History*, New York, 1978. An attempt to restore forgotten women from Jewish history to our consciousness with accounts of unknown women from ancient times through the nineteenth century.

Heschel, Susannah, ed, *On Being a Jewish Feminist: A Reader*, New York, 1983. A good collection of articles with an update on Koltun which is particularly strong in the area of theology. See next entry on Koltun volume.

Koltun, Elizabeth, ed, *The Jewish Woman*, New York, 1976. The first compendium of articles on all aspects of the Jewish feminist movement in the 1970s; contains several "classics."

Meiselman, Moshe, *The Jewish Woman in Jewish Law*, New York, 1979. This book is a right-wing Orthodox polemic against the Jewish feminist movement, the most coherent of its type.

Monson, Rela Geffen, *Jewish Women on the Way Up*, New York, 1987. A study of nearly a thousand Jewish career women, married and single, focusing on dilemmas of dual-career families and policy implications of changing roles of women for the Jewish community.

Schneider, Susan Weidman, *Jewish and Female: Choices and Changes in Our Lives Today*, New York, 1984 (paperback ed. 1985). An excellent review of all the issues raised by the Jewish feminist movement in readable style by the editor of *Lilith* magazine.

Biblio Press has published a series of bibliographies on Jewish women, including a book of syllabi. I recommend the following:

The Jewish Woman, 1900–1985. A Bibliography (2d ed.), ed. Aviva Cantor. New York, 1987; and, Elwell, Ellen Sue Levi. ed., *The Jewish Women's Studies Guide*. New York, 1988.

Abortion and Birth Control: The Contemporary Debate

DAVID M. FELDMAN

Pronatalist is the contemporary word describing the classic Jewish tradition on childbirth. Procreation is counted as a positive mitzvah, given pride of place at the top of rabbinic lists of biblical commandments. *P'ru ur'vu* in the first chapter of Genesis is taken as a blessing to other creatures, whereas to humans it is a command to reproduce. The commentaries explain this difference on its own terms and as negating antiprocreative or celibate views in other cultures. The command is needed because man, created in the image of God, might seek to devote himself entirely to the spiritual and intellectual and neglect the material and physical. Alternatively, only man is aware of the consequences of his sexual activity; he might seek to avoid the attendant responsibilities of childbirth while indulging his sexual drive. Yet another rabbinic comment observes that throughout Genesis I, "The Lord saw that it was good" is repeated for each element of creation. With man, the Lord said, "It is not good that man should be alone." Only that which can endure is good; if man does not procreate he will not endure.

Nor will God Himself endure without us to acknowledge Him: "He who does not engage in procreation diminishes the Divine image. The verse 'for in the image of God has He created man (Gen. 9:6)' is immediately followed by 'be fruitful and multiply.' " Or the later verse (17:7) introduces the Lord Who will be "thy God and [that] of thy descendants after thee." But "if there are no 'descendants after thee,' demands the Talmud, "upon whom will the Divine Presence rest? Upon sticks and stones?" Without human descendants, there is no one to worship God. Without the physical body there is no soul.

Specifics of the Mitzvah

In spelling out the details of this commandment, the rabbis set forth the halakah of birth control by requiring that a couple at least replace itself, that is, give birth to at least a son and daughter. Having either several sons or several daughters does not fulfill the commandment. But "grandchildren are like children," so parents with children of one gender can be comforted that they have a second chance with the grandchildren. Yet two children is the minimum; remaining with that number, according to *Tosafot*, could lead to national extinction. Infant mortality, or uncertainty if the offspring themselves will be viable persons or parents, requires that more than the minimum be sired.

This rabbinic dimension of the mitzvah was called, in brief, *la-shevet* or *la-erev*. The first comes from the verse in Isaiah 45:18: "Not for void did He create the world, but for habitation [*la-shevet*] did He form it." The second is from Ecclesiastes 11:6: "In the morning sow thy seed, and in the evening [*la-erev*] do not withhold thy hand [from continuing to sow], for you know not which will succeed, this or that, or whether they shall both alike be good." This is now part of the mitzvah. To illustrate, a Sefer Torah may be sold only to finance education in Torah or the dowering of a bride; it may be sold for the latter when just the rabbinic dimensions of procreation—*la-shevet* and *la-erev*—remain to be fulfilled. The Jewish pronatalist stance perceives barreness or infertility as a condition to be remedied no less than illness or pathology.

The technical requirements of Jewish law place the responsibility for procreation on the man rather than the woman, though of course it takes two to fulfill the mitzvah. This law may have its basis in the theoretical permissibility of polygamy, or polygyny as opposed to polyandry, whereby a man could marry more than one wife. Each wife could then defer to the other. This sex-role difference is associated with the wording of "Be fruitful and multiply, fill the earth and conquer it"—that is, he, being the more aggressive of the two, the conqueror, must worry about procreation, whereas she, the more passive and coy, should not have to "go seeking in the marketplace." These anthropological reasons are improved upon by the suggestion of a recent Bible commentator, Rabbi Meir Simchah of Dvinsk (d. 1927): both the pain and the risk of childbearing are borne by the woman, not the man. Since the Torah is not only fair but "its ways are ways of pleasantness and all its paths are peace" (Prov. 3:17), the Torah could not in fairness command a woman to undergo pain and risk; this must be her choice. For the man, however, exposed to neither pain nor risk, there is the command and the responsibility to fulfill the command.

Beyond the Halakhah

It goes without saying that attitudes to procreation were not shaped or nurtured through law alone. Abraham protests to God (Gen. 15:2): "What canst Thou give me, seeing that I go childless?" The anguish of the barren woman is a recurrent theme in the Bible and beyond. The most cherished blessing, on the other hand, is fecundity, which is exemplified idyllically in the Psalmist's (Ps. 128) image of one whose "wife is a fruitful vine" and whose "children are as olive plants around the table" and whose ultimate satisfaction is the sight of "children [born] to thy children."

Historical circumstances of frequent massacres and forced conversions, with their resulting decimation of Jewish communities, served to elicit compensatory tendencies and to strengthen the procreative desire. The people's will to replenish its depleted ranks gave added dimension to the instinctive yearning for offspring. This contrasts, for example, with the antiprocreational stand, born of despair, taken by the first-century Gnostics, the fifth-century Manichees, or the twelfth-century Cathars, who taught and lived by the teaching that procreation is to be avoided in an evil world.

Avoiding procreation for the sake of the world, however, is a contemporary issue, seen by the Jewish community as an ethical concern related to available resources. Constituting less than 1 percent of the world's population, the Jewish people could double its present numbers without affecting the world's problems of space and resources and without undermining objectives of zero population growth. Replacing our losses does not upset the numerical balance; it merely keeps us alive. Other minorities should similarly be allowed to maintain their numbers. Our aspirations, as reflected in the liturgy, are not that we overtake the world but merely that "the remnant of Israel" be preserved.

In the face of a precarious future—to return to internal history—procreation is essentially an act of faith. Maternal and religious imperatives defied adverse economic or political realities. From the standpoint of medical considerations, even normal pregnancy is dangerous, and these normal risks are incurred by necessity or desire. With real risk, in clearly hazardous situations, the rabbis legislated against fulfilling this commandment while violating another one, to "take good heed of yourselves." Since the Torah is to be "set aside" when one's life or health is threatened, medical indications are the primary basis for the provision of contraception.

Onanism

Opposite to positive procreation for all its reasons is contraception, which might imply a form of onanism. Though "the act of Er and Onan" is condemned in the Bible—more so in the Talmud, and even more so in the Zohar, the mystic tradition—the word *onanism* was coined as a result of literary and theological references in Christianity to Genesis Chapter 38. Tamar, the childless widow of Er, was brought to his brother Onan so that offspring would be born in Er's name. But Onan, declining to fulfill this "levirate" duty, "when he went to his brother's wife, would spill it on the ground, lest he should give seed for his brother. And the thing which he did was evil in the sight of the Lord, and He slew him also."

The passage served as the basis for condemnation of several related evils in church doctrine. In the fourth century, Epiphanius, bishop in Cyprus, invoked the story of that "immense and frightful crime" of Onan; and St. Jerome writes that Onan "did a detestable thing." But it was the influential St. Augustine who applied the passage to contraception in marriage: it is lawless and shameful to lie with one's wife and avoid the conception of offspring; "this is what Onan, son of Judah, did, and God slew him for it." From then on, Catholic moralists in various times and places condemned either contraception or coitus interruptus as the sin of Onanism, culminating in the citation by Pope Pius XI in *Casti Connubii*, his all-important encyclical on marital conduct (1930), which affirms: "Holy Writ itself testifies that the Divine Majesty pursued this wicked crime with destestation and punished it with death, as St. Augustine recalls." In the Protestant tradition, it is primarily John Calvin who adverted to the passage, writing that Onan both defrauded his late brother of his right and "no less cruelly than foully" committed the crime of contraception. Jeremy Taylor, an Anglican bishop of the seventeenth century, censured Onan, who "did separate his act from its proper end."

The story of Er and Onan served as basis for condemnation in the Jewish tradition as well, but with interesting differences. Er, too, is presumed to have practiced contraception, though his motives were obviously different from those of Onan. He must have done so, says the Talmud, to avoid marring Tamar's fabled beauty with a pregnancy; or, as a twelfth-century Bible commentator, Rabbi Joseph Bechor Shor, suggests: "Er didn't want the trouble of raising children, for there *are* such people who care only about their own convenience." But these and other homiletic interpretations aside, the point of the Onan story is clearly not about contraception in principle or even a particular means of contraception but about motive. Hence the application of its pejorative teaching to means, such as coitus that is, interruptus, in Jewish literature is by *remez* only, solely by intimation or homiletic suggestion.

The clue to the story is its levirate context. Onan was given his late brother's wife for purposes of levirate mitzvah only. In his marital relations with her, he frustrated the levirate purpose. The punishment was accordingly severe because he subverted the only legitimate purpose that could save what he was doing from the category of a capital crime. The code of sexual ethics in Leviticus and Deuteronomy forbids marriage to a brother's widow on penalty of death, except for the special levirate circumstances. When the brother leaves his widow childless, marriage to her for this purpose becomes a mitzvah. Even "Noahides," the people of the generations before Sinai, were, from the Talmud's point of view, commanded concerning such incestuous marriages. Hence the sin of Onan is to have committed, by subterfuge, a capital offense; his means of doing so serve, by intimation, to suggest something unseemly and objectionable in and of itself. It must incidentially be added that a contemporary rabbinic writer untypically resorts to a

wholly naturalistic reading of the story, seeing in it neither violation of marriage law nor condign punishment by the wrath of God.
"We do not have to assume childishly that a thunderbolt de-
scended from heaven and struck Onan dead," he writes. The Bible
is merely relating the natural effect of so unhealthy a practice as
coitus interruptus: Onan suffered a heart attack from the nervous
strain of it all.[1]

But the idea of something unseemly in and of itself does find full
measure of censure in the Talmud and in the mystical tradition
based on the Zohar. Here, masturbation as well as coitus
interruptus and other forms of thwarting the natural manner of coitus are subsumed under "the act of Er and Onan," with consequent implications for contraception. In responsa on birth control,
the rabbi consulted would not recommend abstinence to the couple for whom another pregnancy would be hazardous, nor can he
allow them to place themselves in hazard. The alternative is contraception; but that would involve onanism, at least in premodern
times before the availability of oral contraceptives such as the pill.
The condom and similar means do entail onanism, hence the dilemma reflected in much of the responsa literature.

But with medical risk as the alternative, even the objection
against onanism must be set aside. Antiabstinence considerations
are not set aside, but those of onanism are. Concerning that basic
talmudic source-passage, the *Baraita* of the Three Women (T.B.
Yevamot 12b), the various levels of interpretation all revolve
around whether the three categories of women may or must, or
may not or need not, practice contraception before, during, or
after, with this, that, or the other contraceptive principle. The
undesired alternative to all these is marital relations without contraception, never abstinence.

In-Vitro Fertilization

With so pronatalist a general and specific tradition, the Jewish
response has been understandably affirmative to new reproductive
techniques such as in-vitro fertilization. Other faith groups at first
demurred: how can one violate natural law or deviate from the natural process, whereby husband and wife, unassisted, see to the
conception and gestation of the embryo? But this matter need not

be affected by concepts of natural law. We do not worship nature nor do we regard its laws as unbreakable. On the contrary, the process of creation is ongoing, and we seek to be "partners with God" in conquering and controlling nature. Hence we applaud efforts to dam the rivers and prevent flooding, to use lightning rods, or even air conditioners, to overcome the tyranny of natural elements. We circumcise infant males, rather than stand back and declare nature perfect. The climax of the Creation narrative in Genesis describes the Sabbath as ordained at a point in Creation when God had, in the literal translation, "ceased from His work which He had created to do." "Created to do"? What does that mean? the rabbis ask. It means that God created much yet to be done, much for us to do now that we are here on earth to be partners in the continuation of the creative process.

Hence to give nature a little help when, for example, Fallopian tubes are blocked, by circumventing this impediment through use of the Petri dish, is acceptable, even meritorious. Furthermore, we have already "improved upon" nature by the very institution of marriage. Man is not naturally monogamous; primitives used to mate indiscriminately. Religion and civilization have advanced beyond all this by instituting marriage and known paternity. Most important, the desire of a woman for offspring is a deeply human one, and helping her realize this desire, even through recourse to the laboratory but with safeguards against abuse, is a positively human deed. Similarly, in vivo fertilization, where the ovum is lavaged out and implanted in the womb of another, can be acceptable. But then the question of maternity is raised: Who is the real mother?

In the Talmud's imagery, "there are three partners in the birth of the human child"—the father, the mother, and God. The mother actually gives more. The genetic endowment of the father is matched both by the mother's genetic endowment, the ovum, and by her gestational environment, the womb. If these two contributions are divided between two women, one supplying the ovum and the other the womb, which one is the mother? Moreover, in the case of surrogate mothers, who offer both of these contributions to their sponsors, what maternal claim accrues to the sponsor?

Even these ultramodern phenomena have their precedents in scripture. Rachel and Leah had their own children, but before and in between these births, they "sponsored" children through their handmaidens Bilhah and Zilpah. These handmaidens, as well as Hagar in Abraham's day, were prototypes of surrogate mothers. But they were free of the sociological problems that complicate the picture today. The "surrogates" did not have a change of heart and insist on keeping the babies, nor did the sponsors renege because the babies were not up to their expectations. Also, there was no financial arrangement. Safeguards are needed against complications or abuses so that these procedures might be available in the absence of the "natural" alternative. England's Warnock Commission, in its report of July 1984, recommended against surrogate mother arrangements because the potential of abuse is so great. Its chief rabbi, Immanuel Jakobovits, endorsed that verdict, adding: "To use another person as 'incubator' and then take from her the child she carried and delivered, for a fee, is a revolting degradation of maternity and an affront to human dignity." In America, the Michigan Court of Appeals in 1981 viewed the surrogate arrangement as a form of forbidden "baby bartering," although supporters maintain that the payment is for "services" rather than for the baby, which belonged to the sponsors to begin with. In an increasing number of state legislatures legal notice is being taken of growing public opinion against the practice of surrogate parenting.

The question of maternity in in vivo fertilization can be resolved in favor of the sponsoring mother by arguing that the genetic, as opposed to the gestational, contribution is the dynamic one, giving the all-important genetic code. Also, the donated zygote can be said to be a nascent being, with the identity of the mother already intact. From another standpoint, the first mother's role is not replaceable by technology but the host mother's is; the gestation could conceivably be done in the laboratory. Yet maternity can be argued for the host mother on the ground that a transplanted organ becomes an integral part of the body of the recipient, which means that the recipient of an ovarian transplant becomes the mother. Also, the host mother gives both nurture and gestation to the embryo. As a congressional committee was told in August 1984, "The biological fact is that the gestational mother has contributed more of herself to the child than the genetic mother, and therefore has a greater biological investment and interest in it." Moreover, the legal presumption in favor of the host mother "gives the child and society certainty of identification at the time of birth, which is a protection for both mother and child." Nine months of responsible nurture is a far greater "gift" than the surrender of an ovum, entitling the host far more clearly to acknowledgment of parenthood. Israeli hospitals, where such in vivo fertilization has taken place, have listed both mothers on the birth certificate, helping us find our way through the mind-boggling implications of new developments in reproductive technology. Two maternal relationships, like that of mother and father, may exist simultaneously.

Of course, Jewish law would never sanction recourse to any such methods merely to spare one the inconvenience of pregnancy and childbearing and certainly not to ensure some package of genetic characteristics such as blue eyes or tall stature. But when there is no natural alternative enabling a woman to fulfill her maternal yearning, or 'a couple to fulfill the mitzvah, of procreation, this procedure is permissible. Today we view "barrenness" to be an "illness," a loss of normal health. Accordingly, all the principles of setting aside the ritual and other laws of the Torah prevail here, too: the same may and should be done to help overcome infertility as would be done for any other pathological condition.

Artificial Insemination

Before in vitro or in vivo fertilization was a gleam in anyone's eye procreation assistance was found in artificial insemination. A husband's immotile sperm (AIH), or a donor's sperm (AID) when the husband was both infertile and impotent, was inseminated in a clinical procedure. These practices bring in a different set of halakhic and moral problems, though AIH much less so.

Problems in connection with artificial insemination by the husband involve mainly the procurement of the semen, that is, the avoidance of onanism. The unwitting or deliberate admixture of the semen of another to increase fertility strength is unacceptable. AID presents the greater number of problems. Some rabbinic authorities declare the process adulterous and the offspring illegitimate. Others remind us that adultery is a conscious violation of the marriage vow by illicit intimacy, which does not take place in this clinical procedure; hence no adultery or illegitimacy can be associated with artificial insemination by donor. Nonetheless, it does sever the human, family bond, and it does conceal paternity, an important consideration in Jewish law. When the children are grown they may unwittingly marry their siblings so that unknown paternity has led to the grave sin of incest.

Adoption might seem the far better alternative, though the objection to unknown paternity applies here, too. Hence the identity of natural parents should be knowable to the child or to a readily accessible friend to avoid the possibility of incest. One psychological school of thought prefers adoption because it avoids resentment by the husband. If his wife had to be artificially inseminated by another, the child will bear her genetic endowment, which is a plus; but the husband is left out entirely, which is a minus. When the child is adopted, neither parent has genetic input, which is a minus; but there is no resentment or jealousy and no reminder of the husband's disproportionate inadequacy, which is a plus. Again, none of the medically resourceful alternatives would be chosen, or permitted to be chosen, when conception and birth in the normal way are possible.

An additional consideration for this point of view is the concept of lineage, an important one in Jewish tradition. To know and identify one's ancestors and to hope to give them immortality by advancing their righteous aspirations lends another spiritual dimension to one's own life and places it in a larger context of significance. Hence, in Jewish life we have the prevalent custom of naming a child after a grandparent, giving both a second chance to the ancestor and an inspiration to the descendant.

The Abortion Question

The moral and political debate in the United States on the subject of abortion continues unabated. Ultimate answers remain elusive years after the implementation of *Roe* v. *Wade* of January 1973. Abortion played a major role in the political campaigns of 1984 and 1988, pointing to public review of that 1973 decision. The right to take advantage of its permissive ruling was the subject of debate, with efforts increasing to remove that right by constitutional amendment or by a full or partial reversal in new Supreme Court rulings, such as that of July 1989.

At public hearings on the question, I have made the point that the rights of women, or reproductive freedom, cannot be admissible as an argument in favor of abortion if abortion is indeed murder. Just as a mother cannot put to death a grown child on the grounds that he or she is the fruit of her womb, neither can she do so before birth on grounds of the right to privacy or freedom to do with her body as she sees fit—if abortion is murder. Feticide is then as forbidden as homicide, and there are no personal rights of the mother. But if abortion is not murder—and only then—other considerations, such as the prior welfare of the mother, can come into play. In the Jewish legal-moral position, the principle is *tza'ara d'gufah kadim*, her welfare, avoidance of her pain, comes first.

Abortion is not murder, vociferous and repeated claims to the contrary notwithstanding. Abortion cannot be murder in Jewish law because murder is one of the three cardinal sins which require martyrdom. Rather than commit murder of the innocent, public idolatry, or gross sexual immorality (adultery-incest), one has to surrender his own life in martyrdom. All the rest of the Torah is under the category of *ya'avor v'al ye-hareg*, "let one transgress rather than die," but not for murder of the innocent. Hence if abortion were declared murder, a mother would not be allowed to have an abortion even to save her life, which is obviously not the case.

There is—need it be stated?—no commandment that reads "Thou shalt not kill." It reads "Thou shalt not murder." The difference is in the circumstances. Killing is allowed in self-defense, in war, perhaps by the sentencing court, even against the prowler in one's home. In these situations the victim is no longer innocent; he has forfeited his protection under the commandment. He must, of course, do so consciously. He must have deliberately placed himself in a position of attack or threat in order to lose his protection. Another such category is that of *rodef*, the aggressor, who also may be killed if there is no other way to halt his pursuit or aggression of a third party.

The Talmud considers declaring the fetus a *rodef*, an aggressor, against its mother and making that the reason for permitting abortion to save her life. (The idea entered the writtings of St. Thomas Aquinas through its citation in the works of Maimonides.) But the Talmud proceeds to reject that reasoning, even suggesting that the mother is the pursuer by virtue of her physical condition that makes the pregnancy life-threatening. God may be the pursuer, says the Talmud, the situation an "act of God." The only valid ground, it concludes, for permitting even therapeutic abortion is that the fetus is not yet a human person. This means killing is admittedly involved, but not murder. Killing is the taking of life of, say, an animal or a chicken, or of a human who forfeits his immunity by an act of aggression. We keep ourselves from the cardinal sin of murder if the victim is either not human or not innocent. And the difference between fetal life and human life is not determined by the biologist or the physician or the court but by the metaphysician. It is the determination of the culture or the religion that declares not when life begins but when life begins to be human.

Background in Jewish Law

To trace the issues from the start, the abortion question in talmudic law revolves around the legal status of the embryo. For this the Talmud has a phrase, *ubbar yerekh immo,* which is a counterpart of the Latin *pars viscerum matris.* That is, the fetus is deemed a "part of its mother" rather than an independent entity. This designation says nothing about the morality of abortion; rather, it defines ownership as, for example, in the case of an embryo found in a purchased animal. Because it is intrinsic to its mother's body, it belongs to the buyer. In the religious conversion of a pregnant woman, her unborn child is automatically included and requires no further ceremony. Nor does it have power of acquisition; gifts made on its behalf are not binding. These and similar points mean that the fetus has no "juridical personality" but say nothing about the right of abortion. This question turns, rather, on whether feticide is or is not homicide.

The law of homicide in the Torah, in one of its formulations, reads (Exod. 21:12): "*Makkeh ish*" "He who smites a man." Does this include any man, even a day-old child? Yes, says the Talmud, citing another text (Lev. 24:17): "*ki yakkeh kol nefesh adam*" "If one smite any *nefesh adam*"—literally, any human person. (We may not be sure that the newborn babe has completed its term and is a *bar kayyama,* fully viable, until thirty days after birth, but it is fully human from the moment of birth. If it dies before its thirtieth day, no funeral or *shivah* rites are applicable. But active destruction of a born child of even doubtful viability is here definitely forbidden.) The *any* is understood to include the day-old child, but the *nefesh adam* is taken to exclude the fetus in the womb. The fetus in the womb, says Rashi, classic commentator to Bible and Talmud, is *lav nefesh hu*, not a person, until it comes into the world.

Feticide, then, does not constitute homicide, and the basis for denying it the status of a capital crime in Jewish law—even for those rabbis who may have wanted to rule otherwise—is scriptural. Alongside the above text is one in Exodus 21:22, which provides: "If men strive, and wound a pregnant woman so that her fruit be expelled, but no harm befall [her], then shall he be fined as her husband shall assess. . . . But if harm befall [her], then shalt thou give life for life." The Talmud makes this verse's teaching explicit: only monetary compensation is exacted of one who causes a woman to miscarry. Though the abortion spoken of here is accidental, it contrasts with the homicide of the mother, which is also accidental. Even unintentional homicide cannot be expiated by monetary fine.

Extra Rabbinic Views

This critical text has an alternate version in the Septuagint, the Greek translation of the Bible produced in Alexandria in the third pre-Christian century. Change of just one word there yields an entirely different statute on the subject. Professor Viktor Aptowitzer's essays analyze the disputed passage: he calls the school of thought it represents the Alexandrian school, as opposed to the Palestinian—that is, the talmudic—view set forth above. The word in question is *ason*, rendered here as *harm*; hence, "if [there be] no harm [i.e., death, to the mother], then shall he be fined. . . . If [there be] harm, then shalt thou give life for life." The Greek renders *ason* as form, translating roughly: "If [there be] form, then shalt thou give life for life." The "life for life" clause is thus applied to the fetus instead of the mother *and* a distinction is made—as Augustine later formulated it—between *embryo informatus* and *embryo formatus*. For the latter, the text so rendered prescribes the death penalty.

Among the Church Fathers, the consequent doctrine of feticide as murder was preached by Tertullian in the second century, who accepted the Septuagint, and by Jerome in the fourth, who did not and whose classic Bible translation renders the passage according to the Hebrew text accepted in the church. The *Didache*, a handbook of basic Christianity for the instruction of converts from paganism, follows the Alexandrian teaching and specifies abortion as a capital crime. Closer to the main body of the Jewish community, we find the doctrine accepted by the Samaritans and Karaites and, more important, by Philo, the popular first-century philosopher of Alexandria. His younger contemporary Josephus, however, bears witness to the Palestinian (halakhic) tradition. Aside from its textual warrant, this tradition is more authentic than the later tendency, "which, in addition, is not genuinely Jewish but must have originated in Alexandria under Egyptian-Greek influence."[2]

In the rabbinic tradition, then, abortion is a noncapital crime at worst. But a curious factor further complicates the question. One more biblical text, this one in Genesis and hence "before Sinai" and part of the Laws of the Sons of Noah, served as the source for the teaching that feticide is indeed a capital crime—for non-Jews. Genesis 9:6 reads, "He who sheds the blood of man, through man [i.e., through the human court of law] shall his blood be shed." Since the "man, through man" [*shofekh dam ha'adam ba'adam*] can also be rendered "man, in man," the Talmud records the exposition of Rabbi Ishmael: "What is this 'man, in man'? It refers to the fetus in its mother's womb." Being in Genesis—without the qualifying balance of the Exodus (Sinaitic) passage—this verse made feticide a capital crime for non-Jews (those not heir to the covenant at Sinai) in Jewish law. Some hold this exposition to be more sociological than textually inherent, voicing a reaction against abuses among the heathen. In view of rampant abortion and infanticide, they claim, Rabbi Ishmael extracted from the Genesis text this judgment against the Romans.

Regardless of rationale, the doctrine remains part of theoretical Jewish law, as Maimonides, for example, codifies it. "A 'Son of Noah' who killed a person, even a fetus in its mother's womb, is capitally liable." Therapeutic abortion is not included in this Noahide prohibition, nor is an abortion during the first forty days, according to some. The implications of this anomaly—a different law for the Sons of Noah than for Israel—were addressed in a responsum of the eighteenth century: "It is not to be supposed that the Torah would consider the embryo as a person [*nefesh*] for them [Sons of Noah] but not for us. The fetus is not a person for them either; the Torah was merely more severe in its practical ruling in their regard. Hence, therapeutic abortion would be permissible to them, too."³

If abortion is not murder in the rabbinic system, neither is it worse than murder. It is worse than murder in religious systems that are concerned with "ensoulment" of the fetus. At a conference several years ago on the subject, I made bold to say that the discussion for the past several sessions of the conference was essentially irrelevant. They had been debating the time of ensoulment—whether the soul enters the fetus at conception, at the end of the first trimester, or at birth? From the Jewish standpoint, this issue must be declared irrelevant. The question is not when the soul enters but what kind of a soul enters. Classical Christianity teaches that a tainted soul informs the fetus, which must be cleansed by baptism to save it from eternal perdition. In line with the doctrine of original sin, each soul inherits the taint of its primordial ancestors. When St. Fulgentius, sixth century, was asked when that stain attaches to the person, he replied that it does so with conception. Hence the concern with allowing the fetus to be brought to term so that it can be baptized; otherwise it is condemned to death in both worlds, making abortion clearly worse than murder. It must accordingly be said that when Catholics reputedly decide to "let the mother die" rather than allow an abortion, they are not being cruel but merely consistent with a logical concern. The mother presumably was baptized as an infant; it is all right to let her die and "go to her reward." But the child must be brought to term and baptized and saved from perdition. So sincere was this concern that theologians at the Sorbonne in the nineteenth century invented a baptismal syringe, wherewith to baptize a fetus in utero in the event of a spontaneous abortion, a miscarriage.

But this is surely a concern that the Jewish community cannot share. Having no such concept of original sin, we recite daily in our prayers words that come verbatim from the Talmud: "My God, the soul thou hast endowed in me is pure." We inherit a pure soul, which becomes "contaminated" only by our own misdeeds. By that token, early abortion would send a fetus to heaven in a state of pristine purity. Although the Talmud does discuss the time of ensoulment—whether it occurs when the child is conceived, or at the first trimester, at birth, or, as one opinion has it, when the child first answers Amen—it dismisses the question as both unanswerable and irrelevant to the abortion question.

Abortion, then, is neither murder nor worse than murder, nor is it an acceptable option when this alternative is death to the mother. Since the mother may not choose suicide, abortion in that extreme case becomes mandatory. This is the sense of the fundamental talmudic passage bearing on the subject. The Mishnah puts it this way: "If a woman has [life-threatening] difficulty in childbirth, the embryo within her must be [aborted, even, if necessary] dismembered limb by limb, because her life [*hayyeha*] takes precedence over its life [*hayyav*]. Once its head (or its greater part) has emerged, it may not be touched, for we may not set aside one life [*nefesh*] for another" (*Mishnah Ohalot* 7:6).

The justification for abortion, then, is that before the child emerges we do not have a *nefesh*. The life of the fetus is only potential; it cannot compete with actual human life. As cited at the outset, the Talmud considered grounding warrant for abortion on the idea that the fetus is a *rodef*, an aggressor or pursuer. The Talmud dismissed that line of reasoning; neither fetus nor mother can be defined as pursuer.

Yet Maimonides, in his great summarizing Law Code, seems to retrieve the rejected argument. He formulates the talmudic law as follows: "This, too, is a [negative] Commandment: Not to take pity on the life of a pursuer. Therefore the Sages ruled that when a woman has difficulty in giving birth, one dismembers the fetus in her womb—either with drugs or by surgery—because it is like a pursuer seeking to kill her. Once its head has emerged, it may not be touched, for we may not set aside one life for another; this is the natural course of the world" (*Hilchot Rozeach*, I:9).

Further Implications

At a conference in Rome under the auspices of the Vatican, I pointed out that a life-threatening pregnancy is certainly warrant for abortion. A Catholic woman physician rose to challenge my position. She told of a difficult pregnancy she herself had sustained: the doctor counseled abortion, but the priest forbade it. She obeyed her priest, and the child was born without incident. But a priest present at that conference turned to address her and explained: "Yes, as a Catholic woman you are duty-bound to listen to your priest, who will tell you abortion is wrong. But a Jewish woman is equally duty-bound to listen to her rabbi, who will tell her that Jewish law forbids her to put her life in danger; that it requires her to obey the doctor in such a case, even if he later turns out to have been mistaken."

Another such clarifying confrontation took place back home in New York City, when another Catholic woman rose to question the point of view. She began: "Don't you believe in the Bible? The Bible says, 'Therefore, choose life.' Since abortion is the taking of life, how can you allow it?" "Because," I replied, "when you see 'choose life' in the Bible and when we see it, we are seeing different things. From a Catholic standpoint, essentially otherworldly in orientation, you see 'life' as life in the next world. Otherwise, why would you allow the death of the mother? That, too, is taking life. Yet you feel that the mother, already baptized, can 'choose life' in the next world. But when *we* see those words, we think of life in this world, and so we strive to save the mother, to save existing life. How do I know this? Because the Talmud gives a rationale for its principle that 'saving life sets aside all else in the Torah,' that the Sabbath and even Yom Kippur must be desecrated in order to protect or preserve life or health. The rationale is simple: 'Violate [for the patient] this Sabbath, so that he will be able to keep many Sabbaths.' In other words, we want to 'choose life' here on earth, and a therapeutic abortion is therefore indicated, even mandated."

Since abortion is not murder, and Maimonides could not have ruled otherwise, the commentators to his code explain that he made figurative use of the pursuer idea to buttress the case for abortion. Hence his formulation *k'rodef,* that the fetus is "like a pursuer."

Illustrative of the difference, albeit technical, between murder and killing is the following report: Rabbi Issac Unterman, late chief rabbi of Israel, was firmly opposed to abortion except under extreme circumstances. He labels it "akin to murder" but preserves the distinction. He tells of a Jewish girl made pregnant by a German soldier during World War I. She asked the soldier for support of the child to be born; he instead took her to a physician to abort. The physician, Jewish, declined to perform the abortion, insisting it was against his principles. The soldier then drew his gun and threatened the doctor: Either you abort or I will shoot you. Rabbi Unterman declared that, had he been asked the question by the doctor, he would have told him to abort. If abortion were really murder, the doctor would have to martyr himself, to lay down his life rather than comply. Much as I would like to call it murder, he said in effect, the clear sense of Jewish law is that it is not.

Also in this connection, Rabbi Joseph Rosin of Rogatchov responded, in the early part of this century, to a query as to whether a man may divorce his wife because she brought about an abortion. His answer was no: although abortion is "akin to homicide," it is not a real enough homicide or offense to make it permissible to divorce her against her will.

Rabbi Unterman stood squarely in the tradition of Maimonides and, in fact, all rabbinic teaching on the subject of abortion can be said to align itself with either Maimonides, on the right, or Rashi, on the left. The "rightist" approach begins with the assumption, formulated by Unterman, that abortion is "akin to murder" and therefore allowable only in cases of corresponding gravity such as saving the life of the mother. The approach then builds *down* from that strict position to embrace a broader interpretation of lifesaving situations. These include a threat to her health, for example, and perhaps a threat to her sanity if she is contemplating suicide where suicide is a possibility but excludes any lesser reasons.

The more "liberal" approach, based on Rashi's affirmation that the fetus is not a human person, is associated with another former chief rabbi of Israel, Benzion Uziel. This approach assumes that no real prohibition against abortion exists and builds *up* from that ground to safeguard against indiscriminate or unjustified thwarting of potential life. This school of thought includes the example of Rabbi Yair Bachrach in the seventeenth century, whose classic responsum saw no legal bar to abortion but would not permit it in the case before him of a pregnancy conceived in adultery; the woman, "in deep remorse," wanted to destroy the fruit of her sin. The responsum concludes by refusing to sanction abortion, not on legal grounds but on sociological ones, as a safeguard against further immorality. Other authorities, such as Rabbi Jacob Yavetz, disagreed on this point, affirming the legal sanction of abortion for the woman's welfare, whether life or health or even for avoidance of "great pain."

Maternal rather than fetal indications are the rule for both schools of thought. The rightist position certainly considers only the mother, but so does the leftist one. The latter school includes even the mother's less than life-and-death welfare, expressed in the words *great pain,* and based on the principle that *tza'ara d'gufah kadim.* Rabbinic rulings on abortion, when collated and distilled, are thus amenable to the generalization that if a woman were to come before the rabbi and seek permission for an abortion by saying, "I had German measles, or I took thalidomide, during pregnancy, and the possibility is that the child will be born deformed," rabbi would decline permission on those grounds. "How do you know," he might say, "that the child will be born deformed? Maybe not. And if so, how do you know that such is worse for him than not being born?" Why mix in the "secrets of God"? But if the same woman under the same circumstances came to the same rabbi and expressed the problem differently, saying, "The possibility is that the child will be born deformed, and that possibility is giving me extreme mental anguish," the rabbi would then rule otherwise. Now the fetal indication has become a maternal indication, and all the considerations for her welfare are now brought to bear. The fetus is unknown, future, potential, part of the "secrets of God"; the mother is known, present, human, and seeking compassion.

One rabbinic authority, writing in Romania in 1940, responded to the case of an epileptic mother who feared that her unborn child would also be epileptic. He writes: "For fear of possible, remote danger to a future child that maybe, God forbid, he will know sickness—how can it occur to anyone to actively kill the fetus because of such a possible doubt? This seems to me very much like the laws of Lycurgus, King of Sparta, according to which every blemished child was to be put to death. . . . Permission for abortion is to be granted only because of mental anguish for the mother. But for fear of what might be the child's lot?—The secrets of God are not knowable." He was basing his decision on an explicit ruling in 1913 by Rabbi Mordecai Winkler of Hungary: "Mental-health risk has been definitely equated with physical-health risk. This woman, in danger of losing her mental health unless the pregnancy is interrupted, would therefore accordingly qualify."[4]

The emphasis on maternal as opposed to fetal indications caused a dilemma with regard to such tragic, but clearly fetal, afflictions as that of Tay-Sachs. Screening of prospective mates or parents is recommended; but after a pregnancy begins, may amniocentesis be performed to determine if the cells of the fetus have been affected?

Having limited the warrant for abortion to maternal indications, and the birth of a Tay-Sachs child presents no risk to the mother's life or health, the answer would be negative. And since abortion is ruled out, amniocentesis would be halakhically proscribed as a gratuitous invasive assault, with its own attendant risks, on the womb. The dilemma, however, is resolved by a perception on the part of the mother that this is really a maternal indication. The present knowledge that the child will deteriorate and die in infancy, although the birth itself will be safe for her, gives her genuine mental anguish. The fetal indication has become a maternal one. Alternatively, though the majority of halakhic positions are as described here, there are at least two eminent authorities who rule that some fetal indications, such as this one, are serious enough to warrant an abortion. Rabbi Saul Israeli of the Jerusalem Rabbinical Court and Rabbi Eliezer Waldenberg, an expert in medical ethics, have so ruled.

The spectrum of Jewish positions on the matter of abortion, from right to left, all stand in sharp contrast to any liberal position on neonatal defectives. The point is that the Jewish tradition is the real "right to life" affirmation. Another look at the passage from the *Mishnah* proves that all this concern for the welfare of the mother obtains prior to birth. From the moment of birth, the life of the infant is as inviolate as that of the mother. Its right to life is then absolute. Before birth, however, right to life is not the applicable concept; it is "right to be born." The right to be born is not absolute but relative to the welfare of the mother. No one has a right to be born any more than a right to be conceived. But just as the *Mishnah* makes the fetus secondary to the mother before birth, so it rejects any distinction after birth. This contradicts another popular slogan, "quality of life." If quality of life were a factor, it would be absurd to say that the newborn babe is equal to its mother. The mother has her achievements and her interconnected dependencies; the infant has none of these yet. Still, we reject any considerations of relative quality; the operative slogan is rather "sanctity of life." From the moment of its birth, the life of the newborn is sacred, as indivisibly and undifferentially sacred as that of the mother. This is the true "right to life" position. Whereas *right to be born* is relative to the welfare of the mother, *right to life* is not relative to the mother's or anyone's welfare. Right to life means that no person need apologize for living, neither to parents, to physicians, to society, nor to self.

The great pains this chapter takes to prove abortion warrantable under some circumstances would seem to obscure the fact that it remains stigmatized except as a last resort. Procreation is a positive mitzvah, and potential life has the sanctity of its potential. The Talmud uses the dreaded word *murder* in a figurative, hyperbolic sense even in connection with not conceiving. The bachelor and the couple who decline to conceive are called "guilty of bloodshed" for their sin of omission. Procreation is a desideratum as well as a mitzvah, and casual abortion is accordingly abhorrent. There may be legal and moral sanction for abortion where necessary, but the attitude remains one of solemn hesitation in the presence of the sanctity of life and a pronatalist respect for new life.

Accordingly, abortion for population control is repugnant to the Jewish mind. Abortion for economic reasons is also not admissible. Although taking precaution by abortion or contraception against physical threat to the mother remains a mitzvah, this cannot be said when the problem is financial difficulty. Material considerations or career concerns are improper in this connection, especially when there are others eager to adopt or nurture. A degree of brutalization is scarcely avoidable in the destruction of even potential life or in the rejection of a precious gift of God. But when the reasons for considering abortion are overwhelming, the right to do so remains hers after all.

In the course of the 1984 presidential campaign, Archbishop John O'Connor of New York made an impassioned plea for people of all religious and political persuasions to join in the struggle against abortion on demand and in support of reverence for life. The Jewish community applauds and shares in the battle for reverence for life but also in the pluralistic concern for individual liberty. Some contemporary rabbis welcome the strong stand of the antiabortion groups and regard the leniencies of traditional Jewish law as either too subtle or too dangerous for broad consumption. Others see the right of choice as inherent in the Jewish treatment of the subject and stress the noncapital nature of the offense. Either way, it is important that political factors not be allowed to equate abortion with murder and prochoice people with murderers or outlaws or proabortionists as such. Murder is a fundamental evil which no civilized society should tolerate, but abortion can be understood in more than one way; the right to do so must not be unfairly compromised or stigmatized.

Notes

1. Nathan Drazin, *Marriage made in Heaven* (New York, 1959), p. 59.
2. Victor Aptowitzer, "Observations on the Criminal Law of the Jews," *Jewish Quarterly Review* 15 (1924), pp. 111 ff.
3. R. Isaac Schorr, *Koach Sharr* (Kolomea, 1888), vol. 1, No. 20.
4. Mordecai Winkler, *Levushei Mordechai* (Mad, 1913), No. 39.

FOR FURTHER READING

Bleich, J. David, *Judaism and Healing: Halakhic Perspectives*, New York, 1981. A brief but substantive introduction to twenty-seven issues in Jewish medical ethics.

Feldman, David M, *Health and Medicine in the Jewish Tradition*, New York, 1986. The mandate to heal and its implications for reproductive technology, therapy, the treatment of the dying, and the like.

_____. *Marital Relations, Birth Control and Abortion*, New York, 1974, (Paperback version of *Birth Control in Jewish Law*. New York, 1968.) Classic analysis of these and other matters, with comparative reference to Christian tradition.

Feldman, David M., and Fred Rosner, eds. *Compendium on Medical Ethnics*, New York, 1984. The sixth edition of a handbook on theoretical issues, with recommended hospital procedures.

Gold, Michael, *And Hannah Wept: Infertility, Adoption and the Jewish Couple*, Philadelphia, 1988. Deals with procreation and its problems, medical solutions to infertility, and the emotional and practical factors in adoption.

Jakobovitz, Immanuel, *Jewish Medical Ethics*, New York, 1975. Updated edition of the pioneering study in the field, with history and source reference.

Meier, Levi, ed, *Jewish Values in Bioethics*, New York, 1986. Transcripts of papers delivered at the annual Max Martin Salick Lectureship at Cedars-Sinai Hospital, treating twelve themes by various authorities.

Rosner, Fred, *Modern Medicine and Jewish Ethics*, Hoboken: 1986. A comprehensive treatment of a range of familiar and novel questions in medicine and religious practice.

Rosner, Fred, and David J. Bleich, eds, *Jewish Bioethics*, New York, 1979. A collection of basic texts on a wide range of medical ethics questions, from perinatal problems to issues of death and dying.

AIDS: The Contemporary Jewish Perspective

DAVID NOVAK

Current Public Concern with AIDS

Since the discovery, less than ten years ago, of the growing health problem of Acquired Immune Deficiency Syndrome (AIDS), public concern with this new phenomenon has increased significantly, far outstripping discussion of any other health problem in our society. The media are constantly filled with everything from personal testimonies by and about AIDS sufferers and their loved ones to predictions by various experts on the future course of this problem and how we might best cope with it. Indeed, interest in AIDS is so widespread, and fear about it so rampant, that the surgeon general of the United States has prepared a booklet about AIDS and how to avoid contracting it. This booklet has been sent to every American household, no doubt at considerable expense to the taxpayers.

If AIDS were simply a health problem, that is, a physical disease (actually, it is the result of a virus that weakens the natural immune system of the body to such an extent that there is no effective defense against any infection that might attack the body), the degree of public concern that has been expressed heretofore would be totally out of proportion to the actual danger. Despite the growing number of patients dying as the result of AIDS-related diseases, their number is much smaller than the number of patients who die as the result of cancer, heart disease, and other, more familiar, fatal maladies. Moreover, despite warnings by some experts, which other experts consider grossly exaggerated, that the general population is at an increasing risk, the disease has been largely confined to male homosexuals and intravenous drug users.[1] Therefore, there must be something about this malady that inspires more than just the fear of imminent physical contagion in the general population, the overwhelming number of whom do not fall into the two highest-risk groups. For most of us, AIDS has created more of a spiritual problem than a physical one. As such, any human approach to this disease—certainly any religious approach, which must deal with concerns of both body and soul—will be inadequate if it deals with AIDS as it would with any other epidemic or threatened epidemic. Indeed, it would seem that the very phenomenology of AIDS involves religious questions in a more immediate way than any other modern health problem. And because so much of the population has been so thoroughly secularized, certainly in attitudes toward health and disease, our culture has been ill prepared for the religious phenomenology of AIDS.

The religious phenomenology of AIDS becomes evident in three spiritual questions AIDS inevitably raises.

First, AIDS seems to question the prevailing hedonism of our culture. Before its appearance, it was far easier to argue that our bodies are simply there to be used for our pleasure, that there are no bodily impediments per se, and that we can do with our bodies whatever we will. The availability of antibiotic drugs that have supposedly cured the old venereal diseases such as syphilis and gonorrhea, birth control drugs and devices, and legalized hygienic abortion certainly made the arguments for a "sexual revolution" more compelling, although the dangers of the relationship of drugs to this hedonistic revolution were becoming increasingly evident even before AIDS came on the scene. AIDS has now demonstrated that the promiscuity that generally characterizes those at greatest risk of contracting it (including heterosexuals) is physically dangerous. In other words, the old warnings about the physical consequences of hedonistic promiscuity ("you'll get a terrible disease if you do that!") suddenly have a new truth to them. AIDS has shown us that the body is not just the tool of the soul's willful capacity but that it has an inherent integrity that must be respected for the sake of the good of the whole human person. And it has shown that the human will is only part of a larger created nature and that the will's pretensions to omnipotence, which are supremely manifest in hedonism, are mortally dangerous on the most immediate physical level.[2] Furthermore, our lack of preparation for the AIDS crisis because of our hedonism is in essence akin to our lack of preparation for the ecological crisis because of our uncritical faith in technology.[3] In both cases, human pretensions of omnipotence are being directly challenged by the biological order of nature, which is beyond our control.

Second, AIDS seems to raise an issue that was thought by most moderns to be an ancient superstition long behind us: God's punishment of sin through physical maladies. As anyone with either therapeutic or pastoral experience well knows, the first question most often raised even today, even by many "nonreligious" people, who have discovered serious disease in themselves is, What did I do for God to do this to me?[4] In the case of most other diseases, whose epidemiology is totally external, one can attempt to reason with the patient by showing that the disease was contracted through no fault of his or her own. (Whether such reasoning is psychologically helpful to the patient is another question.) The AIDS patient, however, most often does indeed know just what he or she did that caused his or her body to be so receptive to the AIDS virus and thus set in motion the deadly syndrome.

This knowledge entails considerable guilt, for most of the people in our culture, however otherwise secularized they may be, still regard homosexual acts and the use of narcotic drugs to be not only immoral but sinful; that is, they are acts for which God will punish us. Therefore, the cultural message about AIDS seems to be not only that is it caused by one's own acts but that it is caused by one's immoral or sinful acts. Indeed, one need no longer argue for the immorality of these acts based on abstract philosophical or theological definitions; rather, one can now point to concrete and seemingly inevitable consequences. Arguments on behalf of AIDS sufferers which ignore these indisputable facts can only be regarded as rationalizations motivated by pathological denials of empirical reality.

Finally, that children can be born with AIDS because of the acts of their parents seems to raise the old fear that "God punishes the children for the sins of the parents."[5] This fear also applies to those who have contracted AIDS because of having been infused in one way or another with the bodily fluids of someone who did contract AIDS because of his or her own acts. In other words, we not only suffer for our own sins, but we suffer for the sins of others before us. This raises the question of "original sin," a doctrine most Jews (at least most liberal Jews) are surprised if not shocked to learn that Judaism affirms, as does Christianity after it, albeit with some important differences.[6]

It is because of these considerations that a Jewish approach to the problem of AIDS must incorporate both the immediately practical norms of Jewish law (halakhah) and some of the more theoretical reflections of Jewish theology (Aggadah) about disease in general, reflections that can be seen as informing the normative process of which halakhah is always the most evident aspect.[7] For an adequate Jewish discussion of AIDS must address not only the bodily needs of those specifically afflicted with it but their spiritual needs and, indeed, the spiritual needs of all those for whom the social presence of AIDS has raised some old religious questions in surprisingly new ways.

Indiscriminate Treatment of the Sick

In traditional Judaism (to which this author is personally committed), male homosexual acts are absolutely prohibited, both for Jews and for non-Jews as well. (Female homosexual acts are also prohibited, but their prohibition is based on quite different sources. Moreover, since female homosexuals are not a high-risk AIDS group, we need not be concerned with them in this specific context.[8]) According to one major authority in the Talmud, both Jewish and non-Jewish males are proscribed from homosexual acts by the scriptural prohibition, "you shall not lie with a man as with a woman; it is an abomination (*to'ebah hi*)" (Lev. 18:22).[9] According to another authority, this verse specifically proscribes Jewish men only, non-Jewish men being so proscribed by the scriptural verse "a man ... shall cleave to his wife [and they shall be one flesh]" (Gen. 2:24), which is interpreted to mean "but not with a male [*zakhar*]."[10] This latter interpretation, which is taken to be the normative one, entails the view that the Jewish proscription of such homosexual acts is a reaffirmation of a more general human proscription, whereas the former interpretation sees the Jewish proscription as being primary and the general human proscription as being derivative. The acceptance of this latter interpretation is important in emphasizing that, for subsequent Jewish tradition, the proscription of male homosexual acts is neither something applying only to Jews nor something specifically Jewish to be imposed on the general population by Jews or by the influence of Judaism. It can be addressed as a human issue. Therefore, traditional Judaism can make common cause with other religious and ethical traditions that affirm the same human proscriptions, without any one of them subordinating its own moral authority to the other.[11]

The same moral presentation can be seen in the prohibition of acts that are clearly destructive of life and health, of which intravenous drug use is an obvious example. One of the main grounds given in the Talmud for this prohibition is the verse addressed to Noah and his sons (for the rabbis, "sons of Noah" is a synonym for humankind). "Surely I shall hold you responsible for your own lifeblood" (Gen. 9:5).[12] Indeed, in a famous passage in the Talmud, in which a rabbi being martyred is urged to shorten his suffering by hastening his own death while being burned at the stake, the rabbi refuses, arguing along general human lines that "it is best that He who gave life take it, but that a person not destroy himself."[13]

The majority of AIDS sufferers are considered to be in the category of sinners, and it is irrelevant whether they be Jews or non-Jews. Full care should be extended to AIDS patients, even though sympathy with their plight must never lead to approval of their way of life. I must emphasize this point because I strongly suspect that there is a concerted attempt on the part of apologists for homosexuality to extend normal human sympathy for AIDS suffering in particular to a more general human sympathy for all aspects of the lives of those suffering from AIDS. In Jewish teaching as well as ordinary human reason, such an extension of sympathy is totally misplaced. It is as misplaced as attempting to extend our normal human sympathy with smokers suffering from lung cancer to their practice of smoking cigarettes. Nevertheless, our obligation to AIDS patients must be internalized as sympathy with them for three reasons.

First, according to Jewish tradition, everyone is essentially a sinner. "There is no person [*'adam*] on earth who is so righteous that he will do only good and not sin" (Eccles. 7:20).[14] And even certain extraordinary scriptural personalities, who are seen by the Talmud as being without sin, are still included in the mortality decreed for all humankind because of original sin.[15] Furthermore, the Talmud sees all human suffering as a means for intensifying our relationship with God. This turns out to mean that even if one cannot discern specific sin in oneself when suffering, one is to act as if he or she were a sinner, namely, he or she must return to God (the Hebrew for "repentance" is *teshuvah*—return).[16] Therefore, sin is so pervasively human that the difference between the right-eous and the wicked is ultimately one of degree, not of kind. This does not, of course, excuse anyone's particular sin, but it does in-dicate that the self-righteous confidence that assumes its own se-curity because it is not suffering at present as is someone else is religiously abhorrent. As the atonement liturgy used on Yom Kip-pur succinctly puts it. "We are neither so arrogant or so stubborn as to say before You O' Lord our God and God of our ancestors that we are righteous [*tzadiqim 'anahnu*] and have not sinned."[17]

Because we are all, therefore, subject to both disease and death because of our sins, we are in an existential position to *sympathize* with (literally *feel with* from the Greek *sympathein* as in the Ger-man *Mitgefuehl*) those suffering from any disease, including AIDS. This is brought out in the rabbinic treatment of the scriptural norms concerning the disease *tzara'at* (wrongly translated *leprosy*; actually a far less fatal disease than what is for us leprosy, namely, Hansen's Disease). According to the rabbis, the reason why Scrip-ture specifically singles out this disease for its concern is because it is the punishment for a number of antisocial vices, most espe-cially slander.[18] The community is commanded to quarantine those suffering from this disease.[19] It would seem that this action is for the sake of the community to avoid contamination by contact with lepers, either physically or spiritually. "And the one who is af-flicted with the disease [*ve-ha-tzaru'a*], his clothes shall be rent and his head disheveled, and he shall cover his upper lip and cry 'unclean! [*tam'e*]' " (Lev. 13:46). The rabbis emphasize, however, that this is not done to humiliate the *tzara'at* sufferer but to give him the public opportunity to express his pain and anguish and to beseech others to "seek compassion [*rahamim*] for him."[20] This compassion is to be exercised both in prayer (beseeching God) and personal attention (beseeching man). These acts are the two parts of the overall commandment to attend to the needs of the sick (*biqur holim*).[21]

The treatment of the one suffering from this disease is more for his sake than for the sake of the community in which he lives. The community clearly has both a physical and spiritual responsibility for him. Furthermore, this concern is not limited to sufferers from this specific disease. In a parallel passage, the Talmud extends this procedure to those suffering from any other disease or misfortune.[22] Finally, once again emphasizing the general human problem involved in AIDS, Jews are to be indiscriminate in terms of those who are the object of their medical attention, be they Jews or non-Jews.[23]

A serious problem does arise, however, when confronting the Talmud's rule that in the case of a "provocative sinner" (*mumar le-hakh'is*), one is not only not to help such a person, but one is actually not to save his life (*moridin ve-lo ma'alin*).[24] The question that must be honestly faced by all those who accept the authority of Jewish law, despite its obvious difficulty, is twofold: (1) whether the male homosexual or drug user suffering from AIDS falls into this category; and (2) whether the enforcement of this rule still applies under contemporary conditions.[25]

As for the first question, the provocative sinner is contrasted with the "sinner for appetite" (*mumar le-te'abon*). At first glance, it would seem that since both active homosexuals and drug users are seemingly motivated by "appetite," their immediate gratification takes precedence over the observance of moral restraints. If this is the case, the drastic action mandated by this Talmudic rule does not apply to them after all. But the essential distinction between these two types of sinners is not seen to be the motivation behind their respective acts, that is, the former being motivated to rebel against the authority of God by violating what has been revealed in the Torah, the latter being motivated by the desire for instant gratification. Rather, Maimonides interprets the difference between the two types of sinners to be whether or not the sin is habitual and willful.[26] If one sins habitually and willfully, then he or she is considered to be a *provocative* sinner. But if one sins occasionally and with guilt, that person is considered to be a sinner *for appetite*. Actually, the term *appetite* is used here as a euphemism for weakness of will. The Talmudic way of describing such a person is that "he would not eat nonkosher food if kosher food were readily at hand."[27]

Based on this criterion, it would seem that active homosexuals and drug users do indeed fall into the category of provocative sinners. Their actions seem to be both habitual and willful. Furthermore, the attempt of some recent religious apologists for homosexuality to see active homosexuals as being under the influence of an avoidable compulsion (*'ones*) and thus not morally culpable is rationally flawed.[28] For it confuses the state of homosexual desire (or desire for drugs, if one is to follow this same logic of the argument) with homosexual activity. The Torah only prohibits homosexual activity, not homosexual desire, which can hardly be the subject of conscious choice.[29] Of course, since the presence of such homosexual desire makes the avoidance of proscribed homosexual acts quite difficult, one could argue for the moral counsel that someone who is continually experiencing that desire seek professional help in an effort to sublimate it or, optimally, to experience heterosexual desire.[30] To assume that homosexual activity is as consciously involuntary as homosexual feeling and desire is to classify all homosexuals as being deprived of free choice. But that is hardly compassion, for it denies them their moral personality, an essential part of their full human functioning.[31] It erroneously assumes that only heterosexuals can separate between sexual desire and sexual activity. But even though, according to traditional criteria, active homosexuals are provocative sinners, even provocative sinners are capable of repentance and repentance can thus be expected of them.[32] Those who repent require our respect; those deprived of free choice, on the other hand, can only be the objects of our pity. Thus our obligation to care for AIDS patients, even if their disease is the result of grave sin, must not only tend to their bodies but to their souls. The soul of the sinner is of infinitely greater importance than his or her sin.[33]

Even though many AIDS patients do fall into the category of the provocative sinner, there are times when the sanctions entailed by sin are not enforced.[34] Thus in the Middle Ages, it was questioned why all provocative sinners were not included in the category of those whose lives were not to be saved. In fact, it was noted that the rule itself seems to be inconsistent for it included certain persons guilty of relatively minor sins and excluded others guilty of much more grave sins. One exegete explains this seeming inconsistency by noting that the criterion of inclusion is not the inherent nature per se of the proscribed acts being performed, but rather the likely consequences the rabbis thought would result from issuing such a harsh warning.[35] Thus if the rabbis thought that a relatively minor offense was being treated too lightly by the people and that the threat of a severe punishment would have a sobering effect on them, they enacted such a harsh sanction. This action is seen as being justified by the power given to contemporary rabbinical authorities to exercise judgments more severe than those actually mandated by statute, if and when they judged an emergency situation in public morality.[36] Thus this category is subject to a high degree of judicial discretion. Furthermore, it seems that by the time of the Middle Ages, this category was almost exclusively confined to those whose deeds actually endangered the lives and property of the entire community, most notably, informers (*mosrim*).[37] It would seem that a similar reaction could conceivably apply to AIDS patients, who, despite their awareness of their highly contagious condition, still engage in sexual activity with unknowing partners. In the case of other AIDS patients, however, such sanctions, or even the threat of such sanctions, would be counterproductive. In modern times, this latter conclusion was powerfully formulated by the influential Israeli Talmudist and jurist (*poseq*), R. Abraham Isaiah Karelitz (d. 1953), known as the *Hazon 'Ish*. He insisted that the purpose of all such rabbinic legislation is only to be constructive, a matter dependent on a judicial consideration of the times.[38]

The Question of Danger to Health Care Personnel

One of the moral problems that has arisen in connection with the AIDS crisis is the refusal of many health care personnel to treat AIDS patients. They argue that not only is AIDS highly contagious, but the methods of its contagion have by no means been fully ascertained. Without such definition, it cannot be contained within predictable boundaries. Hence the only sure way of not contracting the disease is to avoid any contact whatsoever with those who have AIDS. The question, then, is to what extent may the religiously based duty of self-preservation be invoked as prior to the religiously based duty to treat the sick, especially when one has unique skills for doing so through professional training.[39]

A truly adequate approach to this problem must begin with the question of what is the source of the obligation to treat the sick. This can be the only proper context for dealing with the more specific question of what is required of us in treating AIDS patients. In the classical Jewish sources there are two main theories concerning the source of the obligation to extend treatment to the sick: that of Maimonides (d. 1204) and that of Nahmanides (d. 1267).

In an early work, Maimonides argues that the obligation of the physician (*rof'e*—which in our day can certainly be extended to all health care personnel) is derived from the extension of the scriptural law requiring that we return a lost article to its owner (Deut. 22:2) by the Talmud to include "returning his body to him," that is, saving his life.[40] In a later work, he reiterates the scriptural command, "You shall not stand idly by the blood of your neighbor" (Lev. 19:16), which the Talmud connects with the previous interpretation of returning lost property (including a "lost" body) to its owner.[41] The latter verse is seen as being needed to teach the obligation to engage in such saving action even if it entails considerable effort and expense. Even though Maimonides does not mention the actual duty of a physician in this later text, one can clearly extend the point made in it to include the physician. And as regards our problem of to what extent health care personnel are obligated to treat AIDS patients, who do place them at some risk, the most important commentator on Maimonides, R. Joseph Karo (d. 1575), connects this text with an obscure rabbinic text which states that one is required to "expose himself to possible danger" (*safeq sakanah*) when saving a human life.[42] Needless to say, the difference between "possible" danger and "definite" danger (*sakanah vad'ai*) can be determined only on an ad hoc basis.

There are a number of problems with basing the duty to care for the sick, and especially the duty to care for AIDS patients, on Maimonides' theory.

First, the connection of the duty to extend oneself to someone in physical danger with the duty to expose onself to possible danger is highly tenuous. Moreover, later commentators have great trouble finding this rabbinic text that mandates exposure to possible danger. It is said to be from the Palestinian Talmud, but the great Talmudist R. Naftali Berlin (*Netzib*, d. 1893) can find there only a text that deals with an individual volunteering to risk his life for that of another.[43] Clearly, the permission and even the encouragement of a supererogatory act by a heroic individual cannot be the basis for a general norm requiring everyone in a similar situation to do so.[44]

Second, all of the Talmudic sources deal with situations in which one *happens* to encounter other persons in dangerous situations. None of them deals with any obligation to choose and remain in a health care profession and regularly treat all patients indiscriminately, for there, such encounters are regular occurrences, not chance happenings. This is not to say that Maimonides himself, who was a distinguished physician, did not regard his profession of medicine to be a *vocatio*. From his biographical testimony we know that he did.[45] But his theory of the obligation to extend medical care, indeed to choose to become a professional who regularly does so for better and for worse, does not seem to explain this obligation sufficiently.

To many students of Maimonides' writings, it has seemed odd that he did not quote or even paraphrase the well-known Talmud text which states, "It was taught in the School of R. Ishmael that from Scripture's words, 'he shall surely provide for his healing' (Exodus 21:19) is derived the permission for a physician to heal."[46] Perhaps Maimonides believed that the use of the term *permission* (*reshut*) indicated that such activity is optional; therefore, the *obligation* to heal requires a stronger scriptural and Talmudic ground.[47] Nevertheless, Nahmanides (who was Maimonides' most cogent legal and theological critic) does quote this very text, and his exposition of it shows another theory, one which I believe is more adequate to the task at hand, both in terms of Jewish law and of Jewish theology. The key difference between his theory and that of Maimonides is that he does not base the obligation to heal on an analogy between human life and human property as does Maimonides.[48] Nahmanides writes,

> The explanation of this Talmud text is that the physician might well say, "why do I need this trouble; perhaps I might make a mistake [*'et'eh*] and the result be that I have killed lives through error [*bi-shegagah*]?"; therefore, the Torah authorizes him [*natnah lo reshut*] to heal . . . there are those who say that the physician is like a judge who is obligated to judge [*metzuveh la-doon*]. . . . And it makes sense . . . also that they should not say, "God wounds and He heals" since . . . human beings have become accustomed to medical treatment [*be-refu'ot . . . she-nahagu*] . . . Here "permission" (*reshut*) means an obligation (*reshut de-mitzvah*) . . . which God has designated for him to do.[49]

Here *permission* is not taken in its usual sense of that which is optional, but rather it is taken negatively, namely, that which is not prohibited.[50] It is an authorization to perform a commandment, one which one might think is for God alone to do.

Nahmanides' analogy between a physician and a judge lies at the heart of the theological point he is making here. In both the professions of healing and judging, the activity is regarded as essentially Divine and human only by participation. Thus Scripture assures the judges that they should not be deterred because their efforts have only partial results in this world; indeed, it could not be otherwise because justice is essentially transcendent.[51] "You shall not fear any man for the judgment is God's" (Deut. 1:17).[52]

God is also designated by Scripture as a physician. "Every disease which I placed in Egypt I shall not place on you for I the Lord am your physician [*rof'ekha*]" (Exod. 15:26).[53] Just as, ideally, God should be the only judge, so, ideally, God should be the only physician.[54] The less than ideal conditions of human life on earth, however, require human judges and, for Nahmanides, especially require human physicians.[55] Nevertheless, these human physicians must always appreciate their essentially subordinate role in the true created order.[56]

Nahmanides' theory of the obligation to heal makes it not just an ordinary obligation, but rather an act of *imitatio Dei*.[57] Indeed, what for the rabbis are the two main attributes of God, that of judgment (*'Elohim* qua *midat ha-din*) and that of compassion (*YHWH* qua *midat rahamim*), can be seen as the basis for the participatory status of judges and physicians: judges in the attribute of judgment, physicians (and all other "healers") in the attribute of compassion.[58]

In considering the obligation to treat AIDS patients, this is a crucial point. For AIDS is a disease, and at least for the time being its sufferers can only be treated, not cured. No one's life can be saved. We can only care for these lives in the little time they have left. This requires greater effort; it also entails greater frustration because the phenomenology of modern medicine, like so much of the phenomenology of our technological civilization, is totally success-oriented. We always want lasting results for our efforts, and here there are none. Yet Judaism obligates care, not just cure.[59] Here is where understanding our obligation as a Divine commandment, one which is uniquely grounded in Divine example, not just Divine decree, alone makes sense of it. For it requires the infinite expenditure of compassion rather than the efficacy needed for finite results. That is why it cannot be an ordinary commandment, one simply based on Divine decree.[60] This is important, too, for justifying treatment that is only palliative (alleviating suffering as much as possible) rather than actually curing a disease, which is clearly not the case at present with AIDS patients. In Maimonides' medical model, based as it is on the analogy of returning a lost piece of property, however, we are dealing with a case in which a problem (a lost piece of property) is actually solved (it is returned to its owner). By contrast, Nahmanides' medical model only explains *care* of the sick, even when there can be no successful completion of a procedure.

The true results of our obedience to the commandments, the recompense for our exposure to toil and even danger in order to keep them, we are taught lies in a realm beyond our experience and certainly beyond our grasp.[61] Hence we can care for the AIDS patients because their imminent mortality does not catch us unaware. The commandments are addressed to us as equally mortal persons; we would not need them if we were anything else.[62] And the commandments save us from ultimate despair, which in the case of treating AIDS patients is a strong and ever-present temptation. It saves us from despair because we are involved through the commandments in the very life of God Himself, in which life, not death, is the final victor.[63]

Notes

Thanks to my friends Eugene Borowitz, James Childress, Marc Gellman, David Weiss Halivni, Peter Ochs, and Michael Wyschogrod, whose valuable comments on an earlier draft of this paper helped me improve this version of it.

1. See M. A. Fumento, "AIDS: Are Heterosexuals at Risk?" *Commentary* 84 (November, 1987), pp. 21–27.

2. On hedonism and Judaism, see David Novak, *Halakhah in a Theological Dimension* (Chico, Calif., 1985), pp. 80–81.

3. See David Novak, "Technology and Its Ultimate Threat: A Jewish Meditation," *Research in Philosophy and Technology* (June, 1990).

4. The persistence of this question explains the enormous popularity of Harold Kushner's book *When Bad Things Happen to Good People* (New York, 1981). Rabbi Kushner's conclusion, however, that these things *happen* rather than being *caused* by God (see, esp., pp. 113–131.) is hardly consistent with the emphasis of traditional Jewish theology that everything other than our own free response to God is indeed "in the hands of God" (see B. Berakhot and parallels re Deut. 10:12), and, as we shall soon see, according to that theology, none of us can claim to be "good people."

5. The disturbing message of this verse (Exod. 20:5 and 34:7; Num. 14:18; Deut. 5:9) already troubled the prophets (see Jer. 31:28; Ezek. Chap. 18). The Talmud, in one comment, tries to qualify the message by stating that it applies only "when the children hang onto [i.e., willfully repeat] the deeds of their parents" (B. Berakhot 7a and B. Sanhedrin 27b). Nevertheless, that children do suffer because of their parents' misdeeds is too apparent ever to be fully explained away. See Y. Megillah 4.12/75d and, esp., R. Samuel David Luzzatto (Shadal), *Commentary on the Torah:* Exod. 20:5; also, Novak, *Halakhah in a Theological Dimension,* pp. 11ff.

6. See Gen. 8:21; also Solomon Schecter, *Some Aspects of Rabbinic Theology* (New York, 1936), pp. 242ff.; and Will Herberg, *Judaism and Modern Man* (New York, 1951), pp. 74ff.

7. See David Novak, *Law and Theology in Judaism,* 2 vols. (New York, 1974–76), vol. 1, pp 1ff., vol 2, pp xiiiff.

8. See, e.g., B. Yebamot 76a; Maim., *Hilkhot 'Isuray Bi'ah,* 21.8; also, David Novak, *The Image of the Non-Jew in Judaism* (New York, 1983), pp. 213–15.

9. B. Sanhedrin 57b re Lev. 18:6.

10. Ibid., 58a.

11. See David Novak, *Jewish-Christian Dialogue: A Jewish Justification* (New York, 1989), Introduction.

12. B. Baba Kama 91b.

13. B. 'Abodah Zarah 18a. See B. Berakhot 32b re Deut. 4:9, 15.

14. See B. Sanhedrin 46b.

15. B. Baba Batra 17a. See B. Yebamot 103b and parallels with Maharsha thereon; Wisdom of Solomon 2:24; Nahmanides, *Torat Ha'Adam: Sha'ar Ha-Gemul,* intro., *Kitvay Ramban,* ed. C. B. Chavel (Jerusalem, 1963), 2:12.

16. B. Berakhot 5a–b.

17. *The Authorized Daily Prayer Book,* ed. S. Singer (London, 1962), p. 353. See M. Sanhedrin 6.2; B. Shabbat 32b; Nahmanides, *Torat Ha'Adam: 'Inyan Viduy, Kitvay Ramban,* 2:47; *Shulhan 'Arukh: Yoreh De'ah,* 338.2.

18. See, e.g., T. Nega 'im 6.7; 'Arakhin 15b re Lev. 14:2.

19. See 'Arakhin 16b re Lev. 13:46. The rabbis, however, regarded *tzara'at*'s contagion to be moral rather than physical. See, e.g., M. Nega 'im 3.2; Maim., *Hilkhot Tum'at Tzara'at,* 9.8.

20. B. Mo'ed Qatan 5a. Cf. Maim., *Hilkhot Tum'at Tzara'at,* 10.8.

21. See B. Nedarim 39b–40a.

22. B. Sotah 32b; *Shulhan 'Arukh: Yoreh De'ah,* 335.8.

23. See B. Gittin 61a.

24. B. 'Abodah Zarah 26b.

25. Theoretically, a rabbinic law (such as this one) can be repealed (see M. 'Eduyot 1.5); however, in actual practice, reexamination of the conditions required for the application of the law was the usual procedure for effecting change. See, e.g., M. Kiddushin 4.14; B. Kiddushin 82a; Karo, *Shulhan 'Arukh: 'Eben Ha'Ezer,* 24.1 and Sirkes, *Bach* on *Tur: 'Eben Ha'Ezer,* 24; also, Karo, *Kesef Mishneh* on Maim., *Hilkhot Tefilah,* 11.1.

26. *Hilkhot Rotzeah,* 4.10 and *Hilkhot Teshubah,* 3.9 (see Karo, *kesef Mishneh* thereon).

27. B. Hullin 4a and parallels. For eating as a euphemism for sexual activity, see Semahot 7.8 and B. Kiddushin 21b–22a.

28. See H. J. Matt, "An Approach to Homosexuality," *Judaism* 27 (Winter, 1978), p. 16.

29. See Norman Lamm, "Judaism and the Modern Attitude to Homosexuality," *Encyclopedia Judaica Yearbook* (1974), pp. 194–205.

30. See David Novak, "On Homosexuality," *Sh'ma* 11 (November 14, 1980), pp 3–5.

31. See Maim., *Hilkhot Teshubah,* 4.1ff.

32. See ibid., 7.1ff.

33. For the refusal to equate the sinner with his or her sin, see B. Berakhot 10a re Ps. 104:35.

34. See B. Betzah 28b. For the problem of the administration of punishment in Jewish law, see Menahem Elon, *Ha-Mishpat Ha'Ibri*, 2d ed. 2 vols, (Jerusalem, 1978), vol 1 pp 421–427.

35. R. Joseph ibn Habib, *Nimuqay Yosef* on B. 'Abodah Zarah 26b, ed. Blau, 203 in the name of *Tosfot Ha-R'osh*. Also see *Tosfot Rabbenu Samson of Sens*, thereon, ed. Blau, 82.

36. See B. Sanhedrin 46a; also, Maim., *Hilkhot Sanhedrin*, 24.10.

37. See *Teshubot Ha-R'osh*, 17.1.

38. *Hazon 'Ish:* Yoreh De'ah (B'nai B'rak, 1958), sec. 2, 7d. Cf. B. Gittin 33a, Tos., s.v. "v'afqa'inhu."

39. See *Sifra* re Lev. 25:36, ed. Weiss, 109c; B. Baba Metzia 62a.

40. *Commentary on the Mishnah:* Nedarim 4.4.

41. *Hilkhot Rotzeah*, 1.14 elaborating on B. Sanhedrin 73a.

42. See Karo, *Kesef Mishneh* on Maim., *Hilkhot Tum'at Tzara' at*, 1:14; also Karo, *Bet Yosef* on *Tur: Hoshen Mishpat*, 426 re Lev. 19:16 and M. Sanhedrin 4.5. Along similar lines, see R. Solomon Luria, *Yam shel Shlomoh:* Baba Kama, 6.26 re B. Baba Kama 60b. Cf., however, R. David ibn Abi Zimra, *Teshubot Ha-Radbaz*, 3, no. 627; R. Joshua Falk, *Me'irat 'Aynayim* on *Shulhan 'Arukh: Hoshen Mishpat*, 426.

43. *Ha'Ameq Sh'elah* on *She'iltot de-Rab Hai Gaon:* Shelah, end re Y. Terumot 8.4/46b. Viktor Aptowitzer argued in his "Unechte Jeruschalmizitate," *Monatschrift fuer die Geschichte und Wissenschaft des Judenthums* 55 (1911), pp. 419–425., and in this point he has been followed by other modern critical Talmudists, that when a medieval source quotes the *Yersuhalmi* and we do not have this source in our *Yerushalmi* text, then the citation may very well be from a now lost rabbinic collection (*Qobetz Yerushalmi* on *Sefer Yerushalmi*). See also, R. Zvi Hirsch Chajes's note on B. Megillah 12b, and *'Imary Binah*, sec. 2, in *Kol Sifray Maharatz Chajes* (B'nai B'rak, 1958), Vol. 2, pp 891ff.

44. See Joshua Halberstam, "Supererogation in Jewish *Halakhah* and Islamic *Shari'a*," in *Studies in Islamic and Jewish Traditions*, ed. William. M. Brinner and Stephen D. Ricks (Atlanta, 1986), pp. 85ff.

45. See my late revered teacher, Abraham Joshua Heschel, *Maimonides: A Biography*, trans. Joachim Neugroschel (New York, 1982), pp. 213ff.

46. B. Baba Kama 85a.

47. See, e.g., B. Berakhot 27b; Maim., *Hilkhot Tefillah*, 1.6. For the attempt to see *reshut* as designating a low level of obligation rather than a pure option, see M. Betzah 5.2 and and B. Betzah 36b; B. Berakhot 26a, Tos., s.v. "ta'ah"; ibid., 27b, Tos., s.v. "halakhah." Regardless of which interpretation one accepts, however, the term *reshut* is not strong enough to ground the sense of *vocatio* needed for the practice of medicine as a profession.

48. For the pitfalls of using economic analogies when dealing with the protection of human persons, see Richard Stith, "Toward Freedom from Value," *Jurist* 38 (1978), pp. 48ff.

49. *Torat Ha'Adam:* 'Inyan Ha-Sakanah, *Kitvay Ramban*, Vol. 2, pp. 41–43.

50. For *reshut* in this stronger sense, see, esp., R. Joshua Falk, *Perishah* on *Tur: Yoreh De'ah*, 336, n.4.

51. See M. 'Abot 2.16.

52. See B. Sanhedrin 6b.

53. For God's greater healing power than man's, see *Mekhilta:* Be-Shelah, ed. Horovitz-Rabin, 156.

54. For uneasiness with human authority in relation to Divine authority, see Jud. 8:22–23; 1 Sam. 8:5ff.

55. See, e.g., Nahmanides, *Commentary on the Torah:* Lev. 26:11.

56. For a powerful theological statement against the prevailing medical absolutism of this secular age, see my late friend Paul Ramsey, *The Patient as Person* (New Haven, 1970), pp. 115, 156–57.

57. See B. Shabbat 133b re Exod. 15:2; *Beresheet Rabbah* 8, end.

58. See Arthur Marmorstein, *The Old Rabbinic Doctrine of God* (New York, 1968), 1:43ff.

59. See B. Yoma 85a; B. Yebamot 80a–b and Rashi, s.v. "mipnay sakanah"; B. Shabbat 151b; B. Nedarim 39b (the retort of R. Aha bar Hanina); Sirkes, *Bach* on *Tur: Hoshen Mishpat,* 426 re the limitations of the Maimonidean model for medical treatment.

60. See B. Sotah 14a re Gen. 18:1; B. Baba Kama 99b–100a re Exod. 18:20.

61. B. Kiddushin 39b. See B. Berakhot 34b re Isa. 64:3.

62. See B. Kiddushin 54a; *Shir Ha-Shirim Rabbah,* 8.13 re Num. 19:14.

63. See B. Pesahim 68b.

FOR FURTHER READING

Because the phenomenon of AIDS is rather recent, there has been no sustained Jewish reflection on its moral problems heretofore. This essay constitutes a beginning effort in this area and, therefore, is based exclusively on primary traditional Jewish sources. The articles listed below are some basic treatments of AIDS in the general literature. They proved helpful in formulating the issues that an examination of the classical Jewish texts required in order to be relevant in the contemporary context.

Institute of Medicine/National Academy of Sciences, Confronting AIDS: Directions for Public Health, Health Care, and Research (October 1986).

Institute of Medicine/National Academy of Sciences, Confronting AIDS: Update 1988 (1988).

American Journal of Public Health, 78 (April 1988). Entire issue devoted to AIDS.

Science 239 (Feb. 5, 1988), whole issue, especially LeRoy Walters' essay, "Ethical Issues in the Prevention and Treatment of HIV Infection and AIDS" (pp. 597–603).

"AIDS: Public Health and Civil Liberties," *Hastings Center Report,* Special Supplement (December 1986).

Zuger, Abigail and Steven Miles, "Physicians, AIDS, and Occupational Risk," *Journal of the American Medical Association* 258 (Oct. 9, 1987), pp. 1924–1928 with editorials (pp. 1939–1940).

Emanuel, Ezekiel, "Do Physicians Have an Obligation to Treat Patients with AIDS?" *New England Journal of Medicine* 318 (June 23, 1988), pp. 1686–1690.

Contemporary Jewish Demography

SIDNEY GOLDSTEIN

The current status and future prospects of the Jewish community in the United States are dependent, to a considerable degree, on its demographic structure—its size, distribution, and composition—and on factors affecting changes in these structural features. Like the general population of the United States, American Jewry has been undergoing steady alteration in its demographic structure. We can therefore expect substantial changes in family and household composition, in age composition, in economic activities and familial responsibilities for women and men, and in geographic distribution. The effects on the patterns and levels of births, deaths, and migration and in turn on the size, composition, and distribution of a population have enormous significance at both the local and national levels for the social, cultural, and religious viability of the community.

American Jews constitute the largest Jewish community in the world, but their total number has always been a matter of conjecture because the decennial census has never included a question on religious identity. Over the years, however, social scientists have developed a number of procedures for counting American Jews and estimating past and present Jewish population and trends. It is, of course, risky to project these estimates into the future; nevertheless, some trends are unmistakable.

The Jewish population of the United States grew from about one thousand in 1790 to 1 million by the end of the nineteenth century. This growth was dwarfed by the mass immigration that brought some 3 million East European Jews to the United States between 1880 and 1930 and raised the percentage of Jews in the total population from 0.5 in 1880 to an estimated 3.6 (4.2 million) at the end of the 1920s. The proportion of Jews in the United States population reached a peak of 3.7 percent in the mid-1930s. Over the next fifty years, curtailed immigration, reduced fertility, and the effects of assimilation and intermarriage considerably slowed this growth rate. By 1986, Jewish households (defined as households containing one or more Jews) included approximately 5.7 million Jews. Because of their much slower rate of growth than the total American population, by 1986 Jews constituted only about 2.4 percent of the total population.

The cessation of mass Jewish immigration to the United States affected not only the source of growth but also the generational composition of American Jewry. Despite the influx of refugees after World War II and the immigration of Soviet Jews, Israelis, and others in the 1970s and 1980s, more than 85 percent of the Jewish community today is native-born, and half or more of these are third- and fourth-generation Americans. This means that the American Jewish community must depend demographically very largely on itself to maintain its numbers. It means, too, that the demographic, sociocultural, and religious future of the community will depend, to a great degree, on how its American-born members react to the freedom to integrate spatially, economically, and socially into the larger American social structure.

Marriage and Fertility

American Jews have had the distinction of having smaller families than virtually any other ethnic and religious group in the country. Available evidence from the late nineteenth century points to a Jewish birth rate lower than that of the non-Jewish population; this differential seems to have persisted to the present day, although convergence in fertility behavior between Jews and non-Jews has been taking place as a result of more widespread acceptance of the smaller family and the greater prevalence of family planning. Yet Jews still tend to marry later, desire and expect to have small families, be more approving of contraception, and apparently practice birth control more often and more efficiently than most other groups. These patterns reflect in part the attitudes and practices of a highly urban, educated, and rational population. They may also represent a reaction to minority status and all that such status implies, socially and psychologically. Whatever the reasons, low fertility, particularly when it hovers at or goes below the replacement level of 2.1 children per married couple, could contribute to a decline in the total number of Jews.

Such decline may be accelerated as well by changing marital patterns, especially nonmarriage. In a recent review of fertility in the United States, Charles Westoff concluded that "it seems unlikely that the trend toward postponement of marriage has yet run its course." Citing the growing independence of women, the costs of marriage, and norms that permit couples to live together outside of marriage, he foresees further increases in average age at marriage rather than stabilization or decline.[1] Whether the current concerns with AIDS will change these norms remains to be seen. To what extent do Jews conform to these changing marriage patterns?

Young Jews still seem to place a high value on marriage and the family. A study of high school seniors showed that about 95 percent of the young Jewish men and women expect to marry, more than was true of the members of other religious groups; but a very large percentage of the Jews expect to marry later than non-Jews.[2] Jewish young people, like those in the general population, are postponing marriage, thereby raising serious doubts about whether they will realize the high levels of marriage indicated in their expressed expectations. Pooled national data documenting actual behavior for the 1960s and 1970s pointed strongly to a rise in age at marriage for Jews, a reduction in the percent ever married by the time they reached their forties, and a widening rather than narrowing gap between Jews and non-Jews.[3] In contrast to the 1960s, when 90 percent of Jews aged twenty-five to thirty-four were married, only 74 percent in this age group were married in the 1970s. For those aged thirty-five to forty-four, the level reached 97 percent in the 1960s but only 91 percent in the 1970s, 5 percentage points below the non-Jewish level.

Further evidence comes from the American Jewish Committee's study of Jewish college freshmen.[4] In a 1971 suvey of freshmen only 4 percent of the men and 20 percent of the women reported that they regarded it "essential or very important to get married in the next five years." By 1980, when most of these freshmen were in their late twenties, only 33 percent of the men and 42 percent of the women were married (another 2 and 5 percent had been married and were already divorced). By contrast, among non-Jews 56 percent of the men and 57 percent of the women were married. Only about 5 percent of the Jews were already parents compared to 25 percent of the non-Jews.

Jews' characteristic late marriage and low levels of marriage are also suggested by various recent community studies. The 1986 MetroWest New Jersey study found that whereas two-thirds of those now aged thirty-five to forty-four had been married by age twenty-five, just under half of those now twenty-five to thirty-four married before age twenty-five.[5] Whether the 30 percent in the twenty-five to thirty-four age group who are not yet married will eventually marry and thereby reduce the nonmarriage level to the low of 4 percent now characterizing the thirty-five to forty-four age group remains to be seen. The 1984 study of Philadelphia's Jewish community (Yancey and Goldstein, 1984) found that as many as 11 percent of the women and 16 percent of the men between ages thirty-one and forty had never married.[6]

The comparative data from the 1975 and 1985 Boston surveys are indicative of the recent changes that occurred in marriage patterns.[7] The 1975 study found that among those aged thirty to thirty-nine 88 percent married and only 9 percent were still single. By 1985, only 69 percent in this age group were married; almost one-quarter (23 percent) were still single. The national data and those for MetroWest, Philadelphia, and Boston suggest that, for a rising percentage of Jews, postponement of marriage may lead to eschewal of marriage, at least until the end of the reproductive period. Delay and possible avoidance of marriage may, in turn, have implications for overall fertility levels in the absence of any strong trend toward extramarital fertility among single Jewish women.

Moreover, the impact of changing marriage patterns on fertility may be compounded by the changing divorce rate. Although divorce is considerably lower among Jews than non-Jews, the proportions of divorced Jewish persons and of one-parent households has risen in recent years.[8] For example, in Philadelphia, 6 percent of all women and 7 percent of all men aged thirty-one to forty were separated or divorced. A 1985 study of Baltimore found 5 percent of the adults separated or divorced compared to under 2 percent in 1968; it also found that of those who were married, 15 percent had been married more than once whereas in 1968 only 8 percent of the married adults had experienced multiple marriages, although some of these remarriages undoubtedly involved widowed persons. Among those aged thirty to thirty-nine, the Boston studies for 1975 and 1985 found an increase from 3 to 8 percent in divorced and separated persons, and for those forty to forty-nine that figure had risen from 2 to 12 percent. Increases in percent divorced or separated were also observed for all older groups up to age seventy.[9]

Currently, experts debate whether Jewish fertility is or will be sufficiently high to assure replacement. All seem to agree that, at best, Jewish fertility will not exceed the replacement level of 2.1 children per mother. The possibility of subreplacement levels depends on how much confidence can be placed in past and recent behavior as predictors of future behavior and on whether expressions of fertility expectations are reliable indicators of future childbearing. Steven M. Cohen argued that "on the basis of past experience, it does seem safe to say that the completed Jewish birthrate for today's Jewish parents may remain well below the number needed for replacement." His explanation seems reasonable. "So long as middle-class urbanized Americans experience low birthrates, so will comparable Jews. Jewish birth patterns will generally follow those of the larger society as they have in the past."[10]

More recently, citing data from the 1982 National Survey of Family Growth, as well as from earlier surveys, Calvin Goldscheider and Frances K. Goldscheider argue that Jewish fertility is likely to remain below that of Protestants and Catholics but that the 2.1 average number of children expected by currently and ever married women does not point to below replacement level fertility. They claim that this conclusion is reinforced by the findings that Jews in a 1972 national sample of high school seniors expect about two children on average and continued to do so in 1979.[11]

Yet the Goldscheiders acknowledge that the accuracy of the predictors of replacement level fertility will depend on the proportion of Jewish women who marry. If a substantial percentage of Jewish women do not marry or do not have children outside marriage, the fertility of the married, even if it averages 2.1 children, will not be adequate to replace all the married and unmarried. Moreover, the 2.1 average may itself be too high. For example, a 1985 study of Baltimore found 12 percent of Jewish women aged thirty-five to forty-four still childless and 9 percent of women aged twenty-five to forty-four expecting to remain childless; a substantial percentage expected to have only one child.[12] The 1975 and 1985 Boston surveys also provide some insights into fertility. The comparisons suggest that "Jewish adults, along with postponing marriage, are also postponing having children, and, apparently, more are having no children."[13]

There has been speculation that changing family values associated with the later stages of the feminist movement are leading to a greater acceptance of children in the American family in the mid-1980s than earlier and that this trend may influence Jewish family size as well. Such an expectation is not warranted for the American population, however, according to comparisons of the results of national surveys conducted by the U.S. Bureau of the Census in 1985 and those conducted in earlier decades.[14] For example, in 1976, an average of 2,218 children had been born per 1,000 white women age thirty to thirty-four and a total of 2,390 per 1,000 was expected. By 1985, women in this age group had averaged only 1,612 children per 1,000 and expected a total of only 1,979, which is below replacement.

On the basis of such evidence for the American population as a whole, Charles Westoff (1986:558) finds "little basis for assuming that the low level of fertility in this country is a demographic aberration." To the contrary, he argues that the basic social forces that underlay the historical decline in fertility—industrialization and development of a service economy, the transition of children from being producers to being consumers, universal education, the replacement of traditional values by an ethos of rationality, the changing functions of the family and the improved status of women, and improved contraceptive technology—all point to continuing low level of fertility. He suggests that, if anything, the greater uncertainty is how low fertility will yet fall. Although all predictions are subject to error, Westoff's assumptions, like those cited by Cohen for the Jews, provide forceful arguments against expecting a return to above replacement fertility, particularly among Jews, who have been in the forefront of the decline in fertility. Given the patterns of late marriage and high educational levels that characterize the Jewish population, there is no convincing evidence that Jews will deviate from the pattern of low fertility that seems likely to continue among whites as a whole.[15]

Based on the available evidence, I believe that Jewish fertility levels are highly unlikely to forge ahead of those of non-Jewish whites, for whom below-replacement fertility levels are projected. It seems reasonable to conclude that Jewish fertility will not exceed replacement level in the near future and that, more likely, it will be at somewhat below replacement. It must be stressed that even if fertility is at replacement level, maintenance of population size is not assured if losses occur concurrently through the high mortality of an aging population and the impact of assimilation and intermarriage.

Intermarriage

Until fairly recently, the Jewish community has been much more concerned with the effects of intermarriage than of fertility on demographic survival. If marital assimilation takes place at a high rate, American Jewry faces demographic losses both through the assimilation of the Jewish partner and the loss of children born to such a marriage. Even if the Jewish partner does not assimilate, intermarriage is likely to reduce the Jewish rate of growth unless extensive conversions of non-Jewish spouses occur; intermarriage may also reduce growth because fewer children will be born Jewish. Regrettably, there is no fully reliable and recent set of information on the rates of intermarriage and its impact on identity. The evidence we do have suggests that the level of intermarriage, the extent of conversion, and the impact of conversion and mixed marriage on Jewish identity vary considerably, depending on the size, location, age, and social cohesiveness of a particular community. Despite these variations, virtually every study in recent decades points to rising levels both of intermarriage among young, native-born Americans and of conversion to Judaism. Evidence from the most recent studies, however, suggests that both may have reached plateaus and that conversions may be declining.

The results of the 1970–71 National Jewish Population Study (NJPS) indicated that 7 percent of all Jews married at the time of the survey were in mixed marriages. This overall level was not unusually high, but the study also showed that intermarriages rose sharply from 4–5 percent of those marrying between 1950 and 1959 to 10 percent of the 1960–64 marriage cohort and to 22 percent of those marrying in 1965–69.[16]

The effect of intermarriage on demographic growth is largely determined by the extent of conversion to Judaism by the non-Jewish partner and by the extent to which children born within such marriages are raised as Jews. Overall, the evidence from the NJPS suggested that a substantial proportion of intermarriages resulted in conversion of the non-Jew, especially among the younger groups, which have a higher intermarriage rate. In an even larger number, the non-Jewish spouse identified as Jewish. Furthermore, about half of the children from such marriages were being raised as Jews.

In contrast to the NJPS's relatively optimistic conclusions regarding the impact of intermarriage, a 1976–77 eight-city study of 446 intermarried couples concluded that intermarriage represented a threat to Jewish continuity.[17] The evidence pointed to low conversion rates, a low level of Jewish conduct and practice in mixed marriages, a low proportion of children being regarded as Jewish, and most of the children not being socialized as Jews. The study stressed the need for outreach programs designed to provide more opportunities to enhance the Jewish content of the family life of the intermarried and especially to strengthen the likelihood that children would identify as Jews.

Community studies undertaken since the NJPS show that rates of mixed marriage continue to vary inversely with age and are generally higher among younger persons than those reported in NJPS. But the levels continue to differ considerably from community to community. A reasonable estimate seems to be that the average current intermarriage rate for American Jews is between 25 and 30 percent, indicating that in 45 percent of all newly married couples one partner is not Jewish. For example, in Baltimore, of all married persons, 26 percent aged thirty-five to forty-four and 36 percent of the youngest cohort, aged twenty-five to thirty-four; were not born Jewish; only about 30 percent of non-Jewish partners in the intermarriages of the youngest cohort converted to Judaism.[18] Also important is the evidence that 13 percent of the Jewish partners converted away from Judaism. Significantly, less than a majority of the children in households in which the non-Jewish partner did not convert were identified as Jewish. If rates of conversion are, in fact, declining and if most of the children in such marriages are not identifying as Jews, the impact of intermarriage on Jewish demographics may become more negative than in the past.

The MetroWest New Jersey study also found a steady rise in intermarriages, from only 6 percent of individuals married before 1964 to 14 percent of those married in 1975–80 and one-third of those married since 1980.[19] Concurrently, the proportion of intermarried households in which the non-Jewish spouse converted has declined. From a high of 44 percent of all marriages in 1971–74, the percentage converting declined to 27 percent of those marrying in 1975–80 and only 12 percent of those married since 1980.

The recent Boston data also point to rising levels of intermarriage. The overall level of intermarriage reported for adults married only once is 15 percent, but this figure rises from virtually zero among couples who married before 1956, to 10 percent of those who married between 1966 and 1970, and up to just under 30 percent of those marrying between 1976 and 1985. Moreover, among those married in 1985, only 14 percent of the non-Jewish spouses converted to Judaism; unfortunately, no comparative data are presented for the earlier survey. Among second marriages the percent involving a spouse not raised Jewish rose from none of the small number who entered second marriages before 1965 to over half of those doing so after 1965.[20]

Because of the limitations in the data on intermarriage, however, these patterns are suggestive at best. We do not yet know definitely if intermarriage leads to a quantitative gain or loss for the Jewish community. Of all items that warrant further research, intermarriage undoubtedly ranks among the very highest. And as the views of various segments of the Jewish community diverge with respect to who among the intermarried and their children should be counted as Jewish, the task of undertaking research on the subject will become even more complex.

Residential Mobility

At a time when American Jewish fertility has reached probably its lowest level and when intermarriage and assimilation may be threatening the demographic and socioreligious vitality of the community, increasing levels of mobility and greater geographic dispersion of the population nationally and locally are new threats and new challenges. According to the NJPS, about three-fourths of all adult Jews in 1971 no longer lived in their city of birth, and one-third of all adults had moved within the previous five to six years.[21]

More recent data, albeit at the local level, confirm the mobility patterns identified by the NJPS. Statistics from the 1985 Boston survey indicate that only 45 percent of adults had been living in the same town for ten years or more. This percentage varied from only 22 percent of those aged twenty-one to thirty-nine to over 60 percent of those aged forty and over. As many as 30 percent of all adults had moved into the metropolitan area within the ten years preceding the survey, but the levels were much higher among the younger segments of the population, 60 percent of those aged twenty-one to twenty-nine and 38 percent of those aged thirty to thirty-nine. Furthermore, half of those in their twenties reported that they would likely move out of Greater Boston in the next five years, and 64 percent reported that they were very or fairly likely to do so within the next ten years. The data for Greater Boston corroborate a pattern of relatively high levels of mobility among Jews.[22]

The very features that help explain the mobility of Jews in Greater Boston—being better educated, more professional and managerial, more native-born, and living in smaller households— are also likely to be conducive to higher Jewish mobility nation-wide. The patterns of redistribution shown by the Boston data—strong movement to the South and West by those leaving the area—conform to those characterizing the country as a whole.

For the first half of the twentieth century, Jews were heavily concentrated in the Northeast. In 1930, 69 percent lived in the region. Compared to the general American population, proportionally fewer lived in the North Central (20 percent) and southern regions (8 percent), and about as small a proportion lived in the West (5 percent).[23] By 1986, the Jewish population was distributed more nearly like the total American population. The Northeast still contained a disproportionate share of American Jewry (53 percent) but had declined substantially, as had the percentage in the North Central region (11 percent). Growing percentages lived in the South (18 percent) and the West (17 percent).[24] Since the education obtained by American Jews and the occupations they now enter often lead to movement away from family and out of centers of Jewish population concentration, these shifts in regional distribution are likely to become accentuated in the future.

The migration effects of changing educational and occupational patterns may be compounded by a higher marriage age, a lower percent marrying and a higher percent divorcing, and low fertility, all of which are conducive to greater mobility.

The Jewish population is being redistributed not only across regions but also within and between metropolitan and nonmetropolitan areas. Jewish residential clustering in a limited number of urban neighborhoods is changing as Jews participate in the general suburbanization movement. Jewish neighborhoods in central city areas and in older suburbs have experienced population decline as newer outer suburbs have grown.

The metropolitan and national patterns of dispersion have probably been accentuated by the settlement of growing numbers of Jews in small communities throughout the nation. In the past, small communities have had great difficulty retaining their populations, Jewish and non-Jewish. Like their neighbors, Jews have left to seek better educational, occupational, and social opportunities in larger cities. Many of those who remained small-town residents tended to minimize their Jewishness and often intermarried or assimilated.[25] Beginning in the 1970s, Americans as a whole entered a new pattern of population redistribution with many moving to smaller towns and cities and away from metropolitan centers. Available evidence suggests that, consonant with this general development, a number of small Jewish communities have once again been gaining populations, and more such communities seem to be appearing. Some Jews who have sought the tranquillity and slower pace of small-town life at the same time seem to be developing a more active identification with Judaism in their new surroundings.

According to the *American Jewish Year Book*, there were 469 places with fewer than five thousand Jewish inhabitants in 1985. Indeed, 348 had fewer than a thousand Jews, and, of these, 283 had fewer than five hundred.[26] It is also fair to assume that considerably more such small communities exist which have either not yet entered the statistics of the *Year Book* or are buried in the statistics referring to larger metropolitan areas and states. Overall, the Jewish American population has become more dispersed. Although residential clustering will continue in metropolitan areas with large Jewish populations, Jewish population movement must nonetheless be considered a key variable in any assessment of the future strength of the American Jewish community. On one hand, high levels of movement and especially repeated movement may weaken individual ties to local communities and institutions and reduce the strength of Jewish identity, compounding tendencies to high rates of intermarriage and assimilation. High turnover could also affect the viability of individual communities and of the American Jewish community as a whole. On the other hand, the shifts associated with population movement may give smaller communities the density and diversity of Jewish population needed to maintain and possibly strengthen basic institutions essential for group survival and enrichment. In either case, it seems clear that migration rather than fertility and intermarriage may well be the key dynamic affecting the vitality of Jewish communities and individual Jewish identity in the next several decades. Until we have more insights into its full implications and the extent to which policies can be designed to cope with them, while also recognizing that such movement has contributed to the development of a national Jewish community, dealing with this key demographic process may remain one of the major challenges the community faces.

Structural Variables

Size, distribution, and density are critical variables determining the strength and vitality of any segment of the population, but a wide range of demographic, social, and economic variables also significantly affects the community's current viability and future survival. Among these, age, education, occupation, and generation status have particular relevance for Jews. Emerging as an added variable is the potential religious polarization of the community.

Age. Of all the demographic variables, age is the most basic. Since at least the 1950s, the Jewish population of the United States has had an older age structure than the general white population. U. O. Schmelz and Sergio Della Pergola estimated that by 1980 over 15 percent of America's Jews were aged sixty-five and over; they projected a rise to 17 percent by the year 2000. Equally significant is the projected sharp increase in the "old aged" (seventy-five and over) from about 314,000 in 1980 to 414,000 in the year 2000.[27] Such an aged population will have a depressing effect on growth rates and will raise levels of overall mortality. Aging will also pose special challenges for the Jewish community to find the financial resources necessary to cope with increasing needs for health and social services, especially if a noticeable proportion of Jewish aged live below the poverty level.

Educational Attainment. At the same time that the population has been aging, it has been becoming more educated. The high premium Jews nationwide place on education is documented by several comparisons. The 1980 census reported that 67 percent of the U.S. population had a high school education or less and only 18 percent had at least a college degree. By contrast, not a single Jewish community in the comparative assessment reported in the *American Jewish Yearbook* or in surveys undertaken since then reported more than 45 percent of its population with only a high school or lower education. Most communities reported that close to 50 percent or more of their adult members had a college degree. In fact, in all but three communities, the percent with advanced degrees exceeded the percent in the total population with any college degree.[28]

That such high educational achievement has become accentuated over time is evidenced in the Boston comparative data. The percent with only a high school education or less declined from 55 in 1965 to only 19 in 1985. By contrast, the percent with an advanced degree grew from 12 to 29 percent over the same interval, and those with one to four years of college from 32 to 51 percent. That the trend is likely to persist is suggested by statistics for the twenty-five-to-forty-four-year age group, among whom only 11 percent stopped at a high school diploma or lower level; 42 percent already had advanced degrees, and another 42 percent had some college education.[29] Boston may not be typical of the United States as a whole, but evidence from other communities points in similar directions.

Several implications emerge. First, both nationally and locally, the organized Jewish community faces an ever more educated Jewish public, quite different from the less educated, more largely immigrant population of earlier decades. Second, to the extent that education may be correlated with greater integration into the American scene, educational level becomes a key variable around which to focus efforts to enhance Jewish identity, especially during the four-to-eight-year period when undergraduate and graduate students are away from their family of orientation and before most have formed their own families. Third, since education is the key to occupational choice and will lead many to seek opportunities away from their hometowns, high levels of mobility will continue to characterize the Jewish population. The impact of education will be accentuated as more Jews obtain advanced degrees that lead to professional employment involving working for others—situations in which personal advancement, careers for spouses, and the transfer demands associated with national and multinational enterprises require repeated movement to achieve specified goals. That education has such an effect is reflected by the occupational profile of the Jewish population.

Occupational Affiliation. As has been true for decades, Jews are disproportionally concentrated in high white-collar positions. In 1980, the Bureau of the Census found 29 percent of the adult population of the United States to be in professional and managerial positions. Jewish community studies have indicated that between half and three-fourths of Jews are so employed. By contrast, the 1980 census found just under half of all Americans to be engaged in blue-collar work, but it was a rare Jewish community that reported more than 10 percent of Jews so employed, and for some it was below 5 percent. Obviously, the high education Jews obtain is associated with commensurate placement in the occupational hierarchy—although this does not necessarily imply that specific skills are fully used.

Some indication of the direction of change in occupational affiliation is evidenced by the Boston surveys. Among males, the percent employed as professionals rose from 32 in 1965 to 46 in 1985, while the percent earning a living as managers declined from 37 to 22. For women, the percentage of both professionals and managers increased. Although the percent of males employed as clerical and sales workers fluctuated over the twenty years between 15 and 20 percent, women experienced a substantial shift out of this category, with the percent so employed declining from 53 to 31 percent.

Particularly noteworthy for the Boston data is the increasing participation of women in the labor force, from 51 percent in 1975 to 60 percent in 1985. The differences by age are especially striking, increasing from 57 percent of those aged fifty to sixty-four, to two-thirds of those forty to forty-nine, to 85 percent of those eighteen to twenty-nine. Significant, too, of those employed, two-thirds of all women worked full time, as many as 70 percent of those aged forty to forty-nine and three-fourths of those eighteen to twenty-nine. That only 53 percent of employed women aged thirty to thirty-nine worked full time probably reflects the presence of young children at home.

Clearly, increasing female employment and increased professionalization of the labor force as a whole were the two major changes characterizing employment of Jews in Boston between 1965 and 1985. To the extent that these patterns hold for Jewish men and women in the United States as a whole and that many professional occupations are associated with frequent mobility, the reliance on the professional communities as surrogates in place of the religious group may well increase at the price of less involvement in the local organized Jewish community.[30] Together, the higher education, greater professionalization and mobility, and consequent conversion of the Jewish community from a set of local constituencies to a national community present a major challenge to the vitality of the local community as well as to the strength of individual Jewish identity.[31]

Generational Changes

A major factor affecting the continued vitality of the American Jewish community in the past has been the transfusions received through immigration. Now, increasingly third- and fourth-generation Jews face the American scene without large-scale outside reinforcement. Although this emergent pattern has been somewhat modified in recent decades by the influx of Jews from the Soviet Union, Israel, and Iran, the full extent to which this immigration affects the demographic composition and sociological character of American Jewry, especially at the local level, remains to be documented. These groups may add to the number of Jews or compensate a bit for population declines. But either because of deficiences in Jewish background and experience or lack of integration with the organized Jewish community, their numerical contribution may not be matched by contributions to other aspects of Jewish communal life. Despite the influx of Russian and Israeli immigrants, the foreign-born component is decreasing over time as older immigrants die. In most communities, the foreign-born now constitute only between 11 and 18 percent.[32]

The sharp changes in the generational composition of the population suggest that the community's future depends to a great degree on how its third and higher generation members react to the freedom to integrate into the American social structure. Whether trends toward assimilation are being stabilized, reversed, or accelerated and how the expression of ties to the Jewish community is changing require continuing monitoring and assessment.

Religious Polarization

Concerns with effects of changing patterns of demographic growth and composition may pale in the shadow of what could be a much more serious challenge for American Jewry. As we approach the twenty-first century, Irving Greenberg's key question may be particularly relevant: "Will there be one Jewish people by the year 2000?" If sociological forces are left unchecked, he warns, "the Jewish people will be split apart into two, mutually divided hostile groups who are unable or unwilling to marry each other."[33]

Will divisions stemming from different attitudes toward conversion, partilineal descent, and divorce so affect the definition of who is a Jew that a substantial segment of the projected 5.0 to 5.5 million American Jews will have their status as Jews questioned by another segment? If as many as 15 to 20 percent of all Jews were to be classified as marginal, as Greenberg suggests, the implications for the unity of the American Jewish community and for the potential assimilation of those outside the core group would be very serious indeed. Such polarization of the community would have critical implications for social interaction among Jews, for survival as one people, and, finally, for survival demographically at a level at which we can remain a key segment not only of the total American community but of world Jewry. From a research perspective, such a situation would add immensely to the complex tasks of defining and measuring intermarriage and of ascertaining the actual number of Jews in the United States.

Conclusion

Whether American Jewry faces greater assimilation or is transforming itself into a different but still dynamic community is the focus of ongoing debate in which the community's future demographics are a key concern. In combination, the current patterns of low fertility, high levels of intermarriage, lowered residential density, and changing composition can potentially weaken the demographic base of the United States Jewish population. This need not be so. To the extent that Jews retain a comparatively close-knit, ethnic-religious identification within the total society, the potential for continued vitality remains. Stability of numbers or even declining numbers need not constitute a fundamental threat to the maintenance of a strong Jewish community and to high levels of individual Jewish identity.

A stable or larger population base would certainly make the effort to ensure Jewish identity and vitality easier. Concern with numbers is especially relevant at the local level. It is unlikely, however, that the Jewish American community as a whole can do very much to control the changing fertility levels or the patterns of redistribution because these processes very largely reflect reactions to a wide and complex range of social, economic, and normative changes in the larger American society. It is perhaps more important for the community to undertake and maintain fuller and more scientifically sound assessments of the implications of the whole range of demographic developments and that it be prepared, on the basis of such evaluations, to develop new institutional forms designed, at a minimum, to mitigate the negative effects of population decline and dispersal. Ideally, these efforts should also increase opportunities for Jewish self-identification and for greater participation of individuals in organized Jewish life. Through such steps, the community will help ensure that the changes that do occur still allow for a meaningful balance between being Jewish and being American.

Two recent reviews of the quality of Jewish life in the United States and of the accuracy of projections about the future demographics of American Jewry have very correctly sighted the heart of the issue. Charles Liebman stresses that mere biological survival of Jews in the United States over the next century, a prediction which few, if any, reputable demographers would contest, is not synonymous with assurance of a high-quality Jewish life in these years. As he correctly argues, concern with numbers is relevant only as these numbers affect the quality of American Jewish life.[34] The key concern about the future of the community must focus on maintaining the quality of that life. Although numbers, composition, and distribution are important factors affecting the outcome, they certainly are, as David Gordis has emphasized, "preconditions," not "conditions." As he has effectively expressed it, "The determinant of the Jewish future will not be demography or affiliation statistics. The key will be the internal character of Jewish life, the degree to which it affects the way Jews live their lives, the content of Judaism for Jews."[35] Institutional forces, operating within the constraints as well as the strengths imposed by demographic conditions, can still contribute to a vital, creative community.

Notes

I wish to thank the editors of *Judaism* for permission to use materials from vol. 36, no. 2 (Spring 1987) of that journal for this article.

1. Charles Westoff, "Fertility in the United States," *Science* 234 (October 31, 1986), p. 556.
2. Calvin Goldscheider and Frances K. Goldscheider, "Family Size Expectations of Young American Jewish Adults," paper presented at Ninth World Congress of Jewish Studies, Jerusalem, August 1985.
3. Steven M. Cohen, *American Modernity and Jewish Identity* (New York, 1983).
4. Geraldine Rosenfield, "Jewish College Freshmen: An Analysis of Three Studies," mimeo (New York, 1984).
5. Michael Rappeport and Gary A. Tobin, *A Population Study of the Jewish Community of Metro West New Jersey, 1986* (East Orange [N.J.], 1987).
6. William L. Yancey and Ira Goldstein, *The Jewish Population of the Greater Philadelphia Area* (Philadelphia, 1984).
7. Sherry Israel, "Boston's Jewish Community: The 1985 CJP Demographic Survey," unpublished report, Combined Jewish Philanthropies of Boston, 1987.
8. Gary A. Tobin and Alvin Chenkin, "Recent Jewish Community Population Studies: A Roundup," *American Jewish Year Book* (Philadelphia, 1985), Vol 85, pp. 154–78.
9. Israel, "Boston's Jewish Community."
10. Cohen, *American Modernity and Jewish Identity,* pp. 118. 120; see also Steven M. Cohen and Calvin Goldscheider, "Jews, More or Less," *Moment* Vol. 9 (September 1984), pp. 41–46; Sidney Goldstein, "American Jewish Demography: Inconsistencies That Challenge," paper presented at Ninth World Congress of Jewish Studies, Jerusalem, August 1985.
11. William D. Mosher and Calvin Goldscheider, "Contraceptive Patterns of Religious and Racial Groups in the United States, 1955–76: Convergence and Distinctiveness," *Studies in Family Planning* Vol. 15 (May–June 1984), pp 101–11; Goldscheider and Goldscheider, "Family Size Expectations."

12. Gary A. Tobin, *A Demographic Study of the Jewish Community of Greater Baltimore* (Baltimore, 1986).

13. Israel, "Boston's Jewish Community," p. 19.

14. U.S. Bureau of the Census, "Fertility of American Women: June 1985," *Current Population Reports*, Ser. P-20, no. 406 (Washington, D.C., 1986).

15. Westoff, "Fertility in the United States," pp. 554–59; U. O. Schmelz and Sergio Della Pergola, "Some Basic Trends in the Demography of U.S. Jews: A Re-Examination," paper prepared for AJC Conference on New Perspectives in American Jewish Sociology, Findings and Implications, New York, May 1986. Fertility among the ultra-Orthodox is an exception to the low fertility rates characterizing Jews as a whole. The high birth rates of this group, reflecting their strong emphasis on the family and on traditional roles for women and their much lower use of birth control, do not, however, significantly affect overall Jewish fertility levels because the ultra-Orthodox are a relatively small percentage of the total population. Should this percentage increase in the future, as their growing number of children mature and form their own families, the impact of their higher fertility may be felt more strongly.

16. Schmelz and Della Pergola, "Some Basic Trends."

17. Egon Mayer, *Children of Intermarriage: A Study in Patterns of Identification and Family Life* (New York, 1983).

18. Tobin, *Demographic Study.*

19. Rappeport and Tobin, *Population Study.*

20. Israel, "Boston's Jewish Community."

21. Sidney Goldstein, "Jews in the United States: Perspectives from Demography," *American Jewish Year Book* (Philadelphia, 1981), Vol 81, pp. 3–59.

22. Israel, "Boston's Jewish Community."

23. Goldstein, "Jews in the United States."

24. Barry A. Kosmin, Paul Ritterband, and Jeffrey Scheckner, "Jewish Population in the United States," *American Jewish Year Book* (Philadelphia, 1987), Vol. 87, pp. 164–191.

25. Eugene Schoenfield, "Problems and Potentials," in Abraham D. Lavender, ed., *A Coat of Many Colors* (Westport, Conn., 1977), pp. 7–72.

26. "Jewish Population in the United States, 1985," *American Jewish Year Book* (Philadelphia, 1986), Vol 86, pp. 223–230.

27. Schmelz and Della Pergola, "Some Basic Trends."

28. Tobin and Chenkin, "Recent Jewish Community Population Studies."

29. Israel, "Boston's Jewish Community."

30. Cohen, *American Modernity and Jewish Identity*, pp. 89–92.

31. Sidney Goldstein, "Demography of American Jewry: Implications for a National Society," paper presented at the Sidney Hollander Memorial Colloquium on the Emergence of a Continental Jewish Community—Implications for Federations, Parsippany, N.J., 1987.

32. Tobin and Chenkin, "Recent Jewish Community Population Studies."

33. Irving Greenberg, "Jews in the Year 2000," *Rhode Island Jewish Herald*, July 1985.

34. Charles S. Liebman, "A Grim Outlook," in *The Quality of Jewish Life—Two Views*, Jewish Sociology Papers (New York, 1987), pp. 33–55.

35. David M. Gordis, "Triumph or Tragedy: Contemporary American Jewish Life,"*Women's League Outlook* (Winter 1987), p. 30.

FOR FURTHER READING

1. Schmelz, U.O. and Sergio DellaPergola—"The Demographic Consequences of U.S. Jewish Population Trends" *American Jewish Year Book*, (New York & Philadelphia, 1983), pp 141–187. An excellent overview of American Jewish demographic trends by the top demographers at the Hebrew University in Jerusalem. Raises many important questions and policy issues pertaining to U.S. Jewry.

2. *American Jewish Year Book*—published yearly by the Jewish Publication Society and the American Jewish Committee. This encyclopedic annual contains important articles related to Jewish demography on a regular basis. It also contains estimates of Jewish population in the U.S. and Canada as well as the rest of the world every year. The U.S. estimates are broken down by state and city.

3. *Jewish Continuity and Change* by Calvin Goldscheider. Bloomington, 1986. An examination of the impact of the forces of modernization on the American Jewish community. Demographic changes put into a theoretical framework by an optimist.

4. Tobin, Gary A. and Alvin Chenkin—"Recent Jewish Community Population Studies: A Roundup", *American Jewish Year Book* (New York & Philadelphia, 1985) pp 154–178. A review of the results of the community studies done in most major US communities in the 1970's and 80's. Good summary statement on issues such as household size, age, gender, marital status, education, occupation, income and religious identification of U.S. Jews. Important because there has been no national Jewish population survey since 1970.

5. *Boston's Jewish Community*—The 1985 CJP Demographic Study—Compiled by Sherry Israel (Combined Jewish Philanthropies of Greater Boston: Boston, Mass) 1987. Demographers and sociologists of the Jews love Boston because they did community studies in 1965, 1975 and 1985. The wealth of the comparative data is particularly available in this compendium of the findings of the 1985 survey. A model community study for those interested in reading about one large center of Jewish population in the U.S.

6. *Papers in Jewish Demography*—1985, edited by U.O. Schmelz and S. DellaPergola, Jerusalem, 1989. Papers presented in the demography section of the World Congress of Jewish Studies in Jerusalem in 1985. Many of the articles are about North American Jewry and the methodology used to study it.

7. Goldstein, Sidney—"American Jewish Demography: Inconsistencies That Challenge", *Jerusalem Letter/Viewpoints* (Jerusalem 16 October 1986). A good summary of the policy implications seen by the distinguished author of the article in this book, based on his analysis of the current demographic situation of American Jews.

8. Monson, Rela Geffen and Daniel J. Elazar, "Jewish Demography—Realities and Options", *Jerusalem Letter/Viewpoints* (Jerusalem, December 1987). A good companion piece to number 7. Originally written as a background piece for lay leaders attending the first World Conference on Jewish Demography in Jerusalem in 1987. Provides a summary of the demographic research on American Jewry until that year.

Demography Worldwide

U. O. SCHMELZ

Documentation

The demographic statistics of Israeli Jews are copious and reliable, yet the respective information on the Diaspora is deficient in quantity and quality. By now only a minority of the Diaspora countries specify the Jews as a religious or ethnic group in their population censuses, and hardly any vital or migratory statistics on Diaspora Jews are complied officially. Most of the demographic information available on Diaspora Jews comes from Jewish sources. Particularly important are sample surveys of local or countrywide Jewish populations, but the available information is incomplete, uncoordinated, and of varying quality. It poses serious evaluation problems concerning the comparability of different data sets. Yet through perserving study at the Hebrew University's Institute of Contemporary Jewry in Jerusalem, it has become possible to create a fairly coherent and continually updated body of demographic information on the Jewish Diaspora and, in conjunction with the Israeli data, on world Jewry as a whole.

There is a good deal of similarity between some of the basic demographic trends thus ascertained for most of the Diaspora countries. Correspondence is also found between comparable information on the Jews and the general populations of the developed Diaspora countries. Although the main features of the demographic situation and trends in the Diaspora are sufficiently clear, caution is required as to the exactness of many of the available figures.

Size and Geographical Distribution of World Jewish Population

The world's Jews have numbered about 13 million in recent years. During the 1970s their numbers were still growing slowly because of natural increase in Israel. Although the Diaspora was shrinking, by now a stage of zero population growth has been reached.

The major regional Jewries in descending order of the Jewish population, as estimated for 1985, are (in millions): North America, 6.0; Israel, 3.5; Eastern Europe and the Balkans, 1.7; Western Europe, 1.0. The Jews of Latin America now total fewer than 0.5 million. Only small numbers remain in Asia outside Israel and in Africa outside the Republic of South Africa (see Table 1).

Though the Jews are characterized by unique geographical scattering, marked concentrations are found within this dispersal. Seventy-four countries are known to have more than 100 Jewish residents each, but 83 percent of world Jewry lives in the three countries with over 1 million Jews and 95 percent in the nine

Table 1. *Number of Jews in the World, by Regions and Major Countries (rough estimates), 1985*

Region or country	Absolute number	Percent in world	Percent in Diaspora
World	12,960,000	100.0	—
Israel	3,517,000	27.1	—
Diaspora	9,443,000	72.9	100.0
Americas	6,458,000	49.9	68.4
North America	6,010,000	46.4	63.7
United States	5,700,000	44.0	60.4
Canada	310,000	2.4	3.3
Latin America	448,000	3.5	4.7
Argentina	226,000	1.7	2.4
Brazil	100,000	0.8	1.1
Europe	2,721,000	21.0	28.8
Western Europe	1,046,000	8.1	11.1
France	530,000	4.1	5.6
Great Britain	328,000	2.5	3.5
Eastern Europe & Balkans[a]	1,675,000	12.9	17.7
Soviet Union	1,545,000	11.9	16.4
Asia (excl. Israel)[a] and Africa	184,000	1.4	2.0
South Africa	117,000	0.9	1.2
Oceania	80,000	0.6	0.8

[a] The Asian territories of USSR and Turkey are included in Eastern Europe and Balkans.

countries with 100,000 or more Jews (similarly, 94 percent of Diaspora Jewry reside in the respective eight Diaspora countries). These are, in descending order of Jewish population as of 1985, United States, 5,700,000; Israel, 3,517,000; Soviet Union, 1,545,000;[1] France, 530,000; Great Britain, 328,000; Canada, 310,000; Argentina, 226,000; South Africa, 117,000; Brazil, approximately 100,000. Geographical concentrations of many Jews, despite the scattering of others, are found not only with regard to entire countries but also on the level of cities and neighborhoods. The majority of Jews in the Diaspora and Israel live in metropolitan areas, where their number exceeds 100,000. Within such areas or individual cities, a conspicuous tendency prevails for the Jews to be more densely represented in certain neighborhoods.

In 1985 the Jews formed a majority of 82 percent in Israel (63 percent including the Administered Areas), but in no Diaspora country did their proportion reach as much as 2.5 percent of the total population. It exceeded 1 percent in three countries only: United States, 2.4 percent; Canada, 1.2 percent; and Gibraltar, 2.1 percent. Elsewhere the Jews accounted for less than 1 percent and often far less than one per thousand of the entire population.

Smaller Jewish populations appear to be prone to assimilation and mixed marriage. In the open societies of today, the scattering of a part of the Jews within countries and cities as well as their low proportions among the inhabitants of most of their localities of residence (New York being a notable exception) constitute risk factors for Jewish cohesion. The great geographical mobility of Diaspora Jews within countries and metropolitan areas, which is reported particularly from the United States, creates problems for maintaining existing Jewish institutions or setting up new ones when considerable numbers of Jews move to other localities or neighborhoods.

Demographic Dynamics

Because striking differences prevail between Israel and the Diaspora, they will be considered separately.

Diaspora The demographic continuity of subpopulations such as Diaspora Jewries depends on two sets of factors: (1) biological ones—births and deaths, the former strongly linked to the social institution of marriage; and (2) the ability to preserve group identity and transmit it to future generations.

The general populations of the developed countries, which are the reference frame for most Diaspora Jewries, are experiencing changes in marriage patterns related to greater permissiveness in sexual matters: formal marriages are postponed or not contracted at all, cohabitation of informal couples is on the rise, as are divorces and single-person or single-parent households of divorcées. These features have negative repercussions on fertility that are not offset by some remarriage of divorcées.

Altogether a momentous decline has taken place in the levels of desired and actual fertility, due among other determinants to the changed position of women—regarding educational attainment, labor force participation, career aspirations, and family roles—and the widespread use of modern contraceptives. Since the 1970s the fertility of most developed countries has been below the average of 2.1 children per woman (including the unmarried) that is required, at minimal mortality, for demographic replacement of a population in the long run. For instance, average fertility has been around only 1.7 children among white women in the United States since 1973; in West Germany it is now 1.3. These examples illustrate that in modern populations subreplacement fertility may go together with economic success and affluence. This finding is of relevance for the Diaspora Jews as well.

Prolonged low fertility produces aging of the respective populations. Aging in turn depresses the birth rate because there are relatively fewer people in the reproductive ages but raises the death rate because of the relative frequency of the elderly. It thus impairs the natural increase that can become negative when more persons die than are born, as happens now in many Diaspora populations.

In keeping with these general changes in nuptiality patterns, the Diaspora Jews are less likely to marry or at any rate postpone marriage and get divorced more often than before, with negative effects on fertility. The fertility of Jews is consistently found to be even lower than that of the surrounding population. In particular, analysis of the results of the many local Jewish community surveys conducted in the United States in recent years clearly shows that Jewish fertility is far below replacement level. And the aging of the Diaspora Jews exceeds that of the corresponding general populations.

Moreover, in our secular age and with the Jews being a small minority nearly everywhere in the Diaspora, they are exposed to assimilation with a resultant net loss (more secessions than accessions) to Jewish populations or a weakening of Jewish identity that can lead to the same result later, whether in the present or in a coming generation. Of particular importance in this context are out-marriages of Jews with non-Jewish partners. Nowadays these mostly take place without religious conversion of either spouse before the wedding. If so, a "mixed" couple is formed, and if it remains mixed, the demographic outcome for the Jewish population is deferred to the next generation. There are indications that mixed marriages are even less fertile than homogamous Jewish ones. At any rate, since half of the respective spouses are Jews, also half of the children should be so to avoid demographic losses on this ground for the Diaspora populations. In fact, normally less than half of the children from mixed marriages are themselves Jews. This finding has been contested in the United States, but the fragmentary evidence seems to confirm it there as well. Under such circumstances, the "effectively Jewish" fertility—exclusive of the non-Jewish children of mixed couples—is reduced even further than the full fertility of Jewish women, which is already low.

The frequency of mixed marriages is already very high in some smaller European countries and is increasing elsewhere, rapidly so in the Americas. There is by now widespread social acceptance of such marriages among Diaspora Jews. The levels of total out-marriage, including the conversionary ones, are even higher. It has been estimated that about 30 percent of the currently marrying Jewish individuals in the United States contract mixed marriages, which implies that about 45 percent of the currently formed couples with at least one Jewish spouse are mixed.[2] The consequences for the next generation will be considerable, and even those children who will grow up as Jews are likely to develop some affinity to the religion of the non-Jewish parent and his or her family. Moreover, as out-marriages become more common, the proportion among them that results in accessions (whether formal or informal) to the Jewish populations seems to decline. Jews have had a tradition of restraint regarding proselytism, and modes of conversion are now one of the points contested between the various branches of organized Judaism. Hence there is either little activism in this respect or not a few of the conversions that do take place constitute an element of friction within Jewish society.

Advanced assimilation of Jews, whether combined with mixed marriage or not, leads to complex and unstable situations with regard to the religio-ethnic identity of the individuals in question. It may result in alienation and eventual secession from the Jewish population.

In consequence of these demographic processes, all or nearly all of the larger Diaspora Jewries now have a balance of internal evolution (regardless of external migrations) that is close to nil or negative. Though life expectancies are high, the very low "effectively Jewish" fertility, net assimilatory losses, and the adverse consequences of the already pronounced aging operate jointly to reduce the Diaspora populations. Most demographers believe that low fertility will continue to prevail in the developed countries; if so, Jews will be influenced by this general atmosphere. Aging is bound to continue its rising trend under these circumstances, and out-marriages are on the increase. All these factors combine to intensify the demographic crisis in the Diaspora.

By contrast, there is no uniformity regarding the external migration balance of Diaspora Jewries. Of late, this has been positive in, for example, the United States, Canada, and Australia and negative in the Soviet Union, South Africa, and Argentina. A surplus of immigrants in a Diaspora Jewry will partly or wholly compensate for the effects of a negative balance of internal evolution, whereas a net migratory loss will combine with these effects to reduce even further the overall balance of current demographic changes.

Until the 1970s the migration balance between the Diaspora as a whole and Israel was positive for the latter; that is, there were more *olim* than *yordim*. By now, the potentials for aliyah from the Soviet satellites and the Islamic countries are almost exhausted, and the Jews of the free and prosperous countries have so far shown little propensity to settle permanently in Israel. In the first half of the 1980s, when the exit of Jews from the Soviet Union was virtually barred, international migrations of Jews shrank and, on a multiannual average, the migratory balance between the Diaspora and Israel tended to be nil.

Israel Israel's Jewish population is rather evenly composed of people of European and of Asian-African origin. Since the 1950s the previously dissimilar patterns of mortality, nuptiality, and fertility of these two origin groups have converged. Therefore, Israel's Jews can now be described as demographically one population (of course, with some internal differentiation such as exists within the populations of other countries as well).

Mortality is very low in Israel, nuptiality still very widespread, divorce limited, fertility considerable, and the age composition youthful for a modern country. Therefore, Israel's Jews have now a natural increase of about 1.4 percent annually. Unlike the Diaspora, they do not sustain any net assimilatory losses. As long as a substantial migratory surplus lasted, their overall demographic balance exceeded the natural increase by that amount.

Of special interest, demographically and from the national-Jewish point of view, is the fertility situation in Israel. Jewish fertility in Israel is significantly greater than that not only in the Diaspora but also among the general populations of the other developed countries. As against an average of 1.7 children per white woman in the United States and even lower figures in other countries, Israel's Jewish women—with little differentiation according to their geographic origin—have had a current average fertility of 2.8 children in recent years. Religious Jews have greater fertility than the more secular ones, but the latter display above-replacement fertility in Israel.

The present fertility level was attained in part through a rapid decrease in fertility in the Asian-African origin group, related to the replacement, in the reproductive ages, of many foreign-born by Israeli-born women. Such a decrease, which conformed with the global trend of transition from traditional to modern demographic patterns, was only to be expected from the coexistence with European Jews in the social climate of Israel. A remarkable rise, however, took place in the fertility of the European Jews, with increasing duration of stay in Israel and the intergenerational shift from foreign-born to Israeli-born women. This rise occurred despite hardships of immigrant absorption for many of those concerned and some objective difficulties of existence in Israel. Perhaps the increase in fertility evidences an essentially positive attitude to life and the future that has pervaded large sections of Israel's Jews. Whatever the reasons, the Jews of Israel offer an interesting spectacle on the contemporary demographic scene of a population that widely and efficiently practices family planning but chooses its planning targets above replacement level.

These positive features notwithstanding, the demographic situation of Israel's Jews is not devoid of problems. The previously very high propensity to get married has declined somewhat. Generally the question is unavoidable: will the Israeli Jewish population, open as it is to outside influences, maintain its present edge in fertility vis-à-vis the other developed countries? Moreover, aliyah has contracted to such an extent that, on a multiannual average, it no more than compensates for *yeridah;* both are now around ten to fifteen thousand annually. *Yeridah* is thus limited (three to four per thousand), but not insignificant, especially as part of it is composed of highly qualified individuals attracted by superior career opportunities elsewhere. An immediate potential for larger-scale immigration from Diaspora Jewries in distress is not evident now except in the Soviet Union, whose Jews are virtually debarred from leaving, and, when they could leave in recent years, most preferred to go to other destinations, especially the United States, rather than to Israel.[3]

For many decades immigration of Jews compensated for the far larger fertility and natural increase of the Arabs in Israel and Palestine. This is no longer true because of the reduced aliyah. Fertility and natural increase of the Arabs in the state territory of Israel have decreased dramatically, as the last generation born in the Mandatory period was replaced in the procreative age range by those born and educated in Israel. Yet the Arabs' fertility and natural increase are still considerably greater than those of the Israeli Jews. The respective differentials widen if comparison is made between Israel's Jews and the Arabs in the Administered Areas, though there population growth is slowed by emigration. In the absence of sufficient aliyah, the proportion of Arabs in the state territory of Israel has been growing slowly. There is awareness among the Jewish public in Israel of the problems posed by the low ebb of aliyah and by a shifting demographic balance vis-à-vis the Arabs, and wide consensus on the desirability of Jewish population growth for idealistic Zionist as well as for practical reasons.

Population Characteristics

Diaspora   Wherever data are available on the age composition of Diaspora Jews, these are nearly always found to be more aged than the general population of their country or city of residence. The Jews have smaller proportions of children but larger proportions of late-middle-aged and elderly persons. Although aging of populations is now a common process in the developed countries, its intensity is even more pronounced among Diaspora Jewries. The reasons are, above all, the Jews' particularly low fertility; but also losses of younger adults—and indirectly of their offspring—because of assimilation as well as to aliyah or any other emigration; and aftereffects of the Holocaust (where this applies). It is estimated that in 1975 the numbers of children up to age fourteen and of elderly aged sixty-five and above were roughly equal (15 to 16 percent) in the Diaspora as a whole, whereas there had been a clear surplus of elderly (19 percent) over children (15 percent) until 1985. Besides, the percentage of very old people (aged seventy-five and over) is growing markedly. There are considerable regional differences in these respects; the Jewish population of the United States is less aged than those of many other Diaspora countries.

Aging depresses the birth rates and raises the death rates. At any given level of fertility, an aged population will tend to have fewer people in the procreative bracket and thus a lower birth rate. At any level of life expectancies, an aged population will include more elderly and consequently register a higher death rate. These demographic relationships apply, of course, also to the Jewish populations. Besides, the pronounced aging of many Diaspora populations probably leads to feminization because on the average women live longer than men and hence usually form a majority of the elderly. Aging together with certain changes in marriage patterns such as prolonged singlehood and divorce reduces the average size of Jewish households and raises the proportion of one-person households. Larger numbers of infirm old Jews are likely to increase the respective institutionalization rates.

Beyond such more narrowly demographic consequences, the pronounced aging of the Jews implies fundamental economic and societal changes with widespread ramifications that will extend into the future, for example, regarding labor force participation, income structure, consumption patterns, demand for smaller dwellings or residences in climatically favored zones, and need for geriatric services. The intensified aging will perhaps also have repercussions on the tenor of Jewish communal life and on the Jews' position and participation in the general society in which they live.

The very low fertility and birth rates in the Diaspora during recent decades have already led to a remarkable diminution in the absolute and relative numbers of children. This decline has had strong implications for enrollment in Jewish educational institutions. In the United States, for instance, the number enrolled in Jewish schools and kindergartens dropped by 33 percent between 1966–67 and 1981–82 to 1982–83, but the total of three-to-seventeen-year-old Jewish children is estimated to have declined by as much as 43 percent. According to these figures, the enrollment rates (relative to existing child population) actually rose despite the drastic decline in the absolute size of the enrollment.

The Jewish world population has undergone a far-reaching geographical redistribution during the last generations because of large-scale migrations and the effects of the Holocaust in Europe. Three-quarters of present Diaspora Jewry live in countries where there were still relatively few Jews a century ago or even later—in the Americas, South Africa, and Oceania. As long as the great modern migrations of the Jews lasted, their majority in the countries of destination were foreign-born persons who had immigrated from abroad; most of them originated in Eastern Europe with its tradition-bound and still very religious Jewish population. By now, most of the Jews in the new countries of residence are native-born with the accompanying familiarity with surrounding conditions, proficiency in the national language, involvement in the affairs of their respective countries, and enhanced exposure to assimilation.

The overwhelming majority of Diaspora Jews live in large cities or metropolitan areas and share characteristics of the middle and upper-middle classes there. In some countries, though, and notably in the United States, there is now an opposite tendency for younger Jews with professional qualifications to be sent by large firms or on government assignments to smaller and more remote localities where they are needed in new enterprises or public services. There, too, as well as in any developing countries where

Jews now live, most of them behave demographically according to the patterns of the large-city Jewries of developed countries.

In comparison to the total population of their countries or cities of residence, Diaspora Jews usually have higher formal education, are concentrated in white-collar occupations, and are economically better off. In some countries, most of the younger Jewish generation study at universities. Occupationally, Jews are increasingly found in upper managerial positions, as self-employed professionals, and in professional jobs of public service (education, health, law). Individual Jews are conspicuous for outstanding achievements in the sciences and arts as well as in the public life of important countries.

Because of assimilation or for organizational reasons, Diaspora Jewries often consist of an affiliated sector (possibly with a great variety of institutional links) and completely nonaffiliated margins. Among the former, there is usually variation according to degree of involvement and Jewish commitment. Among the latter, Jewish-born but alienated individuals are found. These are still included, as a rule, in the Jewish population estimates presented in Table 1 (unlike actual seceders, who should be omitted). But not all of them or of their offspring are likely to persevere within the Jewish fold, which operates toward attrition of the Diaspora populations in the longer-term perspective (see demographic projections below).

Israel The current proportion of elderly among the Jews of Israel is smaller than in most developed countries because fertility and natural increase are greater in Israel. Nevertheless, the proportion aged sixty-five and over among Israel's Jews rose from 4 percent around 1950 to 10 percent between 1980 and 1985. This was not caused mainly by reduced fertility, as in the Diaspora, but by a gradual adjustment of the age structure, which had previously been dominated by selectively young immigrants, to the actual fertility level prevailing in Israel.

Israeli Jews reside in more than nine hundred rural localities of less than two thousand inhabitants each, but 90 percent of the total Jewish population congregates in localities above two thousand inhabitants, and 65 percent in the metropolitan areas of Greater Tel Aviv and Greater Haifa and in Jerusalem. Most of the rural localities are kibbutzim and moshavim (voluntary collective or coopera-tive settlements), which are a well-known peculiarity of Israel.

Unlike the Diaspora, where the relatively small Jewish minori-ties can specialize in selective occupations, Israeli Jews provide manpower for the entire national economy. All the same, a shift in the supply of low-skilled manual labor has been unmistakable: in the past this labor was provided by Zionist pioneers, then by Jew-ish mass immigrants, and then by Israeli Arabs. More recently it has been largely supplied by Arabs from the Administered Areas who sought employment in Israel.

The proportion of Jews in Israel who have received a higher ed-ucation (thirteen or more years of study) as well as of academic graduates is continually rising, especially among the younger adults, though it falls short of the very high levels found in some Diaspora Jewries.

A collective cultural achievement has been the revival of He-brew as a fully functioning language and the mother tongue of the younger generations of Jews growing up in Israel.

Demographic Projections

Projections are, of course, not prophecies but serve to show the quantitative changes that will occur in the size and composition of a given population if it evolves according to defined assumptions. If the assumptions reflect the current demographic dynamics, the projection becomes a means for clarifying the longer-term impli-cations of these existing dynamics. In the making of projections it is usual to apply alternative sets of assumptions, both as a precau-tion and to indicate a reasonable range of variation.

I shall present here three versions of projections that are in-tended to illustrate plausible evolutions of the Jewish population in the Diaspora as a whole and the United States particularly, in Is-rael, and in the world during the twenty-five-year period from 1985 to 2010 (see Table 2). The common features of the three ver-sions are low mortality and a nil assumption for the migration bal-ance between the Diaspora and Israel (in keeping with the realities of the early 1980s), whereas a migratory surplus was assumed for U.S. Jewry. If the balance of migrations between the Diaspora and Israel should change markedly, for example, through large-scale aliyah of Soviet Jews, the projected results will have to be adjusted

Table 2. *Predicted Population Trends, 1985–2010*

Region	Version of projection	Fertility	Net assimilatory losses
Diaspora	Medium	Constantly low	Moderate
	Low	Constantly low	Strong
	High	Rising	Moderate
Israel	Medium	Declining somewhat	Nil
	Low	Declining markedly	Nil
	High	Constantly substantial	Nil

accordingly. The scenarios regarding the other parameters of the different versions were essentially as follows:[4]

Diaspora   In consequence of continually low fertility and intensified aging, official population projections for developed countries such as the United States expect that natural increase will cease at some time in the coming decades and, with no or little immigration, the population size will gradually decline. A shrinkage of population is already occurring in a few countries such as West Germany.

The internal demographic evolution of the Diaspora has been negative for some time because of particularly low fertility, strong aging, and assimilatory attrition, which extends to the offspring of mixed marriages. Little wonder that the medium and low versions of the Diaspora projections point to marked decreases in the total of Jews there. This trend appears, though somewhat mitigated, in the high version because the negative influence of aging and assimilatory losses will outweigh the effects of any plausible rise in fertility. For the United States in particular, only a combination of markedly rising fertility and virtual absence of assimilatory losses (including identification of half the newborn from mixed marriages as Jews) could prevent a population decrease. Projections that are not presented here have also been made for all the other major Diaspora regions; in most of them the present demographic situation, and consequently also the future prospects, are more adverse than in the United States. According to the medium version, the total number of Jews in the Diaspora would decrease from somewhat less than 9.5 million in 1985 to 8.2 million in 2000 and about 7.3 million until the year 2010, a decline of 23 percent.

Moreover, not only the size but also the cohesion of Diaspora Jewries will be affected, if assimilation and in particular the frequency of mixed marriages continue to increase.

The percent of elderly (sixty-five years and above) among all Diaspora Jews will not change considerably between 1985 and 2010 and will stay in the range of 19 to 20 percent, according to the medium projection. The reason is that the small cohorts born between the later 1920s and the mid-1940s, during the Great Depression and World War II, will enter the elderly range. When the large cohorts born during the baby boom around 1950 reach ages sixty-five and above beginning in the second decade of the coming century, the proportion of elderly among Diaspora Jews will rise drastically.

Israel   Israel's Jews will continue to increase in numbers, even in the absence of a migratory surplus[5], because of natural increase. Their numbers will expand from 3.5 million in 1985 to 4.1 million in 2000 and 4.5 by 2010, according to the medium projection. In the latter year, the proportion of Jews in the territory of the state (without the Administered Areas) may be about 76 percent unless there is sizable aliyah.

In Israel too the percentage of elderly Jews is shown by the projections to remain stable from 1985 to 2010, for reasons similar to those already stated with regard to the Diaspora. But the level of that percentage will be only half what it is in the Diaspora: 10 percent as compared to 20 percent. A marked increase in the proportion of elderly is also anticipated for Israel after 2010 because large birth cohorts will then reach ages sixty-five and above.

World Jewry   Until recently the substantial natural increase of Israel's Jews offset the adverse internal evolution in the Diaspora and caused a growth of world Jewry, though on a continually decreasing scale. Now, a temporary equilibrium has been reached: the natural increase in Israel approximately equals the diminution in the Diaspora, so that world Jewry is in the stage of zero population growth. This situation will not endure, however, as the projections show. The size of world Jewry will start to shrink, primarily because of intensified rates of diminution in the Diaspora but possibly also because of some lowering of the natural increase among Israel's Jews. The continual growth of Israel's share

Table 3. *Projection of Jewish Population Size, 1985–2010*

Region	Jews (in millions) 1985	2000	2010	Percent of change, 1985–2010
	Medium Projection			
World	13.0	12.4	12.0	−8
Diaspora	9.5	8.2	7.3	−23
United States	5.7	5.4	5.1	−11
Israel	3.5	4.2	4.7	+34
	Low Projection			
World	13.0	12.0	11.3	−13
Diaspora	9.5	7.9	6.8	−28
United States	5.7	5.1	4.7	−18
Israel	3.5	4.1	4.5	+29
	High Projection			
World	13.0	12.8	12.8	−2
Diaspora	9.5	8.5	7.9	−17
United States	5.7	5.6	5.4	−5
Israel	3.5	4.3	4.9	+40

Region	Version of projection	Fertility	Net Assimilatory Losses Newborn	Others (annually)
Diaspora,	Medium	1.5	2.5%–12.5%	0.2%
including	Low	"	5.0%–25/0%	0.4%
United States	High	1.5–2.1	2.5%–12.5%	0.2%
Israel	Medium	2.8–2.4	Nil	Nil
	Low	2.8–2.1	Nil	Nil
	High	2.8	Nil	Nil

The migratory surplus of U.S. Jews was put at 15,000 annually, altogether 375,000 throughout the twenty-five-year projection period.

among world Jewry will not suffice to counterbalance the negative influence of the worsening evolution in the Diaspora. According to the medium projection, the total number of Jews in the world may contract from 13.0 million in 1985 to 12.4 million in 2000 and 12.0 million by the year 2010, an 8 percent decrease over twenty-five years.

As of 1985, 71 percent of the world's Jews lived in the two countries with the largest Jewish populations—the United States and Israel. By 2010 the joint prominence of these two major Jewries will be enhanced so that together they will be home to as many as 81 percent of all Jews, according to the medium projection. Although the relative share of Israel alone may rise substantially from 27 to 39 percent, that of the United States will barely maintain itself (44 percent in 1985, 42 percent in 2010). The number of Jews in Israel will approach that in the United States by 2010, according to all versions of the projections presented in Table 3.

Conclusion

The brief analysis presented here suggests that demographically it is not irrelevant whether Jews live in Israel or the Diaspora. Israel's Jews are not exposed to mixed marriages and assimilatory losses, and the immigrants from Europe and America have attained in Israel a fertility level that much surpasses that in the Diaspora and results in not inconsiderable natural increase. In the demographic balance sheet of world Jewry, Israel's natural increase counteracts the diminution of the Diaspora. Moreover, attachment to Israel has become an important element in the Jewish identity of many Diaspora Jews.

There is wide consensus among Israel's Jews on the desirability of population growth. Demographic policies, partly coinciding with public support for families with children, have been in operation and are likely to be reactivated.

The ongoing numerical decline of the Jewish population in the Diaspora and the future shrinkage of world Jewry, as indicated by the projections, come after the loss of a third of the Jewish people in the Holocaust. Viewed in this perspective, the Diaspora's current demographic problems differ in historical purport from the analogous, albeit less severe, demographic processes prevailing in the developed countries. Larger-scale demographic policies in the Diaspora, which must be on a voluntary basis, are obviously not easy to put into effect. Yet the possibility is not precluded of increasing awareness of the demographic issues and their implications among the Jewish leadership and public. Choices of a marriage partner and of fertility targets are made by a great many individuals and couples, and it is only right that they should know what collective consequences their private decisions may have.

In view of the gravity of the issues involved, it is necessary to improve and update the demographic documentation on Diaspora Jewry. Plans are taking shape for a round of coordinated sociodemographic surveys to be conducted among major Jewish populations of the free world throughout the 1990s.

Notes

1. The three post–World War II censuses of the Soviet Union indicated 2,268,000 Jews in 1959, 2,151,000 in 1970, and 1,811,000 in 1979. These figures are consistent among themselves, if the known changes during the intervals—emigration and a negative balance of internal evolution—are taken into account. Accordingly, though it is likely that some persons of fully Jewish descent existed above the respective census figures, they too were consistent in concealing their Jewishness. Any quantitative clue is lacking for estimating how many among them might still actually be Jews. I have therefore used the census figure of 1979 as the basis for updating the estimate, with this reservation.
2. The proportion mixed is always greater for couples than for individuals because a homogamous Jewish union appears only once in the count of couples but twice in that of the component individuals.
3. This summary was written before the large scale aliyah of the past 2 years and has to be revised accordingly.
4. The projections presented here for the whole Diaspora are actually the sum of ten regional projections (with appropriately differing assumptions). The projections for Israel were adapted from those computed by the Central Bureau of Statistics in 1987. The calibrations for the projection assumptions were approximately as follows (a dash indicates gradual change from the initial to the terminal level of the projection period):
5. Again, this situation has been altered by the large scale recent Russian and Ethiopian aliyah.

FOR FURTHER READING

Bachi, Roberto, *The Population of Israel,* Jerusalem, 1977.

_____. *Population Trends of World Jewry,* Jerusalem, 1976.

Bensimon, Doris, and Sergio DellaPergola, *La population juive de France: Socio-demographie et identite,* Jerusalem, 1984.

DellaPergola, Sergio, and Leah, Cohen, eds. *World Jewish Population: Trends and Policies,* Jerusalem, 1990.

DellaPergola, Sergio, and Uziel O. Schmelz, "Demographic Transformations of American Jewry: Marriage and Mixed Marriage in the 1980s." In *Studies in Contemporary Jewry,* vol. 5, New York, 1988.

Goldstein, Sidney, "Jews in the United States: Perspectives from Demography." In *American Jewish Year Book,* New York, 1981, pp 3–59.

Ritterband, Paul, ed., *Modern Jewish Fertility,* Leiden, 1981.

Schmelz, Uziel O., *Aging of World Jewry,* Jerusalem, 1984.

_____. "Jewish Survival: The Demographic Factors." In *American Jewish Year Book,* 81, New York, 1981, pp. 61–117.

_____. *World Jewish Population: Regional Estimates and Projections.* Jerusalem, 1981.

Schmelz, Uziel O., and Sergio DellaPergola, *Basic Trends in U.S. Jewish Demography*, New York, 1988.

———. "World Jewish population 1986," *American Jewish Year Book*, 88, New York, 1988, pp. 412–427.

———, eds. *Papers in Jewish Demography 1985*, Jerusalem, 1989.

Schmelz, Uziel O., and Gad, Nathan, eds., *Studies in the Population of Israel in Honor of Roberto Bachi*, Jerusalem, 1986.

Assimilation

DEBORAH E. LIPSTADT

Since the Enlightenment many Diaspora Jewish leaders, particularly those in western Europe and North America, have feared the impact of assimilation on the well-being and future of their communities. Although anti-Semitism has long been considered the preeminent external danger, assimilation has been seen as the greatest internal threat. By assimilating, many Jewish leaders feared, Jews would do to themselves from within that which countless enemies had been unable to do from without.[1]

There are those who argue that these fears, particularly as they apply to the American Jewish community, are unfounded. They contend that the Jewish community is currently engaged in a revival that has not only prevented assimilation but has in many cases reversed the process and produced a stronger degree of affiliation.[2]

Those on the optimistic side have sometimes accused communal leaders, who continue to propound the dangers of assimilation, of basing their arguments on ideological beliefs and organizational goals and of ignoring the empirical evidence, which indicates that assimilation is not about to engulf the Jewish community but rather that the community is in the midst of a renaissance. Critics of this theory argue that too much attention is being paid to the form and too little to the substance of the so-called revival. Pointing to the high rate of intermarriage, low levels of Jewish learning, and increasing rates of nonaffiliation, they see ominous threats on the horizon. At the heart of this debate is the question, Is the

American Jewish community in the process of assimilating and
losing its unique identity, or has a uniquely American form of Judaism emerged, which, though it is significantly different from traditional Judaism, is resilient enough to maintain a strong Jewish
identity?

Two sets of observers can look at the same phenomena and
reach radically different conclusions because the ways in which
they assess assimilation and acculturation are so dissimilar. This
essay will explore this controversy. It begins by examining the
meaning of the term *assimilation* and then turns to the relationship
between assimilation and acculturation, the history of the acculturation of the American Jewish community, and the different sociological theories about the process of assimilation.

Assimilation: A Problematic Term

There are a myriad of problems with the use of the term *assimilation*. Daniel Bell has summed them up most succinctly by asking,
"What is there [for American Jews] to assimilate to?"[3] The confusion and debate over assimilation emanates, at least in part, from its
dynamism as a process. People are not assimilated into something
that is static. It changes even as they change. There was a time
when minority groups could be differentiated from the majority
by their language, dress, and names. Today these are no longer reliable standards by which to measure assimilation.

For the purposes of this essay assimilation will be defined as that
point at which a specific minority group no longer constitutes a
significant and identifiable entity in society. This stage can be attained, Marshall Sklare has observed, even though the group still
retains some ancestral memories and uses traditional family
names.[4]

The process is complete when the group has been completely
merged into the general society; when the individual no longer
thinks of himself or herself as a member of that minority group;
when members of the minority group consider the individual to be
part of the majority and when the majority thinks of the individual
as one of its own.[5] At that point the minority member has lost his
or her own sense of identity and has merged completely.[6]

The identifiable manifestations of assimilation vary. They generally include name changing, physical and cosmetic alteration,

learning the majority language (and not that of the minority group), and abandoning attachment to and knowledge of the minority culture. But all these changes can take place without assimilation occurring. It is the "voluntary or involuntary change in personal relationships" that appears to be the real key to complete ethnic conversion.[7] In other words, an individual could change her name or physical appearance and be ignorant not only of the language spoken by her minority group but of its traditions and practices as well. But assimilation may not have occurred if the individual's key personal relationships are with members of the minority group.

Though both religious and lay leaders of the Jewish community have frequently bemoaned the rapid pace of assimilation, in fact, the statistics remain elusive and open to debate. Assimilation generally occurs across extended periods and not at a given point. It is a gradual, multigenerational process, and it is difficult to identify the precise point at which it occurs. Moreover, though assimilationists may be well aware of the process in which they are engaged, the totally assimilated are often not conscious of their situation. Yet another obstacle in measuring assimilation is that in settings in which ethnic and minority identity is valued, as in the contemporary United States, assimilation is often not respected. Consequently, those who are engaged in the process may be conflicted about publicly acknowledging that they are altering their group identity. Few people who have consciously chosen to change their names or religious identity so as to mask their minority heritage will boast that they have done so.[8]

Another reason for the difficulty in assessing the precise extent of assimilation is that it can be reversed. The speed with which it occurs can be affected by many factors, including the general value placed on ethnic identity. In recent decades in the United States, where ethnicity has become a source of pride, one finds members of religious or ethnic minorities reasserting their minority identity after letting it lie dormant for all of their adult lives. In certain cases, parents had rejected the minority identification while their children seek to "reconnect" with a group they never personally abandoned. This process is easier when the individual is not reconnecting with a geographic area, the "old country," but with a religion, culture, and broad, multifaceted tradition, as is the case with Judaism and the Jewish community.

Prejudice and discrimination directed at the group in general or the particular individual who is trying to assimilate can affect the process in two contradictory ways. They can hasten it and prompt the individual to try to shed all identifiable connections with the minority group or they can slow down or halt the process altogether. In recent decades numerous individuals in the American Jewish community have attested to their reconnection with the community after a period of alienation or separation as a result of either personally confronting expressions of anti-Semitism or perceiving a threat to Jewish survival. The latter was particularly the case during the Six-Day War in 1967 and the Yom Kippur War in 1973. Although some might consider assimilation a means of escaping prejudice, others would be reluctant to do so because they would not want to be branded as cowards or as having abandoned fellow members of the minority group.[9]

Assimilation and Acculturation

Ultimately, the most basic reason why the impact of assimilation has been so difficult to assess is the substantial confusion in the minds of many observers of Jewish life between assimilation and acculturation. If assimilation marks the complete disappearance of the minority identity—a sociological death in that the individual is completely lost to the community—then the American Jewish community has not assimilated. Apostasy has been and remains a rare occurrence, and various communal studies conducted over the past decade reveal that most Jews retain some link, however weak and tentative, with the Jewish community or Jewish traditions. In a recent survey, for example, a proportion of individuals who had no synagogue affiliation identified themselves as members of a Reform synagogue even though they were not out of an obvious sense that they should maintain some form of affiliation. Despite the growing rate of exogamy, increasing numbers of intermarried households maintain some expression of Jewish identity. In certain households both religious traditions are practiced. Though there are many people who would dismiss this as a meaningless and confusing act, particularly as it concerns the children in the household, nonetheless it is not the act of an assimilated person. In recent years various studies have pointed to the "survivalist" nature of American Jewish life, rejecting the notion that the American Jewish community is interested only in accommodating itself to majority demands. American Jews have reached a consensus that assimilation is not a desirable goal. Their behavior can be described as "retentivist," in that more than many other groups in the United States they have made retention of their minority identity a communal goal. Rather than assimilate, they have acculturated.[10]

An acculturated community is one that has assumed many of the majority's cultural patterns, including its dress, economic behavior, language, values, and political views. Many of those become meshed with minority values and traditions, producing a distinctive and unique culture. The revival of ethnic identity in contemporary American is a sign that acculturation need not be a way station on the road to assimilation. Contrary to previous predictions by various sociologists, acculturation has not inexorably led the members of the minority group to abandon all their links to the minority.[11] The nature of the relationship may change but the relationship itself may well remain. Herein may lie the crux of the debate over the quality of Jewish life in contemporary America. The links that remain may be celebrated by some, but others see them as of dubious Jewish quality and insufficient to maintain a dynamic and creative Jewish identity. They are, at best, vestiges of what once was. For some they are of great value and for others they are virtually useless. I will return to this point in the final section of this essay.

American Jews have not been alone in successfully acculturating to their host environment. In fact, one of the noteworthy developments in the period since the eighteenth century both in Europe and in North America has been the ability of many members of various minority groups—Jews included—to maintain their links to their group of origin and at the same time assume both behavioral and cultural patterns of the majority society.[12] Nonetheless, it is clear that Jews, particularly in America, have been one of the nonracial ethnic minorities that has been most successful at acculturation.

Theories of Assimilation

American Jewry's successful acculturation—in contrast to assimilation—is eloquent proof that the original theory of assimilation propounded by most American sociologists was incorrect.

Prominent American sociologists had predicted that the total assimilation of minority communities, Jews included, was inevitable.
"Straight line assimilation," as this theory is known, propounded a
three-stage process: self-segregation, acculturation, and ultimately
assimilation. Some sociologists, Robert E. Park, prominent among
them, anticipated a four-step process: contact, competition, accommodation, and assimilation. However many steps were involved, there was no question, according to these theorists, that
assimilation was the inevitable outcome. It was a trend that pro-
ceeded generation by generation until by the third or fourth generation all links to the minority group would be fully dissipated.[13]

Many of these sociologists were members of the dominant
group and were closely tied to White Anglo-Saxon Protestant
(WASP) culture. In certain cases they were attempting with their
theories to reassure those who feared the social consequences of
the massive "new" immigration from southern and eastern Europe
during the latter decades of the nineteenth and the early decades of
the twentieth centuries. According to their theory, there was no
reason to fear the strange customs, traditions, languages, and culture of the new immigrants because they would abandon all these
in the process of assimilation. They were challenged by Marcus
Lee Hansen's hypothesis of "third generation nationalism."
Hansen, who believed that the assimilation of the third generation
was not inevitable, depicted the assimilatory process as a cycle and
not a straight line. The grandchild, who felt fully accepted and absorbed in American life, might, Hansen argued, wish to perpetuate
what his-second generation parent had tried to forget.[14]

In addition to the move from a straight-line theory to Hansen's
cyclical approach, the notion of the melting pot was rejected and
replaced with the idea of cultural pluralism. A turning point in the
conceptual understanding of the assimilatory process was achieved
in 1964, when Milton Gordon's *Assimilation in America* incorporated Horace Kallen's theory of cultural pluralism into the study of
acculturation and differentiated cultural assimilation or acculturation from structural assimilation. (Structural assimilation is a
change in one's primary and institutional relationships.) Gordon
posited that complete assimilation was achieved through structural
change.

The melting pot, in which all groups gave up their distinctive
identity and contributed to the majority identity, was probably an

accurate metaphor for the first generation's hope to be fully incorporated into American society, to "merge into indistinguishable sameness with the real Americans."[15]

The straight-line theory has not proven accurate. As Daniel Moynihan and Nathan Glazer noted in the mid-1960s, ethnicity was alive and well. "The point about the melting pot is . . . that it did not happen."[16] It is true, however, that the initial generations did try to find ways to become part of the cultural majority. William Petersen attributes these attempts to blend into the dominant culture to insecurity. The early generations wished to be accepted as "true Americans" and were convinced that being like the majority, if not more so, was the way to make that happen. The majority was decidedly ambivalent about this nation. It wanted the immigrants to abandon their distinctive ways but was reluctant to welcome them fully. If the early generations wanted to merge into the majority because of their insecurity, subsequent generations' feelings of security led them to a "yearning to distinguish one's group [and one's self] from the mass."[17]

Both the straight-line and the melting pot concepts failed to recognize that third- and fourth-generation Americans were anxious to find a means of differentiating themselves from each other and could maintain an ethnic identity even as their European heritage disappeared. Most important, the straight-line theory did not take into account that the adjustments in religious and ethnic behavior all groups make are nonlinear but can reverse direction from generation to generation. As Steven M. Cohen has noted, though members of the second generation of American Jews observed fewer rituals and were less likely to affiliate with synagogues than their parents, they were more likely to support Jewish charities and join other Jewish organizations. Although traditional religious observances and synagogue affiliation declined from second to third generations, in these categories the fourth generation seemed to stabilize or even slightly increase its activity.[18] Many modern parents who choose a day school education for their children received little or no Jewish education themselves.

These changes reflect a number of different but related developments, including Hansen's cycle and Jews' desire to maintain their identity without feeling that they are at odds with general American society. The uniquely American aspect of this change has been the evolution of the concept of "civil Judaism," which is based on Robert Bellah's idea of civil religion. Practices that were once considered wholly secular such as raising funds for Jewish charities have been infused with a religious significance. They have been transformed from an act of noblesse oblige to one involving an element of personal and communal redemption.[19]

Assimilation and the American Jewish Experience

Why did assimilation not become the mass phenomenon in the Jewish community that sociologists predicted it would? Why have Jews been able to acculturate both themselves and their Jewish tradition with such alacrity? Why has the total loss of Jewish identity been more the exception than the rule? And if this is truly the case, does the American Jewish community have cause for concern about its future?

Unlike in the European Jewish experience, the hostility of the non-Jewish community has played only a minor role in affecting the pace of Jewish acculturation. The Anglo-Saxon Protestant majority has long been decidedly ambivalent about accepting Jews into its midst. Immigrants to this country received mixed messages. They were told to emulate the majority but often found obstacles blocking their way. There were residential areas from which they were barred, schools that would not accept their children, and recreational and social clubs that would deny them membership. Most significant, there were firms that would not hire them and, if they did, hid them in back offices.

Despite these obstacles American anti-Semitism cannot be singled out as a major factor in affecting the pace of assimilation. It was never widespread or sustained enough to do so, and it always had to compete with other discriminatory sentiments that pervaded American culture such as opposition to blacks, Catholics, and Orientals.

Those Jews who, rather than assimilate into the majority, attempted to replace their Jewish identity with another ideology such as socialism or radical liberalism often found the atmosphere inhospitable. After 1967 many Jews were alienated by the New Left's hostility to Israel and reevaluated their relationship with the Jewish community, in some cases moving closer to it.[20]

But one of the more important reasons why assimilation has not become widespread is the deep-seated American tradition of pluralism, the idea that this country was composed of many different types of peoples, with various traditions and cultures, which has been part of the American ethic since this country's founding. There were times when it was only paid lip service and honored in the breach. But it could always be cited as a fundamental principle of American life. Maintaining a minority identity could not be seen as fundamentally at odds with basic American values. Since the 1970s the idea of ethnic identity has become an ideal. In 1988 in his acceptance speech at the Democratic National Convention, Michael Dukakis placed great emphasis on his immigrant heritage. He was the first son of immigrants to be nominated for the office of president.

In contrast to various central and western European countries, America never proclaimed that a unidimensional ethnic or religious character was an objective ideal. Consequently, as Ben Halpern has observed, assimilation never attained the status of a full-fledged ideology in the American Jewish community.[21] The only Jewish expression of assimilation as a desired end was in the Ethical Culture movement, which never had a major impact on the Jewish community or attracted many adherents.

Because Jewish survival is more likely in a multicultural than in a single culture society, acculturation was easier in America than it had been in other countries. In addition, as a result of the long-term Jewish experience with acculturation, Jews were able to adapt their minority identity to America with greater ease than some other groups. Well before their arrival in North America, Jews had had a multigenerational experience of living as a minority in other cultures. Unlike most other ethnic and religious immigrants groups that came to America such as the Italians or the Irish, Jews had previously successfully overcome the challenge of acculturation. Various scholars, including Salo Baron, Jacob Neusner, and Gerson Cohen, believe that the most creative periods in Jewish history were those when Jews maintained long and close relationships with other cultures.

Unlike many other immigrants to America Jews had no intention of returning to their lands of origin. Consequently, they were inclined to find means of adapting their Jewish identity to American demands. They found that many of the Jewish values they brought with them were considered American values as well, for example, education, anti-discrimination, and social welfare. The

Jewish fight against anti-Semitism in America became not just a struggle to protect Jews but a fight against essentially un-American behavior. Rather than being an issue of self-interest, it became "part of a wider issue that involves not only them but all of society, of the war on all social maladjustments."[22]

In contrast to assimilation, acculturation does not call for the individual or the group to sever its association with its minority identity, although in the process of acculturating, the minority may change the way its members identify and associate. The new forms of identification and association may be similar to traditional forms or radically different. Jews who came to America during periods of massive migration were often convinced that to be fully accepted they must give up "everything which America might find foreign," for example, kashrut, and Shabbat. Many hastened to do so. But in response, they created alternatives to traditional Judaism, most notably a communal institutional infrastructure that was far more elaborate than anything evident in previous Jewish communities.[23] Even the German Jewish communal structure, the *Gemeinde*, on which the American was modeled was not as extensive or as elaborate.

Daniel Elazar has observed that public affiliation has become the central mode of being Jewish in America. "Organized activity . . . has come to be the most common manifestation of Judaism, replacing prayer, study and the normal private intercourse of kin as a means of being Jewish."[24] This change was so successful in part because the associational approach is quintessentially American. The "essence of American Jewish identity, the core meaning of Judaism for many American Jews," may well be their social and communal links to one another.[25]

In the process of acculturation American Jews have not only replaced certain traditional behaviors with new patterns of association, but they have selected among the traditional practices those most easily harmonized with American tradition. Over the past four decades there has been a change in religious behavior in the Jewish community. Fewer Jews light Shabbat candles and observe kashrut, but more light Chanukah candles or attend Passover Seders.

Marshall Sklare attributes these changes to Jews' desire to remain Jews while at the same feeling at home in America. According to Sklare, the most frequently observed Jewish rituals meet five criteria: they can be redefined in contemporary terms; they do not demand that the observer be socially isolated or adopt a distinctive lifestyle; they provide an alternative to widely observed Christian holidays, for example, Chanukah for Christmas; they do not have to be observed on a frequent or continuous basis; and they are to some degree focused on children.[26]

One recent development in the American Jewish community breaks with this pattern of selecting rituals based on the degree to which they allow one to feel at home in America. The growth in modern Orthodoxy, the Ba'al Teshuvah movement, has resulted in a significant expansion of Orthodox institutions and practices in the last decade. It is probably too soon to assess, but it has the potential to have a serious impact on the future of Jewish communal institutions. It provides stunning validation of Hansen's theory.

The Debate over the Viability of Jewish Life in America

Controversy regarding the nature of Jewish life in America was sparked by the publication of Charles Silberman's highly optimistic *A Certain People*. Silberman examined a number of recent changes in American Jewish life and argued that, in contrast to the predictions of many leaders of the community, American Jews were exhibiting unprecedented resilience. The community had undergone a transformation and consequently new criteria must be used for judging the quality of Jewish life. Pointing to the emergence of the *Havura* Movement, Federation Young Leadership programs, the women's movement, Jewish studies programs, and the entry of Jews into positions of corporate leadership, Silberman argued that American Jewry was flourishing. He dismissed the laments about assimilation and its various manifestations, including intermarriage, Jewish illiteracy, negative population growth, and many other woes. Silberman was not the only observer of the Jewish scene to argue that rather than undergoing assimilation, the American Jewish community was experiencing a transformation. Steven M. Cohen and Calvin Goldscheider made similar observations.[27]

These optimists were particularly impressed by the willingness of Jews to proclaim their Jewish identity openly, particularly in arenas where they had often been reluctant to do so. No longer was Jewish identity relegated to the home and secular identity to the public sphere. Many people were more expressive of their Jewish identity in the public realm than they were in private. This was a striking change that Silberman hailed as reflective of a new stage in Jewish life.

The change was most evident in areas where Jews had been particularly unwilling to call attention to their minority identity such as the college campus, the political world, and the corporate sector. Jewish college presidents could be found in services on Rosh Hashanah and Yom Kippur and members of Congress attended a weekly class to study Jewish texts. It was these and many similar developments that so excited Silberman and others. They declared that Jewish life had been transformed and should be assessed using a radically different scale of measurement.

There have been serious criticisms of this revival, led by Marshall Sklare and Charles Liebman, along with Ruth Wisse, Arthur Hertzberg, and Samuel Heilman. The critics do not deny that these developments have taken place, but they differ on their implications and significance.[28] They cited disturbing signs, including the growing number of intermarriages and the generally low level of Jewish literacy, and argued that there was no room for rejoicing. They argued that much of what was being celebrated as evidence of the new renaissance was weak and vacuous. Charles Liebman pointed to the qualitative shallowness of this phenomenon. The Judaic content of some of the examples most widely touted as proof of this renewal was quite low. Though there was much good "feeling" about "being and doing Jewish," basic principles, values, and knowledge of Judaism seemed to be evident in only a most general and elementary fashion. Jewish illiteracy seemed to be at an all-time high. Much of what was being celebrated as a Jewish revival, it could be argued, was really an expression of the American *zeitgeist,* "it's in to be ethnic." And, one could legitimately wonder, what would happen if the time came when it was no longer as acceptable?

Ultimately this debate is rooted in fundamental differences in the barometer used to gauge Jewish acculturation. There is no universally accepted mode of measuring Jewish "sufficiency." An act the optimists might consider to be a forceful expression of Jewish identity may be for the critics weak and virtually meaningless.[29] Being willing openly to proclaim an identity that may have been hidden or at best muted is assessed differently by optimists and pessimists. They both would probably see it as a positive act, but the former would attribute to it far greater significance than would the latter. Because acculturation occurs across a spectrum and there is no single standard by which to evaluate it, such radically different assessments are possible.

By all definitions the American Jewish community has not assimilated. It has not disappeared, and virtually all sectors of it, irrespective of their religious, social, or political views, believe that Jewish survival is an important and viable goal. The issue is what it means to survive as a Jewish community. The community may not have assimilated, but it has been transformed. The question that can only be answered in the future is whether that transformation will be of enough depth and cultural wealth and whether it will have enough substance so that Judaism and Jewish life in America do not become shallow reflections of their former selves. If the changes are only in style and not substance, the differences between assimilation and acculturation might well be rendered meaningless and, at least for the American Jewish community of the twenty-first century, the straight-line theory will ultimately have been proven correct. But if it is of real depth and not a passing fad, the fears of assimilation will truly have been rendered moot.

Notes

1. Simon Rawidowicz demonstrated that for centuries, beginning in the early rabbinic period, Jews have commonly feared that their generation would be the last and with its passing devotion to Jewish learning and tradition would dissipate if not vanish. It was a self-inflicted death—suicide not murder—that they anticipated (Rawidowicz, "Israel: The Ever-dying People," *Studies in Jewish Thought,* ed. Nahum Glatzer [Philadelphia, 1974], pp. 210–224.)
2. Charles Silberman's book *A Certain People* (New York, 1985) crystallized this debate, which will be discussed in greater detail at the end of this paper.
3. Stephen M. Cohen, "Reasons For Optimism," *The Quality of American Jewish Life— Two Views,* New York, American Jewish Committee (New York, 1987) pp. 3–31
4. Marshall Sklare, "Jewish Acculturation and American Jewish Identity," in *Jewish Life in America: Historical Perspectives,* ed. Gladys Rosen (New York, 1978), p. 167.
5. Harold J. Abramson, "Assimilation and Pluralism," *Harvard Encyclopedia of American Ethnic Groups* (Cambridge, Mass., 1980), pp. 150–160.; Marshall Sklare, *America's Jews* (New York, 1971), p. 29.
6. David Ellenson, "Modernization and the Jews of Nineteenth Century Frankfurt and Berlin: A Portrait of Communities in Transition" Dworsky Center for Jewish Studies, Occasional Paper 2, University of Minnesota, 1988, p. 6.
7. "Assimililation and Pluralism," p. 157.
8. Sklare, *America's Jews,* pp. 31–33, 40.

9. Sklare, "Jewish Acculturation and American Jewish Identity," p. 168.

10. Sklare *America's Jews*, p. 32; Milton Gordon, *Assimilation in American Life* (New York, 1964).

11. Marsha L. Rozenblit, *The Jews of Vienna, 1867–1914: Assimilation and Identity* (Albany, 1983), p. 3; Ellenson, "Modernization," p. 6.

12. Ellenson, "Modernization," p. 6.

13. Sklare, "Jewish Acculturation and American Jewish Identity," p. 167; Abramson, "Assimilation and Pluralism," pp. 150–154; William Petersen, *Concepts of Ethnicity* (Cambridge, Mass. 1982), p. 13. Neil Sandberg created the term "straight line" theory of assimilation (*Ethnic Identity and Assimilation: The Polish-American Community* [New York, 1974]).

14. Petersen, *Concepts of Ethnicity*, p. 17.

15. Abramson, "Assimilation and Pluralism," p. 154; Petersen, "Concepts of Ethnicity," p. 13 (Encyclopedia, p. 238); Horace M. Kallen, *Cultural Pluralism and the American Idea: An Essay in Social Philosophy* (Philadelphia, 1956).

16. Nathan Glazer and Daniel Patrick Moynihan, *Beyond the Melting Pot: The Negroes, Puerto Ricans, Jews, Italians and Irish of New York City* (Cambridge, Mass. 1964), p. v.

17. Petersen, "Concepts of Ethnicity," (Encyclopedia, p. 239).

18. Steven M. Cohen, *American Modernity and Jewish Identity* (New York, 1983), see introduction by Charles Silberman, p. xiv.

19. Deborah E. Lipstadt, "From Noblesse Oblige to Personal Redemption: The Changing Profile and Agenda of American Jewish Leaders," *Modern Judaism* 4 (1984): pp. 295–309. The most extensive work on civil Judaism in America has is Jonathan S. Woocher, *Sacred Survival: The Civil Religion of American Jew,* (Bloomington, 1986).

20. For an example of how the rejection of Jews by certain black organizations and the anti-Israel attitudes of the New Left affected Jewish attitudes see "The Holocaust: Symbol and Myth in American Jewish Life," *Forum* No. 46 (Winter 1981), pp. 73–88.

21. Ben Halpern, *The American Jew* (New York, 1956), pp. 16–17. Daniel Elazar, *Community and Polity: The Organizational Dynamics of American Jewry* (Philadelphia, 1976), p. 21.

22. Arthur Hertzberg, *Being Jewish in America* (New York, 1979), p. 173.

23. Halpern, *American Jew*, p. 35.

24. Elazar, *Community and Polity*, p. 12.

25. Deborah Dash Moore, *At Home in America: Second Generation New York Jews* (New York, 1981), p. 240.

26. Marshall Sklare and Joseph Greenblum, *Jewish Identity on the Suburban Frontier* (Chicago, 1979), pp. 57–59.

27. Calvin Goldscheider, *Jewish Continuity and Change: Emerging Patterns in America* (Bloomington, 1986); Goldscheider, *The American Jewish Community: Social Science Research and Policy Implications* (Atlanta, 1986); Calvin Goldscheider and Alan Zuckerman, *The Transformation of the Jews* (Chicago, 1984); Cohen, *American Modernity and Jewish Identity*.

28. *New York Review of Books*, November 21, 1985, pp. 18–21; *New Leader*, October 7, 1985, pp. 16–19; *Commentary*, November 1985, pp. 108–114.

29. Cohen, "Quality of American Jewish Life."

FOR FURTHER READING

Milton Gordon's *Assimilation in American Life: The Role of Race, Religion and National Origins* (New York, 1964) remains one of the most influential works on the processes of assimilation. For some of the seminal thinking on the meaning of pluralism in American life see Horace M. Kallen, *Culture and Democracy in the United States* (New York, 1924) *and Kallen, Cultural Pluralism and the American Idea: An Essay in Social Philosophy* (Philadelphia, 1956).

An invaluable collection of essays on assimilation, pluralism, ethnicity, and the myriad ethnic groups represented in the United States is contained in the *Harvard Encyclopedia of American Ethnic Groups* (Cambridge, Mass., 1980). Among the more useful essays are William Petersen, "Concepts of Ethnicity," Harold J. Abramson, "Assimilation and Pluralism," and Arthur A. Goren, "Jews." [Petersen's and Goren's essays have been reprinted as separate paperback volumes.]

For a comparative analysis of the course of the assimilation and acculturation of American Jews, blacks, and Puerto Ricans see the classic work by Nathan Glazer and Daniel Patrick Moynihan, *Beyond the Melting Pot: The Negroes, Puerto Ricans, Jews, Italians and Irish of New York City* (Cambridge, Mass. 1964).

Sociological portraits of the changing nature of American Jews and their communal life are contained in Marshall Sklare and Joseph Greenblum, *Jewish Identity on the Suburban Frontier* (Chicago, 1979); Marshall Sklare, *America's Jews* (New York, 1971); Calvin Goldscheider, *Jewish Continuity and Change: Emerging Patterns in America* (Bloomington, 1986); Calvin Goldscheider, *The American Jewish Community: Social Science Research and Policy Implications* (Atlanta, 1986); Calvin Goldscheider and Alan Zuckerman, *The Transformation of the Jews* (Chicago, 1984); and Steven M. Cohen, *American Modernity and Jewish Identity* (New York, 1983). Arthur Hertzberg's *Being Jewish in America* (New York, 1979) addresses some of the issues Jews in the United States have faced as a result of their acculturation into American life. Jonathan S. Woocher's *Sacred Survival* (Bloomington, 1986) is a valuable portrait of recent changes in American Jewish Communal life.

For studies on intermarriage and its connection to acculturation see Egon Mayer, *Love and Tradition: Marriage Between Jews and Christians* (New York, 1985), and Susan Weidman Schneider, *Intermarriage: The Challenge of Living With Differences Between Christians and Jews* (New York, 1989).

Pluralism

ELLIOT N. DORFF

In political and religious contexts, pluralism is the position that one can affirm one's own views and practices while being open to communication with, and appreciation of, those who think and act differently.[1] Such an open-minded stance, as familiar and attractive as it is to an American audience, entails some serious problems. Specifically, how can I justify my own view while granting legitimacy to others? Will admitting the validity of other views diminish what I am prepared to sacrifice for my own? Are there any boundaries to the legitimacy I should extend to others? That is, when, if ever, should I cease to accept what another says and does and actively fight against it, perhaps even militarily? But if I am not pluralistic, how can I have anything but hostile relations with anyone outside my own group? For Jews, the issue exists on two levels: how Jews should understand and relate to those who are not Jewish; and the subject of this essay, how Jews should interact with their fellow Jews who think and act in a mode different from their own.[2]

Practical Problems and Proposals for Pluralism

Although the philosophical questions entailed in pluralism have been the same for millennia, recent disagreements within the Jewish community have heightened interest in both the practical and theoretical sides of this issue. Problems involving family law have attracted the most attention—definitions of Jewish status, conversions, marriages, and divorces which some recognize and some do not.[3] As bad as these problems are in North America, they are even worse in Israel, where such matters are controlled by the Orthodox chief rabbinate, which is one reason for the alarming disaffection of non-Orthodox, American Jews with Israel.[4]

But other, increasingly vexing, tensions also cause concern for Jewish unity. These include, first, vituperative public outbursts by one group against another, violations of what Charles Silberman calls "the basic rule of American interreligious life"—that is, "one does not publicly deny the validity of someone else's religion, nor does one publicly claim to have a monopoly on religious truth"— whatever one thinks or says in private.[5] A corollary of this is the need to abandon the polemics, distortions, and lies that sometimes characterize presentations of other views—whether in the classroom, in a public oration, or in print.[6] Another corollary of this "religion of civility" is that all groups—including the Orthodox— must stop refusing to sit down together with other Jews within communal agencies such as the local Board of Rabbis or to enter buildings housing other groups for a communal meeting or program.

Aside from eliminating such irritations, laypeople and rabbis now see the need to take positive steps to broaden cooperation and avoid splintering. Rabbi Harold Schulweis (Conservative), for example, has proposed exchanges on a lay level for both youth and adults through joint meetings, socials, retreats, and summer camp experiences.[7] Rabbi Alexander Schindler (Reform) has suggested that rabbis be invited to speak in the synagogues of other denominations; that publications report positive attitudes and activities concerning other denominations; that transdenominational studies be undertaken by members of the faculties of the various seminaries in an effort to resolve the issues of conversion and divorce; and that there be a national forum that meets no less than four times each year to air differences, explore possible compromises, and define issues of common cause.[8] Rabbi Irving Greenberg (Orthodox), who founded the National Jewish Center for Learning and Leadership largely to overcome divisivenesss within the Jewish community, has fostered ongoing meetings of rabbis and academicians in communities across the continent to get to know each other and discuss matters of common concern. He has also suggested that synagogues of various denominations jointly sponsor classes taught by rabbis and others from all institutions involved; that teenagers be brought together to discuss how to work together to further unity in the next generation; and that local communities establish task forces to promote intra-Jewish cooperation and programs.[9]

At the bottom of all of this is the assertion that *Ahavat Yisrael* (love of one's fellow Jews) must be taught as a value that transcends denominational differences. This underscores the need for a theory of pluralism that explains how and why one could adopt a given view and yet be willing—at least within some bounds—to respect as Jews those who have different views.

Rabbinic Approaches to Diversity

The Need for Unity. A play on words based on Deuteronomy 14:1 leads the rabbis to the principle that Jews should not split into factions.[10] The need for unity is, in part, political and social. Only a cohesive community can prevent anarchy and plan joint action to protect and enhance life. For the rabbis, though, the motivation was also theological: "When Israel is of one mind below, God's great name is exalted above, as it says, 'He became King in Jeshurun when the heads of the people assembled, the tribes of Israel together' (Deuteronomy 33:5)."[11] If communities are splintered, the various groups seem to be guided by two different Torahs or even by two different gods,[12] which can undermine respect for religious institutions and, ultimately, for religion itself. Furthermore, a divided Jewish community cannot effectively accomplish its religious mission of being "a light unto the nations" in perfecting the world under the dominion of God.[13]

Those for whom unity is the exclusive or paramount goal sometimes seek to attain it by claiming that there is only one correct view and that all others should be shunned or even attacked. Unfortunately, there is ample precedent for this approach in Jewish history. One account of the relationships between the first-century School of Shammai and its rival School of Hillel, for example, depicts the former as ambushing and killing all but six of the latter,[14] and in the eighteenth century Eastern European Jewry was split between Hasidim and Mitnaggedim, who issued bans of excommunication against each other prohibiting members of each group from engaging in communication or commerce with members of the other.

Rabbinic Endorsements of Pluralism. But that is not the only—and certainly not the predominant—model for attaining unity. Deuteronomy's commandment not to deviate from the words of the court—the basis for judicial authority and communal conformity—is effectively balanced by the command to "fear no man, for judgment is God's."[15] Traditional sources accordingly document a dynamic pluralism *within* the Jewish community. There are seventy faces to each passage in the Torah, according to the rabbis, and Moses was not told the final decision on each matter of law "so that the Torah may be capable of interpretation with forty-nine points *pro* and forty-nine points *contra*."[16] People should listen to each other and be prepared to change their minds on legal matters, says the Mishnah, and the opinion of a dissenting judge is recorded because in a later generation the court may revise the law to agree with him.[17] Just as the manna tasted different to each person, so too, say the rabbis, each person hears God's revelation according to his own ability.[18] The long tradition of finding varying rationales for the laws and varying interpretations of the biblical stories is the sum and substance of the Midrash Aggadah, and the methodology used in Jewish law encourages debate.[19] That may be frustrating at times, but one must learn to live with it and open one's mind to the multiplicity of meanings inherent in the Torah:

> Lest a man should say, "Since some scholars declare a thing impure and others declare it pure, some pronounce it to be permitted while others declare it forbidden, some disqualify an object while others uphold its fitness, how can I study Torah under such circumstances?" Scripture states, "They are given from one shepherd" (Ecclesiastes 12:11): One God has given them, one leader [Moses] has uttered them at the command of the Lord of all creation, blessed be He, as it says, "And God spoke *all* these words" (Exodus 20:1). You, then, should make your ear like a grain receiver and acquire a heart that can understand the words of the scholars who declare a thing impure as well as those who declare it pure, the words of those who declare a thing forbidden as well as those who pronounce it permitted, and the words of those who disqualify an object as well as those who uphold its fitness. . . . Although one scholar offers his view and another scholar offers his, the words of both are all derived from what Moses, the shepherd, received from the One Lord of the universe.[20]

Indeed, one should intentionally expose oneself to diverse approaches by studying with at least two rabbis, for "one who studies Torah from [only] one teacher will never achieve great success [literally, 'a sign of blessing']."[21]

Some, of course, did not like diversity of opinion. In the second century, Rabbi Jose complained that it makes the Torah seem like multiple Torahs, and he attributed the lack of conformity to insufficient study and/or overweening pride on the part of contemporary scholars.[22] Ten centuries later, though, Maimonides pointed out that multiple interpretations are inevitable because of the varying temperaments and intellectual capabilities of the Torah's many interpreters.[23] Rabbi Menahem ben Solomon Meiri (1249–1316) maintained that disagreement is not only inevitable but desirable as an integral part of establishing the truth, for without dispute people are not challenged to test and refine their positions.[24] The talmudic section most quoted on this issue, which presents a totally different view of the disputes between the schools of Shammai and Hillel from the one cited above, understands scholarly arguments as not only rationally but *theologically* necessary, for all sides bespeak "the words of the living God":

> Rabbi Abba stated in the name of Samuel: For three years there was a dispute between the School of Shammai and the School of Hillel, the former asserting, "The law agrees with us," and the latter contending, "The law agrees with us." Then a Heavenly Voice announced, "The utterances of both are the words of the living God, but the law agrees with the School of Hillel." Since "both are the words of the living God, what was it that entitled the School of Hillel to have the law fixed according to them? Because they were kindly and modest, they studied their own rulings and those of the School of Shammai, and they [were even so humble as to] mention the opinions of the School of Shammai before theirs.[25]

The goal is thus to educate people to be open to learning from others, similar to the School of Hillel, and to respect those with whom they disagree—so much so as to cite them first. One wants learning with manners, commitment to finding the truth together with respect for others and love of peace.[26]

If each answer is the word of God, though, why exert oneself in pursuit of truth? Vigorous study of the classical texts is required, according to the rabbis, because that is the way one learns and applies God's will, the postbiblical form of God's revelation.[27] One comes into contact with God in the process of study; it is a religious experience as well as a legal one. Moreover, Jewish law obligates Jews to study the Torah throughout their lives, even if they are poor, and even if such study involves them in debates with their teachers or parents—although there are rules of propriety governing how such debates should be held.[28]

Rabbinic Limitations on Pluralism. The Talmud is full of fractious disputes in which virtually anything could be questioned. There were some limits, though, to this general picture of uninhibited debate. When the Sanhedrin existed, rabbis could challenge decisions in debate, but in practice they had to conform to the Sanhedrin's majority ruling.[29] Rabbinic sources strive to differentiate the high level of dissent to which the rabbis were accustomed and which they thought healthy from that of the biblical figure Korah, whose rebellion the Torah condemns. Korah's dissent, the rabbis said, was not "for the sake of Heaven" but for his own power and love of victory, whereas the disputes of Hillel and Shammai were for the sake of Heaven—that is, to seek the truth. Because that was the case, rabbinic disputes will continue for all time, but Korah's dispute died with him.[30] Thus disputants must argue for the right reasons while following the practice determined by the majority.

Rabbinic literature speaks of Jews whose mode of dissent led the community to exclude them. These include the *min* (sectarian) and the *apikoros* (heretic). In view of the wide latitude of rabbinic debate, one can understand why there is considerable discussion in classical and contemporary literature about exactly what these people held or did that made their modes of dissent unacceptable.[31] Rashi, for example, says that one feature of admissible debate is that "neither side of the conflict cites an arugment from the Torah of another god, but only from the Torah of our God."[32]

In addition to such individuals, there have been groups that splintered off from the Jewish people. These include Christians, Hebrew Christians (from the first through the fifth centuries), Karaites (from the eighth century to the present), and Sabbatians (in the late seventeenth and early eighteenth centuries).

Rabbinic Modes of Accommodation in Practice. Jews ruled the people of these splinter groups outside the bounds. Those who remained part of the Jewish people needed to determine how to interact with those with whom they disagreed.

One rabbinic source addresses the degree to which a community can tolerate diversity of practice.[33] For Rabbi Johanon (third century, Israel) and Abayye (fourth century, Babylonia), the principle that the community should remain united precluded multiple practices in one locale, but communities in distinct areas could follow disparate rulings in observing the law. Rava, Abayye's contemporary and sparing partner, is more permissive. For him the principle only prohibits the members of a given court from issuing conflicting rulings; they may disagree in discussion, but they ultimately have to make one coherent decision. Two courts, however, even within the same city, could issue conflicting rulings without violating the principle. In tolerating this diversity, Rava might have been thinking of the circumstances in large cities, where differing groups of Jews might live near each other but practice Jewish law in varying ways.[34]

Members of the schools of Shammai and Hillel, however, served on the same courts. How did they agree on a ruling—and even permit their children to intermarry? According to one talmudic opinion, since the Hillelites were in the majority, the Shammaites accepted their authority in practice but remained opposed in theory. Pluralism, on this model, stops with thought; uniformity is necessary in action, and that must be determined by the majority of the rabbis charged with making the decision. A second talmudic solution is that God prevented any cases prohibited in one view but not in the other from occurring. The third explanation is that each party kept the other informed of problematic cases, and thus marriages between the families associated with the two schools could continue.[35] In other words, they trusted the majority, they trusted God, or they trusted each other.[36]

Modern Approaches to Diversity

The rabbinic sources, as we have seen, tolerate a wide spectrum of opinion and even of practice, but only within a community that shares a commitment to the fundamental beliefs and practices of Judaism. For contemporary Jews, of course, that no longer is the case. Even if Jews believe in God, they rarely feel commanded to observe the dictates of Jewish law. Thus only a small percentage of the barely half who belong to synagogues observe the dietary or Sabbath laws.[37] Conversely, the Holocaust and the State of Israel have demonstrated that, for better or worse, Jews *are* one, although not on religious grounds. Moreover, the Jewish community is clearly distinct from the various Christian and secular communities in America, and it has rejected the Jews for Jesus.

Any modern theory of pluralism, then, must take account of these new, complicating realities. Specifically, it must explain how we can justify a pluralism within the Jewish community much broader than the rabbinic sources ever contemplated while at the same time excluding those who are not accepted as Jews.

Modern, Orthodox Rejectionism. Some refuse to engage in the effort; they maintain that their view is the only correct one. Most of Orthodoxy has taken this tack, including even the modern Orthodox. Thus Rabbi Norman Lamm, president of Yeshiva University, has claimed that pluralism is not a sacred principle within Judaism. Moreover, "a pluralism which accepts everything as co-legitimate is not pluralism, but the kind of relativism that leads . . . to spiritual nihilism. If everything is kosher, nothing is kosher."[38] Similarly, Rabbi Walter Wurzburger, past editor of the modern Orthodox journal *Tradition*, has said: "Religious pluralism borders on religious relativism, if not outright nihilism. It rests on the assumption that no religion can be true and that it does not really matter what kind of myth we invoke in order to provide us with a sense of meaning and purpose."[39]

Nevertheless, Orthodox spokesmen acknowledge that, as the Talmud puts it, "A Jew, even if he sins, is [still] a Jew."[40] They may not recognize the conversions of non-Orthodox rabbis, but they are also not willing to cut themselves off from those born Jewish, as Wurzburger states positively and passionately: "*Ahavat Yisrael* [love of fellow Jews] is a religious imperative which, according to Rabbi Akiba, consitiues the most inclusive principle of the entire Torah and must be extended to every Jew, regardless of his religious persuasion. . . . But our love for . . . fellow Jews by no means precludes our commitment to Torah as *Torat Emet* [a Torah of truth], which entails the rejection of any article of faith or practice which contravenes the teachings of the Torah."[41]

How, then, should an Orthodox Jew relate to the non-Orthodox movements? Rabbi Avi Shafran of Providence, Rhode Island, put the position of most Orthodox spokesmen succinctly: the Reform and Conservative "movements are not, to me, branches of Judaism. Jewish, perhaps, like B'nai B'rith or the Jewish War Veterans, but not Juda*ism*. That position has long been filled."[42]

Other Orthodox spokesmen create theoretical frameworks that soften the starkness of Shafran's statement but do not alter its substance. Their theories provide for cooperation and even a degree of appreciation of the other movements but deny them legitimacy as expressions of God's will.

Lamm, for example, says that the non-Orthodox movements have "functional validity" and maybe even "spiritual dignity" but not "Jewish legitimacy." Noting that the word *validity* comes from the Latin *validus,* meaning strong, he points out that it is simply a fact that the non-Orthodox movements have both numbers and strength: "From a *functional* point of view, therefore, non-Orthodox rabbis are *valid* leaders of Jewish religious communities, and it is both fatuous and self-defeating not to acknowledge this openly and draw the necessary consequences, e.g., of establishing friendly and harmonious and respectful relationships, and working together, all of us, towards the Jewish communal and global goals that we share and which unite us inextricably and indissolubly." Like Orthodox rabbis, non-Orthodox rabbis, according to Lamm, may or may not have *spiritual dignity,* depending on the sincerity with which they struggle to have their conduct conform to the principles of their faith. Non-Orthodox forms of Judaism and their representatives, however, cannot have Jewish *legitimacy,* for legitimacy (derived from *lex,* law) is a normative and evaluative term, the criterion for which is "acceptance of Halakhah [Jewish law] as transcendentally obligatory, as the holy and normative 'way' for Jews, as decisive law and not just something to 'consult' in the process of developing policy. . . . At bottom, any vision of the truth excludes certain competing visions. And so does the Torah commitment."[43]

Wurzburger's usage of the words *validity* and *legitimacy* is apparently the exact opposite of Lamm's (varying definitions of terms is an ongoing problem in these discussions), but his position is similar: "While I cannot recognize the validity of procedures or practices which contravene *Halakhic* [Jewish legal] norms, I do not seek the delegitimization of non-Orthodox movements. On the contrary, I firmly believe that they can make significant contributions to the extent that they champion causes which reflect the values of our religious tradition."[44]

Liberal Jews have principles that, in some measure, contradict those of the Orthodox. They would therefore reject attempts to reconcile them to Orthodox tenets, practices, or methods, but they are not rejectionists in the sense used above because they would continue to view Orthodoxy as a valid (legitimate), although wrong, version of Judaism.

Covenant of Fate, Covenant of Destiny. A second model also comes from Orthodox spokesmen, but it differs considerably from the first. Rabbi Joseph Soloveitchik suggested in the 1950s that all Jews are bound by two covenants, a covenant of fate and a covenant of destiny (which he also called the covenant of Egypt and the covenant of Sinai).

The covenant of fate is the inescapable unity that binds Jews because of their shared fate in history. This covenant is involuntary; Jews are part of it whether they want to be or not. It has four components: (1) shared historical events (Jews feel that they are part of everything that happens to other Jews); (2) shared suffering (the anguish and pain inflicted on other Jews I experience as mine too); (3) shared responsibility (a sense of obligation to help other Jews and a willingness to do so); and (4) shared actions (activities with and for other Jews).

The covenant of destiny, by contrast, is voluntary. It is the act of commitment of the individual Jew and the Jews as a whole to realize historical Jewish values, goals, and dreams. There are significant differences among Jews as to how best to accomplish this commitment, but such arguments must be carried on within the framework of all those who share the covenant of fate.

Soloveitchik devised this model to explain the ties of religious Jews to secular Zionists, but Rabbi Irving Greenberg suggests applying it to intermovement relationships as well. Note how the slippery words *legitimacy* and *validity* here take on yet another set of meanings:

I would generalize Soloveitchik's insight: one must learn to distinguish validity and legitimacy. Legitimacy is derived from and applies to all groups that share the covenant of fate. Once having extended that legitimacy, one has every right to criticize and disagree with the validity of actions by groups that "violate" the covenant of destiny. . . . All communities, as all marriages, can exist with fights—even hard fights—as long as the fundamental legitimacy of the relationship is not challenged.[45]

Greenberg says that applying this model would rule out Jews for Jesus because by joining Christianity they have separated themselves from Jewish fate. It would also suggest that the Satmar Hasidim, Naturei Karta, radical assimilationists, and anti-Zionist universalists be excluded because of their dissociation from the fate of Jews in Israel.

This analysis examines and articulates more clearly than the rejectionist view the reasons why all Jews feel strong connections to each other and why they should have empathy for other views while also explaining how various groups of Jews can think the others wrong. Jews should not only feel responsibility for each other (the covenant of fate) but genuinely appreciate the many ways they Jews devote themselves to realizing the covenant of destiny.

A Pedagogic Convenant. Rabbi Irving Greenberg suggests another way of justifying pluralism. In the Bible, he points out, God is the dominant partner in the creation and definition of the covenant. Rabbinic literature elevates human beings to a role equal to that of God in determining the law. No voice from Heaven can do that, only the deliberation of the rabbis.[46] Their decisions, however, must be tied to God's revelation in the Written or Oral Torah, and so both God and human beings have a role. In our own time, Greenberg argues, after the Holocaust and the State of Israel, the dominant role has shifted to humanity. The Holocaust has made us question God's willingness (or ability) to intervene in our lives, and the State of Israel has demonstrated that we must take responsibility for ourselves as a people. It is as if God, the ultimate parent, has now given us free rein to make our own decisions, however much we stumble. "To enable people to mature, the teacher/parent/authority must allow them experimentation, even differing judgments, and even the right to err."[47]

In Soloveitchik's model one effectively says of others who differ, "You are wrong, but you are part of my people"; in this model, one says, "We both may be right."[48] The extra bonus in this approach, then, is the positive emotional atmosphere it creates: we share not only mutual responsibility but also a mutual effort to articulate God's will in our time.

Embracing Diversity.   As the Orthodox tend to have a low tolerance for diversity, liberals have a high tolerance for it. This is clearly a matter of degree—everyone wants *some* unity and *some* diversity—and it is not exclusively a matter of psychological temper. It is also a matter of philosophical commitments.

Rabbi Jacob Staub (Reconstructionist), for example, denies the centrality of Jewish law in linking the Jewish people historically: "I do *not* regard commitment to the Halakhic system to be the tie that has always united all Jews. The surviving Halakhic sources represent, I believe, the views of a very small minority of the rabbinic elite." Certainly in our postemancipation world, when "Jews have been freed from Halakhic authorities," we should expect and rejoice at the multiple approaches to Jewish life that have emerged. "I believe that Jews have always been, and will continue to be, divided—that *davka* [indeed] it is because of the passion that motivates our diversity that we are likely to survive with vibrancy."[49]

Aside from the obvious need to coordinate efforts on some matters, this view has at least one other disadvantage, which Staub himself notes. Jews working to implement conflicting views of what modern Jewish life should be cannot help but affront each other: "By our very existence, some Jews are offensive and insulting to others—on all sides." He speaks personally about the disappointment and pain his Orthodox relatives feel about his beliefs and practices, and vice versa. We must therefore, he says, "apply ourselves to recognizing, acknowledging, and bemoaning the inadvertent pain we cause to those whom we love so dearly—even as we remain steadfastly committed to the principles we cherish."[50]

Identifying Shared Convictions.   Some justify pluralism by pointing out how many convictions Jews share; diversity in the areas that remain are then perceived not as deleterious but as enriching and enlivening.

Rabbi David Hartman, for example, says that religious and non-religious Jews share the goals of developing character and rejecting idolatry in all its forms, even if they do not agree on appropriate methods or reasons for doing so. They can thus share both behavioral goals and a common theological language. Rabbi Reuven Kimelman claims that all Jews search for retaining Jewish authenticity within contemporary civilization; they seek a share in holiness through living as part of the Jewish community; they know that separation from the Jewish community is detachment from the covenant with the God of Israel; and they participate in discovering the grandeur of the Jewish tradition and the cultural heroes who emerge from it. Rabbi Eugene Lipman stresses that Jews share a mission, that our purpose is not simply Jewish survival but the creation of God's Kingdom on earth.[51]

Those who take this tack often maintain that to the extent that varying positions do exist, they complement each other—a point which, of course, is available to the other theories as well. Thus Rabbi Abraham Kook, former chief rabbi of Israel, appreciates differing views for revealing various aspects of the truth: "For the building is constructed from various parts, and the truth of the light of the world will be built from various dimensions, from various approaches, for these and those are the words of the living God."[52] Kimelman points out that if synagogue options are reduced, affiliation rates are likely to fall even below the current 50 percent. Reform Jews were the first to establish a synagogue movement and synagogue-centered youth groups; Conservative Jews pioneered in religiously centered camping and teenage pilgrimages to Israel; and the Orthodox have sponsored day schools. These institutions now exist in all three movements to the benefit of all.[53]

God Wants Pluralism. Rabbi Simon Greenberg has suggested a theological justification for pluralism. He defines pluralism as "the ability to say that 'your ideas are spiritually and ethically as valid—that is, as capable of being justified, supported, and defended—as mine' and yet remain firmly committed to your own ideas and practices."[54] He defines *valid* not as a term of power, as it is for Lamm, or conformity to a covenant, as it is for Irving Greenberg, but as designating intellectual credibility and worthiness.

Moreover, in contrast to both Lamm and Irving Greenberg, Simon Greenberg uses *legitimacy* as a synonym for *validity*.[55]

But what bestows legitimacy upon varying views such that a person should be pluralistic? Political pluralism, as mandated in the Bill of Rights, can be justified by pragmatic considerations, as James Madison does, but what legitimizes a spiritual or ethical pluralism? Greenberg says that he knows of no philosophic justification for pluralism, for that would entail the legitimation of accepting a position and its contrary or contradictory. There is, however, a religious justification: God *intended* that we all think differently.

Greenberg learns this from, among other sources, the Mishnah, which asks why God initiated the human species by creating only one man. One reason, the Mishnah suggests, is to impress upon us *the greatness of the Holy One, blessed be He*, for when human beings mint coins, they all come out the same, but God made one mold (Adam) and no one of them is exactly like another. This physical pluralism is matched by an intellectual pluralism for which, the rabbis say, God is to be blessed: "When one sees a crowd of people, he is to say, 'Blessed is the master of mysteries,' for just as their faces are not alike, so are their thoughts not alike." The Midrash supports this further when it says that when Moses was about to die, he said to the Lord: "Master of the Universe, You know the opinions of everyone, and that there are no two among Your children who think alike. I beg of You that after I die, when You appoint a leader for them, appoint one who will bear with (accept, *sovel*) each one of them as he thinks (on his own terms, *lefi daato*)." We know that Moses said this, the rabbis said, because Moses describes God as "God of the *ruhot* (spirits [in the plural]) of all flesh" (Num. 24:16). It is even the case, according to Rabbi Joshua and all of the later tradition, that righteous non-Jews have a portion in the World to Come, for it is only "the nations who ignored God" who will be denied that—again, a theological consideration.[56] Thus God *wants* pluralism so that people will constantly be reminded of His grandeur.

These sources also indicate that pluralism is a divine creation; human beings have difficulty imitating it. To achieve the ability to be pluralistic is, in fact, the ultimate ethical and spiritual challenge, according to Greenberg. Just as "love your neighbor as yourself"—which, for Rabbi Akiba, is the underlying principle of all the commandments[57]—requires a person to go beyond biologically rooted self-love, pluralism requires a person to escape egocentricity. It is not possible for human beings totally to love their neighbors as themselves, and neither is it possible to be totally pluralistic; we are by nature too self-centered fully to achieve either goal. The tradition, however, prescribes methods to bring us closer to these aims. Many of its directions to gain love of neighbor appear in that same Chapter 19 of Leviticus in which the commandment itself appears. The tradition's instructions as to how to become pluralistic are contained in the talmudic source quoted earlier describing the debates of Hillel and Shammai; one must, like Hillel, be affable and humble and teach opinions opposed to one's own, citing them first.[58]

Epistemological and Historical Grounds for Pluralism. Finally, I would suggest yet another approach involving epistemological and historical rationales for pluralism—rationales that have their own theological component.

When speaking historically, one must first remember the organic nature of all communities, including the Jewish one. Every community grows like an organism; it changes over time in response to both internal and external circumstances. As a result, one cannot establish limits on the ideology or practice of a community with any degree of confidence in their accuracy or durability; even Moses could not understand the Jewish tradition as expounded in the school of Rabbi Akiba, according to the Talmud.[59] That does not mean that the community is incoherent; we are a community partly because we share a history and its heroes, partly because we are aware of ourselves and are perceived by others as a community, partly because we work together as a community, and partly because we have shared goals—a shared vision and mission. All the legal and intellectual attempts to define the limits and content of Jewish identity gain whatever authority they have from that shared life.

This broad, historical perspective should impart a degree of humility to those trying to set definite bounds and make one somewhat less earnest in doing so. The community *will* define itself in time in the organic, logically haphazard way it has always used; theoretical attempts to do this are post facto rationalizations of what happens in a largely arational way. That does not mean that they are worthless; on the contrary, efforts to give communal life rational form can contribute immensely to the community's self-awareness and its plans for the future. One just should not exaggerate the degree to which human beings can devise a communal definition adequate to ever-changing historical facts.

Epistemological and theological considerations should also motivate us to embrace a pluralistic outlook. If we have difficulty putting the facts of human history in intelligible form, how much more do we realize our limits when it comes to discovering God and defining what God wants of us. We are not, of course, totally at a loss in either situation; God has given us intellectual facilities and the Torah to guide us. But we each, as the Rabbis recognized, will understand God and His will according to our own individual abilities and perspective.[60] "Every way of man is right in his own eyes, but the Lord weighs the hearts" (Prov. 21:2); as Rashi explains, this means that God judges each of us by our intentions because a human being cannot be expected to know the truth as God knows it.

Commitment to pluralism is motivated not only by the limitations of our knowledge; as we have seen, God intentionally, according to the rabbis, reveals only a part of His truth in the Torah, and the rest must come from study and debate. Even with study there is a limit to human knowledge, for, as the medieval Jewish philosopher Joseph Albo said, "If I knew Him, I would be He."[61] God as understood in the Jewish tradition thus wants pluralism not only to demonstrate His grandeur in creating humanity with diversity but also to force human beings to realize their epistemological creatureliness, the limits of human knowledge in comparison to that of God. One is commanded to study; one *is* supposed to be committed to learning as much of God, His world, and His will as possible. But one must recognize that a passion for truth does not mean that one has exclusive possession of it; indeed, it is humanly impossible to have full or sole possession of it. Moreover, one should understand that everyone's quest for religious knowledge is aided by discussion with others, for different views force all concerned to evaluate and refine their positions. The paradigmatic disputants, the School of Hillel, reverse their position a number of times in the Talmud, in contrast to the School of Shammai, which did so at most once; the Hillelites understood the epistemological and theological value of plural views and the need to learn from others.

Thus an appropriate degree of religious humility would lead one to engage in spirited, spiritual argumentation; one should not assume that one knows the truth and attempt to exclude others by fiat or social pressure. One can and must take stands, but one should do so while remaining open to being convinced to the contrary. One should also recognize that others may intelligently, morally, and theologically both think and act differently. From the standpoint of piety, pluralism emerges not from relativism but from a deeply held and aptly humble monotheism.

The Need for Unity with Diversity

Rabbinic sources demonstrate the necessity and legitimacy of vigorous disagreement within a unified, coherent community. It is, of course, not easy to balance the twin needs for unity and diversity; one needs to discover and examine the grounds for one's own beliefs and practices, stretch to see the reasons for why others believe and act as they do, and determine the limits of dissent a community can tolerate. Modern theories attempt to do this in a much more diversified setting than talmudic and medieval rabbis ever contemplated, one characterized not only by physical dispersion but by widely varying forms of being Jewish. In such circumstances, it is not surprising that the theories differ considerably in the extent to which they validate the beliefs and practices of others, but the very attempt to articulate such theories bespeaks the strongly felt need to retain unity within our diversity.

According to the Talmud, just as Jews put on phylacteries (*tefillin*), so too does God. The phylacteries which Jews wear bear the verse, "Hear O Israel, the Lord is our God, the Lord is one" (Deut. 6:4). God's phylacteries bear the verse, "Who is like Your people Israel, one nation in the world" (1 Chron. 17:21).[62] Neither unity has been sufficiently achieved. Three times each day in the *Alenu* prayer, Jews pray that God's unity might be acknowledged by all people. The unity of the people Israel, with its vigorous diversity intact, must also be the object of our work and prayers, just as it is on the mind of God.

Notes

In the following, M. = Mishnah; T. = Tosefta; B. = Babylonian Talmud; J. = Jerusalem (Palestinian) Talmud; M.T. = Maimonides' Mishneh Torah; and S.A. = Joseph Karo's Shulhan Arukh.

1. The term *pluralism* has historically been used to define a philosophical position affirming that ultimate reality is not one (monism) but many, but that is not the concern of this essay.
2. I discuss theoretical frameworks for the interaction of Jews with non-Jews in "The Covenant: How Jews Understand Themselves and Others," *Anglican Theological Review* 64 (October, 1982), pp. 481–501.
3. See, for example, Irving Greenberg, "Will There Be One Jewish People by the Year 2000?" *Perspectives* (New York, 1986), p. 1.
4. See Steven M. Cohen, *Ties and Tensions: The 1986 Survey of American Jewish Attitudes toward Israel and Israelis* (New York, 1987).
5. See, for example, Charles Silberman's untitled presentation in *Materials from the Critical Issues Conference: Will There Be One Jewish People by the Year 2000?* (New York, 1986), p. 88.
6. This point has been appropriately stressed by Eugene J. Lipman in *A CAJE Symposium: Division, Pluralism, and Unity among Jews* (New York, 1986), p. 1.
7. Harold M. Schulweis, "Jewish Apartheid," *Moment* 11 (December 1985), pp. 23–28.
8. Alexander Schindler's untitled presentation in *Materials from the Critical Issues Conference*, pp. 46–47.
9. Document of CLAL entitled "What Communities Can Do to Advance the Cause of Jewish Unity" (New York, n.d.).
10. *Sifre Deuteronomy,* 96, 346.
11. Ibid., 346.
12. Rashi (Rabbi Shlomo Yitzhaki, 1040–1105) ascribes the fear to the appearance of two Torahs on *B. Yevamot* 13b, s.v. *lo ta'aseh aggudot aggudot*; Ritba (Rabbi Yom Tov ben Abraham Ishbili, ca. 1250–1330) fears the appearance of two gods in *Hiddushei Haritba* on *B. Yevamot* 13b.
13. The image of Israel as a light to the nations is in Isaiah 42:6, 49:6; cf. 60:3. The mission of Israel to perfect the world under the dominion of God is repeated three times daily in the *Alenu* prayer.
14. *M. Shabbat* 1:4; *J. Shabbat* 1:4 (3c); see also *B. Shabbat* 17a and Josephus, *The Jewish War* Book IV, passim.
15. Deuteronomy 17:11, 1:17. David Dishon suggests this juxtaposition, and he collected and analyzed many of the rabbinic sources discussed in Sections 2–4 in his *Tarbut Ha-Mahloket B'Yisrael* (Tel Aviv, 1984) (Hebrew).
16. *Numbers Rabbah* 13:15–16; *Y. Sanhedrin* 4:2 (22a).
17. *M. Eduyot* 1:4–5.
18. *Pesikta d'Rav Kahana*, Massekhet Bahodesh Ha-shlishi, on Exodus 20:2. See also *Exodus Rabbah* 29:1.
19. David Hartman stresses these features of the Aggadah and the halakha in demonstrating the acceptability of pluralism (*Joy and Responsibility* [Jerusalem, 1978], pp. 130–161).
20. *Avot d'Rabbi Natan* 18:3; *T. Sotah* 7:7; *B. Hagigah* 3b; *Numbers Rabbah* 14:4.
21. *B. Avodah Zarah* 19a.
22. *T. Hagigah* 2:9; *B. Hullin* 7b, and see Rashi's commentary on this there. See also *T. Sotah* 14:9 (Erport MSS.).
23. Maimonides, *Commentary to the Mishnah,* Introduction, ed. Kafah, 1:11–12 (Hebrew).
24. Meiri, *Commentary to Ethics of the Fathers* on *Ethics of the Fathers* 5:17.

25. *B. Eruvin* 13b.
26. *Ethics of the Fathers* 1:12; 3:21; *B. Berakhot* 64a.
27. *B. Bava Batra* 12a.
28. *B. Kiddushin* 29a–b, 40b; *Arukh Ha-Shulhan, Yoreh De'ah* 240:12, et. al. See Israel M. Goldman, *Life-Long Learning among Jews* (New York, 1975), esp. pp. 31–68.
29. See, for example, *M. Rosh Hashanah* 2:8–9.
30. Numbers 16:1–35; *M. Avot (Ethics of the Fathers)* 5:17, and see the commentaries of Rabbi Obadiah of Bertinoro (ca. 1450 to before 1516) and Rabbenu Jonah ben Abraham Gerondi (ca. 1200–1263) to that Mishnah.
31. For example, A. Buchler, "The Minim of Sepphoris and Tiberias in the Second and Third Centuries," in *Studies in Jewish History*, ed. I. Brodie and J. Rabbinovitz (Oxford, 1956), pp. 245–74.
32. Rashi on *B. Hagigah* 3b, s.v. *Kulan.*
33. *Sifre Deuteronomy* 96, 346.
34. *J. Pesahim* 4:1 (30d); *B. Yevamot* 14a.
35. *J. Yevamot* 1:6 (3b); *B. Yevamot* 14a–b. See also *T. Yevamot* 1:12.
36. Reuven Kimelman put it this way; see his article, "Judaism and Pluralism," *Modern Judaism* 7 (May 1987), p. 136.
37. See Steven M. Cohen, *American Modernity and Jewish Identity* (New York, 1983), pp. 56, 82, 88, 91, 94.
38. Norman Lamm's untitled presentation in *Materials from the Critical Issues Conference*, p. 56.
39. Walter Wurzburger's statement in *CAJE Symposium*, p. 11.
40. *B. Sanhedrin* 44a.
41. Wurzburger in *CAJE Symposium*, p. 7.
42. Avi Shafran's untitled letter in *Moment* 11 (January–February, 1986), p. 55.
43. Norman Lamm in *Materials*, pp. 59–61.
44. Wurzburger's presentation in *CAJE Symposium*, p. 8; p. 11.
45. Irving Greenberg, "Toward a Principled Pluralism," in *Perspectives*, p. 28.
46. That is the message especially of the famous story in *B. Bava Metzia* 59b.
47. Greenberg, "Will There Be One Jewish People," p. 29.
48. Rabbi Greenberg phrased it this way at a lecture on March 8, 1987, at Camp Ramah in Ojai, California.
49. Jacob Staub's untitled presentation in *CAJE Symposium*, pp. 4–5; see. p. 10.
50. Ibid., p. 5.
51. Hartman, "Halakhah as a Ground for Creating a Shared Spiritual Language," in *Joy and Responsibility*, pp. 143–55; Kimelman, "Judaism and Pluralism," p. 144; Lipman's untitled presentation in *CAJE Symposium*, p. 1.
52. Abraham Isaac Kook, *Olat Rayah* (1939; rpt. Jerusalem, 1962), 1:330.
53. Kimelman, "Judaism and Pluralism," pp. 145–47. He uses the metaphor of an orchestra whose harmony depends on all the instruments playing their different parts but for a common goal.
54. Simon Greenberg, "Pluralism and Jewish Education," *Religious Education* 81 (Winter 1986), p. 23. See also p. 27, where he links pluralism to the absence of violence in transforming another person's opinion.
55. This is indicated by the sentence that follows immediately after Greenberg's definition of *validity* quoted above. That sentence begins, "This implication of the term legitimate. . . ."
56. Greenberg, "Pluralism and Jewish Education," pp. 24, 26. The Mishnah cited is *M. Sanhedrin* 4:5; the blessing cited is in *B. Berakhot* 58a; the Midrash cited is in *Midrash*

Tanhuma on Num. 24:16; and the source granting righteous Gentiles a place in the World to Come is *T. Sanhedrin* 13:2, based on Ps. 9:18.

57. *Sifra* to Lev. 19:18. Ben Azzai instead cites "This is the book of the generations of Adam . . . in the likeness of God He made him" (Gen. 5:1)—a principle that extends love beyond Jews ("your neighbor") and ties it directly to God, whose image should be appreciated in every person.

58. *B. Eruvin* 13b.

59. *B. Menahot* 29b.

60. See *Exodus Rabbah* 29:1 and *Pesikta d'Rav Kahana*, Bahodesh Hashlishi, on Exod. 20:2.

61. Joseph Albo, *Sefer Ha-Ikkarim*, pt. 2, chap. 30, Isaac Husik, trans. (Philadelphia, 1946), 2:206.

62. *B. Berakhot* 6a.

FOR FURTHER READING

Dorff, Elliot N., "The Covenant: How Jews Understand Themselves and Others," *Anglican Theological Review* 64 (October 1982), pp. 481–501. This article explores the theological sources within Judaism which, on one hand, give Jews a sense of their own identity and uniqueness, and, on the other, urge them to appreciate and cooperate with non-Jews. Many of these same sources are relevant to intra-Jewish discussions of pluralism.

Greenberg, Irving. "Toward a Principled Pluralism" and "Will There Be One Jewish People by the Year 2000?" In *Perspectives*, pp. 1–8, 20–31, New York, 1986. These are two seminal papers by the man who has sounded the alarm more than any other on the dangers of fragmentation within the Jewish community and the need for, as he calls it, "a principled pluralism" among Jews.

Greenberg, Simon, "Pluralism and Jewish Education," *Religious Education* 81 (Winter 1986), pp. 19–28. In this essay, Rabbi Greenberg examines how sources within Judaism can and should lead to a pluralistic approach in Jewish education within all denominations of Judaism.

Hartman, David, "Halakhah as a Ground for Creating a Shared Spiritual Language." In his *Joy and Responsibility*, pp. 130–61, Jerusalem, 1978. Rabbi Hartman, an Orthodox rabbi, argues that Orthodox education need not, and should not, educate toward the spiritual isolation of its students from Jews holding other views.

Jacobs, Louis, *A Tree of Life: Diversity, Flexibility, and Creativity in Jewish Law*, New York, 1984. Although this book is ultimately an exposition of Jacobs's own philosophy of Jewish law, it is probably the clearest and most thorough demonstration in English of the openness and flexibility of traditional Judaism, with the stated purpose of recapturing such a nonfundamentalist approach in the contemporary Jewish community.

Kimelman, Reuven, "Judaism and Pluralism," *Modern Judaism* 7 (May 1987), pp. 131–50. In this essay, Rabbi Kimelman examines some of the evidence of a friendly but lively process of debate among the rabbis of the Mishnah and Talmud in arguing for Jewish pluralism today. Much of this article is based on the longer treatment of this subject in David Dishon, *Tarbut Ha-Mahloket Be-Yisrael* (Tel Aviv, 1984), and those who read Hebrew may profitably refer to Dishon's thorough investigation of this evidence.

Matanky, Leonard A., ed, *A CAJE Symposium: Division, Pluralism and Unity among Jews,* New York, 1986. A transcript of a symposium conducted on this subject on August 7, 1986, including presentations by Rabbis Eugene J. Lipman (Reform), Jacob J. Staub (Reconstructionist), Mordecai Waxman (Conservative), and Walter S. Wurzburger (Orthodox), this valuable booklet also includes a record of the question-and-answer period that followed and an annotated bibliography on pluralism.

Materials from the Critical Issues Conference: Will There Be One Jewish People by the Year 2000? New York, 1986. Presentations by Elie Wiesel, Gerson Cohen, Ira Silverman, Alexander Schindler, Norman Lamm, Charles Silberman, and Irving Greenberg, together with a summary of suggestions arising from the presentations and workshops for enhancing Jewish pluralism.

Schechter, Solomon, "His Majesty's Opposition". In *Seminary Addresses and Other Papers,* pp. 239–44. New York, 1915, Reprint. New York, 1959. One of the earliest defenses of Jewish pluralism in English by the Chancellor of the Jewish Theological Seminary of America.

Schulweis, Harold M., "Jewish Apartheid," *Moment* 11 (December 1985) pp. 23–28. An article whose title and substance brought wide attention to the tragedy of "Jewish apartheid" and the critical need to bridge the gaps among Jewish groups.

Europe and the rest of the world on this issue; yes, overt political, structural, and violent anti-Semitism has been much less of a factor here, but that does not mean that America has been free of its influence. To be sure, most social science surveys using such customary indexes as non-Jewish attitudes and stereotypes concerning Jews have shown a decline of anti-Semitism in the post–World War II period. Researchers who have examined other indicators such as Jewish access to political office, college admission, employment, housing, and the like have found similar results. As a group, Jews have achieved great economic, social, and political success in the United States.

Yet a feeling of disquiet still exists because the phenomenon has not disappeared, even in pluralistic, democratic America. A significant percentage of Americans, maybe as high as 20 to 25 percent, still harbor anti-Semitic stereotypes. Gary Tobin has demonstrated that Jews feel that anti-Semitism is still a problem.[2] They point to the increased visibility of neo-Nazi political tendencies in Western Europe, Canada, and the United States and the growth of Holocaust revisionism. In 1985, for example, Canada witnessed the much publicized trials of Ernst Zundel in Ontario and Jim Keegstra in Alberta, both dealing with the denial of the Holocaust. They are disturbed when organizations like the White Aryan Resistance, the Aryan Nations, the Order, and the revitalized Ku Klux Klan promulgate anti-Semitic and racist rhetoric and literature and indicate their intention to do acts of violence against blacks and Jews. They are concerned when bigoted groups of youth known as "skinheads" are growing across the country, possibly numbering as many as thirty-five hundred in thirty-five cities, and are being supported by older racist groups. These youth groups have been blamed for crimes ranging from intimidation and arson to murder. Jews are made anxious by the increased violence directed against them, including such heinous crimes as the bombing of synagogues, the desecration of cemeteries, and the assassination by Aryan extremists of Denver radio personality Alan Berg in 1984. Finally, they are made uneasy by the blurring of the distinctions between genuine criticism of specific Israeli policies and vitriolic anti-Zionist diatribes that go well beyond legitimate political criticism or discourse and that use Israel as a surrogate for traditional anti-Semitic beliefs and attitudes; the rise of a fundamental Christianity that claims that God does not hear the prayers of

Jews; the apparent increase of black anti-Semitism; and the anti-Semitic slurs of a candidate for the United States presidency. To be sure, a difference exists between Europe and America, but has America been different enough? This question has been central ever since a once civilized country exploded in this century in an unprecedented orgy of anti-Semitism and genocide. It is a question that permits no easy answers.

In the face of this reality, the relative neglect of anti-Semitism by students of American history contrasts with the intense fascination it has held for scholars of European history. The latter assigned to anti-Semitism an extraordinary importance, arguing that critical attitudes toward Jews indicate the basic health of any society. As John Higham puts it, "Anti-Semitism, in this view, is not just a serious problem in human relations; it is the very archetype of prejudice."[3] To paraphrase Dostoyevsky, European historians such as Jacob Katz, Yehuda Bauer, and Shmuel Ettinger maintained that a civilization can be judged by how it treats Jews and other vulnerable groups. The study of anti-Semitism for these scholars must be understood not as a parochial concern but as the study of the essence of the culture.[4]

Historians of American Jewry, in contrast, have tended to view anti-Semitism as an exception, a quirk of fate, an abnormal situation caused by temporary social and economic factors. Scholarly literature is scattered and inchoate, focusing on the more tangible aspects of anti-Semitism and prejudice rather than the ideological and psychological consequences of decades of stereotyping and the pressures to assimilate (in Europe there was the stick, in America the carrot).[5] We therefore lack a systematic understanding of the factors that have divided Jew and Christian in America. Another problem involves the uncertainty and theoretical fuzziness surrounding anti-Semitism. Ultimately, we are left with studies that do not define or create working typologies of anti-Semitism, something Ben Halpern has successfully attempted.[6]

Notwithstanding the tendency of many to see anti-Semitism behind every furtive glance and frustrated desire, clearly not every negative statement or sentiment regarding Jews is anti-Semitic. Jewish immigrants to America experienced some hostility simply because they were impoverished, unacculturated foreigners.[7] Pride in America as a haven for the oppressed and the liberal traditions of tolerance, individuality, and equal opportunity helped create, as Jonathan Sarna has pointed out, the ambivalent attitudes Americans have had concerning Jews, often combining feelings of hostility with feelings of friendship and acceptance.[8] Moreover, mitigating circumstances contributed tolerance within the historical tradition of American Christianity. John Higham has argued, for example, that a certain strain of sentiment among American Protestants admired Jews and Judaism. Puritan orthodoxy held that the Jews were God's chosen people, miraculously saved and sustained as proof of God's greatness, a view that lent itself to sympathy and positive identification with the Jews.[9]

Because of this historical tradition, scholars of the American experience did not really look at the issue of anti-Semitism until after the Holocaust. In the wake of that tragedy, prominent social scientists and psychologists attempted to analyze and understand the social, economic, religious, and psychological factors that predispose some individuals and societies to reactions of extreme hostility and hatred toward racial and religious groups. The writings of Theodor Adorno, Bruno Bettelheim, Morris Janowitz, Seymour Martin Lipset, Alan Davies, Gordon Allport, Charles Stember, Rodney Stark, and Harold Quinley are exemplary of the vast social science research that has been done in this area.[10]

In particular, Glock and Stark, in *Christian Beliefs and Anti-Semitism*, propounded a correlation between those professing anti-Semitic beliefs and their Christian beliefs and affiliation. Gary Marx's *Protest and Prejudice* found blacks no more anti-Semitic than whites; to the extent that black anti-Semitism exists, it results largely from unfavorable social and economic contact between Jew and black.[11]

The Tenacity of Prejudice, a survey analysis by Gertrude Selznick and Stephen Steinberg, isolates the independent variables that contribute to anti-Semitism. The researchers developed an "Index of Anti-Semitic Belief," which they submitted to two thousand respondents. Analyzing the results, they found that education, more than age, generation, geographical location, and religious beliefs, was the most important independent variable in determining the extent of anti-Semitic bias. They predicted the gradual disappearance of anti-Semitism with the spread of education.[12]

Anti-Semitism in the United States: A Study of Prejudice in the 1980s, by Gregory Martire and Ruth Clark, is very much in the same tradition. Also using survey analysis, the authors attempt to provide "the first comprehensive trend study of anti-Semitism in the United States, and . . . to examine the factors that are associated with American anti-Semitism in the 1980s."[13] Drawing on the Selznick and Steinberg study, plus a 1977 study on attitudes toward Israel by Yankelovich, Skelly, and White, Inc., Martire and Clark conducted fifty in-depth interviews with Jews and non-Jews from across the nation and compiled a quantitative survey based on 1,215 personal interviews representing a cross section of adults in the contiguous United States.

The authors conclude that, although they are a minority, "individuals holding anti-Semitic beliefs clearly represent a significant social problem in the United States."[14] One in four (23 percent) non-Jews can be characterized as prejudiced. Though anti-Semitic beliefs continue to present a serious problem, the authors found a decline since 1964 in the prevalence of many traditional anti-Semitic stereotypes such as negative images relating to shrewdness, dishonesty, assertiveness, or willingness to use shady business practices. The decline resulted not from changes in the attitudes of individuals but from generational change—the coming of age of those who were children in the mid-1960s, who as young people tended to be relatively unprejudiced and who showed an increased tolerance of diversity.

Martire and Clark did not find any particular correlation between anti-Semitism and political conservatism, energy crisis concerns, dual loyalty fears, or religious fundamentalism. Instead, their study indicates that anti-Semitism is associated most strongly with three demographic characteristics: age, education, and race. "The level of anti-Semitism is higher among adults who are older, less educated, or black," thus pointing to the generational variable as the most important determinant.[15] This finding has several significant implications. "It suggests that an individual's attitude towards Jews is probably relatively enduring. . . . It also suggests that the decline in anti-Semitism should continue as the better-educated and more tolerant young adults continue through the life cycle."[16]

The only exception to this hopeful prognosis is the black community. The authors found that race is the other demographic factor most closely associated with anti-Semitism. About 23 percent of whites can be characterized as prejudiced compared to 37 percent of blacks.[17] Black anti-Semitism appears to stem primarily from the tensions caused by the middleman minority, or retailer-consumer, relationship that characterizes the economic interactions of the two groups.[18]

These studies have made an important contribution to the growing body of social science literature on the subject of anti-Semitism, yet there are some weaknesses in the approach. Because such studies lack a historical orientation and because, as Lucy Dawidowicz pointed out in an important article in *Commentary*, of "its single focus on opinion," the survey analysis method is "not properly geared to study the etiology of anti-Semitism. Useful for periodic pulse-taking, it nevertheless serves ultimately to limit our understanding of anti-Semitism, which is a phenomenon marked by a high degree of multiformity and contradictoriness."[19] Furthermore, these works of social research do not explain the earlier and specifically American manifestations of anti-Semitism.

Beginning in the late 1960s, American scholars apparently became more sensitive to the issue of American anti-Semitism and the role of ideology. Critical of the grading-over process of consensus historiography, they initiated a revisionist critique of the problem. There were several reasons for this development. American historians of the time were engaged generally in a critical rethinking of assumptions long taken for granted concerning the political, economic, and social realities of our past. American Jewish scholars, just beginning to come into their own in academia, were drawn toward previously unexamined aspects of the American Jewish experience. The pluralistic attitudes characteristic of 1960s culture brought Jews and Jewish scholars out of the closet, so to speak, and made it easier for them to discuss issues of Jewish concern publicly. The growing interest in the Holocaust, spurred on by the 1961–62 Eichmann trial, the 1967 Arab-Israeli war and predictions of a second Holocaust, and the emergence of Elie Wiesel as folk hero and witness to atrocity generated interest in the problem of anti-Semitism.

Israel's creation in 1948 posed theological problems for many Christians, who believed that Judaism ceased as a creative and legitimate force with the rise of Christianity and that the destruction of the Temple in 70 B.C.E. had marked the death of Judaism and the Jewish people as viable, living entities. The perception that Jews were "a fossilized relic of Syriac society," as British historian Arnold Toynbee put it, apparently made it difficult for many

Christians to support the modern state created by this "anachronistic" people.[20] Yet these negative factors, one can surmise, facilitated a positive response in some areas, a renewed interest in Jewish-Christian relations in America, and the desire to look closely and critically at the problem of American anti-Semitism.

Elsewhere I have argued that anti-Semitism has been far more important and pervasive in our national history than previous scholars were willing to admit and that its persistence over time in different social and economic contexts throws some doubt on the socioeconomic explanation of its existence. Instead, I draw attention to the role of stereotypes such as the Jew as enemy of Christianity, the deceitful Shylock, the parvenu, the international conspirator, and so forth in perpetuating negative attitudes toward Jews.

Nineteenth-century American society probably was unaware of the European historical background that had built anti-Semitism into its societal structure. Only a few Americans knew of the medieval ecclesiastical statutes limiting the economic activities available to Jews. Although the origins of the structurally created anti-Semitism in European and American society had been forgotten, the symbolic expressions of these origins remained embedded in the literature and sensibilities of Western society in the form of pejorative stereotypes.[21]

What relationship do these images have to the tendency to discriminate against Jews? Do all negative images lead inevitably to discrimination? Are some more dangerous than others? What elements in society benefit from discrimination? What impact have these negative images had on Jewish self-perception and self-esteem? Has their existence fostered the rush toward assimilation?

Among the relatively few books and articles that examine American anti-Semitism from a historical perspective, one finds only tentative answers to these questions. The best-known works—the studies by Oscar Handlin, John Higham, Arnold Rose, Leonard Dinnerstein (*The Leo Frank Case*), Cary McWilliams, and Richard Hofstadter—argue that anti-Semitism is the consequence of objective socioeconomic factors and tensions operative in society that affect marginal groups.[22] Sander Diamond and Leo Ribuffo have extended this analysis of social conflict to include those individuals who have created or joined Radical Right and Christian Right organizations.[23]

Before we can generalize about their findings, we need to know why certain individuals are attracted to extremist movements. As William Schneider has pointed out, Joseph McCarthy, George Wallace, and more recent right-wing ideologues such as Jerry Falwell and Pat Robertson have not been associated openly with anti-Semitic sentiments: "These right-wing figures . . . conscientiously avoided the exploitation of anti-Semitism among their followers. Indeed, some candidates of the New Right have made explicit overtures to Jews, arguing that Jews should consider their self-interest and not merely their ideology."[24]

Similarly, it is not enough to say, for example, that all fundamentalists are anti-Semitic. As Ribuffo has argued, there is "no necessary connection between conservative theology and far right activism . . . nevertheless, the convention associating fundamentalism with bigotry and reaction, created during the 1920s, was widely disseminated. . . . Following World War II, this convention, combined with surfacing suspicion of 'simple folk,' would decisively influence interpretations of the far right."[25] In their study of anti-Semitism in America, Martire and Clark have concluded

> that the relationship between Christian orthodoxy and anti-Semitism is due almost entirely to three demographic factors: education, race, and age. . . . After controlling for education, race, and age, we find that the partial correlation between religiousness and anti-Semitism virtually disappears, indicating that the apparent relationship is actually due to the fact that individuals who are traditional in their religious outlook are more likely to be older, less educated, and black—all factors that are associated with higher levels of anti-Semitic belief.[26]

Finally, anti-Semitic ideology and attitudes are insufficient in themselves to explain America's anti-Jewish tendencies. Most contemporary analyses of American anti-Semitism show, disturbingly, that in the late nineteenth and early twentieth centuries, anti-Semitism was separated from analysis of capitalist development, thereby locating the American-Jewish problem in a structural vacuum independent of other economic or social tendencies.

Much valuable work has been done on the effect of image, ideology, and myth on the development of American anti-Semitism, but there has been insufficient reflection on socioeconomic factors independent of ethnic, religious, or national characteristics.

We know, for example, from sociological literature, that there is a well-established tendency as economic competition increases, albeit real or imagined, for ethnic antagonisms to increase among discernible competing groups. Richard Rubenstein has pointed out this phenomenon in *The Cunning of History*. It is true for wage-labor conflicts, certain economic dependency relationships, and business competition.[27] Max Weber cites the antagonisms that can result if a particular group is identified with a particular economic activity or position such as debtor or creditor.[28] Similarly, sociologists Isidor Wallimann and Edna Bonacich have observed antagonism between retailers and consumers when the two belonged to different ethnic groups.[29]

There is a growing sociological literature on "middleman minorities" and victimization. Were such mechanisms also present in the American-Jewish situation? Was the Jewish community discernible as a competitor of non-Jewish segments of the American society, and could it as such be targeted for political exploitation by a rising anti-Semitic movement? David Gerber suggests that this was the case in antebellum Buffalo, New York.[30] Recent studies indicate that the same phenomenon may be operative in the rising tide of anti-Semitism among blacks. As Gary Marx and others have argued, evidence suggests that, because of their own historically marginal status, Jews have developed a "middleman" role between the black community and white society in occupations such as teachers, principals, merchants, social workers, and doctors. Thus Marx concludes convincingly: "While we do not assume that these contacts are the sole source of Negro hostility, it would seem from the data that they are an important source."[31]

It is true that many immigrant groups underwent attack in America. And it must be said that Jews neither met with as much hostility nor as much acceptance as did certain other minorities. Rapid social and economic advancement exposed Jews to more social discrimination but also left them in a better position to deal with it. Once they emerged from the ghettos into the suburbs in the second generation, their newly attained economic positions, educational levels, and emerging defense organizations served as cushions to deflate prejudice. Their remarkable success in America, a source of mixed admiration and envy, weakened the potential impact of anti-Semitism.[32]

Yet the fact remains that anti-Semitism erupted even in reformist and libertarian sectors of American society. The democratic impulse was not and may not always be resolute enough to overcome the psychological and social momentum of anti-Semitic stereotyping.[33] True, America never visited mass physical oppression upon its Jews. But there are more subtle forms of oppression—economic, social, and cultural—that are also damaging and painful. In addition to the ideological factors, Jews faced the serious problem of social discrimination. Saratoga, Nahant, Newport, Long Branch, Lakewood, even New York City became battlegrounds. Signs like "No Jews or Dogs Admitted Here" were common in many of America's finest resorts. Advertisements in the *New York Times* and the *New York Tribune* often used euphemisms like "restricted clientele," "discriminating families only," and "Christian patronage." Rather than accept this discrimination, some prominent Jews, including Nathan Straus, retaliated by buying several of the leading hotels that excluded Jews.[34]

Discrimination at summer resorts, private schools, and clubs increased during the years before World War I. The Century Club in New York rejected the distinguished scientist Jacques Loeb because he was a Jew. Most Masonic lodges excluded Jews. Some of the most prestigious preparatory schools, such as Exeter, Hotchkiss, and Andover, had small Jewish quotas. After 1900, few Jews were elected to the Princeton clubs or to the fraternities at Yale, Columbia, and Harvard. The literary and gymnastic societies at Columbia excluded Jews. As a result, Jewish students gradually formed their own fraternities, the first appearing at Columbia in 1898. The anti-Semitic feelings also infected college faculties. It was common knowledge that few Jews could gain entry to or advancement in American academic circles.[35]

Social discrimination reached a climax in the quota systems adopted by colleges and medical schools in the years after World War I. Many colleges set limits on Jewish enrollment. Some established alumni committees to screen applicants. Others, under the pretext of seeking regional balance, gave preference to students outside the East, thereby limiting the number of Jews, who were heavily concentrated there. The most common method of exclusion came with the introduction of character and psychological examinations.

Before the 1920s, scholastic performance was the most important criterion in admissions policies. Now admissions committees
devised tests to rank students on such characteristics as "public
spirit," "fair play," "interest in fellows," and "leadership," traits
not usually associated in the popular mind with Jews. Here we see
that negative imagery can have social consequences. According to
the prevailing opinion, "public spirit" and "interest in fellows"
were Christian virtues; Jews were excessively clannish and cared
only for their group. "Leadership" also was seen as a Protestant
virtue; Jews exhibiting it would be regarded as aggressive and
pushy.[36] By 1919 New York University instituted stringent restrictions and introduced psychological testing. Chancellor Elmor
Brown justified this policy, citing the "separateness" of the Jewish
student body.[37] Columbia University cut the number of Jews in the
incoming classes from 40 to 20 percent. At Harvard, where elite
Protestant students and faculty feared the university's becoming a
"new Jerusalem," President A. Lawrence Lowell in 1922 recommended a quota system, openly adopting what other institutions
were doing covertly. "There is a rapidly growing anti-Semitic feeling in this country," he wrote in June of that year, "caused by . . . a
strong race feeling on the part of the Jews."[38] Smaller colleges,
perhaps more rigid than some large, urban ones, used more subjec-
tive criteria such as requiring a photograph of the candidate and
enforcing a geographic distribution. The problem was even
greater in medical schools, which erected formidable barriers
throughout the country, severely limiting Jewish enrollments and
causing undue hardship.[39] The adoption of a Jewish quota that
began explicitly at Columbia, New York University and Harvard
reflected the behind-the-scenes policy between 1920 and the mid-
1940s at most eastern private liberal arts colleges and elite universities, in the major state universities in the South and MidWest,
and nationally in many medical, dental, and law schools. As Marcia
Graham Synnott has argued, the reason for these limitations was
"to perpetuate the economic and social position of middle- and
upper-middle-class, white, native-born Protestants." This policy
also had social and economic implications because "few manufac-
turing companies, corporate law firms, private hospitals, or such
government bureaucracies as the State Department welcomed
Jews."[40]

The 1920s also saw the proliferation of "restrictive covenants" in housing through which owners pledged not to sell their homes and property to Jews and other undesirable groups. Economic discrimination also grew. Jews could not find positions in banking, insurance, and public utilities firms. Employment agencies found that Jews were unacceptable to most employers. The Alliance Employment Bureau in New York City, for example, wrote to Cyrus Sulzberger, president of the United Hebrew Charities, in 1908: "We are finding great difficulty in placing our Jewish boys and girls, an increasing number of employers absolutely refusing to take them." The Katharine Gibbs School for secretarial training informed a Jewish applicant in 1928 that its policy was "not to accept students of Jewish nationality." Insurance companies such as Connecticut Mutual Life Insurance Company, the Shawnee Fire Insurance Company, and the New Jersey Fire Insurance Company, urged their agents not to insure Jewish clients because they were "an extraordinary hazardous class."[41]

The most significant ideological attack against Jews occurred during the 1920s and 1930s. It focused not on religious issues or Jewish social climbing but on race and political subversion. A resurgent Ku Klux Klan activated the myths about Jews as Christ killers and race polluters. More significantly, the country witnessed the resurrection of the international stereotype of the Jew as half banker and half Bolshevik, conspiring to seize control of the nation. This belief, having been foreshadowed during the Civil War, emerged in the 1890s during the Populist ferment and crystallized in the early 1920s around auto magnate Henry Ford. In May 1922, Ford's newspaper, the *Dearborn Independent,* launched an anti-Semitic propaganda campaign without precedent in American history. It lasted for about seven years. In time, the newspaper "exposed" Jewish control of everything from the League of Nations to American politics, from baseball and jazz to agriculture and movies. If any pattern of ideas activated discrimination, it was the conspiratorial ferment to which the Populists, Henry Ford, and the Ku Klux Klan contributed.[42]

With the approach of World War II, these issues were further clouded by events in Europe. As Hitler proved to be virulently anti-Semitic, American Jews began to argue for intervention in the affairs of Europe, a stand resented by isolationists committed to keeping America out of the impending conflagration. On September 11, 1941, American aviation hero Charles Lindbergh warned that the Jews and President Franklin D. Roosevelt were conspiring to bring the nation into a war against Germany and that such a war would prove catastrophic for America.

This sentiment fed into a form of Catholic anti-Semitism best represented by Father Charles Coughlin, who spoke for the beliefs of small-town America. Beginning in 1936, in his journal, *Social Justice,* and on his widely aired radio broadcasts (with 20 to 30 million listeners), he began to argue that European fascism was a legitimate response to the more pernicious threat of communism that was largely inspired by Jews. His diatribes continued until 1942, when he was finally taken off the air. But Fritz Kuhn's German-American Bund, Gerald L. K. Smith, Dudley Pelley, and other pro-Nazi and anti-Semitic groups and individuals kept the issue alive. More than one hundred anti-Semitic organizations were formed in the United States in the 1930s, including the Silver Shirts, the Friends of Democracy, and the National Union for Social Justice.

The situation became more acute when European Jews began to seek refuge in this country. The growing isolationism and xenophobia of the 1930s, as well as public opinion polls of the period, have shown how stereotyping reinforced insensitivity and misunderstanding and contributed to the government's inertia in the face of an unprecedented human tragedy. The critical decade of the 1930s witnessed the rise of Nazism in Europe and a high degree of acceptance and approval of anti-Semitism in America. Although sympathetic to the plight of the refugees, many Americans remained unalterably opposed to admitting them.

Consequently, only approximately 127,000 refugees, or an average of a little over 18,000 a year, came to the United States between 1933 and 1940. Without congressional action, 183,112 could have entered the United States from Germany and Austria. Obstruction and red tape, largely caused by insensitivity to their plight, kept out at least 60,000 deserving others.[43]

The sum of the individual cases of American anti-Semitism before World War II may not seem very significant. But when viewed from the point of view of the callous lack of concern for Nazi refugees and refusal to admit them that led to certain death for countless thousands, the reality becomes painfully disturbing.

Matters did, however, improve dramatically after 1945. Whether as a result of guilt feelings and sympathy for Jews because of the Holocaust, or the greater effectiveness of American Jewish organizations committed to fighting anti-Semitism, or the diminished appeal of ideologies of all sorts in postwar America, the intensity and effect of anti-Semitism in the United States declined significantly in the late 1940s into the 1950s. Universities and colleges began to loosen their quota restrictions. Medical, dental, and law schools showed dramatic increases in the numbers of Jewish students.[44] Public opinion polls in the early 1950s began reflecting the more positive attitudes of non-Jews toward Jews. Major public opinion surveys published in 1964, 1966, 1981, and 1982 indicated that the trend was continuing.[45] Institutional discrimination against Jews in housing and employment was sharply reduced. Jews began to enjoy greater political success, being elected to the House of Representatives, the Senate, and other high political offices in numbers far disproportionate to the size of the Jewish population.[46] In the 101st Congress sworn in on January 3, 1989, there were thirty-one Jewish members of the House of Representatives and eight Jewish senators, one of whom is believed to be the first Orthodox Jew elected to the chamber. By the 1980s, some would feel that anti-Semitism in the United States, once a serious problem, was a thing of the past.

But though there is no question that Americans today are much more accepting of Jews and far less intolerant than they were in the pre–World War II period, there still are some significant areas of concern. One notable exception to the apparent decline of anti-Semitism appears in the black community with which Jews have been historically linked in their collective struggles for civil rights and equal opportunities. Recent public opinion surveys reveal that on almost every indicator blacks, particularly young blacks, hold more negative views of Jews than do whites. This is troubling for two reasons. First, contrary to the trend among whites, black anti-Semitism is inversely related to age and education (the strongest anti-Semitism is expressed by the most educated and by younger blacks).[47] Second, although anti-Semitism is not now generally politically acceptable in America, it is acceptable in the black community. The more politically conscious and active blacks appear to be more negative than the majority of blacks. When so public a personality as Jesse Jackson used the term "hymies" to refer to Jews during his 1984 campaign for the Democratic presidential nomination and when he and other black leaders did not repudiate

Louis Farrakhan, who introduced anti-Semitic rhetoric into national politics, there is cause for concern.

The historic alliance between Jews and blacks, forged during the long civil rights struggle, seems to be drawing to a close. The sources for these tensions go back several decades. As early as the 1960s, many black activists began to feel that Jews in the civil rights movement were patronizing in their attitudes and reluctant to give up leadership roles to blacks. Simultaneously certain developments in American society brought new conflicts between blacks and Jews. The population of blacks in America's northeastern cities, where Jews lived in disproportionate numbers, continued to increase, causing social friction between adjacent black and Jewish communities. Jews, like other whites, tended to link the problem of crime to blacks. Resentment and fear intensified and surfaced with acute force during controversies like the New York City teachers' strike of 1968. That strike developed over the issue of school decentralization. The catalyst was a decision made by the Ocean Hill–Brownsville board of education in April 1968 to dismiss nineteen teachers who were thought to oppose the experimental decentralization project. Almost all of the nineteen were Jews. When Superintendent of Schools Bernard Donovan called for the reinstatement of the teachers, local parents, most of whom were black, prevented them from entering the schools. In September approximately 95 percent of the teachers went on strike. The lines were now drawn between a white, largely Jewish school system and United Federation of Teachers facing a largely black student and parent body. A plethora of racist and anti-Semitic expressions appeared in print and on the radio such as the following anti-Semitic poem, written by a fifteen-year-old schoolgirl and read on WBAI-FM on December 26, 1968: "Hey, Jew Boy, with that yarmulka on your head / You pale-faced Jew boy—I wish you were dead."[48] Remarks like these and the tensions they unleashed led many Jews to fear that black anti-Semitism was a serious concern. Recalling a history of quota systems and anti-Semitic hiring practices in the United States, many felt that the merit system was the Jews' one protection and that it was threatened by differences between the two communities on social issues such as decentralization, affirmative action, quotas, busing, and political and economic competition. Differences over Israel exacerbated the problem. Many blacks identify with liberation struggles around the globe and have aligned themselves with the Arab and Palestine Liberation Organization struggles against Israel. This position is legitimate if it is based on reasoned, careful analyses of the situation. Unfortunately, it often blends into an anti-Zionism verging on anti-Semitism with Israel unfairly described as a conspiratorial state with demonic qualities characterized by its alleged arrogance and its colonialist, imperialist, and racist tendencies.

A second qualifier to these more hopeful signs has to do with the data. Questions have been raised about the validity of opinion surveys. What do they really show?[49] Attitudes cannot always be equated with behavior. Even though the percentage of Americans harboring anti-Semitic stereotypes seems to have declined, significant numbers, maybe 15 to 20 percent, are still affected by the old canards, and on some surveys, as the 1981 Yankelovich study notes, the percentages are much higher. For example, 33 percent of Americans believe that Jews are more willing than others to use shady practices to get what they want, and 43 percent still believe that international banking is controlled by Jews.[50] Furthermore, and more troubling, new stereotypes have emerged and younger non-Jews are more likely than older non-Jews to hold them. Education and generation may not bring the hoped-for end to anti-Semitism. Negative remarks directed toward Jews express anti-Semitism. Stereotypic Jewish American Princess jokes, for example, and "JAP-baiting" may not always be intended as anti-Semitic but may reveal latent prejudice. Ultimately it is the relationship between attitude and behavior that is important, and it may not be much consolation that only 20 percent of Americans have anti-Semitic attitudes in light of the apparent increase of anti-Semitic incidents in recent years. Audits of anti-Semitic incidents produced by the Anti-Defamation League since 1979 show an average of more than 600 reported occurrences a year. The number has grown from about 400 in 1980 to almost 1,000 in 1981 and then down to 638 in 1985, 906 in 1986, and up to 1,018 in 1987. The upward trend continued in 1988 with harassment up 41 percent and vandalism 19 percent, reaching a total of nearly 1,300 incidents. These include arson, cemetery desecrations, anti-Semitic graffiti, threats, and harassment. Some of the more serious vandalism incidents were perpetrated by members of neo-Nazi youth gangs called skinheads in several cities, including Chicago, San Diego, Los Angeles, and Miami. Although vandalism involving hate groups had accounted for no more than one or two incidents over the past several years, the number jumped to about twenty in 1987. There has also been an increase of anti-Semitic incidents on college campuses in 1988 into 1989: drawing of swastikas at Yale University, the State University of New York at Binghamton, and Memphis State University; an attack against a Yeshiva University student in Manhattan by a gang of youths shouting anti-Semitic epithets as they beat, robbed, and stabbed the nineteen-year-old; and a depiction of Dartmouth College's Jewish president, James Freedman, by a conservative college newspaper, *Dartmouth Review*, as another Hitler. When evaluated in the context of the growth of such other extremist groups as the Ku Klux Klan, the Liberty Lobby, the Aryan Nations, the Posse Comitatus, Willis Carto's Liberty Lobby, Lyndon LaRouche's organization, and such pseudo-religious groups as the Sword and the Christian Patriot's Defense League, they may indicate the beginning of a trend. The guilt feelings felt by many non-Jews concerning the Holocaust may be disappearing.

A growing amnesia about the Holocaust has taken various forms. Neo-Nazi tendencies have erupted in Western Europe, Canada, and the United States. Books in the United States, Britain, and France, as well as other countries, have denied or minimized the reality of the Holocaust. The publication of Arthur Butz's *The Hoax of the Twentieth Century* in 1976 and the launching of the Institute for Historical Review in the late 1970s with its sophisticated *Journal of Historical Review* that began in 1980 were designed to earn scholarly and academic acceptance for revisionism. Robert Faurisson's, *Mémoire en défense contre aux qui m'accusent de falsified l'histoire*, with an introduction by Noam Chomsky, gave this thrust even more legitimacy.

In 1985, Canada witnessed two important trials, both dealing with the denial of the Holocaust. In Ontario, Ernst Zundel, a recent German immigrant, was charged with knowingly publishing information likely to cause harm to social and/or racial tolerance by circulating the canard that the Holocaust was a Jewish fabrication. In Alberta, a former high school teacher and mayor of the small community of Eckville, Jim Keegstra, was accused of willfully promoting hatred of the Jews, having taught his students from 1978 to 1982 that Jews had largely made up the "lie" of the Holocaust. Zundel's conviction was overthrown on a technicality and a second trial has been ordered. Keegstra was fined for his offense; his appeal is also pending.

This amnesia has shown itself in other ways as well, including the passion for Hitler memorabilia and the forged diaries purchased by *Stern* magazine; public apathy concerning unpunished war criminals; the controversial invitation by Chancellor Helmut Kohl to President Ronald Reagan to visit the German military cemetery at Bitburg, where members of the Waffen S.S. are buried; the election of Kurt Waldheim as president of Austria and his subsequent audiences with the pope; The controversy over the Carmelite Monastery at Auschwitz; the headlong rush towards German reunification without adequate sensitivity to the victims; and perhaps most disturbing, the tendency on the part of some established and recognized scholars to write about the period in ways that would have been politically and morally unacceptable several years ago.

The actual scandal lies in playing down the Nazi period rather than in its outright denial. Some, like Joachim Fest, Hitler's biographer, have attempted to incorporate Nazism into some universal notion of totalitarianism. This is one side of a growing historical relativism that is unfortunate because it is not firmly grounded in either fact or morality. Other scholars like Ernst Nolte and Andreas Hillgruber have attempted to contextualize the Nazi Holocaust by arguing that Hitler had reason to fear the Jews (Nolte) and that German atrocities must be seen as a reaction to Soviet atrocities (Hillgruber). This revisionist tendency is part of a larger political and historiographical agenda that has as its basis the desire to forget and distort, which is often stronger than the urge to remember. As is clear from the experience of the United States, France, and Germany, such denials and historical relativism are part of a new anti-Semitic subculture, aided by revisionist historians bent on rewriting history.

So there are some dark clouds that punctuate the brighter horizon. Conditions for Jews in America have certainly improved since World War II and anti-Semitism has subsided generally, although it has not disappeared completely. To answer the question posed at the beginning of this essay, yes, America is different, but it is not different enough. To be sure, Jews are more fully accepted in American society than ever before, but there still are areas of inequality, there still is ideologically based anti-Semitism and stereotyping, and there are the new troubling specters of a Holocaust revisionism and an ideologically motivated anti-Zionism that wishes to strip Jews of their particularity, their history, and their right to self-determination in a world that has too often demonstrated its tragic indifference.

Notes

1. J. Milton Yinger, Jr., *Anti-Semitism: A Case Study in Prejudice and Discrimination* (New York, 1964), p. 5.
2. Gary A. Tobin, *Jewish Perceptions of Anti-Semitism* (New York, 1988).
3. John Higham, *Send These to Me* (New York, 1975), p. 174.
4. See Jacob Katz, *Exclusiveness and Tolerance* (New York, 1962); Katz, *From Prejudice to Destruction: Anti-Semitism, 1700–1933* (Cambridge, Mass. 1980); H. H. Ben Sasson and Samuel Ettinger, eds., *Jewish Society through the Ages* (London, 1971); Edward Flannery, *The Anguish of the Jews* (New York, 1965); Uriel Tal, *Christians and Jews in Germany: Religion, Politics, and Ideology in the Second Reich, 1870–1914*, trans. Noah J. Jacobs (Ithaca, 1975); Joshua Trachtenberg, *The Devil and the Jews: The Medieval Conception of the Jew and Its Relation to Anti-Semitism* (New Haven, 1944); Yehuda Bauer, *A History of the Holocaust* (New York, 1982); Jean-Paul Sartre, *Anti-Semite and Jew* (New York, 1965); and George Mosse, *The Crisis of German Ideology* (New York, 1964).
5. Particularly important works on American anti-Semitism include Michael Dobkowski, *The Tarnished Dream: The Basis of American Anti-Semitism* (Westport, Conn., 1979); Leonard Dinnerstein, *The Leo Frank Case* (New York, 1968); Naomi W. Cohen, *Not Free to Desist: The American Jewish Committee, 1906–1966* (Philadelphia, 1972); Saul Friedman, *The Incident at Massena* (New York, 1978); Marcia Graham Synnott, *The Half-Opened Door: Discrimination and Admissions at Harvard, Yale, and Princeton, 1900–1970* (Westport, Conn., 1979); Harold S. Wechsler, *The Qualified Student: A History of Selective College Admission in America* (New York, 1977); Albert Lee, *Henry Ford and the Jews* (New York, 1980). Although not strictly about anti-Semitism, rich sources of documentary evidence are Morris U. Schappes, *Documentary History of the Jews in the United States, 1654–1875* (New York, 1950), which also has a helpful introduction, and Louis Harap, *The Image of the Jew in American Literature* (Philadelphia, 1974). Useful articles have been produced by Leonard Dinnerstein, Leo Ribuffo, Arnold Rose, Morris U. Schappes, Robert Rockaway, David Gerber, William F. Holmes, and other scholars.
6. Ben Halpern, "What Is Anti-Semitism?" *Modern Judaism* 1 (December 1981), pp. 251–62.
7. See John Higham, *Strangers in the Land* (New Brunswick, N.J., 1953).
8. Jonathan Sarna, "Anti-Semitism and American History," *Commentary* 17 (March 1981), pp. 42–47.
9. Higham, *Send These to Me*, p. 121.
10. See Theodor Adorno et al., *The Authoritarian Personality* (New York, 1950); Bruno Bettelheim and Morris Janowitz, *Dynamics of Prejudice* (New York, 1950); Seymour Martin Lipset, *The Politics of Unreason* (New York, 1970); Alan T. Davies, *Anti-Semitism and the Christian Mind* (New York, 1969); Gordon Allport, *The Nature of Prejudice* (Cambridge, Mass., 1954); Charles Stember, *Jews in the Mind of America* (New York, 1966); Charles Y. Glock and Rodney Stark, *Christian Beliefs and Anti-*

Semitism (New York, 1966); Harold E. Quinley and Charles Y. Glock, *Anti-Semitism in America* (New York, 1979); Gregory Martire and Ruth Clark, *Anti-Semitism in the United States: A Study of Prejudice in the 1980s* (New York, 1982). See also Ronald A. Urquhart, "The American Reaction to the Dreyfus Affair: A Study of Anti-Semitism in the 1890's" (Ph.D. disertation, Columbia University, 1972).

11. Gary G. Marx, *Protest and Prejudice* (New York, 1969).

12. Gertrude J. Selznick and Stephen Steinberg, *The Tenacity of Prejudice* (New York, 1969).

13. Martire and Clark, *Anti-Semitism in the United States*, p. 3.

14. Ibid., p. 4.

15. Ibid., p. 44.

16. Ibid., p. 116.

17. Ibid., p. 45.

18. See Edna Bonacich, "A Theory of Ethnic Antagonism: The Split Labor Market," *American Sociological Review* 37 (October 1972), pp. 547–49.

19. Lucy Dawidowicz, *The Jewish Presence* (New York, 1977), p. 212.

20. Arnold Toynbee, *A Study of History*, vol. 1 (London, 1934), p. 90.

21. See Urquhart, "American Reaction to the Dreyfus Affair," p. viii.

22. See Richard Hofstadter, *Age of Reform* (New York, 1960), pp. 92–93; and Hofstadter, *Social Darwinism in American Thought* (Boston, 1955), p. 176.

23. See Sander Diamond, *The Nazi Movement in the United States: 1924–1941* (Ithaca, 1974); Leo Ribuffo, "Henry Ford and the International Jew," *American Jewish History* 69 (June 1980), pp. 437–77; and Ribuffo, *The Old Christian Right* (Philadelphia, 1983).

24. William Schneider, quoted in Martire and Clark, *Anti-Semitism in the United States*, pp. 63–64.

25. Ribuffo, *Old Christian Right*, p. 181.

26. Martire and Clark, *Anti-Semitism in the United States*, pp. 74–75.

27. See Richard Rubenstein, *The Cunning of History* (New York, 1975).

28. Max Weber, *The Theory of Social and Economic Organizations*, ed. Talcott Parsons (Glencoe, Ill., 1957).

29. Isidor Wallimann, "Towards a Theoretical Understanding of Ethnic Antagonism: The Case of the Foreign Workers in Switzerland," *Zeitschrift fur Soziologie* (February 1974), pp. 84–94; Bonacich, "Theory of Ethnic Antagonism," pp. 547–49; and Bonacich, "A Theory of Middleman Minorities," *American Sociological Review* 38 (October 1973), pp. 583–94.

30. David Gerber, "Cutting Out Shylock" *Journal of American History* 69 (December 1982) pp. 615–30.

31. Marx, *Protest and Prejudice*, pp. 154, 165–66. See also Martire and Clark, *Anti-Semitism in the United States*, pp. 44–45, 51–52.

32. Higham, *Send These to Me*, p. 130.

33. Ibid., pp. 131–35.

34. Ibid., pp. 148–49.

35. Ibid., pp. 150–52.

36. See Stephen Steinberg, "How Jewish Quotas Began," *Commentary* 52 (September, 1971), pp. 71–72.

37. *New York University Daily News* 1 (May 11, 1923), p. 4.

38. A. Lawrence Lowell to A. C. Ratshevsky, June 7, 1922, American Jewish Committee Archives, General Correspondence 1906–32 (New York City), folder D-E, s.v. "discrimination."

39. Higham, *Send These to Me*, pp. 159–62.

40. See Marcia Graham Synnott, "Anti-Semitism and American Universities: Did Quotas Follow the Jews?", in David A. Gerber, ed., *Anti-Semitism in American History* (Urbana, 1986), p. 234.
41. American Jewish Committee Archives, G-C 1906–32, Cyrus Sulzberger Folder.
42. Higham, *Send These to Me*, pp. 169–72, 187–88.
43. See Saul Friedman, *No Haven for the Oppressed* (Detroit, 1973); Henry Feingold, *The Politics of Rescue* (New Brunswick, N.J., 1970); Arthur D. Morse, *While Six Million Died* (New York, 1967); David Wyman, *Paper Walls* (Amherst, 1968); Wyman, *The Abandonment of the Jews* (New York, 1984); Walter Laqueur, *The Terrible Secret* (Boston, 1980); Michael Dobkowski, *The Politics of Indifference* (Washington, D.C., 1982).
44. See Leonard Dinnerstein, "Antisemitism Exposed and Attacked, 1945–1950," in Dinnerstein, ed., *Uneasy at Home* (New York, 1987), pp. 178–94.
45. See Tobin, *Jewish Perceptions of Anti-Semitism*, pp. 27–45.
46. See Charles Silberman, *A Certain People* (New York, 1985).
47. See Martire and Clark, *Anti-Semitism in the United States* pp. 43–44
48. Quoted in Robert G. Weisbord and Arthur Stein, *Bittersweet Encounter* (New York, 1972), pp. 175–76.
49. See Tobin, *Jewish Perceptions*
50. Ibid., p. 45.

FOR FURTHER READING

Michael N. Dobkowski, *The Tarnished Dream: The Basis of American Anti-Semitism* (Westport, Conn., 1979), examines the image of the Jew in American popular and high culture in the nineteenth and early twentieth centuries. Marcia Graham Synnott, *The Half-Opened Door: Discrimination and Admissions at Harvard, Yale, and Princeton, 1900–1970* (Westport, Conn., 1979), examines the quota restsrictions imposed on Jews at elite American universities. Harold E. Quinley and Charles Y. Glock, *Anti-Semitism in America* (New Brunswick, N.J.: 1979), describe the nature and extent of contemporary American anti-Semitism. The authors draw their conclusions from major public opinion polls and other survey research. Gregory Martire and Ruth Clark, *Anti-Semitism in the United States* (New York, 1982), provides the first comprehensive trend study of anti-Semitism in the United States based on the national survey conducted in 1964 by Gertrude Selznick and Steven Steinberg published in 1969 as *The Tenacity of Prejudice.* They also examine the factors that are associated with American anti-Semitism in the 1980s. Leonard Dinnerstein, *Uneasy at Home* (New York, 1987), is a collection of essays on American anti-Semitism authored by Dinnerstein over the years. Numbered among them are some of the most important historical essays written on the subject. Gary A. Tobin, *Jewish Perceptions of Anti-Semitism* (New York, 1988), looks at the perceptions that Jews have concerning anti-Semitism and raises some serious questions concerning the validity of previous social science research on the topic. Robert G. Weisbord and Arthur Stein, *BitterSweet Encounter* (New York, Books, 1972), remains one of the most important books on the relationships of blacks and Jews in this country. Herbert Hirsch and Jack D. Spiro, eds., *Persistent Prejudice: Perspectives on Anti-Semitism* (Fairfax, Va., 1988), is a unique, multidisciplinary collection of contemporary essays on the religious, ideological, and cultural expressions of anti-Semitism. Michael Curtis, ed., *Antisemitism in the Contemporary World* (Boulder, Colo., 1986), is a collection of essays by renowned scholars that address such issues as whether there are new forms of anti-Semitism, whether there has been a resurgence in recent years, and whether there is a connection between anti-Zionism and anti-Semitism. David Gerber, ed., *Anti-Semitism in American History* (Urbana, Ill., 1986), is a useful collection of essays dealing with the history of American anti-Semitism. Jonathan Kaufman, *Broken Alliance* (New York, 1988), provides a brilliant analysis of the turbulent relationship between Blacks and Jews in America.

Jewish Education

SAUL P. WACHS

A frame is required to understand the ecology of Jewish education in the United States. That frame is, perhaps, best understood through two concepts: voluntarism and ambivalence.

The modern Jewish community, unlike its medieval predecessors, is totally voluntary in structure. American Jews are not required to pay taxes to the Jewish community. They are under no obligation to support Jewish institutions with time, energy, or money. Unlike the past, for example, the Middle Ages, the community has no sanctions with which to compel such participation. Any Jew can find a place to be married (or buried) whatever the quality of his or her participation in Jewish community life.[1] The community must compete for such participation with other attractive alternatives. The barriers that have traditionally kept Jewish-non-Jewish interaction at a minimum are, for most American Jews, missing (and the overwhelming majority of American Jews would have it no other way). The American Jew, is able to choose from a variety of frameworks within which to organize life. These may be familial, ethnic, religious, cultural, professional, social, political, or ideological. In addition, there is a tension between universal concerns and those that are more narrow in scope. Jews with a very high degree of secular education (the vast majority of American Jews) are particularly aware of these conflicts. Aside from the inherent attractiveness of Western culture, the crucial mediators of that culture (notably the universities and the mass media) often project a bias in favor of the notion that "narrow" loyalties (e.g., to

Jewish tradition) must be transcended when important issue are at stake.

With the exception of that segment of the Orthodox community which avoids contact with these influences, the attitudes of American Jews toward Jewishness (and therefore toward Jewish education) are likely to be shaped, in good measure, by the messages of the educational and cultural media they value. At best, an ambivalence toward Judaism is created. As one leading Jewish educator put it.

> Most American Jews believe in the value of "Jewish continuity"—the maintenance of a distinctive Jewish group identity in America—and want their children to feel likewise. However, most American Jews also believe that Jewish continuity must be achieved without estrangement from the larger society and culture. Hence they insist that their Jewishness be, at a minimum, "comfortable" and "nondisruptive" of their participation in American life, and, at best, actually reinforce their successful integration into the larger society.[2]

Most American Jews are committed to a high degree of personal autonomy and considerable ambivalence as to the role of Jewishness and Jewish culture and/or religion in their lives.

In this essay I will address three questions: (1) What is the reality of Jewish education and the present state of its affairs? (2) What lies behind this reality? How shall we understand the conditions of Jewish education? (3) How could the community move from the present state of affairs to a more effective and satisfying form of Jewish education?

The Present Moment in Jewish Education

Before looking at the world of Jewish education in detail, some generalizations may be be advanced. The rhetoric of support for Jewish education is higher than it has ever been in the history of the United States.[3] Jewish leaders of all persuasions proclaim that education is a high communal priority necessary for the maintenance and renewal of the American Jewish community. Rhetoric is important because it often points to future trends. In this case, rhetoric is accompanied by increased levels of financial support with clear indications of further increase in the future.

At the present time, close to $750 million is spent on American Jewish education in all its forms and settings. Jewish federations, the power centers of local communities, contribute more than $60 million representing almost 30 percent of their local allocations to Jewish education, more than double what they contributed ten years ago.[4]

It is estimated that thirty-nine to forty-three of every one hundred Jewish children aged three to seventeen are enrolled in Jewish schools[5] and that between 70 and 80 percent of all American Jewish children receive some Jewish education before reaching adulthood.[6]

The number of students attending day schools is higher than ever before. It is estimated that over one hundred thousand children and teenagers now attend these intensive schools.[7]

Jewish education in its most intensive forms is flourishing. The number of students involved in yeshivah and kollel (postgraduate yeshivah) education is in the thousands and rivals the figures for European Jewish communities of the past.[8]

Jewish education is expanding into the early childhood and preschool domains. More and more, the Jewish content of these programs is being reevaluated and enriched, both within synagogues and in communally sponsored agencies such as Jewish community centers and child care facilities.[9] A few academic programs to prepare Jewish early childhood educators have been established or are in the process of being established at Hebrew colleges and seminaries, and workshops are conducted for early childhood personnel from around the world every summer at the Melton Centre for Jewish Education in the Diaspora of the Hebrew University in Jerusalem.

Adult Jewish education is also a major growth area, including a vastly increased interest in family education. Federations of Jewish community centers and Jewish organizations as well as synagogues are encouraging members and leaders to increase cultural and religious literacy. Federations' young leadership programs to prepare new generations of community leaders more and more contain a significant element of Jewish study. Jewish community centers are actively involved in this process on the national level.[10] Ironically, this activity has sometimes brought them into conflict with traditional educational institutions (synagogues, Jewish schools), which in the past often derided community centers and federations for the anemic quality of their Jewish programming but which now seem ambivalent about what is sometimes perceived as an invasion of "their turf."[11]

Colleges of Jewish studies such as Gratz College in Philadelphia, the University of Judaism in Los Angeles, and Hebrew College in Boston attract substantial numbers of adults to serious Jewish study programs in addition to their matriculating students.

The development of Jewish studies programs, particularly on the undergraduate levels in secular colleges and universities, has made Jewish studies available to thousands of Jews (and Gentiles), including some who had little or none before. (A study conducted at Brandeis University in 1974–75 indicated that those enrolled in Hebrew language and Jewish studies courses were, overwhelmingly, people who had been students in Jewish schools as children or teenagers. Thus it is incorrect that a lack of Jewish studies as a youngster fosters a sense of deprivation or that attendance at an elementary or secondary program of Jewish education decreases the possibility that a student will enroll in Jewish studies courses on the college level.[12])

With the development of Jewish studies courses at secular colleges and universities, the seminaries and Hebrew colleges have largely evolved into graduate schools with strong programs of continuing education in addition to degree programs.[13] Indeed the largest number of students in these programs had pursued undergraduate Jewish studies on a secular campus in America or Israel before choosing to pursue graduate studies in the rabbinate, cantorate, Jewish education, or Jewish communal service. Thus there currently exists a complementary relationship between institutions of higher learning sponsored by the Jewish community and those under nonsectarian or general sponsorship.

Not all adult education or family education is organized by the community; some is of a grass-roots variety, particularly in connection with the Havurah movement. Here we see energized Jews working to upgrade their literacy in small, intimate groups that offer opportunities for worship and celebration of life-cycle events and holidays as well.

Israel is emerging as an important resource for Jewish education. More than forty thousand North American Jews are involved in study experiences in Israel every year. These programs vary in quality and intensity, but they are considered to be successful.[14]

On the delivery side of Jewish education, a major phenomenon is the development of a grass-roots organization of Jewish educators known as the Coalition for the Advancement of Jewish Education (CAJE). Unlike older professional organizations, CAJE is open to all devotees of Jewish education whatever their qualifications, training, commitments, or institutional loyalties, and it has become a networking of talented educators connected to all groups in the educational spectrum. This is most evident in the annual CAJE national conference, which attracts up to two thousand participants to minicourses, workshops, cultural events, and support groups. This "happening," one of the largest annual gatherings of Jews anywhere, allows for the exchange of ideas, techniques, and resources by people who otherwise might not know of each other's existence, let alone engage in meaningful communication. The "downside" of this phenomenon is that it sometimes mixes kitsch and superficiality with serious study and uses up much of the money available in local communities for teacher training by providing subsidies to teachers who wish to attend. The conference is rotated around the United States, meeting on college campuses each summer for four days. Whatever its weaknesses such as granting instant "peerage" to professors and rabbis, Sunday school teachers, and teaching assistants—with possible detrimental effects on the status of professionalism within Jewish education— CAJE is a tremendous morale builder and has undoubtedly introduced a new vitality into the Jewish educational scene. In addition to the national conference, the organization or its members sponsor local and regional conferences as well as networks that concentrate on specific issues such as research, moral education, and family education. The smaller conferences have been a particularly important outgrowth of CAJE.[15]

Jewish education has also been strengthened by programs of informal education, particularly summer camps. Each movement has developed a network of such camps (e.g., Ramah, NFTY, Morashah; others are sponsored by Hebrew Colleges [Yavneh] or youth movements such as Young Judea, Habonim and Benei Akivah). B'nai B'rith conducts highly successful leadership institutes on both high school and college (Hillel) levels each summer. Orthodox groups such as Habad also conduct programs that offer intensive study of Jewish texts and camp activities. In the total environment of a camp it is sometimes possible deeply to affect the beliefs and values of young people (and older ones who serve on the staff), and these camps are unquestionably among the great success stories of American Jewish education.[16]

There has also been a termendous increase in the number of books and materials available to Jewish educational practitioners through major curricular efforts, an increase in the number of publishers operating in the field, and the establishment of teachers' centers throughout the country.

An emerging development of unknown consequences is the evolution of central agencies of Jewish education from a status of funded, semi-independent units of the organized community to departments of the federations. This development may cause a loss of independence by professional educators but will bring them into closer contact with the power and influence centers of the community.

Finally, for the first time ever, foundations have been created both in America and in Israel that offer the promise and, in some cases, the reality of significant funding for Jewish education. The first grant for research in Jewish education was made by Samuel M. Melton of Columbus, Ohio, in 1959.

During the 1980s, Mr. Melton has been joined by the Bronfman Foundation, the Crown Foundation, the Gruss Fund, the Mandel Associated Foundations, the Pincus Fund, the Joint Fund for Jewish Education, the Wexner Foundation, the Wolf Foundation, and other such groups. In addition to general concerns, some of these funds have undertaken particular problems. For example, the Wexner Foundation offers support for individuals wishing to prepare themselves professionally for the field.

The Problem of Statistics

The current state of Jewish educational statistical information is highly ambiguous and all statistics about to be offered must be regarded as suggestive rather than definitive.

The Supplementary Jewish School

The number of supplementary schools has declined dramatically in recent years. In 1958 there were 3,153 known schools; by

1983 the number had declined to 1,861. Decline in enrollment between 1962 and 1982 amounted to 58 percent.[17]

A Part-Time Enterprise American Jewish education is overwhelmingly, a part-time enterprise. Supplementary schools are the preferred vehicle of education for most American Jewish youth (72 percent). The United States accounts for 85 percent of all supplementary pupils in the Diaspora.[18]

Supplementary School Teachers The teachers are part-timers. In the United States 93 percent of the supplementary school teachers teach ten hours a week or less; 83 percent teach six hours or less a week.[19] The preparation of teachers for these schools is to be understood in this context. Of some 14,550 supplementary teachers surveyed, 83 percent had college degrees but more than half (53 percent) had received no Jewish education beyond high school and only 8 percent were rabbis. In Reform supplementary schools, which represent a large proportion of the total enrollment of these schools, almost three-fourths of the teachers had received no Jewish education beyond the high school years and only 5 percent were rabbis.[20]

Who Are the Teachers? A substantial majority of supplementary school teachers (70 percent) are women.[21] This may reflect the attractiveness of part-time employment for some women or the willingness of some women (whose husbands are substantial wage-earners) to accept work with modest remuneration. Supplementary school teaching also attracts college and professional school students in search of income. Of course, this means that there is a major turnover in staff every year. The Hebrew University study showed that 29 percent of the teachers had taught ten or more years in Jewish schools, 25 percent had from two to four years of experience, and 14 percent were in their first year of teaching. High school students sometimes teach in supplementary schools. They are most often placed in charge of first-year students, thus jeopardizing the establishment of a strong foundation in skills and attitudes on the part of the youngest and most vulnerable of Jewish students.[22]

As might be expected, salaries are very low, ranging in the New York study, for example, from less than $10 an hour to $13,000 per year for experienced full-time teachers.[23] Benefits for supplementary school teachers are largely lacking.[24] As a profession, Jewish supplementary school teaching is almost nonexistent in most parts of the United States.[25]

Who Are the Principals?   Although national data about principals of supplementary schools are not available. We have some data from the study of supplementary schools in the Greater New York area. It was found that one-third of the principals were full-timers with "fairly good secular educational backgrounds" (35 percent had earned master's degrees and 10 percent doctorates). In contrast, with the exception of those who were ordained rabbis (25 percent), the Jewish educational backgrounds of the principals were "minimal." The principals studied were equally divided in gender. The average principal had seven and a half years of experience. Half of them principals had served for five or fewer years in the current position. Given the weakness of the Jewish educational background and the part-time nature of the administrator's position, it is not surprising that teachers surveyed felt that they received insufficient help from their principals.[26]

According to the New York study, principals' compensation in the New York City area has improved during the past decade. In 1981–82, the annual salaries of full-time principals ranged from $6,900 to $15,200 averaging $12,500. The study showed that by 1986, full-time principals earned from $23,000 to $52,000 and averaged $26,500. Life insurance, as well as medical and pension programs,[27] were available from the Federation of Jewish Philanthropies' Fund for Jewish Education.

Structural Problems   In addition to issues of staffing, supplementary Jewish schools tend to be small. More than 70 percent of the schools studied by the Hebrew University had 250 or fewer students.[28] Efforts to merge small, inefficient units have met with moderate success in recent years, but congregational leaders, professional and lay, generally resist such efforts even when change is patently necessary, out of fear that "separation of the school from the Shul" will harm the interests of the latter institution.[29]

Schools averaged from three to five hours of weekly instruction usually offered from one to three days a week. In recent years, there has been a drop in the number of one day programs (predominantly, the province of Reform Jewish education).[30] In Reform Jewish education, midweek instruction is usually tied to *bar-bat mitzvah* preparation, and the popularity of this ceremony among Reform Jews in recent years has helped to strengthen multiday programs in Reform Jewish schools.

Who Are the Students?   The overwhelming majority of students (82 percent) in supplementary Jewish schools drop out after the *bar* or *bat mitzvah* ceremony.[31]

Reform schools have a better retention level, possibly because of the importance placed on the confirmation ceremony in the Reform movement. Typically, such preconfirmation programs are conducted one day a week. Thus we see that supplementary Jewish school students attend for a few hours per week for a few years. Because much importance is placed in educational circles on the concept of "Time on task" in promoting academic achievement, it is not surprising that testing of supplementary school students (when it occurs) shows very modest accomplishments on their part.[32]

Who Sponsors Supplementary Schools?   The vast majority (almost 85 percent) of these schools are sponsored by congregations. It is believed that 4.4 percent are under Orthodox sponsorship, 35.4 percent under Conservative sponsorship, and 49.3 percent under Reform sponsorship.[33] Congregational sponsorship of a supplementary school has advantages and disadvantages. The school may function as part of a system of education in which congregational educators work with members of the family in both formal and informal frameworks. When these frameworks are integrated in the service of a unified vision, the educational impact can be very powerful, and some very successful supplementary schools have been sponsored by congregations.[34] Yet the school may and often does suffer from a need to serve the perceived interests of the host congregation even when these interests conflict with sound educational theory and practice. Not only do the physical facilities of these schools not meet the standards required for "real" schools, but when conflicts develop over priorities in cleaning of the facilities or the use of multipurpose rooms, too often the school's requirements are judged to be less important than those of the congregation or its constituent groups such as the sisterhood.[35]

The issue goes deeper than the question of facilities. Because of the voluntary nature of supplementary education and the chronic shortage of funds to maintain all of the synagogue's programs, it is not unusual for a school to feel pressure to be flexible in establishing or maintaining standards for learning. Thus, for example, on the day a standardized test of Jewish attitudes and knowledge was administered as part of a study of Jewish education in Greater New York City, about 30 percent of the students were absent.[36]

Rabbinic Leadership   The quality of rabbinic, religious and managerial oversight in these schools leaves much to be desired. Educational administration, supervision, curriculum, and instructional methodology are sorely neglected in rabbinic education unless the rabbinical student chooses to give special attention to education.[37] The congregational rabbi is subjected to many pressures stemming from the perceived and actual needs of all the constituencies he or she serves.

It is not surprising that, in the words of the New York study, "When rabbis feel comfortable with their principals, they generally do not 'interfere with the school program.' This often leads to lack of rabbinic involvement in the school."[38] Thus, though the rabbi is the chief professional officer of the congregation and is expected to offer overall guidance, particularly in the areas of ideology and religious practice, there is a general sense that often he or she is felt to be remote from the life of the school. An important exception is the involvement of many rabbis in at least sharing in the teaching of confirmation classes. Depending on the size of the congregation and its school, this may or may not foster the development of a special relationship between the rabbi and the teenagers in such a class. The lacunae in the Jewish educational background of many supplementary school principals is so serious that it is particularly unfortunate that the rabbis—who have good backgrounds—are seldom available to help the teachers.

Lay Leadership   According to the New York study, congregational lay leaders "do not consider the school a priority activity of the synagogue and do not seem ready to increase financial support for its educational program."[39] Lay leaders are generally concerned with meeting budgets. They wish to keep costs down.

School budgets are seen as part of congregational budgets and must be rationalized in keeping with the overall financial needs of the congregation. This typically works to the detriment of the curricular and instructional dimensions of education. Rare is the congregational school that will allocate funds for research and development, in-service training of staff, or the purchase of texts and materials. Lay leaders are usually poorly informed about the curriculum and remote from the classroom. They rely on reports at meetings. Often there is a bifurcation between lay leaders who are concerned about education and who usually sit on school boards and those who seem to be concerned almost exclusively with budgets and who sit on boards of trustees.

Too many lay leaders seem to regard the congregational supplementary school, in business terms, as a "loss leader," a subsidized service that will attract and retain the loyalties of members. This attitude does not lead to serious concern for educational standards or the expectation that the school will have a lasting impact on the commitments and value systems of the students or their families. Finally, the school board chairperson in supplementary schools may be interested in education but lack any expertise or educational vision to contribute to educational deliberations. This is very unfortunate. The school board can serve as a "sounding board" for an ongoing discussion of the educational health of the congregation and deliberations about its long-range goals. Where good supplementary schools were developed, it was often as a result of alliances between competent professionals and strong lay leaders who shared an educational vision.

The Role of the Parent Perhaps the most serious problem facing the supplementary school is a lack of parental support for and involvement in the education of their children. Deliberately or not, parents often transmit messages to the effect that Jewish education is of peripheral importance. What is taught in the school—prayer, study, mitzvah observance, the importance of Jewish culture—is too often not reinforced at home. Parents do not clearly understand the goals of the school. When asked, they usually list their own goals, particularly in connection with the *bar/bat mitzvah* ceremony and the acquisition of some sense of Jewish identity. One of the tragedies of contemporary Jewish life is that, when divorce takes place, the Jewish school often becomes the screen on which residual angers and misunderstandings are played out by the estranged former spouses. Thus a parent may insist on negating the value of a child's Jewish education if that education is valued by the other parent. This can also happen when a child is enrolled in a day school, but the negativity can take the form of scheduling visitation hours that conflict with class sessions or synagogue attendance. If the parents are of different religious backgrounds, the problems are compounded.[40]

If parents support a supplementary Jewish education program actively, it can have a strong impact even though other factors are negative such as facilities or quality of materials. If parental support is lacking, it is very difficult for even a good program to affect the students positively.

Despite all their problems, it seems likely that the overwhelming majority of Jewish children in America will continue to receive their elementary Jewish education in supplementary schools. These schools are a distinctively North American institution, and they are increasingly facing fundamental reevaluation.[41] The congregational school has been called the "stepchild of the synagogue."[42] It can be rehabilitated and can function as an effective educational structure but only within the framework of a systemic attack on the problems enumerated above.

Day Schools

The Jewish day school has experienced impressive growth in recent years. In 1958, at the peak of enrollment in American Jewish schools, there were 248 day schools in the United States. Today, the figure is over 500. About 28 percent of all students between the ages of three and seventeen receiving any Jewish education attend day schools.[43] This figure is relatively low among diaspora communities.[44]

The growth of the day school has been explained in many ways. First, some parents have given up on the supplementary schools. (The removal of the children of those parents most interested in Jewish education has been a factor in weakening supplementary Jewish education.) For parents seeking a serious form of Jewish education, the day school has increasingly come to be be seen as the most effective structure for delivering such an education.

Second, there has been a great interest in private education in the United States. Since the 1960s, with the onset of school busing and the introduction into the urban public schools of social problems, many of which reflected the breakdown of social norms in the family and society, confidence in urban public schools has begun to wane for Jews as for other groups. Some have turned to private education, including Jewish day schools, as routes to the best colleges and providers of a desirable form of education. Nonsectarian and church-sponsored schools have significant Jewish populations; for many of whom, the "Jewish issue," is not important.

Third, attitudes as reflections of feelings of Jewishness of parents and community leaders toward day schools have changed. Once they were seen as "ghettoizing," but now there is an appreciation of their ability to provide harmonious educational environments that combine outstanding general studies programs with stronger Jewish educational programs than are available in most supplementary schools.

Fourth, funding has become available for Jewish day schools. Most of it has come from the Jewish community, among which earlier attitudes of indifference and hostility toward this form of education have all but vanished, and some from the public sector in the form of special grants and ancillary services. The vast majority of day schools are housed in good or excellent facilities and, unlike most supplementary schools, project the image and foster the ambience of real schools.

Finally, many families have discovered that a child may feel more comfortable with a day school education than one involving two institutions. The day school student can reserve late afternoons and Sundays for sports and family outings without cost to his or her Jewish education.

Whereas once day schools were exclusively Orthodox in orientation and generally confined to a few cities (notably, New York), today they are found in all parts of the United States and serve a broad constituency. Three-quarters of the schools are under Orthodox sponsorship. The Conservative Solomon Schechter Day School network includes more than sixty schools, and there are ten Reform day schools. The movement is committed to supporting significant growth.[45]

In sum, Jewish day schools have gained a high degree of acceptability on the elementary level and reach a small number of students (almost exclusively Orthodox) on the secondary level as well. It would appear that non-Orthodox parents, when faced with the choice between offering intensive Jewish education during the crucial teen years and using the resources of the best public or private (non-Jewish) secondary education, overwhelmingly choose the latter to fulfill the educational agendas for their teenage children. It is problematic since a Jewish education terminated during the early teen years is radically incomplete.

Structure and Staffing In contrast to most supplementary schools, the typical day school offers career opportunities for teachers. Of the 6,663 teachers who responded to the Hebrew University census, 37 percent taught more than twenty hours a week, and for Jewish studies teachers the figure was 44 percent.[46] Forty percent of those surveyed had been teaching ten years or more. Only 6 percent were in their first year of teaching. Career preparation is also more professional than for supplementary schools. Most teachers in both types of schools have college degrees. Some Orthodox day schools do not expect Jewish studies teachers to progress beyond seminary education, but 55 percent of the day school Jewish studies teachers had at least some Jewish studies on the college level and another 27 percent were ordained rabbis.[47]

Like supplementary teachers, most day school teachers had received their Jewish education in the United States (76 percent). Of the remainder, 21 percent had done most of their studying in Israel.[48]

Finally, unlike supplementary school teachers, almost all of whom are women, men are represented (albeit as a minority) in day schools. Men make up 40 percent of the Jewish studies faculties of day schools. Many Orthodox schools separate boys from girls for Jewish studies instruction and insist that *Limuedi Kodesh* (sacred studies) for boys be taught by men.[49]

Day schools offer many more hours of Jewish studies than do most supplementary schools, but they vary from school to school. The average figure for all day schools is about sixteen hours a week, ranging from five in some Reform day schools to seventeen in Orthodox schools. Conservative schools average thirteen and a half hours per week of Jewish studies.[50]

Salaries and benefits have improved in the past decade. In the early 1980s, full-time salaries averaged around $18,500. Now they are closer to $25,000, which is still well below the salaries of public school teachers or other Jewish professionals.[51] Day school teachers are more likely than their supplementary school colleagues to receive medical benefits and pensions, but this is far from assured.[52] The salary level generally limits entry into the field to those who have other sources of income (e.g., spouses of doctors or lawyers), recent immigrants, those lacking other career opportunities, candidates for future administrative and supervisory posts, and highly idealistic individuals.

Problems of dignity and morale are felt keenly by teachers. Many are frustrated by the lack of opportunity to have any effect on communal policy regarding Jewish education and by the lack of shared goals with others who affect the world of Jewish education.[53]

Who Are the Principals? There are no hard data to answer this question. Based on visits to almost all of the Schechter schools and other sources of information, the following sketch may be offered. Orthodox schools, when possible, typically call upon rabbis to act as educational directors. Rabbis also headed about one-fifth of the Schechter schools and some of the Reform day schools. About one-third of the Schechter schools were headed by women as were several of the Reform and communal day schools. The principals generally have strong general or Jewish educational backgrounds. Most were trained in the United States; Israel was the second most common source of their studies. A college degree is required in all but right-wing (*Haredi*) institutions, and graduate degrees are common. Some schools employ individuals trained in general education and engage a Jewish studies coordinator to supervise the Jewish studies program. It is not unusual for the general studies principal to be a gentile. Salaries of day school principals are handsome today—mid-$50,000 and higher—comparing favorably with other nonprofit, social service professions. Medical and other benefits as well as pension plans are common. Day school principals, however, suffer from a particular form of burnout. In addition to the frustrations faced by teachers, they must deal with uncertain mandates and accountability to multiple constituencies, all pressing for the advancement or blockage of curricular or instructional programs. In addition, many principals are expected to help raise funds for the school, which may affect the relationship of the principal to the families served. Needless to say, not every educator is a gifted fund-raiser, and problems in that area may affect educational performance.

Sponsorship Non-Orthodox day school education is conducted almost completely on the elementary level; 80 to 90 percent of all secondary day school education in the United States is conducted in Orthodox institutions.[54] There are no available statistics to indicate how many non-Orthodox students are enrolled in Orthodox or communal secondary day schools or what happens to those who end their day school studies at the elementary level.

The matter is of some importance because obviously a Jewish education that ends as a serious enterprise after the sixth or eight grade is seriously deficient, particularly as regards any engagement with the ideas of the Jewish tradition.

As with the supplementary school, the question of sponsorship of day schools is a major issue in Jewish education. The vast majority (88.5 percent) are religiously (but not congregationally) sponsored, though most receive communal funds such as federation allocations. (In the Reform movement, all schools are congregationally sponsored; elsewhere, most schools are under communal or intercongregational sponsorship.) Each pattern has advantages and disadvantages.[55] If the school is part of a congregation, there is the potential for the development of an organic relationship between school, home, and synagogue. But as with the supplementary school, the needs of the day school may be subjugated to those of the congregation because the needs of the school must be balanced against those of other affiliates of the congregation.

If the school is independent of congregational control, it is more likely to be in command of its own budget. Synagogue leaders, professional and lay, however, may feel a sense of distance if not alienation from the day school even though both are part of the same movement. Thus, for example, if some day school parents within a congregation choose a life-style or observance pattern that is more intensive than that of other members, this may be seen as threatening by the majority of the membership and its lay leaders.

This problem is particularly noticeable in the Conservative movement, which is characterized by diversity of life-style and belief. Thus Schechter parents who observe Kashrut engage in Jewish studies or regularly attend Shabbat and festival services with their children may be seen as "Orthodox."

Even if a few of the day school parents maintain these patterns, all members of a congregation choosing the day school may be "tarred" with that image. When the day school is not part of a congregation, there may be other manifestations of a sense of distance between the school and the congregation as well.

In some congregations the rabbi will not mention the name of the day school at the *bar/bat mitzvah* ceremony of one of its students because to do so might, "evoke comparisons between the Schechter school and the congregation school."

In other congregations Schechter students are not encouraged to participate in Shabbat services that are led by the youth of the congregation for the same reason. In general, the "we" and "they" attitude voiced by some congregational members and leaders in regard to members who choose day school education has led some Schechter families to feel uncomfortable within their own congregations.

The issue of the relationship between the synagogue and the day school is complicated. The most powerful form of education takes place within a *system* in which students learn ideas and skills in formal settings (classes) and test out those ideas in the "real world"—youth groups, activities, social action projects, family life, and so on.

The best congregational schools day or supplementary, offer such an integrated system with formal and informal educational and religious programs relating to each other organically in the service of a total institutional mission to create a sense of community. In the present era, given the part-time staffing pattern of most congregations, such a system is lacking and the various activities sponsored by the congregation are not integrated.

The day schools have been willing to increase their educational effectiveness by providing educational and religious activities that might threaten the status of the synagogue as a total community. Most day schools do not offer youth groups, extensive adult education, or Shabbat and festival religious services. They thus have little educational impact. Unfortunately, most congregational leaders do very little to support the day schools. Many rabbis and congregational lay leaders act and speak as if the day schools were in competition with them for the same "customers." This problem occurs primarily among non-Orthodox congregations. In general, Orthodoxy has placed education at the heart of its activities in the United States and takes great pride in the development and expansion of its day schools and Yeshivot. Since almost all Orthodox children attend these schools, there is little potential for the development of a "we-them" attitude between congregations and day schools.

Parents and the Day School   Parents are more-involved in day schools than in most supplementary schools. These parents consider the day school a real school. They take a serious interest in what their children are learning at least in the secular area. Parent meetings tend to be well attended. Students attend classes regularly and meet work assignments, and the schools are generally characterized by an ambience of seriousness and productivity.

This parental involvement is generally positive, but it can lead to a situation of overaccountability, particularly in non-Orthodox schools. (Orthodox schools are typically begun by a small group, usually led by one or more Rabbis. It is generally understood and accepted that educational policy, particularly when it impinges on Jewish studies and Jewish practice, will be controlled by rabbinic leadership and that parents who are uncomfortable with or hostile to Orthdoxy should not enroll their children in the school. Thus many Orthodox schools may be accused of a lack of accountability to parental input, though this will vary from community to community and from school to school.)

There is little consensus among non-Orthodox Jews as to the proper mission of a Jewish day school. (This is not to suggest that non-Orthodox schools are totally lacking in conflict but merely that the area of consensus is significantly broader, for example, the general need to abide by halakhah [Jewish law], and so it is far easier for the school to develop a social climate and a distinctive culture than is true in non-Orthodox schools.) They agree on the need for excellence in secular studies and will not tolerate second-rate standards in that area. They want a school atmosphere that is humane and favorable to individualized learning opportunities. They want the school to promote a positive Jewish identity and a sense of responsibility to other Jews (including *Tzedakah*) with particular emphasis on the needs of the state of Israel. They want the students to master basic Jewish skills and to participate in Jewish communal activities. They also want the students to feel a part of the larger American culture. (Not surprisingly, these ideas are very similar to those cited by Woocher as characteristic of American Jews.[56]) These points are important, but they do not alone add up to a clear sense of mission for a school.

Within these basic perimeters there is a great deal of room for misunderstanding and conflict. One issue has to do with the amount of time and effort to be devoted to Jewish studies because this will inevitably affect time-on-task in the secular studies area.

One Reform educator reported that some parents timed the Jewish studies sessions with a stop watch to make sure that that they did not "detract" from general studies. This is an extreme example, but it reflects an attitude that is not limited to one school or denomination. The question of what kind (if any) of religious services to conduct can be a major issue in a community school. The question of which Mitzvot to emphasize and how to emphasize them can deeply exercise some parents. Subjects such as Bible, rabbinics, Jewish thought, and Jewish practice are foci of tension between parents, teachers, lay leaders, and administrators, who, too often, do not share a common vision of Jewish education. Any decision in those and other areas is a potential cause for conflict. One result of this tension is that professional burnout, is exacerbated, particularly among administrators, who must respond to the demands of all the constituencies that make up the day school community. Another result is the tendency within many non-Orthodox day schools to "soft-pedal" areas of potential conflict. Clear norms of ritual behavior are not established, and there is a tendency to avoid texts and topics that might sharpen an awareness of religious issues. This tends to reduce the affective "bite" of the curriculum and to turn much of the program into information about Judaism without helping students struggle with its demands and expectations.[57] In this, of course, the schools mirror many of the congregations whose children they educate. The need to develop a clearer sense of institutional mission is one of the most pressing tasks facing non-Orthodox schools today. The "Effective

Schools" literature demonstrates that, without a clear sense of institutional mission, it is very difficult, if not impossible, to develop the social climate, values, expectations, image of the good life, and passion that are part and parcel of educational excellence.[58] The ultimate impact of denominational (as opposed to communal) schools and their survival may well depend upon their moving toward greater clarity in determining the ideas, values, and patterns of behavior that they associate with normative Jewish life.[59]

What Should Be Done?

In this section, some proposals are presented to help raise up some of the "valleys" in American Jewish education.

Professionalism Professionalism should be expected of Jewish educators, including the holding of credentials and the mastery of subject matter and professional methodology. It is important that teachers, however experienced return to the classroom periodically to renew their professional skills and knowledge. This activity should be expected and supported.

Dignified career opportunities must be provided for those who wish to dedicate their lives to Jewish education professionally. At this time, there is a dangerous gap between teachers' salaries and those paid to administrators of Jewish schools. Of course, some gap is appropriate. Principals are not tenured. They often must work under tremendous pressures. They are usually the single most important influence on the culture of the schools they head. Their professional preparation requires them to master many disciplines and skills. But the gap between teachers' and administrators' salaries is, in many places, unreasonable. One suspects that a "corporation" model has been applied to Jewish schools. In a corporation, it is assumed that the chief operating officer is capable of rescuing an ailing company and maintaining its health. Such a philosophy cannot be applied to a school. The teacher is responsible for direct delivery of the educational service, and the quality of instruction is of tremendous importance to the educational experience of the student. No one suggests that administrative salaries be lowered. Teachers' compensation packages should be raised significantly.

Most American Jews are part of the middle class today. In examining career possibilities, they know that teaching will not bring them monetary wealth. But teachers have a right to live with dignity. Unless they can do so, good people will avoid the profession or trade the classroom for the principal's office (for which they may or may not be qualified) as soon as possible. In addition, provision for ongoing opportunities for professional renewal must be provided such as support of and expectation for periodic return to the classroom as well as opportunities to interact with colleagues in workshops and conferences.[60] Many of the cadre of professional educators will choose to serve in day schools, but the community should also support high-quality supplementary schools. Where large units can be created, offering formal and informal learning experiences for children, youth, and adults, these institutions can create "packages" that represent full-time employment for qualified educators while at the same time providing high-quality Jewish education.[61]

Experimentation and Accountability   Because "effective schools" are (partly) characterized by a clear sense of mission, the community should support different models of educational theory and practice that are well conceived and that represent alternative visions of Jewish life and education.

Students of Jewish education in recent years have become concerned with the question of the cardinal focus for such education. Some would argue that Jewish education is primarily a cognitive venture, designed to teach texts, ideas, skills, and facts that contribute to Jewish literacy. Others believe that because of the anemia of other arenas of Jewish life today, school must undertake the primary task of socializing Jews into the Jewish community. Some believe that the best a school can do is to provide skills and an intellectual underpinning to support feelings of Jewishness. Socialization is best accomplished through family, neighborhood, synagogue, and organizational life.

Others answer that in the reality of Jewish life in America, the school must assume the primary task of instilling attitudes of belonging for Jews and that this is a necessary prerequisite for further study and enrichment. Curricula for schools based on these alternate visions would be quite different. Staff, use of time, experiences and evaluation of learning would reflect the basic divergence of these views.

Moreover, even within the cognitive view, many different approaches are possible. For example, some educators believe that it is possible to teach children to speak, read, write, and understand the Hebrew language with an immersion model. Others believe that the curriculum should be built around Jewish history and contemporary issues involving the local, national, and international Jewish community with particular emphasis on our relationship to Israel. Other educators believe that the most important approach to Jewish education is through the mastery of Jewish texts. (This classical view is, of course, particularly prevalent within the Orthodox community.)[62] Others would pay particular attention to the liturgical side of Jewish life: prayer, the calendar, the life cycle, and the observance of Mitzvot (including those concerned with interpersonal behavior and social ethics).

All of these approaches can generate models of excellence if staffing is appropriate (competent and dedicated to the vision of the school) and if parents support this vision as well. Each of these types of school can be a magnet drawing to itself a particular population of professionals and laity who want to create a distinctive educational and social climate together. Some of these schools could be fully communal in sponsorship, others could result from the joint efforts of congregations with communal support. A judicious combination of incentives and sanctions would enable the community to support such efforts.

To summarize, many Jewish educational models are defensible and the community has a stake in providing reasonable opportunities for experiments in alternate modes. It is suggested that the community should also demand accountability. Thus groups of Jews have the right and the responsibility to establish educational goals to be concretized within alternative institutions. The community should hold these groups responsible for reaching these goals through periodic joint assessment.

The community should also tie the granting of funds to other more general indexes of educational quality such as facilities and learning schedules that are adequate to accomplish the stated objectives of the school. (There is a connection between quantity and quality.) Concrete learning objectives that help translate a broad vision into learning experiences should be established. The community should work within the traditional American framework of respect for local rights and decentralization of decision making, but it should expect periodic self-evaluation by each institution as well as joint evaluation (institution and community) for each institution it supports. (When a religious educational institution is involved, which is part of a larger group such as Union of American Hebrew Congregations, it is appropriate that that group be invited to participate in this process of evaluation as well.[63])

Early Childhood and Adult Education

One of the unfortunate facts of Jewish life is that early childhood education has not been taken seriously as an integral part of the Jewish educational network. Some people fail to realize that the early childhood years offer a prime opportunity for the immersion of the child in Jewish educational experiences.[64]

There has been some movement to change this unfortunate situation, but much more must be done. An unfortunate myth to the effect that early childhood education is merely a fancy and expensive form of baby-sitting still persists among people who should know better. The success of the Head Start program points to the possibility of dramatically affecting young children and their families. The community should both expect and support efforts by early childhood and preschool educators to enrich their knowledge of Jewish culture and tradition. Each of these educators should obtain a Jewish educational credential, which should be respected and honored as an index of professionalization in the field. Curriculum and instructional materials to support early childhood educators are still insufficient. It is important that adequate budget be provided to enable good materials to be created, tested, and revised as necessary. This is part of a larger problem that affects the entire field of Jewish education.

At the other end of the spectrum, a major problem in adult education, aside from the failure to reach many adults, is the lack of full-time positions to attract good educators to the field. At best, adults classes are taught by qualified individuals who make a living teaching in day schools or in some other aspect of Jewish education (or another field).

Jews by Choice

Adult Jewish education has been mentioned as a growth area. An important segment within the adult population is the group known as Jews by Choice. They face special problems in integrating themselves within the Jewish community. This group seems likely to grow and can enrich the community with a sense of zeal and freshness that flows from a life choice filled with meaning. Some who convert, however, do so only to satisfy a spouse's parent or grandparent and lack any real sense of commitment. A (future) *Ger* or *Geioret* may be conflicted or ambivalent about the entire matter of Jewishness.

Too often, courses for converts are occupied chiefly with the imparting of (important) information without allowing students to "ventilate" feelings connected to past experiences with Judaism or the reactions of their families (or those of the Jews they hope to marry) to the projected conversion. At present, support groups for converts (and/or their families) do exist, but much more must be done to welcome and orient Jews by choice if they are to fulfill their potentially positive role within the Jewish community.[65] In this connection, there is a subtle but important problem that has not received adequate attention. Judaism and Christianity are quite different. Judaism is not only a spiritual tradition of ideals, beliefs, and rituals; it also contains ethnic, national, cultural, and Zionistic components. A former Christian may appreciate the importance of the purely associational ties of his or her new religion but have difficulty identifying with the communal aspects of the tradition. Jews resonate to the Shoah and to *Medinat Yisrael;* they are central to the identity of many Jews. New Jews, lacking memories and blood ties to the past, may not automatically share these responses. It is suggested that the community create a mini-mission program that would take a candidate for *Giyyur* (conversion) to Israel to visit Yad Vashem, Kibbtuz Lohamei Haghetta-ot, and other important sites. Ideally, this visit would begin at one of the death camps. Contact could be made with survivors and/or their children. Thus the candidate for *Giyyur* would be helped better to understand Jewish attitudes and sensitivities and begin to develop "Jewish" responses to issues of vital concern to the community. The great success of the United Jewish Appeal missions gives reason to believe that such a program could make a major difference in the attitudes of Jews by choice. If this is not possible, contact with individuals who survived the Shoah or have been closely involved with the building of the state of Israel is too important to be left out of the study process that precedes being accepted into the Jewish community.

Israeli-Americans

No one knows how many Israelis live in the United States. Scholars and community leaders have not agreed on a common definition for the population. Yet a large population of former Israelis does exist, and it varies greatly with regard to feelings of Jewishness, attitudes toward Judaism, and ultimate plans for residence. The organized community has made few efforts to reach out to these people, who (except for the Orthodox) have generally avoided active involvement in Jewish activities. In New York City, many are *Haredim* (Ultra-Pietists). Elsewhere, Los Angeles and Philadelphia, for example, they are not religiously involved.[66] Many do not send their children to Jewish schools. Aside from economic and cultural issues (in Israel, education is free), to do so would be to acknowledge that they plan to remain in the United States, which many seem unable to do.[67] Furthermore, the religious nature of Jewish education in the United States makes it problematic for many Israelis. The word *Dati* in Hebrew, usually translated as *religious,* is understood by most Israelis as meaning Orthodox. Most Israelis in America are *Hiloni-im* (secularists) or *Mesorti-im* (traditionalists, who observe some religious traditions as a form of identification). Non-*Dati* Israelis in Israel seldom send their children to religious schools. Most follow the same pattern in the United States. Unfortunately, many Israelis are not accustomed to thinking about Jewish identity. They may believe that their children will retain an attachment to Israeli culture (and some form of Jewish identity) based on the home.

Experience has shown that immigrant children usually identify with the host culture and minimize or reject any effort to preserve an immigrant culture at home, for example, by speaking the immigrant language. Many of these children are growing up with no support for feelings of Jewishness.

Minimally, there is a need for a thorough study of Israelis to discover their involvement, perceptions of America and the American

Jewish community, future plans, and concerns about their children's Jewish identity. Because the dangers of loss to the community through assimilation or (where there is a sense of spiritual vacuum) conversion, the community has a stake in extending itself on their behalf. Opening preschools, supplementary schools, and day schools with a strong Hebrew language and Zionistic culture merits special consideration as well. For those who are not open to Orthodoxy, non-Orthodox groups should reach out and help acquaint this group with other religious options within Judaism. The Israeli government has not encouraged efforts to make Israelis in America "too comfortable." This policy of "benign neglect" requires reevaluation.

Soviet Jews

The Soviet Jews have also had a (Jewishly) problematic history in America. The American Jewish community has responded magnificently to the opportunity to help Soviet Jews who chose to come to America through many of the initial problems of adjustment. Vocational guidance, English language courses, housing aid, and a host of other services have been provided. Up until recently the community, has, for the most part, eschewed active efforts to help Soviet Jews recover their heritage. Only when significant financial aid was available did the children of this immigrant group enter the local day schools. (Soviet Jews valued private schooling for their children.) Because of the perennial shortage of communal funds, most communities were not willing to provide full scholarships for any but the poorest of these children. Ever wary, communal leaders eschewed a policy of scholarships for all Russian children whose parents requested them. (Only the Orthodox schools, notably those sponsored by Habad Hassidim, sought these children at all costs.) Here, as with the Israeli situation, a grave danger exists that the children will be lost.

For most Soviet Jews, Jewishness was a liability. It subjected them to many disabilities. Its sole "virtue" was that it allowed them to apply to leave the USSR, particularly those who came to the diaspora since Israel was available for Russian Jews desiring to live in a Jewish land.

Without intervention, this negative attitude toward Judaism will remain as a chronic problem. Despite the cost, it would be a wise investment to ensure that the maximum possible number of children and adults be provided with serious Jewish education including Jewish summer camps, trips to Israel, and planned contacts with the organized Jewish community. Without a serious reevaluation of current policy, there is danger that an entire group of Jews will be lost and the responsibility will fall upon the host community that failed to understand the need of the hour. In the recent past, it would appear that such a reevaluation is under way.

A Literature of Success

One of the dangerous myths sourrounding Jewish education is that it is doomed to fail. This essay has pointed to many problems, but it is also true that there are important successes in the field. Unfortunately, little money, time, or energy has been expended for the purpose of documenting these successes. Thus people who are in a position to invest in the future of Jewish education may hesitate to do so for fear of "throwing good money after bad."

The community should honor local, regional, and national educational groups as well as individuals for excellence. Each group could submit descriptions of formal or informal programs of Jewish education for assessment. The group would lay down the goals of the program, and the assessment would have to be consistent with those goals. Minimally, this would enable information about local and national programs to be disseminated widely and would generate contributions toward the literature of success that is required if new sources of support for Jewish education are to be developed.[68] Jewish education badly needs a literature of success.

Closely related to this issue is the lack of a cadre of researchers and academics working in the field of Jewish education. The community supports only a handful of individuals who are free to study and propose solutions to the long-range problems that affect Jewish education. Education requires maintenance and renewal. Almost all of the energy and funding in the field go to maintain what we have. No serious enterprise, business, or academic can make progress under such conditions. There is a need for fellowships to allow for the preparation of a cadre of senior educators who are knowledgeable in research methodology and are placed in positions that allow them to apply appropriate solutions gained from a study of the Jewish tradition, general education, the social sciences, and the field of not-for-profit management to the problems of Jewish education. Most graduate students in the field are attending school while also holding full-time positions. The most attractive opportunities for full-time study are in Israel, but only a small number of people can be accommodated from the pool of those who would pursue such study were it available closer to home. For most people, Israel can provide only a part of the preparation that is needed; ideally, cooperative planning between diaspora institutions and those in Israel would allow each to make a distinctive contribution to a first-class program of professional training.[69]

There is a need for greater support for research both theoretical and involving action.

For example, several important curricula have been developed by national agencies of Jewish education. In all cases, those responsible for developing the curricula did so as part of, or in addition to, other full-time responsibilities. Money was not available to provide for independent evaluation of the impact of the curricula or to disseminate the results of the evaluations that were conducted.

Family Education

One of the chief recommendations of the New York study was that synagogues "transform [their] educational thrust from Supplementary schooling to Jewish Family Education."[70]

It is clear that a healthy child asked to choose between a value system modeled by a school and one modeled by the family will choose the latter. This is less true of teenagers, particularly when they feel a sense of spiritual vacuum.

Thus Jewish family education is a very high priority for the community and deserves support. A literature of Jewish family education is beginning to emerge, and creative educators are beginning to devote themselves to this area.[71]

This form of education requires skills and competencies that are somewhat different than those traditionally needed to work in Jewish education. Colleges of Jewish studies are beginning to offer courses in family education, and it is important that capable professionals in synagogues and in the community be encouraged to equip themselves to work with Jewish families. One approach is for teams of professionals from formal and informal education and communal service backgrounds to work together in family education. This will also allow for a breaking down of barriers that for too long have separated Jewish professionals and prevented joint effort on behalf of the community.

Summary

As one examines the way Jewish education is treated by the community in light of what is needed to make it succeed, the question that arises is "why?"

Serious enterprises, whether private, public, or governmental, do not operate this way. Thus the question remains—why does Jewish education? It is a cliché to say that people get the (Jewish) education they deserve. Sometimes they put up with with a level of Jewish education for years that they would not tolerate for one day in a public school.

The Frame: A Reprise of the Basic Theme   American Jews want to be Jewish, but they are not sure how Jewish they want to be. They want to preserve tradition, but they also want to be free to choose a life-style.

Erev Shabbat or New Year's Eve?   Perhaps the best paradigm for this ambivalence is the behavior of American Jews whenever New Year's Eve falls on Friday evening. For some Jews, Friday evening—*every* Friday evening—is Erev Shabbat, the time for *kiddush* and prayers and rest and family togetherness. For some Jews as for other Americans, New Year's Eve is an important social occasion, one that often has personal, professional, or political meaning.[72] When those two events come together, American Jews find out who they are, for in that confluence of "sacred" occasions, two worlds and two sets of values come into conflict and the claims of each must be addressed.

But if individuals are forced to choose, communities and their leaders prefer not to do so. Even the leaders of the Jewish community have been reluctant to address issues of basic identity. Fundraising, apparently, is most effectively carried out through consensus, and this often requires the avoidance of a sharpening of issues of ideology.

From a historical point of view, Judaism developed through elites and their ability to attract masses to their views. What is needed today is for the leadership of the community to recognize that without a compelling vision, eventually people lose the desire (the need) to give of themselves.[73]

Postscript

Today, with all of our commitment to alternate visions and alternate ideologies, it is suggested that the leadership could make *one* change that might work a revolution in American Jewish education. *That change would be to honor Jewish learning.* It would mean that the leaders would be expected to study, and that would be public knowledge. It would mean honoring knowledgeable people (including teachers) by recognizing their contributions publicly in prestigious settings. It would mean providing knowledgeable people with input into decision-making fora. Traditionally, the community was led by an alliance of the wealthy and the learned, each with certain powers or qualifications to influence policy. Together, they maintained community standards.[74]

The young want to know what works in life. When they see an appreciation of those who study and teach, it conveys the message that Jewish knowledge is valuable and important. Beyond that, it is obvious that learned Jews may contribute insights that will enrich the deliberations of those who set policy and allocate resources of the institutions of the Jewish community.

This essay ends as it began by reiterating the frame for this analysis of contemporary American Jewish education: ambivalence and voluntarism phrased by one of the most astute students of (American) Jewish political history: understood as a convention

Meeting Jewish educational needs is somewhat problematic for the community, since it exposes all the ambivalences . . . of contemporary Jewish life, creating a clash between the desire for survival as a people with the desire for full integration into the general society. Jewish education therefore requires a great measure of commitment to the notion that Jews are different and must educate their children (and themselves) to be different. All agree that Jewish education is important, but the character of the commitment is a different matter. American Jewish education reflects all the ambiguities, and that is one reason why major decision-makers rarely play any real role in the educational

field, and why those who are professionally involved in Jewish education are not major decision-makers in the community.[75]

Some of these judgments, which were rendered in 1973, are no
longer completely true. Nevertheless, the thrust of the statement is
as true in 1988 as it was fifteen years earlier.

The present moment in Jewish education seems to be one of
danger and opportunity. The forces of identity erosion and of acculturation grow daily as generations arise that do not know of the
Shoah or of a world without the state of Israel. The statistics are
alarming. Too many people, including many of talent and ability,
are choosing to drop out of the community. Others want to be
Jewish and work to create a distinctive Jewish life-style, sometimes at great personal sacrifice.[76] In an open society, people are
free to come and go as they wish. The Jewish community can sit
back and go about its daily pressing tasks of maintenance, living
off its spiritual capital providing activities for those who seek
them, or it can take the long view and try to ensure its future
through investing enough of its intellectual, personal, financial,
and organizational resources to make Jewish education a success.

If it does opt for the future, it may yet win a place in the history
books as the premier diaspora community of the ages. If it does
not, it will have played an important if diminishing role in world
Jewish history. Voluntarism and ambivalence are the hallmarks of
our community. It seems appropriate to close this essay by quot-
ing the prophet Elijah, who addressed the Children of Israel who
were ambivalent and confused as to their loyalties and their commitments: "How long will you keep hopping between two opinions?"[77] On the answer to the question may hang the future of the
American Jewish community and the quality of American Jewish
life in the twenty-first century.

Notes

1. See Jacob Katz, *Tradition and Crisis: Jewish Society at the End of the Middle Ages* (New York, 1974).
2. Jonathan Woocher, *Mountain High, Valley Low: The State of Jewish Education Today* (New York, 1988), p. 12.
3. Thoughtful summaries of the status of Jewish education have occasionally appeared in the *American Jewish Yearbook* and Jewish educational journals, notably *Jewish Education*

and *Shevilei Hahinukh*. Some of the most thoughtful analyses have been done by Walter Ackerman, Samuel Dinin, Alexander Dushkin, and Alvin Schiff.

4. Woocher, *Mountain High*, p. 3.

5. Allie A. Dubb and Sergio DellaPergola, *Jewish Educational Statistics, Research Report 4, First Census of Jewish Schools in the Diaspora 1981/2–1982/3, United States of America* (Jerusalem, 1986), p. 5.

6. Woocher, *Mountain High*, p. 3.

7. Barry Chazan, *The State of Jewish Education* (New York, 1988), p. 1. Sources for all statistical information presented by Chazan are found on p. 18. n. 4.

8. See William Helmreich, *The World of the Yeshiva* (New York, 1983).

9. Woocher, *Mountain High*, p. 4.

10. *Maximizing Jewish Educational Effectiveness of Jewish Community Centers* (New York, 1984). Organizations such as the American Jewish Committee, B'nai Brith, and Hadassah increasingly sponsor programs of adult Jewish education. They also contribute to the explosion of publications in this area.

    On Jewish family education see Janice P. Alper, ed., *Learning Together: A Source Book on Jewish Family Education* (Denver, 1987). For a comprehensive guide to materials in the field, see Barbara Eidelman Wachs, "Annotated Bibliography on the Jewish Family," ibid., pp. 425–463.

11. Conflicts have developed between synagogues and federations as well as between synagogues and Jewish community centers. For example, see "Symposium on Relationships between Synagogue and Center," *Conservative Judaism* 16 (Winter–Spring 1962); Jacob Neusner, "Synagogue and Center: The Symposium in Retrospect," *Conservative Judaism* 17 (Fall 1962). For a recent proposal for cooperation, see Melvin Libman, "Creating a New Partnership between Federations and Synagogues," *Journal of Jewish Communal Service* 64 (Summer 1988).

12. Saul P. Wachs, "Backgrounds of Students Enrolled in Jewish Studies and Hebrew Language Courses at Brandeis University," unpublished manuscript, 1973–74.

13. See, for example, *Self-Study Report of Gratz College Submitted to Middle States Association of Colleges and Secondary Schools* (Philadelphia, 1987).

14. Woocher, *Mountain High*, (3) p. 5. See also Haim Aronovitz, Sari Gillon, and Batya Stein, Resource Booklet no. 2, *Background Documents for the Israel Experience Project, Senior Personnel for Jewish Education* (Jerusalem, 1987).

15. The major professional organizations are the Council for Jewish Education, made up of educators of all groups but primarily consisting of those serving in communal settings; the Educators Council of America (Orthodox), Jewish Educators Assembly (Conservative), and National Association of Temple Educators (Reform). The initial reaction of the Jewish educational establishment to CAJE was ambivalent and, in some cases, negative. Today the groups cooperate through the Coalition of Jewish Educational Organizations (COJEO).

16. On the extraordinary success of the Brandeis-Bardin Camp Institute summer program, see Saul P. Wachs, "Educating for Jewish Living and Jewish Population," in *Jewish Population* (New York, 1978). On the effects of a religiously sponsored summer camp, see Janet Aviad, "Subculture or Counterculture: Camp Ramah," in Janet Aviad, ed., *Studies in Jewish Education*, Vol. 3 (Jerusalem, 1988), and references listed there.

17. Chazan, *State*, p. 4.

18. Dubb and DellaPergola, *Jewish Educational Statistics*, p. 4.

19. Ibid. The response rate for topics relating to teachers was particularly low (ranging from one-third to two-thirds of known schools) so these data should be regarded as suggestive rather than definitive.

20. Ibid., p. 61.

21. Ibid., p. 58. The feminization of the teaching profession is not limited to Jewish teaching or to any one country. The same study showed that in independent preschools 98 percent of the teachers were women. Only in the day schools was the situation different, particularly among Orthodox Jewish studies teachers.

22. Ibid., pp. 60–61. Research has documented the unique importance of teachers of the first grade. See Eigil, Pedersen, Therese Annette Faucher, and William W. Eaton, "A New Perspective on the Effects of First-Grade Teachers on Children's Subsequent Adult Status," *Harvard Educational Review* (February 1978). For a popular treatment of the same idea, see Robert Collins, "Miss Apple Daisy," *Reader's Digest*, September 1976.

23. Alvin I. Schiff, *Jewish Supplementary Schooling in Greater New York: An Educational System in Need of Change* (New York, 1988).

24. Saul P. Wachs, "The Jewish Teacher: Professional Status," in *Background Papers in Jewish Education* (New York, 1984).

25. See also Susan L. Shevitz, "The Deterioration of the Profession of Jewish Supplementary School Teaching: An Analysis of Communal Myths on Policy and Program." (qualifying Paper, Harvard University Graduate School of Education, 1983).

26. Schiff, *Jewish Supplementary Schooling*, pp. 72, 70.

27. Ibid., pp. 71–72.

28. Dubb and DellaPergola, *Jewish Educational Statistics*, p. 26.

29. See Susan L. Shevitz, "Supplementary School Consolidation in the Jewish Community: A Symbolic Approach to Communal Decisions" (Ph.D. dissertation, Harvard University, 1987).

30. In 1958, 47 percent of the supplementary schools met two to five days a week, and 47 percent offered classes once a week. In 1983, 76 percent of the schools offered programs two to five days a week and 24 percent had one-day programs (Chazan, *State*, p. 4).

31. Dubb and DellaPergola, *Jewish Educational Statistics*, p. 30.

32. Schiff, *Jewish Supplementary Schooling*, chap. 6. The number of hours judged to be necessary if formal Jewish education is to have an impact far exceeds those available in a typical elementary Jewish supplementary school. See, for example, Harold S. Himmelfarb, "The Impact of Religious Schooling: The Effect of Jewish Education upon Adult Religious Involvement" (Ph.D. dissertation, University of Chicago, 1974); Geoffrey Bock, "The Jewish Schooling of American Jews: A Study of Non-Cognitive Effects" (Ph.D. dissertation, Harvard University, 1976). For a different view, see Steven Cohen and Paul Ritterband, *The Impact of Jewish Education on Jewish Identification: Positive Effects of Part-Time Schools* (Jerusalem, 1984).

33. Dubb and DellaPergola, *Jewish Educational Statistics*, p. 49.

34. Barry Chazan, "The Transformation of the Synagogue Supplementary School," in Jack Wertheimer, ed., *The American Synagogue: A Sanctuary Transformed* (Cambridge, 1987); Saul P. Wachs, "The Impact of the Pilot School of the Melton Research Center on Congregation Tifereth Israel, 1960–1966," in Alexander M. Shapiro and Burton I. Cohen, eds., *Essays in Jewish Education and Judaica in Honor of Louis Newman* (New York, 1984). Other studies have suggested that the major positive impact of these schools is on the identification of the students with the community.

35. On the issues of school sponsorship, see Ronald Lewis Reynolds, "Organizational Goals and Effectiveness: The Function of Goal Ambiguity in Jewish Congregational Afternoon Schools" (Ph.D. dissertation, University of California, Los Angeles, 1982). For an example of educational sponsorship as a major community issue see Saul P. Wachs, Diane A. King, and William B. Lackritz, "Jewish Education in Philadelphia, 1940–1985," in Murray Friedman (ed.) *Philadelphia Jewish Life* (Philadelphia, 1986).

36. Schiff, *Jewish Supplementary Schooling*, p. 62.
37. Ibid., p. 73. Hebrew Union College and Jewish Theological Seminary allow rabbinical students to major in education or to pursue graduate work in education while pursuing rabbinical studies.
38. Ibid., p. 75.
39. Ibid., p. 77.
40. See, for example, Schiff, *Jewish Supplementary Schooling*, pp. 63, 74.
41. Ibid., chap. 8 and 9.
42. Alexander Dushkin, "Congregation and Community in Jewish Education," *Jewish Education* 1, no. 2 (1929).
43. Chazan, *State*, p. 1, no. 4.
44. In some countries such as Colombia, 100 percent of reported enrollment is in day schools. In Canada, almost two-thirds of the students attend day schools. In Great Britain, the figure is between 55 and 60 percent. See Harold S. Himmelfarb and Sergio DellaPergola, Jewish Education Statistics Research Report no. 1, *Enrollment in Jewish Schools in the Diaspora: Late 1970s* (Jerusalem, 1982), pp. 35, 42; Allie A. Dubb, Jewish Educational Statistics, Research Report no. 5, *First Census of Jewish Schools in the Diaspora 1981/2–1982/3, Canada* (Jerusalem, 1987), p. 1.
45. Dubb and DellaPergola, *Jewish Educational Statistics*, p. 47
46. Ibid., p. 59.
47. Ibid., p. 61.
48. Ibid.,
49. Ibid., pp. 61, 58.
50. Ibid,. p. 76.
51. Chazan, *The State*, p. 12.
52. See, for example, *Faculty Salary Schedules—School Year 1986-7* (New York, 1987).
53. Wachs, "Jewish Teacher," pp. 15–23.
54. Dubb and DellaPergola, *Jewish Educational Statistics*, p. 50.
55. Ibid., chap. 5. The following observations reflect visits to almost all of the Schechter schools and numerous conversations with parents, students, rabbis, educators, and lay leaders associated with the schools and the Solomon Schechter Day School Association.
56. Woocher, *Mountain High*.
57. Saul P. Wachs, "Affective Learning and the Teaching of Jewish Tradition," *Jewish Education* 43 (Spring, 1974).
58. Saul P. Wachs, "Jewish Education: Myth and Reality," Dedication of the Rosaline B. Feinstein Chair in Jewish Education, *Community and Culture: Essays in Jewish Studies in Honor of the Ninetieth Anniversary of the Founding of Gratz College*, ed. Nahum Waldman (Philadelphia, 1986), and references therein. See also Schiffs *Jewish Supplementary Schooling* chap. 3.
59. In several cases lay leaders of denominationally sponsored schools agreed to the attentuation or elimination of the ideological thrust of the school so as to gain additional community support. It would appear that when a school deemphasizes its ideology, there is little passion to maintain the ideology it does support or an affiliation that reflects that ideology.
60. A detailed set of proposals aimed at enhancing the personal and professional dignity of Jewish teachers is found in Wachs, "Jewish Teacher," pp. 24–35.
61. For models of such "packages," see *ibid.*, pp. 5–7.
62. See Michael Rosenak, *Commandments and Concerns: Jewish Religious Education in Secular Society* (Philadelphia, 1987). This is the most important book related to topics in Jewish education to appear in a very long time.

63. See Adrianne Bank, "Evaluation: Is It Good for Jewish Education?" In Janet Aviad, ed., *Studies in Jewish Education*, vol. 3 (Jerusalem, 1988).

64. See, for example, Ruth Ravid and Marvell Ginsburg, "The Effect of Early Childhood Education on Family Jewish Practices," *Jewish Education* 53 (Fall 1988), pp. 12–15.

65. The issue of halakhic vs. nonhalakhic conversion is very painful and continues to divide some Reform and Reconstructionist Jews from other religious Jews. Tragedies sometimes occur when *Gerim* are unaware of the issues that surround this matter. It would seem only fair that all candidates for *Geiur* be fully aware of the questions that attach to halakhic and nonhalakhic conversion and the attitude of the Israeli official rabbinate in this matter.

66. See Steven Huberman, "Jewish Megatrends—Planning for the Twenty-First Century," *Journal of Jewish Communal Service* 64 (Summer, 1988). The *Haredi* (Ultra-Pietist) community of New York (e.g., Hassidim) does contain Israeli citizens (whose role was a factor in the 1988 election). Other Israelis in New York use an Orthodox synagogue on the (rare) occasions when they pray or in connection with a life-cycle event. Elsewhere, where the number of *Haredim* is smaller, religious involvement is weak. See Ester G. Smith and Rita J. Simon, "Israelis in the United States: Their Adjustments and Intentions," ibid.

67. In the Smith and Simon study, more than 90 percent said that they "definitely plan to return" to Israel or plan to return "sometime in the future." The facts of repatriation and emigration by this population suggest a process of psychological denial.

68. The *Pedagogic Reporter,* a journal published by JESNA, presents an annual "roundup" of interesting programs in Jewish education. Unfortunately, there is no evaluative component in the "roundup" and thus it risks lumping together descriptions of programs of varying levels of quality. See Shimon Frost, "Four Successful Jewish Supplementary Schools," in *Jewish Education Forum* (New York, 1984).

    The Conservative movement presents Solomon Schechter awards for programs it deems to be outstanding, including many in educational categories. The National Association of Temple Educators (NATE) also recognizes outstanding curricular projects. More awards and with provision for visitation to sites noted are needed so that wider dissemination of information about important efforts can take place.

69. For example, the clinical part of professional education is best carried out in settings that resemble those in which the trainee expects to work, but Hebrew language learning and the study of Israel as a resource are examples of areas in which a study period in Israel can be very valuable.

70. Schiff, *Jewish Supplementary Schooling*, pp. 133–34.

71. See above, note 10.

72. It is not unusual for a synagogue to sponsor a New Year's Eve dance for its members. "Setups" may be added to the "Oneg Shabbat" when the two occasions coincide.

73. See, for example, Arthur J. Magida, "Is Jewish Philanthropy Declining," *Baltimore Jewish Times*, September 2, 1988, pp. 64–67. The key point is that the erosion of Jewish values has led to an erosion in giving to Jewish causes.

74. Wachs, "Jewish Teacher," p. 25. See also Katz, *Tradition and Crisis*. Respect for the learned was limited to those whose learning was truly advanced because a basic level of Jewish literacy was expected of all males in that society. Elementary school teachers were not included in that category. In America, even highly learned Jewish educators were treated badly during the early years of the twentieth century. There was no golden age in American Jewish history before the current era. See Menachem Edelstein, *History of the Development of the Jewish Teaching Profession in America* (New York, 1956); Hutchins Hapgood, *The Spirit of the Ghetto* (New York, 1902, rpt. 1965). See also Susan Shevitz, "Communal Responses to the Teacher Shortage in the North American

Supplementary School," in *Studies in Jewish Education*, vol. 3, pp. 50–51. According to Shevitz, the myth of the Jewish school (and the Jewish teacher) as a threat to Americanization was alive and well in the early decades of the twentieth century. The supplementary school offered a structure to permit Jewish education without limiting full participation in American life (ibid., p. 51).

75. Daniel J. Elazar, *Community and Policy: the Organizational Dynamics of American Jewry,* (Philadelphia 1976), p. 289

76. In this connection, the community would do well to support the efforts of people who wish to intensify their lives Jewishly. Jews who are not interested in Jewish survival probably cannot be convinced to have children. People who are committed to Jewish survival can be helped to enlarge their families. (Day school tuitions are a powerful form of birth control)

77. Jewish Publication Society Translation of *The Prophets*, I Kings 18:21.

FOR FURTHER READING

Books

Alper, Janice P., ed., *Learning Together: A Sourcebook on Jewish Family Education*, Denver, 1987. A guide to the most important new development in Jewish education in North America.

Rosenak, Michael, *Commandments and Concerns: Jewish Religious Education in Secular Society,* Philadelphia, 1987. The most important book on Jewish educational theology and philosophy written in many years, it presents a systematic analysis of the issues facing Jewish educators as they seek to negotiate the tensions between tradition and modernity.

Conference Report

Riemer Joseph, ed., *To Build a Profession,* Waltham, Mass., 1987. A collection of essays dealing with the profession of Jewish education based on a conference of academics and community leaders.

Festschrift

Shapiro, Alexander M., and Burton I. Cohen, eds., *Studies in Jewish Education and Judaica in Honor of Louis Newman,* New York, 1984. The first American Festschrift honoring a Jewish educator contains studies covering the many aspects of American Jewish education touched by the work of its most profound theoretician. Topics include Jewish summer camping, supplementary and day school education, curriculum development, and communal coordination of Jewish education.

Journals

Jewish Education, the most important professional journal in American Jewish education, explores issues from a communal viewpoint.

Compass, a journal for Reform educators, touches on practical aspects of Reform Jewish education.

Melton Journal, a highly literate publication, focuses on a specific aspect of Jewish education in each issue.

Pedagogic Reporter, designed to be read by laity and professionals, is a veteran publication that represents a communal viewpoint in all areas of Jewish education.

Religious Education, the Journal of the Religious Education Association, provides essays dealing with theoretical issues of interest to students of religious education. It does not deal with instructional methodologies or implementation of programming.

Monographs

Ackerman, Walter I., "Jewish Education Today." *American Jewish Yearbook* (1980). Offers a readable summary of the current status of Jewish education.

American Jewish Committee, *Background Papers in Jewish Education,* ed. Yehudah Rosenman and Steven Bayme. A series of monographs issued during the 1980s, each of which deals in some depth with a specific aspect of Jewish education.

Reports of Research

Board of Jewish Education of Greater New York. *Jewish Supplementary Schooling: An Educational System in Need of Change.* Alvin I. Schiff, Study Director. A study of selected supplementary Jewish schools in the New York metropolitan area. Despite some criticism from the field regarding the relationship of findings to recommendations, the study is important for the issues it raises.

Schiff, Alvin I., "Jewish Day Schools in the United States." *Encyclopedia Judaica 1974 Yearbook,* Jerusalem, 1974.

The Hebrew University of Jerusalem, the Melton Centre for Jewish Education in the Diaspora. *Studies in Jewish Education,* vol. 1. Edited by Barry Chazan, Jerusalem, 1983. *Studies in Jewish Education,* vol. 2. Edited by Michael Rosenak, Jerusalem, 1984. *Studies in Jewish Education,* vol. 3. Edited by Janet Aviad, Jerusalem, 1988. These three volumes contain a variety of research papers dealing with all aspects of Jewish education.

Statistics

Jewish Education Statistics. Hebrew University of Jerusalem, Institute of Contemporary Jewry, Project for Jewish Educational Statistics, and Jewish Education Service of North America. A series of research reports dealing with Jewish education around the world. Research report 4 deals with the United States; all five volumes issued to date contain materials of interest.

Dissertations

Several important dissertations have appeared in recent years attesting to the sophistication and vitality of a new generation of theoreticians and practitioners in the field. Summaries of these dissertations appear periodically in the journal *Jewish Education*. The following are among the most important of recent years.

Bock, Geoffrey E., "The Jewish Schooling of American Jews: A Study of Non-Cognitive Effects." Ph.D. dissertation, Harvard University, 1976. This study is devoted to the nature of the impact Jewish education can have on its clients.

Himmelfarb, Harold S., "The Impact of Religious Schooling: The Effect of Jewish Education upon Adult Religious Involvement." Ph.D. Dissertation, University of Chicago, 1974. This study raises the issue of the number of hours of exposure to formal Jewish education are needed for a person to be affected significantly.

Reynolds, Ronald L., "Organizational Goals and Effectiveness: The Function of Goal-Ambiguity in Jewish Congregational Afternoon Schools." Ph.D. Dissertation, University of California, Los Angeles, 1982. This study examines the questions of goal-setting by congregational schools and of the relationship of such schools to the sponsoring congregations.

Schoem, David, "Ethnic Survival in America: The Ethnography of a Jewish Afternoon School." Ph.D. dissertation, University of California, Berkeley, 1979. This "ethnographic" study was designed to uncover the reality of a congregational school with particular attention to its informal as opposed to its official culture.

Shevitz, Susan L., "Supplementary School Consolidation in the Jewish Community: a symbolic Approach to Communal Decision." Ph.D. dissertation, Harvard University, 1987. This study explores the often puzzling decisions made by lay leaders in regard to issues in Jewish education and the political framework behind those decisions.

Zeldin, Michael, "Change in Jewish Education: The Development of a Comprehensive Theory." Ph.D. dissertation, University of Southern California, 1979. Many a talented educator has experienced difficulty in translating an educational vision into a theory of practice. This study seeks to understand how change can and does take place.

The Threat of Nuclear Destruction

DANIEL LANDES

Certainly Jews are no different than any other people in confronting the nuclear threat. *Omnicide*—the total destruction of all human life—is by definition democratic. Nonetheless, omnicide poses a particular challenge to Jewish theology. Judaism posits a God who loves life, is the source of life, and indeed is identified with life. Ultimately, this faith means the overcoming of death as contained in the dogmatic promise of bodily resurrection in the end of days. In the meanwhile, humankind is enjoined to participate in the process of *tikkun olam bimalkut shad-dai*—perfecting the world under the Kingdom of the Almighty. In the face of the constant possibility of a sudden horrific end to humanity, such ideals can seem absurd and meaningless. Judaism, however, in its long history has confronted other challenges to its desire for *tikkun olam*. An inspection of this struggle might enable us to contribute to a solution for the peril we encounter today.[1]

The promise of *tikkun olam* implies the premise of a tear and rent within reality. Jewish consciousness is multilayered, containing five such traumas. The first is ontological. God commands, "Let the earth put forth grass, herb yielding seed and *fruit-tree* bearing fruit" (Gen. 1:11), but the earth does not (cannot) comply: "And the earth brought forth grass, herb yielding seed after its kind, and *tree* bearing fruit" (1:12). The Midrash explains that the intention of a "fruit tree" was "just as the fruit is eaten, so should the tree be edible," but only a "tree" emerged meaning that "the fruit could be eaten and not the tree." Rav Kook understood this

defeat to represent the experiential and essential distinction between practical means and idealistic ends—even when the former
successfully led to the latter. The universe of moral action is not
integrated, and even the tree (means) bearing the most worthy
fruit (ends) is dry, hard, and tasteless.

The second rent is the existential trauma of the Golden Calf.
More than the Garden of Eden story this is the paradigm of sin and
fall from stature. An entire nation, created to embody the mono-
theistic ethical ideal, rejects its purpose by choosing idolatry.
More than sin, it is a (self)-denial of essence, which in the Judaic
consciousness precedes being.

The prime national tear is the destruction of the Temple and resulting *Galut*. The term *diaspora*, reflecting a scattered existence,
does not manifest the chief pain of exile of being cut off from
one's roots. The *Galut* by definition is unnatural—no matter how
normal a life and how normative a cultural expression can be developed within a host civilization, it is experienced as somehow
truncated and not fully right.

The Holocaust is the tear in the divine image of the human. As a
victory of absolute evil, it demonstrated that in their own unique
ways the *tzelem elokim* (divine image) of victims, persecuters, and
bystanders could be perverted and destroyed. We now know that
there are no limits to degradation imposed from without, created
from within, or accepted in apathetic complicity.

The fifth and final tear has a future directionality. It is the hole
man intends to punch within the very physical fabric of reality
through nuclear war. Omnicide is a quantum leap into the abyss
which is daily planned for, played at, and evidently accepted by all.

Each tear represents a diminution of humankind. Each is a constant, not only in memory or in anticipation but in action. Physically and spiritually we undergo a constant reenactment of these
woundings, which breaks through the healing and even the
scarring.

The last two tears are particularly connected. The Holocaust as
absolute genocide is a microversion of omnicide in magnitude of
destruction. Moreover, a strong claim could be made that the
former's facticity made the latter more possible. At the least, the
Holocaust, as other manifestations of horror, paradoxically made
societies less sensitive even though it sounds the warning alarm.

What needs to be done is to isolate those lessons from the Holocaust that bear on our present situation.

Degradation precedes destruction. For Europe to turn so violently upon its Jewish neighbors, it had first to undergo a process of education for hatred, which included the long history of church anti-Judaism which perceived Jews as rejecting the basis of society—Jesus Christ. The Nazis further labeled Jews as pests—implying the need for extermination—and as a cancer within the body of society, which could only be burned away. This education consisted of three components: psuedo-scientific studies proving the Jews to be humanity's enemy; popular propaganda invoking fear and disgust of them; and professional, cultural, and finally physical isolation, removing the Jewish people from the normal bonds of social intercourse and mutual responsibility. All this enabled destruction to take place. We can see the parallel today. Ememies of the superpowers are frequently depicted in harsh and unsympathetic terms. There is a steady process here of demonization, which diminishes the perception of a shared humanity. And when that happens, every insult and injury to the other becomes permitted. That is why athletic, cultural, and social exchanges, though often trivial in themselves, are powerful reminders of a human commonality and inhibitors of our worst prejudices being manifested into action.

Destruction is not carried out by crazed killers. The Holocaust was run by a bureaucracy that kept the trains running and the gas chambers supplied with Zyklon B. The men and women of this bureaucratic structure were cogs in a machine, following orders and attempting to get along. For the great majority the destruction of the Jewish people was an insignificant issue. Today we see the same submersion of responsibility within a technocratic structure. Citizens of a free society do their part for the system and usually well so they can get ahead—without regard to where that system is leading. The vastness of the U.S. military-industrial complex tragically serves to excuse individual responsibility.

Technology distances man from the effects of his actions. The procedure of the gas chamber separated the executioner from his victims. The swiftness and successive nature of gassings along with the large number of people killed made for an assembly line effect. The victims were abstracted into numbers, size, weight, and product—smoke and fertilizer. Today this distancing has gone several steps further. Those who sit watch in the underground hardened silos are to respond faithfully to precisely ordered commands, following an intricately detailed procedure to activate a complicated nuclear force. Here man and machine are one. Neither they nor their superiors will see the faces of their incinerated victims. War games are played in strategic centers in denominations of tens and hundreds of millions; it is doubtful if victims are even imagined. Self-alienation and abstraction of the other is complete.

Man possesses no "fail-safe" mechanism that will shut off his destructive potential at some perceived level of horror. Indeed, the notion, however hopefully and well intentioned, that this will happen is in fact dangerous. A significant reason why the Nazi genocide of the Jews was not really opposed was that men of goodwill could not imagine such evil and therefore would not believe that millions were being gassed and burned. Psychological denial is also prevalent in the face of nuclear destruction. People refuse to imagine that it could happen to them and their loved ones; those who do so frequently are frozen by the vision and eventually choose not to think about it. The result is the same—abdication of responsibility for meeting the issue head-on.

These four considerations could lead one either to surrender to the unavoidability of nuclear destruction or to choose a radical and swift course of unilateral abandonment of nuclear weaponry. Before such alternatives are decided upon, three further lessons from the Holocaust, which exist in a dialectical tension with the first four, must be drawn.

Destruction is not an inexorable process. It was a twisted road to Auschwitz, and a determined opposition both within the fascist state by clergy, men of letters, and common citizens, as well as a movement from without in the early stages, could have prevented much tragedy. As it was, where opposition to destruction was raised—for example, Axis-allied Budapest, fascist Spain, Catholic Italy, and Japanese controlled Shanghai—many were saved. Our first determination today needs to be that nuclear war is a real possibility that *must* be prevented.

To survive is paramount. Inmates of the concentration camps often did not know what drove them to survive; after all, life as they knew and cherished it was over with the death of their families and the obliteration of their communities. Nonetheless, from a dozen shattered groups came a saving remnant that was instrumental for the resurrection of the Jewish people. In our present situation, as we seek total solutions, we must not discount ways of reducing the danger and the scope of potential destruction.

Weakness is an invitation to destruction. Six million Jews were killed because they had no army to defend them, no air force to ferry them away, and no homeland to go to automatically. They had no deterrent or alternatives. They were powerless and weak. As Western democracies seek to reduce the nuclear threat, they must do so out of strength and with a sense of possible alternatives of a military, economic, and political nature.

Tikkun, as a process, is meant to correspond to these tears. It is the movement, step by backward step, away from the brink of complete death. It is every action that enhances the human and thereby the divine. An act of *tikkun* is a return to one's collective roots and nature and an acting in radical faith in utter rejection of all idolatries. In fine, it induces the practical means to parallel and embody within oneself the lofty end to which it aspires.

Tikkun, classically, is manifested both on the macro level—the ultimate repair of the tear—and on the micro—the doing of concrete acts that lead to the ultimate repair. *Tikkun* has two dialectically related models: the Kabbalistic, the origin of the term and theory, and the halakhic, which contains the behavioral substance molded and defined by the Kabbalistic.

Within the Kabbalistic paradigm, performance on the micro level is essentially bypassed by the macro promise. The significance of doing concrete acts lies in their inherent and derivative transcendence, which will ultimately coalesce to overwhelm and heal the whole. When one acts with Kabbalistic intent one already operates and lives within the promised repaired and perfected reality.

The Kabbalistic paradigm has a dangerous side to it. It leads to a leveling wherein all acts have equal weight for they already are within the new reality. Indeed, nonrational, asocial, and apolitical acts because of their removal from this (temporal) worldliness are held to have the greatest significance. Thus many have preferred to bring the new reality through the continuity of symbolic actions and political quietism (the latter creating the circumstances for the former) rather than facing the hard questions of history. The polar opposite of quietism—the political messianic frenzy—is also a legacy of Kabbalistic *tikkun.* It consists of an excited waiting and preparation for existence to make that jump into the new reality. All contemporary problematics of this world are seen as trials, not so much to be resolved but transcended (that is, ignored) and denied real significance. This attitude provides the confidence and the imperative to do foolish acts and create dangerous public policy.

In sum, Kabbalistic *tikkun* is not a helpful posture for the nuclear age. It either means a "mitzvah as usual" approach purposely irrelevant to social crises or it creates a disposition for rigorously righteous decisions that in fighting evil does not shrink from "taking it to the brink" or even over. Either way is disastrous.

Halakhic *tikkun* is the way of living within the fragments of this broken reality. In attempting to improve and knit the fragments together and thus mend the tear one inevitably does some straddling. It is a precarious existence wherein one's efforts can fall between the cracks and disappear. Nonetheless, halakhic *tikkun* is resolutely optimistic within its realistic context. It assumes that we are commanded and able to act, that this world is a proper locus for activity, and that a better reality can be created here now in anticipation of the new reality that will come in God's own good time. An accessible model of this is *shabbat,* which allows for personal, familial, and community integration within the legal structures of rest, honor, and joy.

The power of halakhah lies in a fourfold modality of achieving effectiveness. It emphasizes responsibility over rights; restriction over license; the creation of a personality conscious of bearing *tzelem elokim* (God's image) and seeing this inherent dignity in others as opposed to **nomos,** which is interested only in regulation; and employing covenant as the dominant model for binding and defining relations rather than contract or pact.

The use of halakhic categories can have a positive effect on the search for solutions to the nuclear threat. The notion of *brit* (covenant) assumes equality of both worth and responsibility between the two partners to the agreement. Applied to the goal of achieving nuclear disarmament, this eliminates two possibly destabilizing alternatives: first, pressure for a unilateral disarmament or radical reduction without the promise/guarantee of similar action on the other side, which is dangerous, for it can either signal weakness to the other or eventually engender resentment from within; second, an obsessive need for finding a commanding edge of superiority, which locks the opposing sides into fixed positions and encourages cheating, chicanery, and general bad faith.

Two formal procedures of Jewish law caution one from achieving perfection: legislatively, halakhah employs the concept of the *geder* or "fence," a series of restrictions enacted solely to protect a vital principle, which in the nuclear situation would mean an outer layer or etiquette of inhibitions strictly enforced by agreed-upon sanctions if violated; and judicially, when conflicts between two parties come to arbitration, strict justice is not the preferred option of the court. Instead, *pisharah*—compromise—is advocated. The underlying assumption is that a decision is best when agreed upon by both sides who feel that they can live with it. This attitude employed within a mechanism of a world court is the only viable way of adjudicating dangerous disputes.

The halakhah mandates dialectical concerns even at a point of conflict. Thus at the same time that it mandates that a *Rodef* (pursuer) be stopped from murdering or raping an innocent victim even at the cost of the *Rodef*'s life, it prohibits this action when a less extreme intervention would avail. In other words, if you could stop him by shooting him in the leg but instead you shoot him through the heart, you are morally guilty of murder. This means that although protection of self and the innocent is primary, one still has obligations to the enemy. Adapting this ethic to the present international arena would mean a gradual abandonment of *MAD*—Mutually Assured Destruction—as the cornerstone of peace. Weapons should be negotiated to smaller sizes, targeted to each other, and moved out of populated areas.

The *Mishnah* prohibits the breeding of wild dogs unless they are kept on a chain. The commentators understand this to mean both that it is crucial to restrain an inherently unstable and violent agent of death from wrongfully attacking the innocent and that by its very presence an unrestrained danger creates a debilitating and injurious climate of fear. New weapon systems with "hair triggers" are our wild dogs. Even if not (mis)used, they are, by their existence, frightening. They poison the atmosphere creating a (true) sense of loss of control and, in its wake, despair and apathy. A cap on new and dangerous weapons is a desideration of arms negotiation.

Given the people Israel's experience of genocide, in what sense are they charged with the prevention of omincide? An approach is suggested by a passage describing the essence of Israel in the writings of Abraham Isaak Kook, the early twentieth-century European talmudist, thinker, and later chief rabbi of *Erez Israel* (the land of Israel). Rabbi Kook's works are not readily accessible to many readers. The writing is allusive, evocative, and mystically charged. It posits an underlying unity to reality having been created by One God. His thought, in addition (or in consequence), conveys an unbounded optimism. Writing before the Holocaust, Rabbi Kook held what in retrospect was a naive confidence in the progress and moral ascent of man.[2]

Rabbi Kook's theory of Israel, nevertheless, presents a vivid depiction of its chosenness in relation to mankind. Further, Kook's mysticism does not obscure but rather heightens Israel as an immanent entity, acting out its destiny within this world. Any definition of chosenness will entail a transcendent purpose, but Rabbi Kook's formulation of this doctrine is accomplished not at the expense of history but rather through it. With this acceptance of history, Kook's theory allows for the Holocaust to be confronted. In so doing, the theory is transformed from a spirited optimism into a sober realism redeemed by a radical belief in God and His promise.

Knesset Israel (the people of Israel) is a microcosm of all existence. This refers, in a worldly context, to Israel's material and spiritual dimensions both in its saga and its faith. Israel's history is the ideal microcosm of universal history. There is no social fluctuation among the peoples of the world that you will not find its prototype in Israel. Its faith is the well-sifted essence as well as the influential source of the good and the ideal of all faiths. In this sense, Israel's faith serves as a resource that reviews belief systems with the goal of elevating their discourse so that all may call in the Name of the Lord; your God, "the Separate One of Israel, shall be called the God of the entire earth."

Knesset Israel is the sublime revelation of the spirit within human existence. One does not doubt that the manifestations of life contained within the brain and the heart are not to be found to a similar degree elsewhere in the body. Identically, one cannot doubt—although a sensitive soul and a thoughtful mind will marvel at—the manifestations of life, wonders, miracles, prophecy, the highest degree of divine inspiration, eternal hope, victory over every obstacle, revealed in an exalted form within Israel. *Knesset Israel* is the revelation of the arm of the Lord within the world, His hand in existence and His participation within the development of nations. It is ultimately connected to all that is exalted, venerable, holy and lofty within the entire physical and spiritual scope of reality. It is impossible to think otherwise. (*Orot*, p. 118)

Underneath Rabbi Kook's extravagant language is the rejection of any absolute disjunction between Israel and mankind. Israel is not a different form of man; he is a man. This is more than a state of being. Israel's vocation and destiny is *to be* human and to share in all that is human, both materially and spiritually. The truth of the Torah is not separate from the truths contained within other systems, nor are the latter considered to be deviant forms of Torah. Rather, it is Israel's task to engage in a critical dialogue with mankind to declare monotheism—people's responsibilities to one another and to God. All nations and peoples share in the *zelem elokim* in that reality is a creation of God and man the crowning jewel. The meaning of Israel's election is to be the flesh-and-blood bearer of monotheism's message: to cherish the human and the transcendent.

Israel's election does not assure an easy triumph for *zelem elokim*. The Jewish people were not incidental victims of World War II. The attempt to exterminate them went beyond political expediency and was even counterproductive to the German war effort. Nazi hatred for the people of Israel had a unique intentionality and was the very basis of its ideology and purpose.[3] Standing at the center of mankind, Israel became the target. The Nazi attack on Israel was thus an attack on humankind. By denying humanity to the Jews, the Nazis denied their own. Ultimately, their program was one of self-hatred.

What is the source of this self-hatred? Judaism has maintained that violence perpetrated upon man is rebellion against God because man is God's image on earth. The refusal to consider another as in His image is the desire to cast off the yoke of His image that the hater himself bears and the manifold ethical responsibilities that he is charged with. It is a rejection of meaning and responsibility and a descent into nihilism. A religious understanding of the Final Solution yields this cursed equation: hatred of Israel = hatred of man = self-hatred = hatred of God.

The Holocaust is a paradigmatic event for all mankind. It is a microcosm of ultimate violence and tragedy within the modern nation-states of the West. The Holocaust was not a sacrificial event in which the death of 6 million Jews expatiates the possibilities of such murder of others. It was, rather, a breakthrough event that threatens its own uniqueness by setting a genocidal pattern for other peoples in other situations. The Holocaust is a dark revelation of man's capacities for participating in (the Nazis and their followers) and acquiescing to (the Allies and others) systematic and total destruction. The Holocaust of that people dedicated to bearing the human and divine image heralds the Nuclear Age, when man's self-destruction is contemplated, planned for, and even played at in war-game scenarios. It announces a technological era in which means of dehumanization and methods of torture are mass produced, increasingly sophisticated, and generally ignored. What befell the Jews now threatens all people.

It is at this juncture that we recognize that the "progress" of postmodern man seems to be inexorably grinding to a conclusion, although we do not know the precise result. To the Jew, however, this perplexing situation seems strangely familiar, as if it is embedded within an even larger story whose contours we can somehow intuit if not fully delineate. We are again drawn to the matrix of biblical narrative and rabbinic interpretation as the hermeneutic for and of our times. The biblical text assumes a contemporaneity with its reader (or listener). The process of interpretation should not be a passive suspension of current realities but rather demands a forthright recognition of present concerns alongside an honest exploration of the Bible. Within the consciousness of the Jew, what happened "back then" is a present reality and challenge. This is true of the Bible generally, but it is especially true of early Genesis, where essential issues of creation and destruction as well as morality and responsibility are boldly dealt with and interwoven within the fabric of human existence. Thus the Flood story seems rooted within our social being and identifiable with our situation as its message of covenant and reassurance, at first glance, strikes us as insufficient and discomforting.

The Flood adumbrates nuclear destruction in three ways. The most obvious is its totality: "And all flesh that stirred on earth perished, birds, cattle, beast, and all the things that swarmed upon the earth, and all mankind. All in whose nostrils was the merest breath of life, all that was on dry land, died. All existence on earth was blotted out from the earth" (Gen. 7:21–23a). Besides, for being the recipient of God's special grace, "Only Noah was left, and those with him in the Ark" (7:23). The only species to beat death were sea creatures, who will also be doomed in nuclear war. A hidden similarity is the anonymity of those destroyed. Genesis provides no account of the piteous death struggles of the earth's inhabitants; even their cries are drowned out by the incessant beat of the rain. As in a nuclear holocaust, civilization simply disappears without a trace or memory. Finally, the Flood foreshadowing nuclear winter wreaked havoc not only with life but with the very structure of earth and its atmosphere as seen by God's resolve afterward never again to "curse the earth" or to allow "Seedtime and harvest, cold and heat, summer and winter, day and night" to cease (8:21–22). We know what nuclear war means because of the Flood's totality and anonymity of destruction of life and its transformation of the world.

The responsibility for the destruction of the Flood is laid directly at man's feet. This is done both cognitively and linguistically. Man is punished with the Flood for he has filled the world with *chamas,* generally interpreted as violent robbery. This disregard for a fellow's person and property is a rejection of God's majesty over the world. It is the definition of anarchy and lawlessness. Moral destruction is the precipitate of physical destruction. Linguistically the Bible conveys this point through the word SHaCHaT to convey the sense of how corruption is identical with ruin: "The earth became *spoiled* (vateSHaCHaiT) before God; . . . When God saw how *spoiled* (niSHCHaTah) the earth was, for all flesh had *spoiled* (hiSHCHeT) its ways on earth, God said to Noah 'I have decided to put an end to all flesh . . . I am about to *spoil* (maSHCHeTam) them and the earth' " (6:11–13). Man cannot relegate destruction, flood or nuclear, as "an act of God" in the commonsense meaning as fated and beyond human control. In the biblical-rabbinic view it is *middah kineged middah,* a cosmic tit for tat activated by man himself.

In recreating the social order when the waters recede, morality is given the central role. Man is blessed, in terms reminiscent of the charges to Adam, as ruler of the world. Indeed, his authority is extended in that he may now eat of animal flesh whereas Adam was permitted only the vegetable realm. His sole restriction is not to eat "flesh with its life-blood in it" (Gen. 9:3). But life is exalted more than in this symbolic prohibition. Human life is sacred, and God will not stand for it being causelessly destroyed by either beast or man. Further man himself is enjoined:

a. whoever sheds the blood of man
b. By man shall his blood be shed
c. For in his image
d. Did God make man (9:6)

Lines *c* and *d* explain the heinous status of line *a*, the crime of murder, in that one has violated the image of God that every man bears. But does that very point contradict the injunction of line *b* to shed blood of the murderer who prima facie also bears the divine image?

Evidently the Bible assumes that because of his crime the murderer has lost the image of God. Further, the poetic parallelism and legal intent of lines *a* and *b* reinforce the lesson of the Flood, that is, of *middat kineged middah*. But now mankind becomes the responsible agent for justice as the expression of his image of God.

The moral command to man is preceded by a decision: "And the Lord said to His Heart: 'Never again will I doom the earth because of man, for the blessings of man's mind are evil from his youth, nor will I ever again destroy every living being as I have done' " (8.21). Although God's personal resolve and His command are connected by the theme of reverence for life, there is a certain tension between these two sections which reflect respectively mercy and justice. These two attributes of God, which are derivative to man, who bears the divine image, are not given to an easy or final resolution. They remain in tension within the *ot* (sign) of the covenant between God and man with all creatures "that the waters shall never again become a flood to destroy all flesh" (9:15).

The natural desire that mercy fully triumph over justice is expressed in a reading of "This is the *ot* [sign] of the covenant that I set" (8:21) as the rainbow only *now* coming into existence. The underlying idea is that God, after the Flood, restructures all existence so that destruction will never again occur. It renders the *ot* into a divine fail-safe mechanism. But one can question whether this mercy is truly merciful. If given a safety net, will man be inspired into proper actions or will he more probably have the brazen confidence to push wrongdoings to their limit, since the alternate consequences of his actions will not be borne by him?

A more productive reading of 9:12 has existence not being changed at all by the covenant. Instead, God now imposes a meaning upon the natural occurrence of sunlight reflected and refracted through raindrops. The rainbow is a proper *ot* not only because it comes at the cessation of a heavy rain, as if God states, "see I have not repeated the Flood," or for its attractive splendor. According to Nachmanides, the inverted warrior's bow was a universal call for peace. The rainbow is God's warrior's bow inverted (not pointing to earth, where His arrows of punishment could be shot) and unstrung. It is a perpetual call for peace.

The inverted bow is a two-sided call to peace. It is hung in the sky to remind the world, according to Rabbenu Bachya, of God's intentions to renounce ultimate violence. At the same time it intends to bring forth a similar renunciation from mankind. This follows the logic of *Brit* (covenant), which the bow represents. A *Brit* by definition is mutual, demanding obligations from both sides. Moreover, this *Brit* has a special significance in that it replicates the original relationships with Adam in this period of recreation and the evocation of man (Noah and his descendants) bearing the divine image. *Imago Dei* in a covenantal perspective means *Imitatio Dei*. God demands from man what He demands of Himself. As God curbs his full expression of justice, which would mean full destruction of the world, so too must man curb his destructive potential. This means that mankind must renounce the use of nuclear weapons even if provoked and in accord with the sense of a "just response."

The inverted bow is the symbol of this process. And as Paul Tillich has noted, "every symbol is two edged. It opens up reality and it opens up the soul."[4] The inverted bow, the *KeSH*et, according to Genesis Rabbah, is Mu*KaSH* akin to God's own reality. As His reality is opened we stand in awe. That is why the Talmud (*Haggigah* 16:a) prohibits unrestrained gazing at the rainbow. We are not to reflect obsessively upon God's justice, which would freeze us into inaction and radical pessimism; nor are we to be lulled into passivity by his promise of mercy. Rather we are to look upon the inverted bow, modestly avert our gaze, and bless: "Blessed art thou, O Lord our God, King of the Universe, who remembers the covenant, is faithful to thy covenant, and keepest thy promise." And as God constantly renounces ultimate destruction in the act of divine self-limitation, so too, must man created in his image imitate God, engage in holy self-limitation, and step back from death.

Notes

1. See my discussion on *tikkun,* in *Tikkun* 1, no. 1 (1986), pp. 116–17.
2. See my "The Threefold Covenant: Jewish Belief after the Holocaust," in Alex Grobman and Daniel Landes, eds., *Genocide: Critical Issues of the Holocaust* (New York, 1983), pp. 402–9.
3. Steven T. Katz, "The Unique Intentionality of the Holocaust," *Modern Judaism* (September 1981), pp. 161–83.
4. Paul Tillich, *The Essential Tillich,* ed. F. F. Church (New York, 1989), p. 48.

FOR FURTHER READING

Literature covering the Jewish reactions to the nuclear threat are sparse. A new book on the subject is *Confronting Omnicide: Reflections on the Nuclear Threat from Jewish Thought and Experience,* edited by Daniel A. Landes. Contributers include Jon Levenson, David Novak, Reuven Kimelman, Eliezer Berkovits, J. David Bleich, Irving Greensberg, David Ellenson, Elliot Dorff, Immanuel Jakobovits, Renee Sirat, Michael Wyshogood, Maurice Friedman, Walter Wurzburger, Pinchas H. Peli, and others.

Several books and articles will be helpful to a reader formulating his or her own opinion. In *Creation and the Persistence of Evil: The Jewish Drama of Divine Omnipotence* (San Francisco, 1988), Jon D. Levenson, understands God in the Bible and in rabbinic literature as having not destroyed chaos but having circumscribed it. The battle will be won by God at the end of time, but in the meantime, evil will still be encountered. "War and Peace", in *Contemporary Halatchic Problems* by J. David Bleich (New York, 1977), pp. 180–82, gives a brief review of basic Jewish legal terms regarding warfare. "The Mission of Israel in a Nuclear Age" by Levi Olan in *Judaism* 32 (Winter 1983), pp. 27–33 presents a plan for the Jewish people to take up again the calling of prophetic ethical monotheism, in the current world crisis. *Violence and the Value of Life in Jewish Tradition and Religious Thought,* edited by Yehezkel Landau (Jerusalem 1984), includes articles by Immanuel Jakobovits, Uriel Simon, Emanuel Rackman, and David S. Shapiro on Jewish legal and philosophic sources relating to war and peace. "Confusion of Good and Evil", in *The Insecurity of Freedom* by Abraham J. Heschel (New York, 1967), pp. 127–49, is a Jewish reflection on the moral realism of Protestant theologian Reinhold Niebuhr. Herschel elucidates the concept of mitzvah (the deed) as a way out of our morass. "Peace" by Aviezer Ravitzky in *Contemporary Jewish Religious Thought,* edited by Arthur A. Cohen and Paul Mendes-Flohr (New York, 1987), pp. 685–702, is a beautiful synoptic entity on the variety of Jewish views and visions.

War

REUVEN KIMELMAN

Types of Wars

The Jewish ethics of war focuses on two issues: its legitimation and its conduct.

The Talmud classifies wars according to their source of legitimation. Biblically mandated wars are termed mandatory (*milḥemet mitzvah or milḥemet ḥovah*). Wars undertaken at the discretion of the Sanhedrin (or its legal equivalent such as the modern Israeli Knesset)[1] are termed discretionary (*milḥemet reshut*).

There are three types of mandatory wars: Joshua's war of conquest against the seven Canaanite nations, the war against Amalek, and a defensive war against an already launched attack. Discretionary wars are usually expansionary efforts undertaken to enhance the political prestige of the government or to secure economic gains.[2]

The first type of mandatory war is only of historical interest. Since the Canaanite nations lost their national identity in ancient times they are not on the postbiblical agenda.

This ruling, which appears in both mishnaic and talmudic sources,[3] is part of a tendency to blunt the impact of the seven-nations policy. The Bible points out that these policies were not implemented even during the zenith of ancient Israel's power.[4] And an ancient midrash explicitly excludes the possibility of transferring the seven-nations ruling to other non-Jewish residents of the Land of Israel.[5] Maimonides is just as explicit in emphasizing that all trace of them has vanished.[6] Limiting the jurisdiction of the seven-nations ruling to the conditions of ancient Canaan precludes it from serving as a precedent for contemporary practice.

The second category of mandatory wars, that of the war against Amalek, has been rendered operationally defunct either by comparing them with the Canaanites[7] or by viewing them as the embodiment of sheer evil and postponing the battle to the immediate premessianic struggle.[8]

The two remaining categories, reactive defensive wars (which are classified as mandatory) and expansionary wars (which are classified as discretionary) remain intact. So, for example, King David's response to the Philistine attack is termed *mandatory*[9] while his wars "to expand the border of Israel" are termed *discretionary*.[10] Intermediate wars such as preventive, anticipatory, or preemptive defy so neat a classification. Not only are the classifications debated in the Talmud,[11] but commentators disagree on the categorization of the differing positions in the Talmud.

The major clash occurs between the eleventh-century Franco-German scholar Rashi and the thirteenth-century Franco-Provencal scholar Meiri. According to Rashi, the majority position in the Talmud deems preemptive action to be *discretionary* whereas the minority position expounded by Rabbi Judah considers it to be *mandatory*.

According to Meiri,[12] a preemptive strike, which he describes as a military move against an enemy who it is feared might attack or who is already known to be preparing for war, is judged to be *mandatory* by the majority of the rabbis but deemed *discretionary* by Rabbi Judah. According to this reading, Rabbi Judah defines as mandatory only wars in response to an already launched attack. Maimonides also limits the mandatory classification to a defensive war launched in response to an attack.[13]

The remainder of the present analysis will focus on the ramifications of the distinction between *mandatory* and *discretionary* war with regard to the following four issues: May the classification of a defensive war as mandatory be extended to include preemptive strikes? Which branch of government makes the decision to wage war? How may war be conducted? Who is subject to the draft?

Preemptive Strikes as Self-Defense

It is widely held that national self-defense is a moral right just as is personal self-preservation. Not only Machiavellians view the security and survival of the state as nonnegotiable. The question is whether the inalienable right of self-defense is limited to an already launched attack. This apparently is the majority talmudic position according to Rashi and that of Rabbi Judah according to Meiri. This position is seconded by Article 51 of the United Nations Charter, which states: "Nothing in the present Charter shall impair the inherent right of individual or collective self-defense if an armed attack occurs against a member."

The minority position of Rabbi Judah, however, according to Rashi, and the majority position, according to Meiri, hold that a preemptive strike against an enemy amassing for attack is close enough to a defensive counterattack to be categorized as mandatory. This position holds that to wait for an actual attack might make resistance impossible. Such an argument was championed by Lord Chancellor Kilmuir before the British House of Lords when he remarked with reference to the aforementioned Article 51: "It would be a travesty of the purpose of the Charter to compel a defending state to allow its opponents to deliver the first fatal blow."[14]

This judgment lies behind the endorsement by the United States House Appropriations Committee of the concept of a preemptive attack. Its conclusions were formulated as follows: "In the final analysis, to effectively deter a would-be aggressor, we should maintain our armed forces in such a way and with such an understanding that should it ever become obvious that an attack upon us or our allies is imminent, we can launch an attack before the aggressor has hit either us or our allies. This is an element of deterrence which the United States should not deny itself. No other form of deterrence can be relied upon."[15] This understanding of anticipatory defense allows for a counterattack before the initial blow falls.

Under the terms of modern warfare, for example, if an enemy were to launch a missile attack, the target country could legitimately retaliate even if the enemy missiles were still inside their borders. The doctrine of anticipatory defense would allow for a preemptive strike even if the missiles were still on their launching pads as long as the order had been issued for their launching.

The Decision to Wage War: Who Is Authorized to Declare War?

A mandatory war is declared by the chief executive. A discretionary war requires the advice and/or consent of the Sanhedrin[16] or its judicial legislative equivalent.

There are several reasons for requiring the involvement of the Sanhedrin in the decision to undertake a discretionary war. The first is its role as the legal embodiment of popular sovereignty, the *edah* in biblical terms.[17] Maimonides, who understands this to imply that the high court was the legal equivalent of "the community of Israel as a whole,"[18] uses interchangeably the phrases "according to the majority of Israel" and "according to the high court."[19] This equivalency enables former Chief Rabbi Shlomo Goren to explain that the requirement to secure the Sanhedrin's approval in a discretionary war derives from its representative authority.[20]

The second reason for involving the Sanhedrin is its role as the authoritative interpreter of the Torah-constitution. Since the judicial interpretation of the law is structurally separate from its executive enforcement, the Sanhedrin can serve as a check on executive power.

The involvement of the Sanhedrin in a discretionary war safeguards the citizenry from being endangered without the approval of those who represent them. The obligation of citizens to fight in a discretionary war can be based on the biblical perspective which considers the people and the monarch to be bound by a covenant,[21] each side of which possesses certain obligations. Statehood involves a mutual security pact: the people commit themselves to the state, which protects them as long as it does not risk their lives unnecessarily. Ideally, the people are obliged to support the king just as he is forsworn to uphold the constitution.[22] Allocating some war-making authority to the Sanhedrin guarantees the presence of a countervailing force to the ruler to preserve the inviolability of the social contract.

Before granting authorization to wage war, the Sanhedrin must weigh the probable losses, consider the chances of success, and assess the will of the people. As David Bleich writes, "The

Sanhedrin is charged with assessing the military, political and economic reality and determining whether a proposed war is indeed necessary and whether it will be successful in achieving its objectives."[23] Since wars are always costly in lives, the losses have to be measured against the chance of success. Preventive warfare is unwarranted if the number of lives saved does not significantly exceed the number of lives jeopardized. Calculations of victory alone are not determinative; the price of victory must be considered. The great third-century Babylonian talmudic authority Mar Samuel condoned the loss of up to one-sixth of the fighting forces before subjecting a government to charges of misconduct.[24] Thus a government is not only required to project future losses but to take precautions to limit them. Nonetheless, precision is well-nigh impossible. The gap between plan and execution characterizes the best of military calculations. Linear plans almost always fail to deal with the nonlinear world that rules strategy and war. Rabbi Eleazar in talmudic times noted, "Any war which involves more than sixty thousand is necessarily chaotic."[25] Modern warfare has not significantly changed the equation. In the words of Prussian Field Marshal Helmuth von Moltke, "No plan can survive contact with the battle."[26]

These calculations are the province of that objective body that represents the people. The ruler may be insufficiently disinterested, predisposed to perceive war as an opportunity for enhancing personal prestige, for stimulating the economy, or for consolidating his political base. As the Talmud notes, nothing diverts public attention and deflects the opposition while simultaneously creating the need for a strong leader as war.[27] Reflecting a similar insight, Josephus—well aware of the machinations of opportunistic rulers—pointed out that the biblical laws of warfare are meant to deter conquest by preventing war "wage[d] for self-aggrandizement."[28]

The ruler may be reluctant to commit his army out of fear of compromising his affluence in the defense of the citizenry. The exclusion of the king from certain official decisions is attributed by the Talmud to the concern that the expense of maintaining a standing army would unduly influence his judgment.[29]

In sum, before the populace may be endangered, the ruler's reasons for waging war should be checked by the Sanhedrin's assessment of the people's interest. Through such a system of countervailing powers, the interest of the state and the interest of the people can be balanced.

The Ethical Conduct of War

The estimation of one's own losses and one's own interests are insufficient for the determination of discretionary war. The total destruction ratio required for victory must be considered. This assessment involves a "double intention," that is, the "good" must appear achievable and the "evil" reducible.

Thus, for example, before laying siege to a city, it must be determined that it can be captured without destroying it.[30] There is no warrant for destroying a town for the purpose of *saving* it.

The other rules for sieges follow similar lines of thought. Indefensible villages may not be subjected to siege. Negotiations with the enemy must precede subjecting a city to hunger, thirst, or disease for the purpose of exacting a settlement. Emissaries of peace must be sent to a hostile city for three days. If the terms are accepted, no harm may befall any inhabitants of the city. If the terms are not accepted, the siege is still not to begin until the enemy has opened hostilities. Even after the siege is laid, no direct cruelties against the inhabitants may be inflicted, and a side must be left open as an escape route.[31]

Philo warns that national vendettas are not justifications for wars. If a city under siege sues for peace, it is to be granted. Peace, albeit with sacrifices, says Philo, is preferable to the horrors of war. But peace means peace. "If," he continues, "the adversaries persist in their rashness to the point of madness, they [the besiegers] must proceed to the attack invigorated by enthusiasm and having in the justice of their cause an invincible ally."[32]

Although the purpose of an army at war is to win, both Philo and the ancient rabbis rejected the claim of military necessity as an excuse for military excess. Although victory is the goal, indeed victory with all due haste, aimless violence or wanton destruction is to be avoided. As the Spanish commentator Nahmanides makes clear, acts of destruction are warranted only insofar as they advance the goal of victory.[33] Weapons calculated to produce suffering disproportionate to the military advantage are not allowed.

Since excessive concern with moral niceties can sometimes be morally counterproductive, moral compunctions must not appear as timidity and moral fastidiousness must not be seen as squeamishness, lest such misunderstandings invite aggression. To ensure that it be perceived as issuing from a position of strength, moral preparedness must go hand in hand with military preparedness.

Philo, well aware of the military ambiguity of moral concerns, sounds a note of caution in the following summary of the biblical doctrine of defense: "All this shows clearly that the Jewish nation is ready for agreement and friendship with all like-minded nations whose intentions are peaceful, yet is not of the contemptible kind which surrenders through cowardice to wrongful aggression."[34]

The Immunity of non-combatants cannot be sacrified on the altar of military necessity. Such a principle discriminates in favor of those who have done no harm. As Philo notes, "the Jewish nation, when it takes up arms, distinguishes between those whose life is one of hostility, and the reverse. For to breathe slaughter against all, even those who have done very little or nothing amiss, shows what I should call a savage and brutal soul."[35]

Philo extends the prohibition against axing fruit-bearing trees (Deuteronomy 20:19–20) to include vandalizing the environs of the besieged city. "Indeed so great a love for justice does the law instill in those who live under its constitution that it does not even permit the fertile soil of a hostile city to be outraged by devastation or by cutting down trees to destroy the fruits. . . . Does a tree, I ask you, show ill will to the human enemy that it should be pulled up roots and all, to punish it for ill which it has done or is ready to do to you?"[36]

In a similar vein, Josephus expands on the biblical prohibitions to include the incineration of the enemy's country and the killing of beasts employed in labor.[37] Despoiling the enemy countryside for no military advantage comes under the proscription of profligate destruction.

Maimonides takes the next step in extending the biblical prohibition to exclude categorically wanton destruction. "Also, one who smashes household goods, tears clothes, demolishes a building, stops up a spring, or destroys articles of food with destructive intent, transgresses the command 'You shall not destroy.' "[38]

If one can control the destructive urges provoked by war against nonhuman objects, there is a chance of controlling the destructive urge against humans. The link between these two forms the basis of two a fortiori arguments for the immunity of noncombatants.

Since the prohibition against destroying trees is formulated in a rhetorical manner, namely, "Are trees of the field human to withdraw before you under siege?" (Deuteronomy 20:19), it is deduced that just as a tree—had it fled—would not be chopped down, so a person—were he to flee—should not be cut down. As the fifteenth-century Spanish-Italian exegete Isaac Arama notes, after mentioning the prohibition against the wanton destruction of trees, "all the more so it is fitting to take care that no preventable injury come upon humans."[39]

The immunity of noncombatants is further supported by the ruling that a fourth side of a besieged city be left open. Commentators are unclear whether the motive here is humanitarian or tactical. In either case the opportunity to escape saps the resolve of the beseiged to continue fighting.[40] Thus it is important that the option to flee not be used for the purpose of regrouping to mount rear attacks.[41] If (unarmed) soldiers have the chance to become refugees, then all the more so noncombatants and other neutrals. Thus the prohibition of weapons directed primarily at civilian targets. This position precludes the military option of warfare in conventional war as well as mutually assured destruction (MAD) in nuclear warfare. Multimegaton weapons whose primary goal is civilian slaughter and which are only secondarily used against military targets would be totally proscribed. As there are unacceptable weapons, so there are unacceptable targets.

These ethical intrusions in the waging of war have two major foci: to safeguard the moral character of the soldier and to preserve the human image of the enemy.

Any system that appreciates the realities of both the moral life and the military faces a dilemma in promoting the moral perfection of the individual while allowing for military involvement. Some systems forswear war as the price of moral excellence. Others apportion the moral life and the military life to different segments of the population. If the two are mutually exclusive, then a division of labor is a possible solution.

Neither alternative is acceptable in Jewish ethical theory. Regarding forswearing war, Maimonides pointed out that to renounce defense is to guarantee occupation, conquest, and exile. Realizing that dispersion is an unnatural political condition for Israel, Maimonides, in his *Epistle to the Sages of Marseille,* attributed the loss of the second Jewish commonwealth to the neglect of the art of war. Clearly Maimonides would find it, in the words of Abba Eban, "hard to see why the advocates of unilateral renunciation are more 'moral' than those who seek to prevent war by a reciprocal balance of deterrents and incentives." Solutions to conflict have to be judged by their effectiveness, not only by their virtue. Indeed, there is no reason to concede, as Eban continues, "that prevention of conflict by effective deterrence [is] less moral than the invitation to conflict by avoidable imbalance." For deterrence to be credible, the capacity to make war must be credible. Paradoxically, as Raymond Aron notes, "the possibility of unlimited violence restrains the use of violence without any threats even being proffered."[42]

Unilateral disarmament cannot be judged more moral if it invites attack. A policy of abdication of power that results in condemning others to subjugation has a questionable moral basis. For a leader of a beleaguered nation political naiveté can result in moral sin. Maimonides concludes his critique of the political sagacity of ancient Israel's leaders by lamenting, "Our fathers have sinned, but they are no more."[43]

With regard to a division of labor on ethical lines, Jewish theorists have generally been inclined to reject solutions predicated on the exemption of the ethical elites from the maintenance work of society. Instead, they have been struggling with the challenge of sustaining the moral stature of the soldier. As far back as the first century, Philo explained that the prohibition against slaying the defenseless derives from a concern with the savagery in the soul of the soldier. Indeed, even kings were condemned for their ruthlessness in the slaying of an enemy.[44]

For centuries, ethicists have been concerned with the brutalization of character that inevitably results from the shedding of blood in wartime. In the thirteenth century, Nahmanides, who elsewhere expressed his apprehension that "the most refined of people become possessed with ferocity and cruelty when advancing upon the enemy,"[45] opined that the Torah wants the soldier to "learn to act compassionately with our enemies even during wartime."[46] As Isaac Arama noted two centuries later, "War is impossible without murder and hatred of humanity . . . there is nothing like it to undermine all sense of right and wrong."[47] In the eighteenth century, Hayyim Attar underscored how killing, however justified, "gives birth to a brutalization of sensibilities," which requires special divine grace to be palliated.[48]

In the nineteenth century, Samuel David Luzzato argued that since the Torah's purpose is to strengthen the forces of compassion and to counter the natural drive for only self-serving acts, it is concerned that we not become ingrates by casting stones into the well from which we drink. Such would be the case if, after eating the fruit of a tree, we were to chop down that very tree.[49] Jewish agonizing over the moral stature of the soldier is summed up, in the twentieth century, in the words of Justice Haim Cohen of the Israel Supreme Court: "It seems that constant violence, even in self-defense, is not easily compatible with moral sensitivity."[50] All the more reason to promote an ethic of soldiery.

The concern with the humanity of the enemy has also engaged Jewish ethical reflection. Two of the most poignant comments hark back to the first century. Referring to Deuteronomy 21:10ff., Josephus says the legislator of the Jews commands "showing consideration even to declared enemies. He . . . forbids even the spoiling of fallen combatants; he has taken measures to prevent outrage to prisoners of war, especially women."[51]

Consideration for the humanity of the enemy forms the basis of Philo's explanation for the biblical requirement in Numbers 31:19 of expiation for those soldiers who fought against Midian. He writes: "For though the slaughter of enemies is lawful, yet one who kills a man, even if he does so justly and in self-defense and under compulsion, has something to answer for, in view of the primal common kinship of mankind. And therefore, purification was needed for the slayers, to absolve them from what was held to have been a pollution."[52]

Since, alas, there are times when evil has to be used to hold evil in check, the problem, as Rabbi Abraham Kook noted in his book *Lights*, is how to engage in evil without becoming tainted. One tactic, as noted here by Philo, is to require rites of expiation even after necessary evils. There is no war that does not require penance. According to some, this approach was implemented after the slaying of the Golden Calf episode.[53]

The ongong dialectic between the demands of conscience and the exigencies of the hour was caught by Martin Buber in the following words:

It is true that we are not able to live in perfect justice, and in order to preserve the community of man, we are often compelled to accept wrongs in decisions concerning the community. But what matters is that in every hour of decision we are aware of our responsibility and summon our conscience to weigh exactly how much is necessary to preserve the community, and accept just so much and no more; that we do not interpret the demands of a will-to-power as a demand made by life itself; that we do not make a practice of setting aside a certain sphere in which God's command does not hold, but regard those actions as against his command, forced on us by the exigencies of the hour as painful sacrifices; that we do not salve, or let others salve our conscience when we make decisions concerning public life.[54]

Necessary evils remain evils.

These concerns for the moral quotient of the soldier and the life of the enemy inform the "purity of arms" doctrine of the modern Israel Defense Forces. The doctrine of purity of arms, an expression apparently coined by the Labor-Zionist idealogue Berl Katznelson, limits killing to necessary and unavoidable situations.[55] How successfully it has been maintained under wartime conditions is illustrated by the following account of an Israeli unit entering Nablus during the Six-Day War: "The battalion CO got on the field telephone to my company and said, 'Don't touch the civilians . . . don't fire until you're fired at and don't touch the civilians. Look, you've been warned.' 'Their blood be on your heads.' . . . The boys in the company kept talking about it afterwards. . . . They kept repeating the words. . . . Their blood be on your heads."[56]

According to Israeli colonel Meir Pa'il, the purity of arms doctrine maintains the moral stature of the soldier without seriously compromising his fighting capacity. "There can be no doubt that the turning toward extreme and consummate humanism can endanger the I.D.F.'s [Israel Defense Forces] ability to function, but experience has proved that the proportions of this danger are extremely small and that it does not constitute a phenomenon that really endangers the operative capacity and the efficiency of the defense forces."[57]

A consistent thread weaves its way through Jewish ethical thought from biblical ordinance to modern practice, as noted by ancient as well as medieval and modern observers. Just because an army is legitimately repelling an aggressor does not mean it can recklessly violate civilian life. The warrior is the enemy, not the noncombatant civilian. A just war does not justify unjust acts. If peace is the goal, the reality of war is to be conditioned by the vision of the reconciliation between the warring populations. Education for peace is also part of military preparedness.

Many of these considerations for maintaining the moral stature of the soldier and the humanity of the enemy received their initial stimulus from those biblical passages on war that have been categorized as discretionary. Nonetheless, many of them became applicable to mandatory wars. Although the better-known tendency distinguishes between the two types of war, the inclination to underscore the overlap between them also figures prominently in the classical discussion.[58]

This drive toward moral convergence between the two types of war finds its roots in the Bible. Thus in 1 Samuel 15:6 provisions are made to evacuate neutrals from the battle area even in the biblically mandated war against Amalek.

In addition to some moral considerations, the two types of war share some strategic considerations. Since the statement by Rabbi Eleazar in the *Midrash* about the chaotic nature of warfare derives from the numbers involved in the conquest of the Land of Israel, it follows that even the mandatory war of the original conquest of Israel required a weighing of victory against losses not unlike those of discretionary wars.

The *Midrash* traces the blurring of the distinctions between the two types of war back to the Torah. It finds in the following dialogue a way of parrying the assumption that overtures of peace are limited to discretionary wars. "God commanded Moses to make war on Sihon, as it is said, 'Engage him in battle' (Deuteronomy 2:24), but he did not do so. Instead he sent messengers . . . to Sihon . . . with an offer of peace (Deuteronomy 2:26). God said to him: 'I commanded you to make war with him, but instead you began with peace; by your life, I shall confirm you decision. Every war upon which Israel enters shall begin with an offer of peace.' "[59] Since Joshua is said to have extended such an offer to the Canaanites and Numbers 27:21 points out Joshua's need for applying to the priestly Urim and Tumim to assess the chances of victory, it is evident that also a divinely-commanded war is to be predicated on an overture of peace as well as on a positive assessement of the outcome.[60] Moreover, as discretionary wars require the assent to the

Sanhedrin, so mandatory wars require the concurrence of priestly appurtances. In either case, chief executives lack *carte blanche* to commit their people to war.

The move to impose upon mandatory warfare the procedural or moral restraints of discretionary warfare counters the sliding scale argument, namely, the belief that "the greater the justice of one's cause, the more rights one has in battle."[61] The move from convictions of righteousness to feelings of self-righteousness is slight. The subsequent move of regarding the enemy population as beyond the pale of humanity is even slighter. Since this tendency is especially pronounced in ideologically and religiously motivated wars, any countermove is especially salutary.

The greater the blurring of distinctions between discretionary and mandatory war, the greater the chance of removing from the military agenda the option of total war. Strapping mandatory wars with some of the considerations of discretionary wars prevented them from becoming holy wars. According to John Yoder's *When War Is Unjust*, holy wars differ from just wars in the following five respects:

1. holy wars are validated by a transcendent cause
2. the cause is known by revelation
3. the adversary has no rights
4. the criterion of last resort need not apply
5. it need not be winnable.

The above discussion illustrates how the antidotes to 3-5 were woven into the ethical fabric of mandatory wars. To repeat, the fallen of Amalek were not to be disfigured, the resort to war even against the Canaanites was only pursuant to overtures of peace, and even the chances of success against Midian were weighed by the Urim and Tummin. By replacing the category of holy war with that of mandatory war and subjecting it to many of the limitations of discretionary war, all war became subject to ethical restraint. Since an ethic of unlimited warfare is a contradiction in terms, only a sliding scale of limited warfare is ethically feasible. It is therefore not surprising that the category of holy war is absent from the Jewish ethical or military lexicon.

Exemptions from Military Service

The obligation of the citizen to participate in a mandatory defensive war flows from three assumptions of which the first two are that national defense is based on an analogue of individual self-defense[62] and that national defense is required by the verse "Do not stand idly by the blood of your neighbor."[63] The implication is that the duty to come to the rescue of compatriots under attack is comparable to the duty to intervene to rescue an individual from an assailant.[64]

These two assumptions alone prove inadequate. After all, if escape is available, self-defense is optional. Moreover, classical legal opinion is divided on the obligation of risking one's life for another.[65] The upshot is that the domestic analogy alone remains insufficient. The right of national defense cannot be facilely extrapolated from the right of home defense.

Justifying risk of life in the name of national defense requires the assumption that the duty to save the community is sufficient to authorize risk of life. As Maimonides notes at the end of his *Epistle to Yemen*, "the public welfare takes precedence over one's personal safety."[66] This responsibility to defend the community increases when the community is the state, whose mandate includes the protection of the total citizenry.[67]

In a defensive war, the lives of the citizens are imperiled with the first attack. The counterattack is undertaken to diminish the risk to life. Such is not the case in discretionary wars, which seek to extend the political or economic influence of the government. Even in a preemptive attack, according to one school of thought, the lack of imminent danger to the population prevents the executive from independently deciding to endanger the lives of the citizenry. Whether a policy of war should be endorsed is left to the discretion of the Sanhedrin.

The deliberations of the Sanhedrin include weighing popular support in its endorsement of a war policy. This does not imply a government by referendum. Even those who maintain that sovereignty ultimately rests with the community hold that during their tenure, representatives are authorized to express the collective will.[68] Even democracy, the contemporary halakhist Eliezer Waldenberg notes, does not necessarily entail government by referendum. Representative government is not government by the people, but government by their agents.[69]

Nonetheless, concurrent with theories of majority rule are provisions for minority rights.[70] As there is general agreement that the majority cannot impose unfair rules that discrimminate against the minority, so is there a consensus that the majority has the right to impose on the minority in matters that are clearly for the benefit of the community. Legal opinion, however, is split on whether the minority can be imposed upon in those discretionary areas (*devar hareshut*) which though desired by the majority are not clearly for the benefit of the community as a whole.

Whether such provisions would apply in war is open to question. It would appear that once the government has complied with proper procedure, the individual would have no recourse but to fight. After all, if the duly constituted authorities have determined the necessity of war, how could the individual have the right to review the government's decision? This surely holds in defensive wars when none is exempt from the obligation of self-defense, the duty to rescue others, and the need to come to the defense of the state whose very existence serves to protect all.

The question is whether these considerations apply equally in a discretionary war or whether majority rule is limited by the discretionary nature (*devar hareshut*) of the war and thus must meet the requirement of benefit to the community as a whole. Although these considerations are not made explicit, they may help us understand the peculiar biblical rules of warfare with regard to exemptions from military service.

According to the Torah, before commencing hostilities, the officials must address the troops as follows:

> Is there anyone who has built a new house but has not dedicated it . . . or planted a vineyard but has never harvested it . . . or spoken for a woman in marriage but has not married her . . . let him go back home, lest he die in battle and another [do] it.
> The officials shall go on addressing the troops and say, is there anyone afraid and tender-hearted: Let him go back to his home, lest the courage of his comrades flag like his. (Deut. 20:5–9)

Individuals in these categories are required to report for duty first before being assigned alternative service.

Another category not only is exempt from reporting for duty but is excused from all alternative service such as provisions and weapon supply, road repair, special security expenditures, or even oversight of defensive installations.[71] This category derives from the following verse: "When a man has taken a bride, he shall not go out with the army or be assigned to it for any purpose; he shall be exempt one year for the sake of his household, to give happiness to the woman he has married" (Deut. 24:5).

According to the *Mishnah*, the absolute exemption of one year for one who has consummated his marriage applies also to "one who has built his house and dedicated it" as well as to "one who has planted a vineyard and harvested it."[72]

All the exemptions are characterized by their universal access. There are no exemptions based on birth, education, professional class, or even on religious status.[73] This fits the moral purpose of conscription, which is to universalize or randomize the risks of war across a generation of men. By not creating a special exclusion even for religion, the Torah underscores that when life is at stake there can be no respecting of persons.

The purpose of all of the exemptions is not made explicit, although the value of removing from the field those who cannot concentrate on the battle is alluded to. The presence of such people increases fatalities resulting from disarray and failure of nerve. Other explanations for the exemptions include the need to mitigate individual hardship, to give courage to those who remain, to maintain the sanctity of the camp,[74] or to prevent depopulation of urban areas.[75]

The talmudic rabbis, by grasping each case as illustrative of a principle, extended the exemptions to cover four categories of handicaps: the economic, the familial, the psycho-moral, and the physical.[76] Claims for economic and familial exemptions are subject to substantiation. The other two are assumed to be self-evident.[77]

Although the psycho-moral exemption does not require independent confirmation, its meaning is far from self-evident. The Torah mentions two categories: "afraid" and "tender-hearted." According to Rabbi Yose Hagalili, *afraid* means apprehensive about his sins; *tender-hearted* means fearful of war lest he be killed. According to Rabbi Akiva, *afraid* means fearful of war; *tender-hearted* means compassionate—apprehensive lest he kill.[78] Taken together, there would be grounds for exempting the psychologically timid as well as the morally scrupulous.[79]

Besides having to be substantiated, the economic and familial exemptions share another common denominator. Projects such as starting a house, beginning a vineyard, or getting engaged mostly affect men in their prime, which is the age of maximum combat readiness. These are also the people who would be most willing to fight a necessary war and most reluctant to fight an optional one. A large number of exemptions for this age group can so hamper mobilization efforts as to impair the military effort, as Nahmanides implies when he notes, "Were it not for [the requirement of substantiation], a majority of the people would seek exemption on false pretenses."[80] Nahmanides' fears were borne out by the experience of the biblical judge Gideon, who, upon making provisions for the psycho-moral exemption, lost two-thirds of his fighting force.[81]

But this is precisely the point. There is a loophole in the war legislation, a loophole so gaping that it allows those not convinced of the validity of the war to reassert their sovereignty through legal shenanigans. Doubts about the validity of the war will stir up their own social momentum and induce many to seek wholesale exemptions. The result is a war declared by the executive and approved by the Sanhedrin which sputters because the populace has not been persuaded of its necessity.[82]

Mobilization cannot succeed without a high degree of popular motivation. Many will express their halfheartedness by dragging their feet in the hope of being, as the Talmud says, "the last to go to war and the first to return."[83] Through expressing their reluctance to fight, the populace retains a semblance of sovereignty. By allowing them, however indirectly, to pass judgment on whether the military venture is necessary and serves legitimate political ends, the Torah underscores the interdependence between military readiness and popular readiness. Indeed, for conquered territory to enter the public domain, the military venture must command the approval of the majority.[84]

The upshot is that both mandatory and discretionary wars require both a moral and a political base.[85] Otherwise, the war effort threatens to be undermined by the morale of that community which constitutes the resource of power. David Ben-Gurion summed it up well when he said, "Two-thirds of military prowess is popular morale."[86]

In the final analysis, the issue is not only the justice of the war (*jus ad bellum*) nor the conduct of the war (*jus in bello*) but the ends and purposes for which war is used. Just because a war can be justified both by cause and by conduct does not make it necessary. Although final judgments of necessity are always retrospective, life-and-death decisions in the interim remain subject, in part, to review by the governed.

In sum, it is not enough that wars be justified by reference to ends and means. They must also be justified in the eyes of those who are called upon to make the supreme sacrifice.

Epilogue

In answer to the question why the Torah records those occasions when God's orders on the conduct of war were rescinded in favor of Moses' counsel of restraint, the Midrash states, "Even war is recorded for the sake of peace."[87] If the reality of war is to be conditioned by the vision of peace, then restraint in both the recourse to, and the conduct of, war is imperative to keep ajar the openings of peace.

Notes

1. See Reuven Kimelman, "The Ethics of National Power: Government and War from the Sources of Judaism," in Daniel J. Elazar, ed., *Authority, Power and Leadership in the Jewish Polity: Cases and Issues* (1991) chap. 2, end of part 2.

2. *J. Sotah* 9:10, 23a, *B. Berakhot* 3b, *B. Sotah* 44b, *B. Sanhedrin* 16a, and Maimonides, *Hilkhot Melakhim* 5:1. See Chanoch Albeck, *Seder Nashim* (Tel Aviv, 1958) pp. 390–391.

3. *M. Yadayim* 4:4; *B. Berakhot* 28a; *B. Yoma* 54a cf. *T. Yadayim* 2:17

4. 1 Kings 9:20–21; 2 Chronicles 8:7–9.

5. Following David Hoffmann, *Midrash Tannaim* ad Deuteronomy 20:15, p. 121, n. 10. On the nontransferability of the seven-nation rulings to others, see Joseph Babad's *Minḥat Ḥinukh*, to *Sefer HaḤinukh, mitsvah* #527, Pardes (New York, n.d.), pp. 154–155.

6. Maimonides, *Hilkhot Melakhim* 5:4; *Sefer HaMitsvot, mitsvah* 187.

7. *Minḥat Hinukh, mitsvah* #425 and #604.

8. Mosés bén Jacob of Coucy, *Sefer Mitsvot Gadol (Semag)*, negative commandment, #226; and the *Maimonidean Glosses ad Hilkhot Melakhim*, chap. 5, letter alef, cited by M. M. Kasher *Torah Shelemah* Vol. 14, p. 340.

9. *Midrash Samuel* 22:2, ed. S. Buber, p. 110.

10. *Midrash Lekah Tov,* ed. S. Buber, *Deuteronomy,* p. 35a. *Leviticus Rabbah* makes the distinction between David's wars "for Israel" and those "for himself." Cf. Rashi to *B. Gittin* 8b and 47a, s.v. *kibush yahid;* and *B. Avodah Zarah,* 20b, end.

11. *B. Sotah* 44b, and *J Sotah* 8:10; 23a.

12. *Beit HaBehirah ad Sotah* 42a, *Or Zaru'a* as cited in the gloss to the *Shulkhan Aruk, Orakh Hayyim* 329:6, also permits a preemptive strike against a hostile intention. The *Levush, ad loc.,* limits this to defense of strategically vulnerable areas.

13. Maimonides, *Hilkhot Melakhim* 5:1, according to Avraham Karelitz, *Hazon Ish, Al HaRambam,* B'nei B'rak, 5729, p. 841. Maimonides, *Commentary on the Mishnah ad Sotah* 8:7, lines up with Rashi.

14. Quoted in Barry Feinstein, "Self-Defence and Israel in International Law: A Reappraisal," *Israel Law Review* 11 (1976), p. 531.

15. Ibid., p. 533.

16. *M. Sanhedrin* 1:5; 2:4, see *B. Sanhedrin* 16a, *B. Berakhot* 3b along with Rashi *ad loc.,* and *Genesis Rabbah* 74:15 and parallels. Similarly, the Dead Sea *Temple Scroll (11 QT* 58:15–21) allows for immediate mobilization in a defensive war, but requires consultation with the High Priest and the Urim and Tummin as does the Talmud when waging an offensive war. It has been argued that the requirement of consulting with such hieratic institutions, in any case, applies only when they are in existence, see Moshe Soloveitchick, *Kovets Hidushe Torah,* (Jerusalem, n.d.), p. 31.

17. *B. Sanhedrin* 16a. For the biblical material, see Abraham Malamat, "Organs of Statecraft in the Israelite Monarchy," in *The Biblical Archaeologist Reader 3,* ed. E. F. Campbell, Jr., and D. N. Freedman (Garden City, N.Y., 1970), pp. 167–68.

18. Maimonides, *Commentary to the Mishnah, Horayot* 1:6, ed. Kafih, *Nezikim,* p. 309, see Gerald J. Blidstein, *Political Concepts in Maimonidean Halakha* (Hebrew) (Ramat Gan, 1983), p. 58.

19. Following Gerald J. Blidstein, "Individual and Community in the Middle Ages," in Daniel J. Elazar ed., *Kinship and Consent. The Jewish Political Tradition and Its Contemporary Uses.* (Ramat Gan, 1981), p. 247, n. 62.

20. Shlomo Goren, *Mashiv Milhamah,* vol. 1 (Jerusalem, 5743), pp. 127–130. See Blidstein, *Political Concepts,* p. 58, n. 19.

21. 2 Kings 11:17 and 2 Chronicles 23:3 along with 2 Samuel 5:3. On the problems involved in the term covenant for the Israelite polity, see Malamat, "Organs of Statecraft," pp. 164–65, and Hayim Tadmor, " 'The People' and the Kingship in Ancient Israel: The Role of Political Institutions in the Biblical Period," in H. H. Ben-Sasson and S. Ettinger, eds., *Jewish Society through the Ages* (New York, 1971), pp. 59–62; and F. M. Cross, *Canaanite Myth and Hebrew Epic* (Cambridge, Mass, 1972), p. 221.

22. See the example in Josephus, *Antiquities* 9.7.4 (153).

23. David J. Bleich, "Preemptive War in Jewish Law," *Tradition* 17 (1983) p. 25. According to one source, assessing the chances of victory falls within the province of the priestly Urim and Tumim, whereas the endorsement of a war policy falls within judicial jurisdiction (*B. Eruvin* 45a, see Rashi *ad B. Berakhot* end of 3b) in *J. Sabbath* 2:3;5b= *Midrash HaGadol ad* Numbers 27:21, p. 483, the judgment of the Urim refers to the judgment of the court on high.

24. *B. Shavuot* 35b, following *Tosafot, s.v., deqatla.* cf. *Responsa Hatam Sofer ad Orakh Hayyim* 208, p. 77a.

25. *Midrash Song of Songs Rabbah* 4:4.

26. For the so-called "Clausewitzian friction" that distinguishes the fluid and chaotic nature of real war from war on paper, see Gordon Craig, "The Political Leader as Strategist," in Peter Paret, ed., *The Makers of Modern Strategy from Machiavelli to the Nuclear*

Age (Princeton, 1986), pp. 481–509; and Edward N. Lutwach, *Strategy: The Logic of War and Peace* (Cambridge, Mass., 1987), pp. 10–15.

27. *B. Temurah* 16a. Cf. Aristotle's, *Politics* 1313b, observation that a tyrant needs to be a warmonger to enhance the need for a leader.

28. Josephus, *Contra Apion* II.272 and 292.

29. *B. Sanhedrin* 8b, following *Arukh, s.v., apsania*. In a similar vein, *Numbers Rabbah* (22:6) notes how executive dilly-dallying can be a ruse to extend tenure in office.

30. *Sifre Deuteronomy* section 203, ed. Finkelstein, p. 239, with *Midrash HaGadol ad* Deuteronomy 20:19, ed. Fisch, p. 451.

31. Ibid., and *Midrash HaGadol ad* Numbers 31:7, ed. Rabinowitz, p. 538, n. 17. see David S. Shapiro, "The Jewish Attitude towards Peace and War," in Leo Jung, ed., *Israel of Tomorrow* (New York, 1946), p. 239 and Lawrence K. Milder, *Laws of War in the Bible and Formative Rabbinic Literature*, (ordination Thesis, Hebrew Union College, 1983).

32. Philo, *The Special Laws*, IV. 221.

33. Nahmanides, *Commentary ad* Deuteronomy 20:19.

34. Philo, *The Special Laws*, IV. 224.

35. Ibid., 224–5.

36. Ibid., 226–27.

37. Josephus, *Contra Apion* II.212–214.

38. Maimonides, *Hilkhot Melakhim* 6:10. See also his *Sefer HaMitzvot*, negative *mitzvah* 57.

39. Isaac Arama, *Akedat Yitshak*, chap. 81 (rpt. Jerusalem, 1961), p. 97b.

40. Ramban's addenda to Rambam's *Sefer HaMitzvot*, ed. Chavel (Jerusalem, 1981), the fifth *mitzvah*, p. 246. The Bible (2 Kings 6:21–23 with RaLBaG) and *Midrash* (*Seder Eliaha Rabbah* 8) promote the immunity of noncombatants on both ethical and tactical grounds.

41. Based on *Targum Onqelos, Targum Pseudo-Jonathan*, and *Midrash Leqah Tov ad* Numbers 33:55.

42. Abba Eban, *The New Diplomacy: International Affairs in the Modern Age* (New York, 1983), p. 325; Raymond Aron, *Clausewitz: Philosopher of War* (Englewood Cliffs, N.J., 1985), p. 345.

43. Maimonides' *Collected Epistles and Responsa*, vol. 2 (Hebrew), ed. A. L. Lichtenberg (Leipzig, 1859), p. 25. Maimonides is alluding to Proverbs 20:18 which concludes saying, and we bear their inquity. The Maimonidean explanation of the fall of the second Jewish Commonwealth on political and military grounds is picked up in the fifteenth century by Solomon in Verga's *Shevet Yehudah* and in the following century by Simone Luzzatto's *Discourse on the Condition of the Jews*. Compare this with Hecataeus of Abdera who said of the Jews some eighteen hundred years earlier (ca. 300 BCE) "Their lawgiver was careful to make provisions for warfare and required the young men to cultivate manliness, steadfastness, and generally the endurance of every hardship;" (*History of Egypt* in Diodorus Siculus, *Library of History* 40:3) The general Galut-reluctance to deal with the realities of power against which Maimonides is fighting is so deep-seated that it informs the political thought of Zionist thinkers as diverse as Herzl, Kook, and Magnus. Theodor Herzl's *Altneuland* makes no provision for a professional army. Rabbi Abraham I. Kook argues that the exile had been extended so long to allow for the advent of a time "when government could be conducted without ruthlessness and barbarism" ("The War," in A. Hertzberg, ed., *The Zionist Idea* (New York, 1959), pp. 422–23). And Judah L. Magnes felt that if the Jewish national home cannot be established through "peace and understanding . . . it is better that the Eternal People that has outlived many a mighty empire should possess its soul in patience and wait" (*Dissenter in Zion*, ed. A. Goren (Cambridge, Mass., 1982), pp. 34–35).

44. *Midrash Lamentations Rabbah,* Introduction, section 14. Cf. 2 Kings 6:22 with 1 Kings 20:31.

45. Nahmanides, *Commentary ad* Deuteronomy 23:10.

46. See above n. 40.

47. See above, n. 39.

48. Ḥayyim Attar, *Or HaḤayyim ad* Deuteronomy 13:18.

49. S. D. Luzzato, *Commentary to the Pentateuch* (Hebrew) (rpt. Tel Aviv, 1965), pp. 537–39.

50. Haim Cohen, "Law and Reality in Israel Today," in S. Baron and G. Wise, eds., *Violence and Defense in the Jewish Experience* (Philadelphia, 1977), p. 332.

51. Josephus, *Contra Apion* II.212–13. Similarly, Rabbi Joshua claimed that the biblical Joshua took pains to prevent the disfigurement of fallen Amalekites (*Mekhilta Amalek* 1 ed. Horovitz-Rabin, p. 181; ed. Lauterbach vol. 2, p. 147.) For a more recent reflection of this view, see Naftali Zvi Berlin, *Ha'ameq Davar ad* Deuteronomy 17:3 (Professor Isadore Twersky drew my attention to this source).

52. Philo, *Moses* I.314.

53. So *Targum Yerushalmi, Or HaḤayyim ad* Exodus 32:29; and A. Ehrlich *ad* Numbers 31:50, *Mikra Ki-phshuto* vol. 1 (New York, 1969) p. 301. For Rabbi Abraham Kook's explanation of the apparent cruelty of biblical wars, see *Rav A. Y. Kook Selected Letters,* trans. and annot. Tsvi Feldman (Ma'aleh Adumim, 1985), [Igrot 89]), p. 180.

54. Martin Buber, *Israel and the World* (New York, 1963), pp. 246–47. A similar reluctance to attribute political evil, however necessary, to divine command apparently lies behind the refusal of *Seder Eliahu Rabbah* 4, ed. Friedmann, p. 17, to ascribe to God the Mosaic command of the Levites to slay their brethren.

55. See Ehud Luz, "The Moral Price of Sovereignty: The Dispute about the Use of Military Power within Zionism," *Modern Judaism* 7 (1987), pp. 51–98, 76. Luz's fine discussion cites many of the aforecited Zionist thinkers. It was Prime Minister David Ben Gurion who made the purity of arms doctrine one of the dogmas of the Israel Defense Forces (Cohen, "Law and Reality in Israel Today," p. 332).

56. Avraham Shapira: *The Seventh Day: Soldiers' Talk about the Six-Day War* (London, 1970), p. 132.

57. Meir Pa'il, "The Dynamics of Power: Morality in Armed Conflict after the Six Day War," in Marvin Fox, ed., *Modern Jewish Ethics: Theory and Practice* (Columbus, 1975), p. 215.

58. For Rashi and Nahmanides, see Yehudah Girshuni, *Sefer Mishpat HaMelukhah* (Jerusalem, 5744), pp. 130–34. For Maimonides, see *Hilkhot Melakhim* 6:1, 6:7, and 7:1 (following Blidstein, *Political Concepts,* p. 221, n. 34; and Soloveitchik, *Kovets Ḥidushei Torah* pp. 128–31).

59. *Deuteronomy Rabbah* 5:13 and *Midrash Tanḥuma Tsav* 5

60. *Leviticus Rabbah* 17:6, ed. Margulies, p. 386 and parallels. The position that all wars must be preceded by an overture of peace was accepted by a wide range of medieval authorities including Maimonides, *Hilkhot Melakhim* 6:5; Nahmanides *ad* Deut. 20:10; *SeMaG* positive mitsvah 118; *Sefer HaḤinukh, mitsvah* 527 along with *Minhat Ḥinukh, ad loc.*; and posibly Sa'adyah Gaon, see Yeruham Perla, *Sefer HaMitsvot LeRabbenu Sa'adyah* (Jerusalem, 1973), pp. 251–252.

61. The expression and definition are found in Michael Walzer, *Just and Unjust Wars: A Moral Argument with Historical Illustrations* (New York, 1977), p. 246.

62. *Midrash Tanḥuma, Pinḥas,* 3, p. 90.

63. As Leviticus 19:16 was understood; see Reuven Kimelman, "Judging Man by the Standards of God," *B'nai B'rith International Jewish Monthly,* May 1, 1983, pp. 12–18.

64. See Reuven Kimelman, "Torah against Terror—Does Jewish Law Sanction the Vengeance of Modern-Day Zealots?" *B'nai B'rith International Jewish Monthly*, October 1984, pp. 16–22; and Itamar Warhaftig, "Self-Defense in the Crimes of Murder and Injury" (Hebrew), *Sinai* 81 (5737), pp. 48–78.

65. The debate concerning the duty to risk one's life for another revolves around the opinions of David Ben Zimra, *Teshuvot Radbaz* vol. 3, #1052, who denies such a duty, and Joseph Karo, *Kesef Mishnah ad Hilkhot Rotzeah* 1:14, who affirms it.

66. See Abraham Halkin and David Hartman, *Crisis and Leadership: Epistles of Maimonides* (Philadelphia, 1985), p. 131. Cf. *Genesis Rabbah* 91:10: "It is preferable that one life be in doubtful danger than all be in certain danger;" and Halevi, Kuzari 3:20.

67. Following Abraham Avidan (Zemel), "Risking Oneself in the Saving of Another in the Light of the Halakha" (Hebrew), *Torah SheBa'al Peh*, vol. 16 (Jerusalem, 5734), p. 133; and Abraham Kook, *Mishpat Kohen* (Jerusalem, 5724), sections 142–44. For a discussion of the special prerogatives of the community, see Sha'ul Yisraeli, "Mandatory War and Discretionary War" (Hebrew), *Torah SheBa'al Peh*, vol. 10 (Jerusalem, 5728), pp. 46–50; and Judges 5:23. For the issue in Western political theory, see Michael Walzer, *Obligations: Essays on Disobedience, War, and Citizenship* (New York, 1970), pp. 77–98.

68. The sources are discussed by Blidstein, *Political Concepts*, pp. 225–27; and Samuel Morell, "The Constitutional Limits of Communal Government in Rabbinic Law," *Jewish Social Studies* 33 (1971), pp. 87–119. The principle of representative government was articulated in a most influential manner by the thirteenth-century rabbi R. Solomon ben Aderet (Rashba) in his *Responsa* vol. 1, #617, and vol. 3, #443. Both responsa are conveniently juxtaposed in Menachem Elon, *Jewish Law: History, Sources, Principles* (Hebrew) (Jerusalem, 1973), 2:588–89.

69. Eliezer Waldenberg, *Sefer Hilkhot Medinah*, vol. 3 (Jerusalem, 5712), pp. 90–97.

70. As noted by Blidstein, "Individual and Community," pp. 235–37, 252–53; and Morell, "Constitutional Limits," pp. 90–96. The decisive figure in articulating the principle of minority rights was the twelfth-century rabbi Rabbenu (Jacob) Tam; see Elon, *Jewish Law*, pp. 580–87.

71. Maimonides, *Hilkhot Melakhim*, 7:11. See Saul Lieberman, *Tosefta Ki-fshutah* (New York, 1973), vol. 8, p. 695, l. 246.

72. *M. Sotah* 8:4.

73. Viewing the Levites as ideal types, Maimonides argued for their military exemption; see *Hilkhot Shemitah VeYovel* 13:12 followed by *Midrash HaGadol Numbers* 1:49, ed. Rabinowitz, p. 10 and n. 8. It has been difficult if not impossible to substantiate this position from classical rabbinic sources; see Shlomo Zevin, *Le'Or HaHalakha*, (Tel Aviv, n.d.), pp. 27–28; and Girshuni, *Sefer Mishpat HaMelukhah*, p. 425. Shmaryahu Arieli, *Mishpat HaMilhamah* (Jerusalem, 1971), pp. 37–42, concludes a survey of the evidence contending that if there were such an exemption it applied only as long as the Levites served in the Temple. In any case, it has been argued that such exemptions are revoked in religiously motivated wars: see *Rambam Le-Am ad loc.*, p. 646, n. 54; and Menachem Schneersohn, *Chidushim U-Bi'urim Be-Shas U-Be-Divre HaRambam Z"L* (Brooklyn, 1985), pp. 216–221. The exemption is even more problematic in the light of Maimonides' ruling (*Hilkhot Shabbat* 2:23) that when life is endangered by hostile military action all able-bodied persons are mandated to go out and help; see Eliezer Waldenberg, *Responsa Tsis Elizer* (Hebrew) (Jerusalem, 5745) vol. 3, *siman* 9, pp. 34–35.

74. On the religious dimension of the army, see Eliezer Waldenberg, "The Religious Dimension of the Army of Israel" (Hebrew), *HaTorah VeHaMedinah* 4 (5712), pp. 197–216.

75. *Sifre Deuteronomy*, section 192, p. 233, cf. *The Temple Scroll* 58:9–11.

76. Shlomo Goren, *Torat HaShabbat VeHaMoed* (Jerusalem, 5742), p. 369.
77. See *Sifre Deuteronomy,* section 192, p. 233; and S. H. Kook, *Iyyunim UMehkarim*, vol. 1 (Jerusalem, 5719), pp. 235–37.
78. Following David Halivni, *Mekorot UMesorot, Nashim* (Tel Aviv, 5719), *ad Sotah* 44a, pp. 473–74. Compare the contrasting glosses of Abraham Ibn Ezra and Hizkuni *ad* Deuteronomy 20:8.
79. Following Abraham Hen, *BeMalkhut HaYahadut*, vol. 1, (Jerusalem, 5719), pp. 36 and 101.
80. Nahmanides, *Commentary ad* Deuteronomy 20:8. See *Bekhor Shor, ad loc.*
81. Judges 7:2–3.
82. This helps explain why *M. Sotah* 8:7 and *T. Sotah* 7:24 locate the exemption specifically in a discretionary war. According to Meiri, the exercise of the exemptions is optional (see Saul Lieberman, *Tosefta Ki-fshutah* vol. 8 [New York, 1973] p. 695, n. 38) and according to "Hazon Ish," "there should be no embarking on a discretionary war if it is impossible to fight without the exemptees" (*Orakh Hayyim, Moed* [Bnei Brak, 5733], *Eruvin, siman* 6, p. 167b).
83. *B. Pesahim* 113a.
84. See Maimonides, *Hilkhot Terumot* 1:2 and *Hilkhot Melakim* 5:6; *Sifre Deuteronomy* 51 (ed. L. Finkelstein), p. 116, esp.nn. 13 and 16, and *Shetat HaQadmonim al Massekhet Avodah Zarah*, ed. M. Blau (Brooklyn, 1969), pp. 51–52 esp.n. 93. along with the discussion of Samuel Atlas, *Pathways in Hebrew Law* (Hebrew) (New York, 1978), pp. 66–75.
85. According to *1 Maccabees* (3:56), draft exemptions were activated in the rebellion against the Syrians. It is possible that *1 Maccabees* holds that the exemptions obtain in all wars, see Yigael Yadin, *The Scroll of The War of the Sons of Light Against the Sons of Darkness* (Hebrew) (Jerusalem, 1957), p. 64. The other possibility is that since the inception and timing of the war was at Maccabean initiative and initially increased the peril to life, it needed to allow for the exemptions. For an application of these criteria, especially the populace principle, to the wars of modern Israel, see Reuven Kimelman, "Judaism and the Ethics of War," in Jules Harlow, ed. *The Rabbinical Assembly Proceedings 1987* (New York, 1988), pp. 22–24.
86. David Ben Gurion, *BaMa'arakhah*, Vol, 5 (Israel, 5710), p. 292. For an American application of the "Clausewitzian trinity" of people, politicians, and army, see Harry Summers, Jr., *On Strategy: A Critical Analysis of the Vietnam War* (Novato, 1982).
87. *Midrash Tanhuma, Tsav* 3.

FOR FURTHER READING

Artson, Bradley Shavit, *Love Peace and Pursue Peace: A Jewish Response to War and Nuclear Annihilation,* New York, 1988. An argument that only conventional defensive wars are permitted.

Bleich, David J., "Preemptive War in Jewish Law," *Tradition* 21 (1983), pp. 3–41. This traditional study of the halakic categories of war was instigated by the Israeli incursion into Lebanon in 1982.

Blidstein, Gerald J., "Individual and Community in the Middle Ages." In *Kinship and Consent: The Jewish Political Tradition and Its Contemporary Uses,* ed.

Daniel J. Elazar, pp. 217–56. Ramat Gan, 1981. An analysis of the conflict between individual rights and communal prerogatives as seen by medieval legal authorities.

Feinstein, Barry, "Self-Defence and Israel in International Law: A Reappraisal," *Israel Law Review* 11 (1976), pp. 530ff. An understanding of Israeli wars in the light of international law.

Gendler, Everett, "War and the Jewish Tradition." In *A Conflict of Loyalties: The Case for Selective Conscientious Objection,* ed. James Finn, pp. 78–102. New York, 1968. This study makes the case for selective conscientious objection in Judaism based on sources for legitimate and illegitimate warfare.

Kimelman, Reuven, "The Ethics of National Power: Government and War from the Sources of Judaism." In *Authority, Power and Leadership in the Jewish Polity: Cases and Issues,* ed. Daniel J. Elazar, chap. 2. Forthcoming. A monograph on the Jewish understanding of the problematics of power, government, and war followed by an assessment of the various Arab-Israeli wars.

————. "Judging Man by the Standards of God," *B'nai B'rith International Jewish Monthly,* May 1983, pp. 12–18. A study of the doctrine of indirect responsibility as applied to the Israeli Army by the Kahan commission in the wake of the Christian massacre of Arab refugees in Beirut.

————. "Torah against Terror—Does Jewish Law Sanction the Vengeance of Modern-Day Zealots?," *B'nai B'rith International Jewish Monthly,* October 1984, pp. 16–22. A protest against Jewish sources being abused in order to lend legitimacy to terrorism.

Luz, Ehud, "The Moral Price of Sovereignty: The Dispute about the Use of Military Power within Zionism," *Modern Judaism* 7 (1987), pp. 51–98. A history of the reflections on force in Zionist thought.

Pa'il, Meir, "The Dynamics of Power: Morality in Armed Conflict after the Six Day War." In *Modern Jewish Ethics: Theory and Practice,* ed. Marvin Fox, pp. 191–220. Columbus, Ohio, 1975. An argument for the applicability of Israeli military ethics to real war.

Shapiro, David S., "The Jewish Attitude towards Peace and War." In *Israel of Tomorrow,* ed. Leo Jung, New York, 1946, pp. 215–254. A survey of traditional legal and homiletical material on peace and war.

About the Contributors*

S H L O M O   A V I N E R I is Herbert Samuel Professor of Political Science at the Hebrew University of Jerusalem and former Director General of Israel's Ministry of Foreign Affairs. He is author of *The Social and Political Thought of Karl Marx* and *The Making of Modern Zionism*.

M I C H A E L   D O B K O W S K I is Professor of Religious Studies at Hobart and William Smith Colleges. He is the author of *The Tarnished Dream: The Basis of American Anti-Semitism* and *The Politics of Indifference: A Documentary History of Holocaust Victims in America*.

E L L I O T   N.   D O R F F is Provost and Professor of Philosophy at the University of Judaism in Los Angeles. His books include *Jewish Law and Modern Ideology, Conservative Judaism: Our Ancestors to Our Descendants*, and *Mitzvah Means Commandment*.

E M I L   L.   F A C K E N H E I M is Professor of Philosophy, University of Toronto; Fellow, Institute of Contemporary Jewry, Hebrew University; and, author of *What is Judaism? An Interpretation for the Present Age, To Mend the World* and *The Jewish Bible After the Holocaust*.

D A V I D   M.   F E L D M A N serves as rabbi of the Jewish Center in Teaneck, New Jersey. He is the author of *Birth Control in Jewish Law: Marital Relations, Contraception and Abortion, as set forth in the classic texts of Jewish law*.

S I D N E Y   G O L D S T E I N is G.H. Crooker University Professor and Professor of Sociology at Brown University. A past-president of the Population Association of America, he is recognized worldwide as a leading expert in Jewish demography.

B L U   G R E E N B E R G is a lecturer and author of articles on Jewish women and the Jewish family. Her works include *On Women and Judaism: A View from Tradition, How to Run a Jewish Household*, and *A Special Kind of Mother*.

*The contributors are identified by their occupations at the time of the writing of the essays.

SUSANNAH HESCHEL is an Assistant Professor in the Religious Studies department at Southern Methodist University, Dallas. She is the author of *On Being a Jewish Feminist: A Reader*.

REUVEN KIMELMAN is a professor of Near Eastern and Judaic Studies at Brandeis University. He is author of *The Ethics of National Power: Government and War in the Jewish Tradition* and *Judaism and Pluralism*.

DANIEL LANDES is University Professor of Jewish Ethics and Values at Yeshiva University's Los Angeles Branch and the Director of National Educational Projects at the Simon Wiesenthal Center. He is the editor of a volume entitled *Confronting Omnicide: Jewish Reflections on Weapons of Mass Destruction*.

DEBORAH E. LIPSTADT is a Director of Research at the Skirball Institute on Academic Values, an Adjunct Professor of Religious Studies at Occidental College, and the author of *Beyond Belief: The American Press and the Coming of the Holocaust, 1933-1945*.

RELA GEFFEN MONSON is Professor of Sociology and Dean for Academic Affairs at Gratz College in Pennsylvania. Her major works include *Jewish Campus Life* and *Jewish Women on the Way Up*.

DAVID NOVAK is the Edgar M. Bronfman Professor of Modern Judaic Studies at the University of Virginia in Charlottesville. He is author of *Law and Theology in Judaism* (2 volumes) and *Morality: The Image of the Non-Jew in Judaism*.

MICHAEL ROSENAK is Mandel Associate Professor of Jewish Education at the Hebrew University's Melton Center for Jewish Education in the Diaspora. *Commandments and Concerns: Jewish Religious Education in Secular Society* received the National Jewish Book Award for Jewish Thought in 1989.

NORBERT M. SAMUELSON is a professor of religion at Temple University. He is a founder, past chairman, and current secretary-treasurer of the International Academy of Jewish Philosophy.

U. O. SCHMELZ is a Professor at the Hebrew University of Jerusalem. He is the author of *World Jewish Population — Regional Estimates and Projections* and *Modern Jerusalem's Demographic Evolution*.

SAUL P. WACHS is Rosaline B. Feinstein Professor and Chair of Education, at Gratz College. His publications include *Curriculum for the Jewish Day School; Mitzvah;* and, *Curriculum for the Afternoon Religious School*.

Index

About the Editor

Steven T. Katz is Professor of Jewish Studies at Cornell University. He received his Ph.D. from Cambridge University in 1972 and in 1991 became the first Jew ever to be awarded a Bachelor of Divinity Degree by Cambridge University. Before coming to Cornell he taught at Dartmouth College for more than a decade, and he has also held visiting teaching appointments at Yale, the Hebrew University of Jerusalem, Harvard, the University of Pennsylvania, the University of California at Santa Barbara, William and Mary, and the University of Lancaster (England).

A prolific author, Professor Katz has edited and written many important works in various areas of Jewish thought and comparative mysticism. Among these are *Jewish Philosophers* (1975); *Jewish Ideas and Concepts* (1977); *Post-Holocaust Dialogues*, which won the National Jewish Book Award in 1984; *Historicism, the Holocaust and Zionism* (1992); *Mysticism and Philosophical Analysis* (1976); *Mysticism and Religious Traditions* (1983); and *Mysticism and Language* (1992). He is also the editor of the prize winning journal *Modern Judaism*. At present, he is completing a three volume study entitled *The Holocaust in Historical Context* which is to be published in 1992.